THE ARTS
OF MANKIND

EDITED BY ANDRÉ MALRAUX

AND ANDRÉ PARROT
Member of the *Institut de France*

EDITOR-IN-CHARGE
ALBERT BEURET

FRONTISPIECE – FRAGMENT OF BRONZE STATUE, TRADITIONALLY IDENTIFIED AS THE ELDER BRUTUS. ROME, PALAZZO DEI CONSERVATORI

ROME: THE CENTER OF POWER

500 B.C. to A.D. 200

RANUCCIO BIANCHI BANDINELLI

ROME

THE CENTER OF POWER

500 B.C. to A.D. 200

TRANSLATED BY PETER GREEN

GEORGE BRAZILLER · NEW YORK

In memory of George Salles,
who would have liked this book

Translated from the French
ROME. LE CENTRE DU POUVOIR

Standard Book Number: 0-8076-0559-X
Library of Congress Catalog Card Number: 70-116-985

Printed in France

Contents

Introduction   ix

PART ONE

1   Birth of a Town, a Society, and a Culture   1

2   Two Traditions: Plebeian and Patrician   51

3   Problems of Pictorial and Architectural Space   107

4   From Neo-Atticism to Neo-Hellenism   177

5   The Creation of an Imperial Art: Trajan and Hadrian   223

6   The First Crisis in the Hellenistic Tradition: The Antonines   281

Conclusion   341

PART TWO: GENERAL DOCUMENTATION

Supplementary Illustrations   345

Plans   353

Chronological Table   363

Genealogical Tree of the Antonines   386

Ancient Sources   387

Bibliography   389

Notes on the Illustrations   397

Glossary-Index   417

Maps   439

Introduction

THE art of the Roman period, like Greek art, is part of a widely disseminated cultural pattern. It is precisely for this reason that the underlying historical truths have acquired such a thick incrustation of commonplace judgments, affecting the specialist as much as the man in the street. Such preconceptions are less amenable than most to modification; their removal would call for a detailed work of scholarship, which the present volume does not set out to be. Nor is it possible to write a true work of synthesis, since a survey presupposes a certain level of achievement in analytical research, which as yet has not been attained. In any case, most of the best recent studies are primarily archaeological, whereas here (in accordance with the theme of the series) what was envisaged was a volume of art-history.

The aim of the present work, then, is to trace the origins, development, and increasingly dominant influence of a mode of artistic expression that was bound up with the specific historical phenomenon of a certain society and culture. This society and culture looked to Rome for their political direction, and were quite distinct, as regards structure and organization, both from Greek civilization (whether classical or Hellenistic) and from those other civilizations which sprang up in ancient times around the shores of the Mediterranean. Rome regarded herself as the residual heir to some of these civilizations; their discoveries and achievements, those of the Hellenistic world in particular, bequeathed numerous structural elements to the new cultural edifice being erected. Yet what emerged was something quite different and individual. To isolate and describe the specifically artistic manifestations of this complex culture, with its diverse and often ambiguous characteristics, has been my primary object throughout. I have not, therefore, attempted an aesthetic analysis (much less an aesthetic eulogy) of Roman art. Nor has it been my aim to produce a textbook, which would have meant including a selection, set out in chronological order, of all the most historically important examples of Roman art within the period covered by this book – that is, from the origins to the end of the second century AD.

I have tried to restrict myself to writing art-history. By this I mean putting oneself in the place of those who produced the works in question, with the object of finding out just which cultural and traditional elements, and what sort of motives (whether rational or irrational), helped to determine each artifact's form and meaning. Finally, I have sought to pin down their special significance, not only for those who commissioned or created them, but also for our own generation.

To clarify my programme I need only recall the title I have chosen. My context for Roman art is 'the centre of power' – in other words, Rome itself. This topographical limitation was imposed in order to underline the close connection between the birth and development of art in the Roman period, and the birth and development of the city of Rome. In fact, Rome was to remain the hub of Roman history for over eight centuries – despite many vicissitudes, not to mention the predominantly tribal and political features of its earliest period. In the brief space of a few generations, Rome rose to economic supremacy; all the wealth of every Mediterranean country, and many further afield, passed into Roman hands. Rome provided the point at which countless cultural cross-currents met and blended, never emerging with any clarity, but acquiring certain specifically Roman characteristics in the process. Our task is to discover when this quality of Roman-ness, *Romanitas,* first appeared, how it took shape, and just what its historical and artistic significance may have been.

That is why the present work treats art produced *at Rome* – whether it derived from local or imported elements is relatively unimportant – as the creative determinant for Roman civilization until the end of the second century AD, and refers to artifacts from other areas only when they shed light on what was happening in Rome.

The end of the second century, which saw the principate of Commodus (180-92), the last Antonine, also witnessed the onset of a great crisis in the ancient world – a crisis which culminated some hundred years later, and subsequently prepared the way for a transition to the new world of the Middle Ages. Rome was still the administrative centre of the Empire; but from now on the provinces participated more and more in the city's political and cultural life. Once the privilege of Roman citizenship had been granted to all provincials (by the *Constitutio Antoniniana* of AD 212), their influence increased by leaps and bounds. This was particularly true of the Eastern provinces. Finally, in 324, the administrative centre was transferred to Byzantium, on the Bosphorus. On 11 May 330, this 'New Rome' was formally incorporated as the capital of the Empire and known henceforth as Constantinople.

During the period of Hellenistic expansion in Greek art (which dates from Alexander of Macedon's conquest of the Achaemenid Empire), every Mediterranean country regarded naturalism as the one valid form of artistic expression. Under Commodus new elements were introduced, which ran directly counter to naturalism and tended to undermine its hitherto unquestioned effectiveness.

Never, perhaps, in all history has a crisis in art coincided so obviously with political, economic and spiritual upheavals as during the Roman Imperial epoch. This is why I am devoting a separate volume to the later history of ancient art, from its turning-point under Commodus until the emergence of what was primarily a Christian rather than a Roman empire.

There are two sides to the role which Roman art played in history. Looked at in one way, it is the art which took shape by absorbing the heritage of Greece, and transmitted that heritage to the West; but from another viewpoint it is also the art which precipitated a breakaway from Hellenism, and prepared the ground for the Middle Ages. Though originating in Mediterranean civilization, its final flowering anticipates a shift in the centre of artistic gravity: with Byzantine and Carolingian art, the cultural focus moves from the Mediterranean to Europe.

Certain well-nigh ineradicable misconceptions have worked their way into our picture of Roman art. These can be summed up under two general headings. First, there is a belief that art throughout the Roman epoch was simply Greek art under Roman domination. Second, there is the tendency to see Roman art as a direct product of some specifically Roman creative spirit, or even of the Roman 'race' (however mixed its composition), which, so the argument runs, must have set up a strong reaction against any contact with the Hellenistic cultural tradition: a reaction aimed, consciously or unconsciously, at preserving the ethnic elements in Roman art. This latter theory reveals lingering traces of the old romantic concept which credits each nation with special qualities, the so-called *génie de la nation* – a notion which is incompatible with rigorous historical standards.

For art, as for history, the truth is far more complex. There is only one adequate method of studying it: rather than reduce the subject to mere critical formulas, we must examine its more important manifestations case by case. Such a process is valuable when applied to any creative tradition, but especially so as regards Roman art, which was always explicitly linked to *ad hoc* contingencies and never dominated by any kind of aesthetic programme. Great individual artists were rare, and, for the most part, we do not know their names. During the limited periods when they appeared, they found scope for self-expression through the commercial studio-workshops, which turned out figurative or merely ornamental art in sculpture, painting and mosaics. These studios continued to embody the quasi-industrial tradition of mass-produced artifacts which had first come into being during the Hellenistic period, and which lasted from the end of the fourth century BC until the middle of the first. Roman art, as we shall see, was invariably affected by the changing events of history, and that is why it is so important to examine it in the historical and political context of Rome.

The Romans' concern with art came about in an unforeseen and disorganized fashion. Other cultural traditions suggest a deep, spontaneous emotion struggling to assert itself, and advancing – slowly for the most part, but sometimes, as when a great artistic mind brings its unpredictable genius to bear on the scene, with surprising speed – towards a maturely formulated mode of expression. The Romans, by contrast, began by feeling that a style had been foisted upon them by political circumstance. A coherent evolutionary process cannot be traced in Roman art; only architecture shows any signs of it. Yet here, too, it was a long while before aesthetic awareness dawned. For centuries architects remained content to put up Roman buildings with a top-dressing of Hellenistic decoration. Since Roman art did not embody an emotional attitude rooted in the psyche of its social groups, but rather sprang from an *external* contact with Greek art, its character was eclectic *ab initio*. It could thus at once be tailored to suit the needs of any given social programme, a useful medium for disseminating the official party-line. It was produced, for the most part, by artists who stood in a very special relationship to the patrons commissioning their work. These artists were often prisoners-of-war or even slaves; their position *vis-à-vis* their patrons was one of social inferiority. As resident aliens, they did not enjoy Roman civic rights, and could at any time be deported to their country of origin.

During this initial phase of art in the Roman epoch, the patron's desire to abide by a specific programme carried exceptional weight. This is why, in certain works, we find a general concept dictated by exclusively Roman ideas, which is then overlaid by a formal Hellenistic style. Yet because of this forced adaptation, Hellenism comes to lose its individual character. By a slow process of transformation, it turns into what we call 'Roman art'. This grafting of the Hellenistic creative tradition took place within a limited area, which already had a modest but well-defined tradition of its own, known as Mid-Italic, and never totally suppressed or obliterated. This early Italic influence is an important constituent of later developments in Roman art; for reasons of space, however, it is not possible to discuss it in this book. Nor is it possible to survey the final developments of Roman art – a process of expansion from the Mediterranean basin over the greater part of those countries which, a few centuries later, were to constitute Western Europe as we know it. Both these topics will form the subject of further books in this series.

The phase of ancient art to be examined in this work falls between two distinct periods. During the first, the Italian peninsula – rooted at its northern extremity in continental Europe, and bordering towards the south on the Mediterranean – was experiencing the dawn of true civilization, and forming its first scattered cultural nuclei. The second saw the provinces of the Roman Empire making ready to transfer their centre of power from the Mediterranean to Central Europe (a process which reached completion only with the Carolingian era, but began in the third to fourth centuries A D). It was the period when human thought looked for deliverance to the hereafter, rather than to any earthly reality (which, with the decline of ancient science, soon became incomprehensible). This new approach to existence, with its predominantly irrational motivation, first appeared at the end of the period covered by this book. Its influence over the ancient world was to become progressively greater as time went on, and pointed the way towards the Middle Ages.

PART ONE

1   Birth of a Town, a Society, and a Culture

ROME was not born on the Palatine Hill, as we used to be taught in school – even though it is true that traces of early Iron Age huts have been found there, datable to a period which precedes the traditional foundation-year of Rome (753 BC) by over a century. The clusters of dwelling-places which gradually developed on this and neighbouring hills would have remained no more than a centre of secondary importance, had it not been for two things: the existence of the Tiber, and the fact that the Insula Tiberina offered a convenient point at which the river could be bridged. It was here that Rome came into being.

Traditional accounts of the city's origins were handed down by old men who took pride in their arduous past as herdsmen and farmers, in the victory they had wrested from the harsh soil of the Roman Campagna; to them, Rome was an agricultural centre. Yet her spectacular success was due, first and foremost, to the fact that she formed a natural centre for trade. Throughout the world, wherever two important roads cross or a bridge exists, people stop, meet each other; a market springs up. Where you have a bridge, you must also have a public organization to maintain it. In the earliest period, before the law had been codified, all matters of importance to the community acquired religious connotations: thus the person made responsible for the bridge possessed priestly authority; his official title was *pontifex* (bridge-maker).

One cannot overemphasize just how important this bridge was for Rome. Still in the Imperial period it stood there, beneath the steep volcanic slopes of the Capitol and Palatine, debouching on the Forum Boarium and the Forum Olitorium – the old cattle and vegetable markets. From here a gentle slope led down into the valley which, after serving as a cemetery in archaic times, has subsequently become the Forum Romanum. This, originally another market, evolved into Rome's main commercial and political centre.

The Insula Tiberina, and other such outposts of firm ground in what was virtually swampland, provided the only crossing-points between north and south along the entire

4 ROME: THE PALATINE HILL. FOUNDATIONS OF PROTOHISTORICAL HUTS

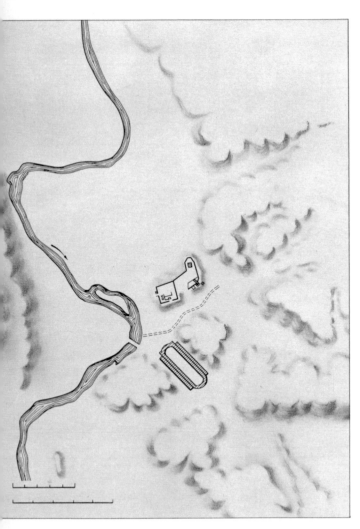

3 THE SEVEN HILLS OF ROME

5 ROME: THE CAPITOL. THE TARPEIAN ROCK

6 ROME: THE INSULA TIBERINA

lower course of the Tiber. The right bank – modern Trastevere – was still known in Horace's day as the 'Etruscan shore' (*litus tuscum*) or the 'Veian bank' (*ripa veiens*), which shows that it had formerly been territory belonging to the Etruscans: Veii was the city of Etruria nearest the Tiber. Etruria was enclosed within two rivers, whose waters flowed down opposite sides of the same mountain range: the Arno in the north, the Tiber to the east and south. Their western boundary was formed by the coast of what the Greeks called the Tyrrhenian Sea, *Tyrrhenoi* being their name for the Etruscans.

The bridge, then, linked Rome with Etruria, which was occupied by a wholly alien non-Latin race. It therefore had to be made in such a way that it could be easily dismantled if trouble broke out between them. It was a bridge of planks, fastened together with rope: hence its name, *Pons Sublicius* (the pile-bridge). To use iron when restoring it was strictly taboo (which suggests that it predates the introduction of iron), and every year, on 14 May, straw dolls were thrown from it into the river, a practice commemorating the age-old sacrifice of human victims to the Tiber, by way of tribute for having got

3

7 ROME: THE FORUM ROMANUM LOOKING TOWARDS THE CAPITOL (17TH C.). ROME, ANTIQUARIUM DI FORO

safely across. It was on this bridge that, according to legend, Horatius Cocles beat off the whole Etruscan army single-handed while his companions broke up the ropes and beams.

On the left – or Roman – bank, the road which crossed the bridge joined an important highway: the Via Salaria, or 'Salt Route'. It was along this road that the precious yield of the Tiber saltern was carried from the Tyrrhenian coast to the inland regions of the peninsula, and thence over the mountains to the shores of the Adriatic.

Rome is virtually encircled by the harsh Sabine mountains, which also hem in the greater part of Latium, descending to the sea at Terracina (Anxur). Because of the commercial expansion of the Etruscans in Campania, all round the Gulf of Naples, Rome became indispensable as a staging-post. In general, when the goods of a trading power have to pass through a particular geographical location, the power concerned makes sure that it does not have to ask anybody's permission. Rome thus came directly under Etruscan influence.

Since the middle of the seventh century BC, the confederation of Etruscan cities had attained a remarkable degree of economic power, mainly through exploiting the copper-

4

8 HORATIUS COCLES HOLDING THE TIBER BRIDGE. PARIS, BIBLIOTHÈQUE NATIONALE

mines on the coast of Tuscany. This economic power had led to the development of a civilization formed largely through regular contact with countries in the Eastern Mediterranean, where artistic motifs that went back to the end of the second millennium BC, deriving from Mesopotamian, Hittite or Caucasian cultural patterns, still flourished. These motifs were spread abroad as a result of trade with Cyprus, Phoenicia, Egypt, and later, above all, with Greece. They appeared on artifacts in bronze, gold, silver, ivory and ceramic. These were luxury products, designed for an aristocratic clientele. Also in this category was the high-class painted pottery imported from Greece: Corinthian ware to begin with, though from about 650 BC onwards Athens took over more and more of Corinth's overseas trade. When this happened, a number of Greek artists – mostly Corinthians – emigrated to Etruria and opened studio-workshops there, which were eventually taken over by their local apprentices.

Southward from harsh Latium, beyond the cross-range of Terracina and the Gulf of Caieta, Campania opens out like the Promised Land. The River Silaris (Sele) marked the southernmost point of Etruscan expansion in this area. Immediately beyond the river lay such flourishing centres of Greek culture as Paestum, and, further south, all the wealthy Greek cities of Magna Graecia and Sicily. Thus Greece and Etruria between them determined the pattern of artistic development in this territory.

From our literary sources we learn that towards the end of the sixth century BC, when the citizens of Rome decided to build a bigger temple in honour of the three Italo-Hellenic deities venerated on the Capitol – Jupiter, Juno and Minerva – this temple was decorated in the Etruscan style. To adorn the pediment and roof-frieze, Etruscan artists were brought over from Veii, where painted terracotta statues had become a speciality. The discovery, at Veii, of terracotta statues representing Apollo, Hermes,

5

9 THE SHE-WOLF OF ROME. ROME, PALAZZO DEI CONSERVATORI

Heracles and other figures, as well as traces of roof-decoration from a late sixth-century temple, confirm this tradition.

Superficial analogies with the Veii terracottas have led scholars to posit an Etruscan origin for the bronze Capitoline wolf. Actually there is nothing specifically Etruscan about this statue; it could just as well have been the work of a Campanian, a Sicel or a Greek artist settled in Italy. As a representation of an animal totem, it may well look back to a period which antedates the legend of the city's twin founders, Romulus and Remus, and their supposed suckling by a wolf.

10 LARINO (LARINUM). SHEPHERDS DISCOVERING THE SHE-WOLF AND TWINS. LARINO: TOWN HALL ▶

11 PRACTICA DI MARE (LAVINIUM): THE THIRTEEN ARCHAIC ALTARS

The legend linking Rome's origins with Troy first appears in the fourth century: not until then do we hear of the arrival of the Trojan prince Aeneas, his marriage with Lavinia, daughter of the local ruler Latinus, and the foundation of a new town, Lavinium. On the ancient site of Lavinium, now Pratica di Mare, 19 miles south of Rome and three miles inland, thirteen archaic-style altars have come to light: proof that as early as the sixth century this place was what it remained ever after, a centre of Rome's official religion and a focal point for local legends, from the arrival of Aeneas to the murder of King Titus Tatius. It was here that Romans paid homage to the Di Penates brought from Troy, and to Vesta, goddess of Fire and Hearth, whose cult was Greek in origin. Here, too, the Dioscuri, Castor and Pollux, had a shrine: the cult of these protective heroes is attested by an inscription on a bronze plaque found among the Lavinium altars, and datable to about 500 BC. All this points to the existence of direct contacts between Latium and Greece from the sixth century onwards, quite independent of the intermediate link provided by the Etruscans.

Rome, then, besides functioning as a commercial *entrepôt* and a staging-post between north and south, provided a point of contact between the artistic traditions of Etruria and Greece. The early Latin language and culture also reveal certain Celtic affinities; culturally, Latium formed the outermost sector of a zone which has been called 'North-west Indo-European', and which, in the field of art, shows a preference for linear or abstract patterns, as one would expect from a civilization in its pre-logical stage of development. No culture in which the representative arts played so small a role (being limited to the decoration of a few terracotta vases) could long resist the influence

8

12 PRACTICA DI MARE (LAVINIUM). PLAQUE BEARING A DEDICATION, IN LATIN, TO THE DIOSCURI. ROME, MUSEO NAZIONALE

of that vigorous naturalism which had established itself as the medium for creative art throughout the Eastern Mediterranean. Thus, in its earliest years, Rome was a town with a mixed artistic tradition, part Etruscan, part Greek.

Rome's most direct and influential contacts, however, were with Etruscan civilization. Yet Roman art was not a mere extension of Etruscan art. To suggest a continuous process of development – as scholars have often done during the past forty years (in fact, ever since Etruscan art was rediscovered by the archaeologists) – is to present an oversimplified picture of history.

Furthermore, when speaking of Etruscan art, one has to distinguish between two main periods. The first, the archaic, extends from the seventh century BC to the beginning of the fifth; during this time, Etruria was an international commercial power, which meant that her art maintained constant direct contact with Greek civilization, while Greek artists set up schools in Etruria. The second period is that during which Etruria no longer enjoyed economic supremacy, and had become little more than a federation of agricultural towns, with an economy indistinguishable from that of any other such group in the Italian peninsula.

A convenient dividing-line between the two periods is the naval victory which Hieron of Syracuse won over the Etruscans off Cumae, in 474 BC; it was after this that the Etruscans abandoned their settlements in Campania. From now on the Greeks and Carthaginians between them began to take over Etruria's maritime trade. Somewhat later, the discovery of mines (especially in Spain) which offered a far richer yield than those of Tuscany put paid to the economic supremacy of the great Etruscan families. Nevertheless, even during this latter period, Etruria retained her cultural pre-eminence over the various groups which made up the population of central Italy. Her contacts with the civilization of the Greek colonies in southern Italy and Sicily – ensured by centuries of tradition – did not come to an end altogether until their conquest by the Romans.

When brought into contact with Etruria's ruling class, Greek legends took on a harsher quality, and the visual arts showed a preference for representations of cruel, gory battle-scenes, and even of human sacrifice. Local legends were depicted with the same obsessional relish, whether they described battles between Etruscan factions, or the struggles of Etruscans against Rome, such as that led by good King Mcstrna (or Mastarna, generally identified with Servius Tullius). These particular paintings come

9

13 VULCI: ETRUSCAN SEPULCHRE, THE FRANÇOIS TOMB. MCSTRNA AND OTHER CHARACTERS IN THE LOCAL LEGEND. ROME, VILLA ALBANI

14 VULCI, THE FRANÇOIS TOMB. ETEOCLES AND POLYNEICES

10

from an Etruscan tomb in Vulci, the so-called François tomb, and can be dated to between 300 and 280 BC. Similar ones must have existed in Rome, but do not survive today.

The first attempt to mount a theatrical entertainment in Rome (364 BC) was a direct imitation of Etruscan methods, and indeed the performers themselves had to be imported from Etruria for the occasion. Two centuries later Roman patricians were still sending their sons to be educated in Etruria; it was said that the 'ceremonies' (*caeremoniae*) of a good education derived from Caere, the Etruscan town nearest to Rome. Even when direct relations with Greece started a fashion for sending students to Athens instead, the change evoked considerable criticism.

Etruscan art during this second period – in particular that of the third and second centuries BC – offers no more than a local variant on the output, mostly craft artifacts, of what we call 'Italic Hellenism'. This, in turn, is simply a provincial manifestation of that full-scale Hellenistic civilization which flourished from about 300 BC in all Greek cities – not only those of ancient Greece itself, but also, indeed primarily, those which became the capitals of flourishing kingdoms under Alexander the Great's heirs: Pergamum, Magnesia, Apamea, Seleucia, Antioch, Alexandria.

It is hard for the modern student to appreciate just how deep-rooted and widespread an influence the Hellenistic creative tradition achieved, especially at craft level: here its workmanship remained of extremely high quality, despite the introduction of assembly-line techniques, necessitated by the growing demand for such products, and their export to virtually every country of the then known world. A modern parallel may help us to understand the situation better. Until the dawn of the twentieth century, the style of European artifacts was wholly determined by all that had been created during those three crowded centuries which began with the Renaissance and culminated in the baroque. Not only paintings and furniture, but every article in daily use, however small or insignificant, contained some direct reflection of this great creative period. An analogous phenomenon in the ancient world was the diffusion of mass-produced Hellenistic art, whose overall influence was, if anything, even more comprehensive, long-lived and intense.

Southern Italy, which (thanks to colonization and commercial contacts) had maintained close relations with the Greeks since remote antiquity, could hardly have remained immune to this influence. Geography made it the nearest overseas market for Greek goods; and, in addition – certainly as regards the towns of Apulia, Campania and Sicily – it became itself a producer of Hellenistic wares, though on a smaller scale and within a far more limited economic system than Greece. This is what is meant by 'Italic Hellenism': a common artistic language in which one can already isolate, almost everywhere, distinct regional dialects or accents. The Sicilian accent comes closest to its original Hellenistic source; the Apulian displays a rich peasant exuberance, together with certain demonstrably Macedonian traits; the Picenian is cruder; the Campanian and Etruscan are closer to one another than to their source.

It remains to ask at what point one can detect an artistic dialect with an accent that is not merely Latin, but specifically Roman. The answer, quite clearly, is that this was a very late phenomenon; even in the fourth and third centuries BC, sculpture and paintings

15 ETRUSCAN BOWL, WITH INSCRIPTION. ROME, MUSEO CAPITOLINO

produced at Rome were still indistinguishable from those of southern Etruria and Campania. However, unless we try to account for this phenomenon, rather than merely accepting it, we shall be in no position either to isolate the distinguishing marks of the earliest Roman art, or to understand anything of its subsequent development.

Offerings with Etruscan inscriptions have been found in archaeological strata between the Tiber and the Capitoline Hill, at the same time as fragments of architectural sculpture in a Graeco-Etruscan style. The most ancient remains of art discovered at Rome are totally indistinguishable from those that have been dug up at Etruscan cities such as Cerveteri and Veii, or at Velletri, Satricum and Falerii, which belonged to the Latins and the Falisci. The character of these various finds, and their relationship to other material in our possession, enable us to rule out the possibility of Rome having been a centre of production from which other towns imported artifacts. Indeed, the reverse seems to have been the case. At the same time, the fact that these remains turned up in cult-buildings scattered over a wide area of the modern town shows that by the end of the sixth century Rome must already have become the largest city in central Italy. However, the advent of the new consular or Republican regime, together with the Volscian invasion of Campania, which disrupted communications with Magna Graecia, provoked an economic crisis; and throughout the fifth century Rome found herself in a far less advantageous position.

19 THE FICORONI CIST (DETAIL, LID): DIONYSUS BETWEEN TWO SATYRS

16

20 THE FICORONI CIST (DETAIL, LID): THE INSCRIPTION

The first time we find the name of Rome on any *objet d'art* is much later. It forms part of the inscription on the famous 'Ficoroni Cist', found in Palestrina, probably a wedding-present from a mother to her daughter. This is a cylindrical receptacle made of copper (not bronze), finely engraved, and designed to keep trinkets and make-up materials in: a metal mirror, an ivory comb, scent-jars, a little rouge-pot, gold ear-rings and necklaces. The inscription itself reads: *Dindia Macolnia fileai dedit Novios Plautios med Romai fecid* ('Dindia Macolnia gave me to her daughter. Novios Plautios made me in Rome'). But the legend represented on the cylindrical surface of the cist is an Italian version of the Greek myth dealing with the Argonauts, portrayed in the style of Greek painting common to the fifth and fourth centuries; while the bronze group on the lid (Dionysus between two satyrs) is a direct imitation of the style adopted by Greek sculptors in the fourth century. As regards its general form, the cist is typical of the work produced at Praeneste (Palestrina), which in 354 BC, probably just before the cist was executed, had renewed its alliance with Rome. As for the name of the artist, Plautios, it is certainly not that of a 'Roman from Rome' (as the city's true natives still like to call themselves), but that of an *émigré* from Campania. The Ficoroni Cist, then, cannot be claimed as a specimen of Roman art, but only as a specimen of the art being produced at Rome during this period. It has even been suggested that Rome was the production-centre for numerous Praeneste-style cists, which were indistinguishable from those being turned out at this time by various other centres in Etruria. Furthermore, the chances are that the inscription refers to Novios Plautios *qua* manufacturer rather than engraver. Stylistically, the cist can be dated to the end of the fourth century BC, or the beginning of the third.

What had Rome been before this? As we have seen, it began life as an Etrusco-Latin city; and, as far as its earliest history is concerned, it is important to remember that it was a township, not an ethnic group or 'nation'. Rome cannot be identified with the Latins, and is to be clearly distinguished from those other peoples whom we describe as 'Italic'. It constituted a separate organism, and one which was both complicated and fast-developing. Nowadays it is hard to conceive that a single town, surrounded by so little territory, could in itself constitute a state. This can be more readily understood if one reflects that even such a city-state is the result of conscious organization; that already it is a complex entity by comparison with scattered family clans, each living in its separate group of huts, or even clans which have amalgamated to form tribes. The town constitutes a state in so far as it represents the union of a number of tribes which acknowledge one central authority. Originally Rome consisted of three tribes, later of twenty-one, and later still, following further territorial acquisitions, of thirty-five. By then, the idea of a tribe had lost all meaning except in bureaucratic or administrative terms; but originally the tribes were genuine familial groups.

Great artistic civilizations, such as those of Mesopotamia, Egypt, India or China, owed both their initial impulse towards urbanization and their cultural evolution to the existence of a great river: the Euphrates, the Nile, the Indus, the Huang Ho. These rivers, with their seasonal floods (and the possibilities of irrigation which such floods provided), led to the development of stable agricultural systems. As a result, it was possible to create, within a short space of time, a regular surplus of capital, which could be used to construct, and embellish, public buildings, mainly of a religious or monumental nature.

No comparable developments took place in Rome. The Tiber, for one thing, was too small a river – even though the actual volume of water it carried was far in excess of its present-day flow. The soil around Rome was no more than a few inches deep, a top-dressing above layers of volcanic tufa and alluvial limestone. Such land is good for nothing except to provide sheep (and not over-demanding cattle) with meagre pasturage. Admittedly, on the nearby Alban hills, and those of Tibur (Tivoli), the earth is fertile; but already at this time, the middle of the fourth century BC, Tivoli was an independent city-state, renewing treaties with Rome on free and equal terms.

In every community where herdsmen and peasants live together, the former regard themselves as the aristocracy, since they are not tied to the land, nor do they have to till it. The herdsman supervises his flocks on horseback, a vantage-point from which he can look down on the toiling peasant, whose shoulders are always bowed over the furrow. When he is short of grain, he also allows himself the privilege of raiding the peasant's crops. By way of compensation, he defends the peasant against external dangers, riding out, sword or spear in hand, to drive off those who attack him. In such a society, different classes very soon establish themselves: patricians, plebeians and knights; while incursions into enemy territory, and the capture of would-be cattle-raiders, provide a class of servants or slaves.

A society of herdsmen and farmers, living in a comparatively infertile region, cannot produce any significant surplus unaided. A rapid marginal increase appears only when a new element is introduced into this pastoral-cum-agricultural economy: commerce. The farmer takes on the role of middleman. This is the factor which, as we have seen, first set Rome on the road to wealth and progress – mainly through the existence of the Tiber and the Salt Route. On the other hand, trade is less reliable than agriculture.

In this way the sixth century BC saw Rome become the chief city of the Tarquins. These legendary so-called 'kings' were Etruscan, which meant that their expulsion, and the subsequent creation of the Roman Republic, were remembered by all Romans as a turning-point in Rome's history. They marked not merely a change of regime, but freedom from foreign domination. The traditionally accepted date for this great event is 509 or 507 BC. It should be remembered, however, that at a certain point the Romans decided to rewrite their earliest history in such a way as to correlate it with that of the Greeks, their main object being to demonstrate that Roman institutions were as long-established as Greek ones, or even more ancient; traditional Roman dates become comparatively reliable only after the year 300, while those for Greek history are equally trustworthy from about 500. Nevertheless, most modern scholars more or less agree with this date for the expulsion of the Tarquins, although it has also been suggested that it should be brought down at least a decade, so as to link it with another crucial date, that of the Etruscan defeat off Cumae in 474 BC. In any case, these two events between them mark the end of an epoch.

After the expulsion of the Tarquins from Rome, and their abandonment of Campania, a period of economic and cultural regression followed: not only for Rome (thus robbed of her key position on a major trade-route), but for the whole of central Italy. This was the price of independence. Primitive mountain tribes, such as the Volscians and Aequi, now swarmed down into Campania, and cut off almost all Rome's contacts with the Greek world. After 421, even Cumae became Samnite. Linguistic analysis confirms the historical tradition, and we have further proof of its accuracy from another source: whereas throughout the sixth century we find a succession of Greek cults being introduced, this movement stops abruptly at the beginning of the fifth. (The Romans always gave a most hospitable reception to each new divinity; being a practical people, they told themselves that one never knew which god might be kindly disposed, or what he might do if rebuffed. A new cult, even if not of any obvious benefit, at least could do no positive harm.) After the introduction of the cult of the Dioscuri, in 484 (Livy, 2.42.5), there was a long gap. It lasted for close on two hundred years, until 293, when the cult of Asclepius (or Aesculapius) was imported from Epidaurus, and established, significantly, on the Insula Tiberina. Etruscan civilization during this period reveals a parallel lacuna in its contacts with Greece.

Thanks to Plutarch (*Numa* 17.3), we possess a list of the trade guilds which existed in early Rome, probably towards the end of the sixth century. They include flute-players, goldsmiths, joiners, dyers, cobblers, tanners, braziers and potters. Scholars have commented on the absence of bakers, laundrymen, weavers, butchers, and blacksmiths. Such omissions indicate a primitive and rural way of life: bread is baked at home, women do their own washing and weaving. There are no butchers because no one buys meat. Those who own cattle slaughter them privately; lesser folk get meat to eat only when the flesh of sacrificial offerings is distributed. In so restricted an economy it is hardly surprising that the list of tradesmen (which we can reconstruct from several sources) does not include stonemasons, architects, painters, sculptors, or even one guild lumping them all together. Iron, it seems, was still rare, while copper – used by braziers in the form of its alloy, bronze – always came from Etruria. But we do find goldsmiths, and indeed one

21 THE SERPENT OF ASCLEPIUS LANDS ON THE INSULA TIBERINA. PARIS, BIBL. NATIONALE

of the most ancient surviving Latin inscriptions is preserved on a gold brooch, the so-called 'Manios fibula', an article of patently Etruscan design.

During the fifth century, Rome narrowed her sphere of influence, both materially and culturally. There was a danger (of which her leaders were well aware) that, after having been a flourishing commercial city, she would sink back into agricultural obscurity. This was what drove her, from now on, to throw all her resources into the struggle against her near neighbours, and to establish direct relations with any dominant maritime power.

A century later, about 355, the first Roman coins appear. Rome's official emblem was the prow of a ship, symbolizing commerce – though the value of money (*pecunia*) was still determined by a standard based on ownership of livestock (*pecus*). This coinage was not struck but cast, in bronze; it appeared late in the day compared with those of the cities of the Eastern Mediterranean, and was so large and heavy (each coin weighed 272·87 gr.) that it proved highly inconvenient for commercial purposes. As a result the standard was several times reduced.

Rome established permanent contact with the Greek-controlled trading-area of Italy after ratifying a treaty with Neapolis (Naples) in 326. This is why the old, heavy, bronze Italic-style currency was replaced – a unique transition – by a new coinage, Greek in style and based on Greek metrology, mostly silver and bronze, but with occasional issues in gold. In this, as in all else, we see Rome acting, not on any kind of theory or system, but in accordance with the practical requirements of a situation as it arose.

For Rome the fifth century had been, above all, a period of internal consolidation. Her first codification of laws, the 'Twelve Tables', was carried out, while great advances in military organization also took place – largely, it seems, as a by-product of patrician

22 ETRUSCAN-TYPE BROOCH KNOWN AS THE 'MANIOS FIBULA'. ROME, MUSEO PREISTORICO E ETNOGRAFICO L. PIGORINI

23-24 THE OLDEST ROMAN COIN. OBVERSE: HEAD OF JANUS. REVERSE: PROW OF A SHIP. ROME, MUSEO NAZIONALE

25 VEII: A SANCTUARY, WITH A ROMAN ROAD RUNNING PAST IT

26 ROME: DEFENSIVE FORTIFICATIONS (THE SO-CALLED SERVIAN WALL)

22

reaction against the plebs. It was also the period when she first began to establish her great network of contacts throughout the Mediterranean. About the end of the century, or at the beginning of the next, according to tradition, the first treaty with Carthage was signed. Now that Pyrgi, the port of Caere, has yielded inscriptions attesting close links, at this very period, between the Etruscans of Caere and certain Punic-speaking peoples, this tradition has become historically plausible. Also in the fifth century, we find hints of Rome's subsequent head-on clash with the Celtic tribes of Gaul, who had already penetrated as far south as the Po Valley.

The city of Rome had been built on very uneven ground; the Palatine and Capitoline hills were far steeper than they are today, and provided excellent natural defences, while the valley-bottoms linking them were for the most part marshland. It is possible that some of the hills were partially fortified as early as the sixth century; but apparently it was not until Rome had been sacked during the Gallic invasion that her citizens began to build a wall round the entire city (378 BC). This was the so-called 'Servian Wall', firmly based on square-cut blocks of tufa, and enclosed by an outer ditch; numerous traces of the latter still survive, enough to enable us to reconstruct the city's perimeter at this period.

The incursion of the Gauls – a people who were radically different from any local tribe, and had made their long journey for the specific purpose of looting this comparatively wealthy city – left a deep and traumatic impression on the Romans (as, indeed, on all the inhabitants of the peninsula). From now on, Rome's first and most vital task, as her citizens saw it, was to insulate herself by means of a self-sufficient ring of autonomous territory. The first important rival city which fell to her, about the beginning of the fourth century (traditional date: 396 BC) was the Etruscan foundation of Veii, a mere ten miles distant. By 304, at the end of the Second Samnite War, Rome was already a power to be reckoned with in the peninsula; after the victory of Sentinum in 295, she stood supreme.

The character and mentality of these Romans had been formed by an age-long struggle, not only against natural hazards and poverty, but against neighbours very much like themselves. By the beginning of the Republican era they had established a recognizable pattern of behaviour. They were hard men, violent of temper and tenacious of purpose, accustomed to back-breaking work and absolute authority within the family. Mentally and physically they were peasants, who devoted themselves to their own practical and immediate interests, to the profit they might attain through individual effort backed by collective determination in the face of adversity – but also through crafty deceit, their one true Muse. They were hagridden by the belief that vague and uncontrollable forces constantly threatened them: this tended to produce an outlook in which gross superstition was tempered by a streak of surly distrust. So distrustful were they, in fact, that they refused to name the deity under whose protection their city lay, and would not even reveal if this mysterious being was a god or a goddess (Macrobius, *Saturn.* 3.9). Even as late as the civil wars which broke out at the very end of the Republican era, to be accused of having revealed the sacred name furnished an adequate excuse for legalizing political murder. A society composed of men with this kind of mentality would logically regard as superfluous, and perhaps even as incomprehensible, anything not immediately useful or

27 SANTA MARIA DI FALLERI (FALERII NOVI): GATE IN THE CITY-WALL

practical. Again and again, when questions of art or philosophy come up, Roman writers cannot resist a sneering reference to 'those crazy Greeks'; but they must have thought them no less crazy in their attitude to moral and political problems.

Aesthetic speculation was totally alien to these men, as was, generally speaking, any kind of abstract theorizing. (Thus, whereas by this time the Romans had amassed a considerable body of juridical experience, and had established laws and legal provisions, they had notably failed to develop any theory of law. In 173, and again in 161 BC, they expelled numbers of Greek philosophers from Rome as a corrupting influence.) On the other hand, the Romans were quick to appreciate a first-class engineer or master mason. The walls of the settlement at Falerii Novi (built about 210 BC), with their nine gates and fifty guard-towers, show a real flair for building. As had previously been the case with the walls of the Latin settlement at Cosa (273 BC), the constructional technique was still that developed by the Etruscans.

Roman architecture was in existence long before Roman painting or Roman sculpture. Yet even as late as the second century BC a permanent theatre built of stone was condemned as 'useless and morally harmful' (Livy, *Epit.* 48), and demolished, by order of the Censors, while still under construction. (Some scholars argue that in fact the authorities were anxious not to give the people any chance of turning their theatre into a fortress.) It took several further generations – not to mention the establishment of unassailable power and a vast influx of wealth – for the Romans to realize that no one can claim to belong to the civilized world without displaying a certain interest in art. The discovery must have been a disturbing one for the old people, but it held out a considerable lure for the younger generation, who – as Plutarch says in a passage to which I shall return – 'now spent a large part of the day discussing art and artists.'

Throughout the fourth century BC, Rome's horizons were restricted to central Italy. During this period she was allied, by a number of treaties and agreements, to the main cities of Etruria, of Latium

28 DISH WITH WAR-ELEPHANT DECORATION. ROME, MUSEO NAZIONALE (VILLA GIULIA)

itself, and, above all, of Campania. But by the end of the fourth and the early years of the third century, her horizons had begun to expand rapidly and her rigidly patrician society was forced to accept the idea of change, and compound with new social requirements. The plebeians, firmly rebuffed after the first few years of the Republic, now began to hold office in the *collegia* of the pontiffs and augurs. The way they got a foot inside the door – by exploiting cult and ritual – is typical of Roman society.

The war which Rome undertook against Tarentum, the most flourishing and civilized of all South Italian cities, brought King Pyrrhus of Epirus and his army to Italy and Sicily (280 BC). This occasion witnessed the Romans' first encounter with a new and extraordinary instrument of combat, which undoubtedly made a great impression on them: the elephant, guided by armed men who rode inside a little tower on its back. However, the evidence we have to illustrate this event – a piece of Italic craftsmanship perhaps from Latium itself – falls, morphologically speaking, within the context of Hellenistic art. This was the first large-scale direct contact of the Roman people with a totally Hellenized folk. It was soon followed, within a decade, by a treaty with a Greek

29 ROME: TOMB OF THE SCIPIOS. SARCOPHAGUS OF L. CORNELIUS SCIPIO BARBATUS. MUSEI VATICANI

prince of Egypt, Ptolemy II Philadelphus, heir to the African province of Alexander's empire.

There followed the final victory over Tarentum (272 BC), the capture of Rhegium (270 BC), and Rome's alliance with Syracuse at the time of the First Punic War (264-241 BC): to set foot in Sicily led, inevitably, to a show-down with Carthage. Finally, in 228, Romans were granted permission to compete in the Isthmian Games at Corinth – which meant, in effect, election to the closed society of those nations nurtured on Greek civilization.

These early contacts, together with successful campaigns in Sardinia, Corsica and Dalmatia, did not as yet lead to any substantial changes in the pattern of Roman culture. Some of the countries with which Rome now established relations were more backward than those of the Italian peninsula. Near the beginning of the Via Appia (the part which was subsequently enclosed within the city-walls), in a still-accessible family vault, that of the Scipios, stands the sarcophagus of one of these victorious generals, Scipio Barbatus. This sarcophagus, datable to about 250 BC, is clearly directly inspired by Sicilian models: simple and architectural in style, it bears no image of any sort – a point worth noting when one recalls what great advances took place in portraiture towards the end of the Republic.

30 LUCERA: SHEPHERD RELIEF. LUCERA, MUSEO PROVINCIALE

For an example of indigenous art before its encounter with Hellenism, we may turn to a relief in the Museo Provinciale at Lucera, which portrays a shepherd with his sheep – pastoral art in a very literal sense. A fragment of this kind is extremely hard to date, since primitive art, and what we may call 'non-culture', are timeless: their manifestations exist *sub specie aeternitatis*. In an Italic context, such a sculpture could equally well belong to the fifth century BC or the first century AD. The only way of dating it would be through a cross-check with pottery sherds. Were any sherds found at the same time as the relief, and if so, of what type were they? We do not know.

31 ORPHEUS AND THE ANIMALS. ROME, PALAZZO DEI CONSERVATORI

What we do know, from our literary sources, is that as early as the fourth century BC statues honouring legendary or historical persons were often set up at Rome, in the Forum. The earliest extant example records the erection of statues on the Rostra in memory of four Roman citizens, sent as ambassadors to Fidenae and killed by the King of the Veians (438). After this there is a gap of over a century in the tradition before we find a reference to any other such statues. From about 340, however, they are by no means uncommon, and include equestrian groups.

All these figures appear to have been in bronze, and we know that some of them formed part of the plunder taken from cities in Etruria or Magna Graecia. Because they were bronze, they all disappeared during the great metal-shortage which resulted from the final economic collapse of the Roman Empire. Perhaps only one fragment from this period has survived, part of what was probably an equestrian statue. This is the head which, during the Renaissance, was placed on a bust and kept in the Capitol, under the name of Junius Brutus, founder of the Republic – a purely imaginary identification (frontispiece).

To place this remarkable portrait in its stylistic context is difficult. The general background to which it belongs has not yet been seriously investigated, and what work does exist is often marred by preconceptions. Quite certainly it is not an example of Greek art, even if its author took the Greeks as his masters; nor does it belong to Roman art, for what we are entitled to describe as 'Roman' is something essentially different – even though the ethical content discernible in those stern features has a Roman quality. Forty years ago I suggested that it might be Etruscan work; but this was really no more than a way of saying that it belonged neither to Greek nor to Roman art, as had hitherto been supposed. At that time, no one had yet recognized the existence of Mid-Italic art, to be clearly differentiated both from Etruscan and from the sort of Greek art that was imported into Sicily and Magna Graecia. Though it had contacts with both (and picked up useful suggestions from them), its inner strength derived from that austerity characteristic of all mountain

32 ISERNIA: RELIEF OF A BATTLE-SCENE. ISERNIA MUSEUM

peasants. It shows scant sympathy with the elegance of Hellenistic Greek art, and is more inclined to borrow the latter's iconography and composition than its formal language. It covers an area extending from Apulia to Picenum, from Campania to Samnium and Latium; it embodies the common stock of Italy's artistic tradition south of the Apennines, prior to Rome's expansion throughout the peninsula. This Mid-Italic tradition – active about the middle of the third century BC, and always immune to that frivolous elegance characteristic of the Hellenistic Age's predominantly urban culture – was, surely, responsible for our supposed head of Brutus (which, incidentally, well matches the character of the legendary figure to whom it has been attributed).

The Mid-Italic artistic tradition lies outside the scope of this book, and indeed deserves separate investigation; but it does provide the essential antecedents to Roman art. It is within the Mid-Italic culture that one can, at a certain point, isolate a specifically Roman accent; and to define this accent, in terms of its development and character, is the main object of this book.

The Mid-Italic artistic tradition must undoubtedly have had its own studio-workshops in Rome. We have already considered the case of Novios Plautios. Mid-Italic, too, are various works which we know to have been executed *in situ*: witness those architectural and sculptured fragments in calcareous stone (*peperino*), originally part of a tomb belonging to the flute-players' guild on the Esquiline, which can be dated between the end of the second and the beginning of the first century BC. It has often been claimed, erroneously, that this is also the source of a group depicting Orpheus surrounded by animals, found near the Porta Tiburtina. Here we have a basically Hellenistic concept, with flowing, elegant movements – typical provincial Hellenism of the Italic variety – overlaid by a certain rustic heaviness. It is not Etruscan work, and must, once again, be attributed to a Mid-Italic artist.

29

Very much the same effect is produced by a provincial relief from Isernia, portraying a Roman battle. This relief borrows – awkwardly, but not without a certain effectiveness – the basic pattern of a famous late-fourth-century picture depicting Alexander at Issus, of which the great mosaic unearthed in Pompeii is a slightly modified copy. Here we are already on the brink of the Imperial epoch; but Hellenistic influences are still all-pervasive.

This cultural tradition must be very clearly distinguished from the new influx of Hellenism which was occasioned by the removal to Rome of numerous original works of Greek art, and the establishment of Greek artists and craftsmen in what had become the Mediterranean's new political centre. This influx came late in the day, a superficial top-dressing which (culturally speaking) never spread beyond the Rome-based elite who owed their position to a mixture of wealth and social prestige. The tradition of Mid-Italic Hellenism, on the other hand, was born, and grew, in association with Hellenistic art as such, which became the direct, natural mode of expression throughout central and southern Italy. Here Campania played a particularly important role, being the only region to remain relatively unaffected by that general decline which overcame all southern Italy after the Second Punic War (218-201 BC).

Also to Mid-Italic culture must be assigned those coins struck by the Allies during their war against Rome (91-88 BC), on which the name ITALIA appears for the first time. It would be wrong, however, to interpret such a legend as a desperate *cri de coeur* on the part of the Italians, anxious to escape subjection to Rome; what they were fighting Rome for was not independence but integration, and in fact by the law of 90-89 BC all Italians were granted Roman citizenship. After this date there was no legal distinction between Italians and Romans – which meant, also, that the dividing-line between Italian

33-34 COIN. OBVERSE: WOMAN'S HEAD AND INSCRIPTION 'ITALIA'. REVERSE: MILITARY OATH-TAKING. ROME, MUSEO NAZIONALE

35 CERVETERI (CAERE): VOTIVE HEAD. VATICAN, MUSEO ETRUSCO GREGORIANO ▶

36-37 ARICCIA: STATUES OF DEMETER AND KORE-PERSEPHONE. ROME, MUSEO NAZIONALE

and Roman art became increasingly blurred. A whole cultural no-man's-land existed, where – in contrast with the sophisticated urban centres, with their prevalent neo-Atticism – the preference for marble had not yet developed, and the bulk of artifacts were still produced in terracotta.

This is the source of the statues and busts which turn up in large quantities from the sanctuaries of Latium, to the north, east and south of Rome. One typical example is a collection of votive offerings found near Castelletto, in the Ariccia valley, which included bronze coins ranging from the earliest Romano-Campanian issues of the fourth century BC to pieces struck under the Emperor Claudius. Side by side with more modest offerings were two remarkable statues of Kore-Persephone and Demeter, the latter being represented also by a bust. This bust is clearly inspired by Sicilian models, which still retained some trace of that characteristic expression familiar to us from the Demeter of

32

38 ARICCIA: BUST OF DEMETER. ROME, MUSEO NAZIONALE

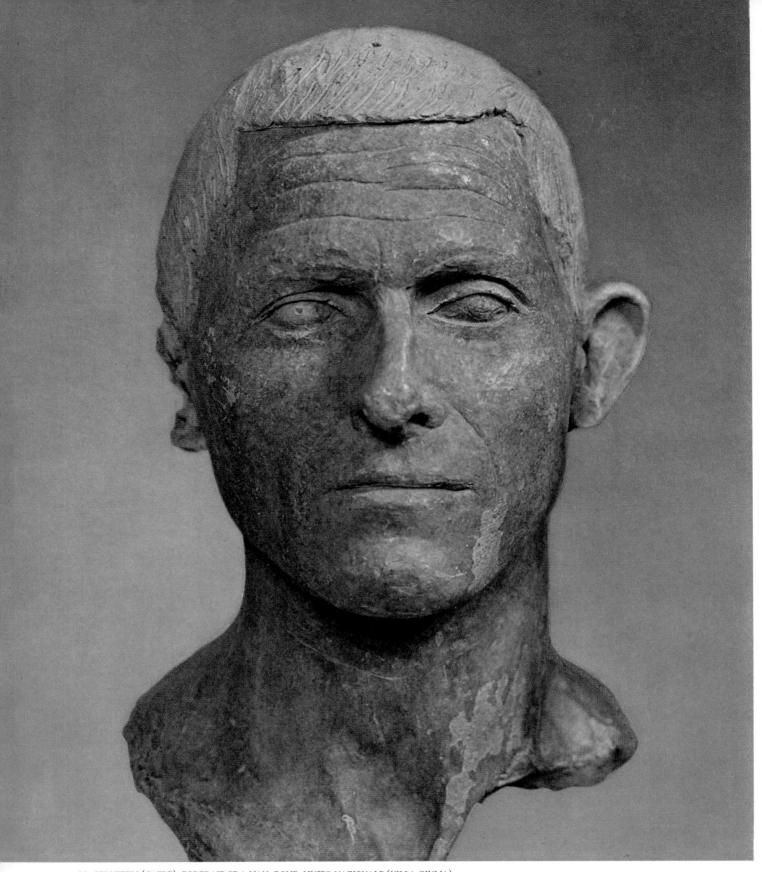

39 CERVETERI (CAERE). PORTRAIT OF A MAN. ROME, MUSEO NAZIONALE (VILLA GIULIA)

40 FUNERARY RELIEF (DETAIL). ROME, PALAZZO DEI CONSERVATORI   41 POMPEY THE GREAT. COPENHAGEN, NY CARLSBERG GLYPTOTEK

Cnidos. Some inscriptions (concerning the Gens Duronia) recall an episode described by Livy (39.9), which may be assigned to the year 186 BC.

These sculptures date to about the middle of the second century BC. They furnish a typical example of an art-form which cannot as yet be termed Roman, but which embodies the artistic tradition then current in Rome – a tradition also responsible for the pedimental decorations of the temples in this town (statues in the Via S. Gregorio). In some other cases the Roman accent is more marked, even affecting non-Roman production-centres round about. The way in which one particular concept of portraiture developed at Rome forms the subject of my next chapter; we can glimpse a reflection of the *genre* in a terracotta portrait-bust from Caere. This belongs to a branch of art which catered specially for the bourgeoisie; a generation or so later, it produced portraits such as that which adorns one of the gravestones belonging to the tomb at the beginning of the Via Praenestina (Via Statilia).

However, during this same period, there were artists at Rome whose education had been more directly Hellenistic – or even Greeks, such as the one who executed a portrait

35

of Pompey the Great, which we can recognize from coins struck in his honour by his son Sextus, when Quintus Nasidius controlled the mint. The capture and subsequent sack of Syracuse in 212 BC, during which Archimedes lost his life, had marked a decisive step forward in Rome's direct contact with Hellenistic art.

Three hundred years later Plutarch wrote a biography of the victorious Roman general, Marcellus, who, he claimed (*Marcell.* 21), 'stripped Syracuse of nearly all its finest works of art to display in his triumphal procession and adorn the City. Hitherto Rome had never seen, much less owned, such luxurious and sophisticated creations; nor, indeed, did Romans have any taste for artistic *chefs-d'oeuvre,* however graceful and elegant they might be. . . . Marcellus therefore won public esteem for having enriched the City with a most enjoyable exhibition, which included every kind of art and was all in the most exquisite Greek taste; but the older generation still thought more highly of Fabius Maximus. After the capture of Tarentum, Fabius had carried off no works of art, but simply laid hands on all the cash and valuables, leaving the statues where they stood, with the remark (or so tradition has it): "Let the Tarentines keep their angry gods." Marcellus was actually criticized to begin with, for having stirred up envy and hatred against Rome, since he gave the impression of leading prisoner in his triumph not only men, but the immortal gods themselves. He incurred further censure for encouraging idleness and gossip in a people more properly accustomed to fighting and tilling the soil, a race that shunned all softness and frivolity, being, like the Euripidean Hercules, "blunt, rough-mannered, good only for great exploits"; and for leading them to waste much of their time in sophisticated chit-chat about art and artists. Nevertheless, [Marcellus] boasted, even to the Greeks, of having taught the Romans to admire and appreciate these marvellous Greek works of art, which hitherto had been a closed book to them.'

This passage might, if unsupported, lose something of its documentary value by reason of being written so long after the event, and by a Greek, who would perhaps take pleasure in emphasizing the rustic simplicity of the early Romans. But the tradition behind it, on which Plutarch drew, was undoubtedly ancient and, moreover, specifically Roman in origin. Livy himself confirms it (25.40.1-3) when he observes that the capture of Syracuse marked 'the beginning of [Roman] admiration for Greek works of art'. Furthermore, the underlying superstition which we can detect in the words attributed to Fabius Maximus, and the criticisms levelled at Marcellus by the older generation, conveys an authentically Roman flavour.

We can, then, accept the fact that from the close of the third century BC people in Rome began to find out that art is something more than a matter of technique, and that the discussion of art is one of the most exciting ways of exploring human nature. At the same time it should be noted that even two generations later the Romans had made singularly little headway in this field; at Rome, art still did not form part of *paideia* (that is, the education and basic cultural background acquired by every person of good family), as it had always done in Greece.

Indeed, the victorious general who, in 146, auctioned off the plundered treasure of Corinth, was so astonished by the high bid made by King Attalus of Pergamum for an ancient picture depicting Dionysus that, says Pliny (35.24), 'suspecting that something of value was hidden in it unbeknown to him (*aliquid in ea virtutis, quod ipse nesciret*), he withdrew it from the sale.' According to tradition, the bid had been one of 600,000 denarii. Working out monetary equivalents for so remote a period always presents difficulties. However, we do know that at the time such a sum was worth 198 kg. of pure gold, or, alternatively, would buy 10,000 oxen. Later, under the Empire, 250,000 denarii was the minimum capital requirement for anyone who aspired to enter the Roman Senate. Under Hadrian, a legionary's annual pay was raised from 225 to 300 denarii. If we convert the sum into modern currency, it amounts, roughly, to $160,000 – about the price one might pay for an authenticated Old Master. Nor can one make allowances for Mummius's ignorance of art on the grounds that he was, after all, a general and not a connoisseur. There was no such thing at Rome as a 'career officer', and this general was also, and at the same time, Consul – that is, one of the two Heads of State, a leading citizen and politician. One is forced to conclude that Mummius's attitude and mentality were typical of the ruling class in his day. Even so, one or two intellectuals may have existed in Rome who knew that the artist who painted this picture, Aristides of Thebes, was the founder of the 'Attic School' of art (early fourth century). But – and this tells us a good deal about Roman society – if such an intellectual *did* exist at the time, he would undoubtedly have felt embarrassed, perhaps even ashamed, to confess such expert knowledge before his fellow-citizens.

After the capture of Syracuse, innumerable further opportunities for examining – and acquiring – Greek works of art presented themselves, though the Romans were thinking more in terms of winning battles than exploring intellectual contacts, and such works of art as were brought to Rome remained public property. The war against Philip V of Macedon ended, in 194 BC, with a great triumph celebrated by the Consul Flaminius, who brought fresh consignments of statues and valuable engraved vessels to Rome. Then there was the war undertaken against Antiochus III, which reached its climax with the capture of Magnesia-by-Sipylus, and resulted in the capture – by another Scipio – of all Hellenized

42 ROMAN COIN: M. CLAUDIUS MARCELLUS. PARIS

43 ATTIC COIN: T. QUINCTIUS FLAMININUS. BERLIN

Asia Minor. This victory sent flooding into Rome the most exquisite products of a nation where Hellenistic art had taken root, and spread, with particular freshness, originality and wealth of imagination. It also, as Livy and Pliny both tell us (Livy, 37.59.3-5; Pliny, *NH* 34.34), 'put an end to wooden or terracotta statues in Roman temples, which were now replaced by imported works of art'. During the triumph there were offered up 224 military standards, 134 models of conquered towns, 1,231 sets of elephant tusks, 234 gold crowns, 137,420 lb. melted-down silver, 224,000 tetradrachms, 321,000 Asiatic coins (cistophori), 140,000 gold pieces (philippi), engraved silver vases to a total weight of 423 lb., and gold vases weighing 1,023 lb., not to mention 134 statues of assorted deities. The overall value of all this loot was an estimated 18,000,000 denarii. The list of war-booty and indemnities for the years 200 and 157 (conveniently set out by Tenney Frank, *Economic Survey of Ancient Rome,* Vol. I, pp. 127-38) gives an impressive picture of the wealth which flowed endlessly into Rome, year after year. During this initial phase of conquest, looting was restricted to the temples. To take over a conquered people's gods was a regular excuse for pillage, and presented a most profitable undertaking, from every point of view.

The climax came in 146 BC, the year when Scipio Aemilianus finally captured Carthage and Lucius Mummius, by reducing Corinth, brought the whole of mainland Greece to heel, Athens included. One example will suffice. Outside the city-walls, in the Campus Martius, there stood an ancient temple of Apollo, which was completely renovated early in Augustus's reign by Caius Sosius, governor of Syria in 38, and a year later the conqueror of Jerusalem. This elegant temple, now rebuilt in the Hellenistic manner, had become a kind of museum. It contained the following items: an Apollo in cedar-wood, brought from Seleucia; twelve statues by the Rhodian sculptor Philiscus – Apollo and Leto, Diana with the nine Muses – which were widely copied and imitated; an Apollo Citharoedus (i.e. as harp-player), executed by Timarchides, an Athenian sculptor of the second century BC; a statue-group portraying Niobe and her children, attributed variously to Scopas or Praxiteles; a picture by Aristeides of Thebes, the fourth-century artist already mentioned; and various other works. Among these last, and still recognizable today, was a statue of Apollo drawing his bow. One ingenious scholar has advanced the theory that this is an original piece by Pythagoras of Rhegium (the most distinguished sculptor in Magna Graecia during the classical period) and was looted from Croton, on the coins of which it is reproduced.

This epoch, then, saw the acquisition, as war-booty, of countless original Greek works: sculpture, paintings, examples of toreutic art (work in precious materials). Given such conditions, a new species inevitably developed: the obsessional collector, whose thirst for *objets d'art* was unlikely to be satisfied by the contemplation of pieces belonging to temples, princes or cities. It was during this second phase that copies of statues and famous paintings and other works inspired by classical art began to be produced and imported on a large scale. They were mainly turned out in the neo-Attic workshops of Athens, a city which still, for the Romans, symbolized art and culture, but was also the nearest convenient market. This passion for collecting made a noticeable impact on the economy, and public opinion began to regard art with rather more respect. But, granted these exceptional conditions, which later ages never equalled for comprehensiveness or

44 HERCULANEUM: HOUSE WITH WOODEN FRAMEWORK

intensity, it is clear that an original, coherent artistic tradition could not possibly develop. Such a *pot-pourri* of styles and periods was bound to produce a highly eclectic taste (eclectic in the same sense as the 'bad taste' of middle-class Europeans in the second half of the nineteenth century) – a taste centred on what was rare, curious or *outré*, rather than open to any real understanding of the meaning of artistic form as such. All these novelties had to become completely absorbed, had to become normal and taken for granted, before they could form the soil from which a new artistic civilization could spring. The conditions under which Roman art took shape are so exceptional that one must never lose sight of them if one wants to grasp the historical significance and value of its development.

Roman society had hitherto followed a patriarchal way of life, and its cultural horizons had been kept deliberately rustic, to match the old tradition of thrift and simplicity – a tradition itself brought into being by Rome's limited economic potential, individual no less than collective. As in Etruria, the temples were built of wood, on an elevated stone stylobate, and decorated with mould-cast, painted terracotta. As for the houses, they consisted of stone and mortar inside a timber framework (as we can still see at Herculaneum). Local pottery was of terracotta, and very coarse. Black glazed Campanian ware, with a few motifs in high relief, imitating bronze, has been found over a wide area. Red-glaze pottery, some of it very unevenly fired, with engraved palm-leaf decorations, was imported from Etruscan factories in the Arno Valley (where later, under Augustus, the *terra sigillata* workshops came into being). Bronze receptacles were used, but seldom adorned with relief-work. As for silver table-ware, this was still such a rarity that on one occasion – circumstantial evidence suggests a date of 150 BC – the members of a Carthaginian embassy to Rome, entertained in turn by various patrician families, always found themselves eating off the same silver dinner-service, which was passed on from one host to the next. This state of affairs is confirmed by another anecdote. In 172 BC, ambassadors from Aetolia were invited to dine with the Consul, Aelius Cato, and served from coarse earthenware platters. Afterwards they sent him a set of silver plate as a present, but he refused to accept it (Pliny, *NH* 33.142-3). This was the son-in-law of Aemilius Paullus, who in 168 BC defeated King Perseus at the battle of Pydna – a victory which led to the dismemberment of Macedonia. At the time of his death, Aelius possessed only two silver cups, and even these were a present from his father-in-law.

Such a parsimonious outlook had been, hitherto, characteristic of Roman society as a whole; but, within the space of a single generation, Rome became the centre of the greatest concentration of capital known to history. This influx of capital more than bears comparison with capital flows of modern times, since what it meant, in effect, was the centralization of all liquid assets from one end of the Mediterranean basin to the other. A proportion of these assets were destined for the State Treasury, but the larger part remained in private hands. In no other place has political power ever been so wholly dependent on wealth. Such was the opulence of Rome at this time that in 65 BC Julius Caesar paid for a gladiatorial show which offered three hundred and twenty matched pairs of fighters, all wearing silver breastplates; on another occasion he exhibited four hundred lions. Entertainment on such a scale is costly, and all this took place *before* the expedition to Spain which marked the beginning of his fame and fortune. The baker and army contractor Marcus Crassus (it was he who crushed Spartacus's revolt, subsequently crucifying six thousand rebels along the Via Appia between Capua and Rome) left, at his death, a fortune amounting to 200,000,000 sesterces, or about 2,000,000 gold sovereigns.

The consequences of this economic explosion have been widely studied from the general historical viewpoint, but they must also be borne in mind when examining the history of art. First and foremost, Rome's age-old political institutions were struck a blow from which they never really recovered. The boom showed up their shortcomings, made it all too clear how inadequate they were for controlling the ultra-complex system of an imperially orientated state. It was only with the Principate of Augustus, who transformed the government into a *de facto* monarchy, based on the strictest bureaucratic organization (though all the time camouflaging his real power behind a smooth legalistic façade) that Rome achieved peace and internal security once more.

The last century of the Republic was a terrible period, during which the political struggle was fought out to its bitter end, with no holds barred and violence as the sole means of deciding each issue. And violence took many forms: brawling in the streets, unprovoked aggression, the assassin's dagger, confiscation of property, exile and civil war. In what is perhaps his earliest surviving poem (Epode XVI), written about the year 41, Horace, then twenty-four, dreams of leading a peaceful, obscure life in the country, seriously considers leaving Rome to her fate and taking off for the blessed isles of the eastern sea.Even though his pastoralism follows a literary fashion copied from Hellenistic models, there is genuine feeling here: a sense of weariness, the urge to escape, a yearning for moral regeneration. One reason why Augustus succeeded was that he not only latched on to this feeling, but found a way of satisfying it.

It was against this background of bitter and bloody conflict, overnight fortunes and unbridled ambition that a new artistic civilization came into existence at Rome. Whereas previously her citizens had merely seen and studied Greek works of art, from now on there would be the heady prospect of *owning* them, either through purchase or by the kind of extortion that the conquest of these Hellenized countries had made all too easy. Every wealthy Roman wanted to emulate the luxury that had been a *sine qua non* of all Hellenistic royal courts. This is the model we need to bear in mind if we want to understand the special preferences shown by Roman connoisseurs during this period, not to mention the character imparted to villas and gardens, even to interior decoration. After the eruption of Vesuvius in 79 AD, certain towns in Campania were buried under a thick layer of ashes. This sudden interruption of daily life has meant that Pompeii and Herculaneum furnish us with evidence that is lacking for Rome, where life has gone on continuously from antiquity until our own day, progressively eliminating the past. Even so, contemporary Rome is richer in ancient monuments than any other city. In Pompeii and Herculaneum, the middle-class houses, surely of modest luxury compared with those owned by Rome's *grand seigneurs*, nevertheless amaze us by the richness of their pictorial decoration. This phenomenon has been well explained as an attempt to equate the house with a *Mouseion,* and to reproduce the description of a royal Hellenistic palace. There is nothing which so vividly recalls the decoration of a Pompeian house as the still-surviving account of the royal pavilion belonging to Ptolemy II Philadelphus (283-221 BC). The pictures in the middle of the panels; the tapestries, woven with lively scenes, which hung in each corner and acted as dividing walls; the metal tripods, the slender wooden columns supporting the tent itself – all are common to both contexts. But what in the actual pavilion was three-dimensional reality is represented, in Pompeii, by *trompe-l'oeil* painting. On other walls we can see great courtyards and colonnades, drawn in retreating perspective, and built around an elegant little circular temple, decorated with garlands – the sort of thing which, at this period, existed neither in Campania nor at Rome.

If the middle classes had to make do with such painted dreams, there did exist a few exceptionally wealthy individuals who could translate at least some of these Hellenistic splendours into reality. In their luxurious homes they accumulated statues, bronzes and silverware – all the more highly valued if they showed signs of long use, which made it clear that they were Hellenistic originals, and not 'modern' derivatives.

45 POMPEII: TOMB OF VESTORIUS PRISCUS. SILVER DINNER-SERVICE ON A TABLE

This obsession with the past remained a characteristic of artistic culture throughout the period we are discussing, including the whole Julio-Claudian epoch. It also crops up again later, giving rise to a series of 'neo-classical' movements which form a basic ingredient in all Roman art up to the time of Constantine and Theodosius – an ingredient which gives away the artificial, theorizing, programme-dictated side of its character. Herein, precisely, lies the weak point of all Roman art. Moments of complete sincerity and genuine creation remain spasmodic, and bound up with the personality of a few artists, while the bigger studio-workshops follow a tradition of anonymity. This also explains why, throughout the second and first centuries BC, we find not one original work, no fresh influx of creative talent – and this despite the availability of innumerable masterpieces from every branch and period of Greek art. It is only from Trajan's reign onwards that a new mode of artistic expression begins to appear; by then the influx of Greek originals had fallen off for a century or more, and the Hellenistic tradition had exhausted itself even in its natural habitat. By then, too, the craze for owning works of art had more or less evaporated, together with the uneasy conscience that such ownership brought.

These qualms of conscience form one of the oddest characteristics of Roman culture towards the end of the Republic. Such hugger-mugger art-collections had something in common with fraudulent letters patent of nobility, obtained by illegitimate means: to be shown off to visitors with pride, yet not without a certain inner uneasiness. To quieten this feeling, people tend to emphasize their family's modest origins, and to make it clear that in their heart of hearts they feel a certain contempt for the framed 'certificate' they are showing off. The practical things of life are more important.

All Roman writers who discuss art – in particular those most involved with it – make an affectation of denying their obvious interest. (I am not concerned here with the grumblings of that stubborn old peasant Cato, who genuinely detested such things.) This trait can be detected even in Cicero, whose understanding of Greek culture is unmatched by any other Roman. He acquired some familiarity with the theories circulating in Hellenistic literature on various problems to do with artistic form, and thus possessed the means to arrive at an independent critical judgment; yet he did not make the slightest effort to do so. Before Plotinus, who wrote at the end of the third century AD, we may search in vain for a theoretical approach to art which differs in any respect from that of the late Hellenistic rhetoricians. There never was a time when Roman society confronted the problem of art on its own terms – least of all during those centuries (third to first BC) which witnessed the final death-throes of the Hellenistic world, and the birth of Roman imperialism.

Cicero himself was an art collector; he asked his friend Atticus, who had become an important publisher, to look round Athens on his behalf and find him some statues that would suit one of his villas. And he could spend money lavishly: in 44 BC his household expenses were 200,000 sesterces (the equivalent of about 2,000 gold sovereigns). His total capital resources amounted to something like 30,000,000 sesterces. He had villas at Tusculum (Frascati), Pompeii and Arpinum, his birth-place (*Ep. ad Att.* 2.1.11), which ran him into considerable debt. One famous extravagance of his was a dining-table in thuja-wood, for which, according to Pliny (*NH* 13.91), he paid 500,000 sesterces.

In his speeches against Verres (70 BC), the governor of Sicily accused of mass embezzlement and extortion, Cicero gives a vivid picture of the collector's mania in action, and also of the museum-like quality which rich men's villas and town houses now began to assume. But he also affects a kind of coy philistinism, which one or two examples will demonstrate. Cicero describes the house of a certain Heius, a Roman living in Messina, who owned a private chapel dedicated to Good Fortune, in which the cult-statue was an ancient figure of wood. Among other statues, he had an Eros by Praxiteles and a Hercules by Myron, while certain rooms in the house were adorned with figure-woven carpets and hangings – 'Pergamene art, very ancient'. In his descriptions of other houses, Cicero gives detailed accounts of tables loaded with silverware – plates, basins, cups, receptacles shaped like animals' heads (*rhyta*) – and sometimes he can even tell us from what antique collections these works derive. Yet every now and then, conscious of the public audience who are listening to his speech for the prosecution, he feels the need to excuse his artistic expertise. He claims to be an ignoramus in such matters, and apologizes for not remembering all these artists' names – though he must have learnt them by heart during his preliminary enquiries into Verres' thefts. While still on the subject of Heius's house, he describes two bronze statues of young girls bearing certain sacred objects on their heads. They were called Canephorae, he says, but the artist – who was the artist? A pause. 'Ah, someone has just reminded me: I am told it was Polycletus.' The name, held thus in suspense and finally whispered in his ear by a clerk, produced the greatest possible effect on his audience: Polycletus was world-famous. Yet we have here something more than a mere advocate's trick.

This pretence of ignorance is absolutely in character. It calls to mind the phrase *nescio quis*, 'some fellow or other', which St Augustine feels obliged to tack on before the name of Virgil or any other great pagan poet whom he cites. But the Christian pretence of ignorance was deliberately contemptuous; it aimed to underline the fact of belonging to a different world, a new culture, even if the attempt was not always wholly successful – as when in nightmares Jerome heard a voice reproaching him for being a Ciceronian rather than a Christian. What we have in the case of Cicero and his contemporaries is something quite different: an uneasy conscience. They felt they had betrayed the austere poverty of their ancestors, the exacting old-fashioned way of life; and to this feeling of guilt was added a constant sense of inferiority, the realization that, despite everything, they had failed to grasp the real *raison d'être* of these works of art, had failed to penetrate their mystery, and had no one, among their own people, capable of creating anything comparable – except by imitation.

Cicero has his clerk read out extracts from registers containing an assessment of these works of art, made 'by those who have a passion for such things'; he himself, he hastens to add, does not value them so highly, and has no personal use for them (*Ego vero ad meam rationem usumque meum non aestimo* [*Verr.* II, 4.7.13]). As we have seen, this is simply not true. Later on (60.134) he endeavours to explain just how serious a matter these thefts by Verres were for the citizens of Sicily and Magna Graecia. 'The Greeks,' he says, 'have an extraordinary passion for these things which we despise' (*quas nos contemnimus*).

This reservation is still discernible in judgments on the character of Agrippa, who died in 12 BC, and whose manners – countrified rather than elegant – won general approval. Yet at the same time the passage to which I refer (Pliny, *NH* 35.26) reveals a new development, one which shows that the 'moment of guilt' had already begun to pass away. Agrippa, in fact, gave it out as his opinion that art-collections should no longer be hidden away in private houses, but should be made accessible to the general public: he gave a lead by releasing his own collection. Here we have the prelude to that taste for public monuments which later ages developed – but also to the decline of private collections.

The number of Greek masterpieces was by no means inexhaustible; moreover, the most famous were either untransportable, or else had been carried off during the period of conquest to be set up in temples and forums, or, again, had been earmarked for the embellishment of some newly founded colony's capital. Thus a time soon came when collectors had to content themselves with copies of the most widely known works. In addition to direct copies, there were variations – replicas of classical iconological types, adaptations of famous statues – designed for functional as well as decorative purposes. In this category are the mirror-image copies that were made of certain well-known statues, the object being to use them as an exact counterpart to the 'straight' copy when decorating a garden or façade. (The replicas of Scopas's *Pothos* are a good instance.) We also have statues like those of Pheidias, or some other classical Old Master, which are copied from an original – or even exactly reproduced by means of a mould – and then

46 POMPEII: EPHEBE LAMPSTAND. NAPLES, MUSEO ARCHEOLOGICO NAZIONALE

cast in bronze, with a gold or silver overlay, and capable of taking a lustre, like the ephebi discovered at Pompeii. This use of reproductions of works by classical Greek masters as elements of interior decoration was characteristic of the opulent society that flourished under Roman imperialism.

Apart from copies, then, there were adaptations and 'pastiches' – that is, a novel re-combination of elements from various different works. Verres, we are told, would have the relief-scenes chiselled off antique gold or silver cups, and incorporated, out of context, on the table-ware being made for him by a large team of high-relief artists, whose exclusive services he enjoyed (Cicero, *Verr.* II, 4.24.54). Here we have direct testimony as to the state of mind in which such pastiches were carried out. Another kind of pastiche was that in which the artist copied some ancient statue of a divinity, but replaced its head with a modern portrait: witness the statue of an orator in the Louvre, reproduced opposite, and bearing the signature 'Kleomenes'. Its head undoubtedly portrays some member of Augustus's family, whereas the body corresponds exactly to that of the 'Hermes as Orator' which stood in Athens.

This insensitivity as regards style is typical of the times, and lasted throughout the entire Roman period. Nothing exemplifies it better than the failure to observe any contrast between a body constructed according to the rules of formal counterpoint (so strictly applied that it produces something wholly intellectualized, almost an abstract composition) and the accidental character, the crude reality of a portrait. From the beginning the Romans were used to this absence of stylistic unity, since it was a fundamental ingredient of Italo-Etruscan art. This trait likewise testifies to the predominantly practical character – functional rather than aesthetic – of artistic production in Rome. The history of Roman art has always been impeded by these commercially produced artifacts, which doubtless constitute evidence for the state of Roman culture, but have nothing to do with the development of Roman art.

While on the subject of copies, pastiches and lists of famous masterpieces – not to mention artistic variations on classically admissible themes, carried out in such a way as to justify calling the result a new creative work – there is one sculptor who should be discussed. He is often referred to by the literary sources, and founded a school, as is evident from the signatures on one or two statues that have come down to us. His name was Pasiteles; he was born in a Greek city of southern Italy, perhaps in Campania, but afterwards took Roman citizenship. He was active during the middle of the first century BC; Cicero knew him, and it would seem that Pompey was his patron. A highly skilled modeller in clay and wax, he was primarily a toreutic artist, besides being a sculptor and a writer on the side. In this latter capacity he dealt with artistic themes, ransacking Hellenistic literature for lists of the most famous masterpieces (*nobilia opera*) and any information concerning them. One anecdote shows him busily copying a lion from the life, using a caged model. He is also mentioned as the creator of certain sacred images in ivory. Technically accomplished, and endowed, it seems, with an eclectic talent, he must have been one of those artists employed by wealthy collectors. Such men 'were like hunting-dogs, sniffing down every trail, following each trifling clue, determined, one way or another, to pick up anything that was going, however unimportant', as Cicero says of those who were in Verres' service (*Verr.* II, 4.13.31). Pasiteles still belongs to Greek art rather than Roman.

We can form no idea of his art, for no work has been identified as his. The portrait of Pompey dubiously attributed to him (now in the Ny Carlsberg Glyptotek, Copenhagen) is, in fact, unlikely to have come from his hand, although it does undoubtedly

48 M. KOSSOUTIUS MENELAOS: ORESTES AND ELECTRA. ROME, MUSEO NAZIONALE

display a characteristic blend of Hellenistic decorative elements and delicate plasticity in the modelling – a sign that its original medium was clay. On the other hand, two works of the school which Pasiteles apparently founded in Rome have been preserved. One is the statue of a young athlete, very typical of the backward-looking neo-classical style, but interesting in that it shows how far the intellectualizing refinement then in fashion had succeeded in imitating, not just the full classical mode, but the severity which had preceded it during the 460s. Such a taste for primitivism soon degenerates into a mannered imitation of the archaic. This ephebe, executed in a style earlier than that of Pheidias, bears the signature of a Greek artist, Stephanos, who proclaims himself Pasiteles' pupil. Another artist, also Greek, who signs himself 'Menelaos, pupil of Stephanos', has left us a frigidly academic group portraying Orestes and Electra. Electra – a very maternal-looking sister – is welcoming Orestes, who here has been conceived as an ephebe. Such an interpretation is highly mannered, and has completely broken away from the characters immortalized by the great Greek tragedians.

Of another sculptor with a Greek name, Arcesilaus, who established himself very successfully at Rome, we again know very little – not even his country of origin. All we have are a few literary references, and perhaps an uncertain reflection in one or two surviving works. He, too, was apparently very expert in clay-modelling, since we are told that his *maquettes* cost as much as any other artist's finished work – and that it was artists who bought them. At least, this is the interpretation currently given to the sources, and to the term *proplasmata* which we find there. But perhaps this referred rather to plaster models for toreutic work, like that which Pliny himself (35.155) later describes, or those that have turned up in excavations throughout the Roman Empire, and even from beyond the frontiers. Arcesilaus was likewise responsible for the statue of Venus which Caesar had placed in the temple at the centre of his Forum: Venus Genetrix, patron of the Gens Iulia. He remained active for some years after Pasiteles, between 55 and 40 BC. Just as Pasiteles' name is linked with that of Pompey, so is the name of Arcesilaus attached to that of Lucullus, the immensely wealthy and refined proconsul of Asia (unless the reference is to his son). It seems probable that Arcesilaus was transplanted to Roman soil from some part of Asia Minor – rather like the first cherry-tree, which was brought over about this time, also by Lucullus. Similarly, we find the name of Mark Antony, the Triumvir, connected with that of Evander, another sculptor and toreutic artist, who was imported from Athens to Alexandria, where he became artistic adviser at Cleopatra's court. He later set up in Rome as a restaurateur and antique-dealer, under the name of Caius Avianus Evander. Cicero himself used to patronize his shop (Cicero, *Ep. ad Fam.* 13.2 c; Horace, *Sat.* 1.3.91; Pliny, *NH* 36.32).

The practice of bringing Greek artists to Rome went back at least as far as Aemilius Paullus, in the second century BC. Several such sculptors, whose works – as we learn from our literary sources – adorned Rome's new temples, probably also established studios in the capital: so successful a power was worth cultivating.

49 M. KOSSOUTIUS MENELAOS: ORESTES (DETAIL)

50 POMPEII: A BAKER AND HIS CUSTOMERS. NAPLES, MUSEO ARCHEOLOGICO NAZIONALE

2   Two Traditions: Plebeian and Patrician

THE HISTORICAL RELIEF

THE second century BC (200-100 BC) was a decisive period as regards Rome's future development. The first two generations of the century carried through the conquest of the Eastern Mediterranean; the third coincided with the revolution that Rome's new economic and political dimensions rendered inevitable – not only at home, within the social class-structure, but also in her dealings with other Italic peoples; it was, in fact, the 'revolutionary generation'.

At the beginning of the century, Rome was taking steps to protect herself, in the north, against the Celts who had occupied the Po Valley. A whole string of Latin colonies were founded, one after the other: in 189, Bononia (Bologna), previously the Etruscan city of Felsina, and after that the headquarters of a Gallic tribe, the Boii; in 183, Mutina (Modena) and Parma; in 181, Aquileia, the northernmost outpost. The colonies of Pisa (180) and Luni (177) fixed the frontiers against the Ligurians. During the same period, thanks to their successful campaign against Philip V of Macedon (200-197), the Romans established a foothold in Greece. The following year they published a declaration of freedom (specifically alluding to Macedonian domination) on behalf of all towns in Greece and Asia Minor – an extremely clever political manœuvre designed to facilitate their own penetration of the area. In 191/0, the war against Antiochus III and the victory at Magnesia-by-Sipylus left Rome mistress of all Asia Minor as far as the Taurus massif. The fateful year 146 has already been mentioned, which saw not only the destruction of Carthage, but also the fall of Corinth – the latter soon to be followed by the occupation of all Greece.

During this period intense activity was going on, for the benefit of the newly-rich, in the world that revolved around art – a world we have already touched on in the preceding chapter. On the one hand, insatiably greedy collectors; on the other, skilled commercial artists, a whole industry of craftsmen who slaved away in their studios, copying, restoring, refashioning. The new masters of the Mediterranean reveal a violent desire to take possession of the entire heritage – over five centuries old – of an artistic civilization, that of classical and Hellenistic Greece, which for sheer intensity and imagination has never been matched in all history. Given these circumstances, it is hardly surprising that by the first century BC no original mode of expression had appeared; nor, indeed, that the scene should be dominated by a peculiar brand of eclecticism which set out to reconcile, in the same work, elements executed in totally distinct and incompatible traditions.

This eclecticism is the first characteristic which allows us to distinguish Roman from Mid-Italic art, the latter having hitherto provided for Rome's artistic needs, such as they were. One can in fact go further, and say that it marks off Roman art from any other artistic culture whatsoever. The eclectic approach normally appears towards the end of a civilization, and is linked with creative exhaustion and intellectualism. Here, by contrast, it appears from the very beginning.

This special quality manifests itself quite unmistakably in a work which may be regarded as the oldest example known to us, in Roman art, of a public monument with sculptured decorations: the so-called 'Altar of Domitius Ahenobarbus'. In fact we have no proof that it was in any way connected with the Ahenobarbus family, or that it was an altar. One of the Ahenobarbi, probably the Consul of 192 BC, rebuilt the temple dedicated to Neptune near the Circus Flaminius; later, in 42 BC, another member of the family won a great naval victory, and it was long thought that the group which stood in the temple, portraying a procession of marine deities following Thetis and Achilles, commemorated this event. It was also thought (Pliny, *NH* 36.26) that this group was the work of the famous Greek sculptor Scopas; but in all likelihood the sculptor was Scopas Minor, active at the very end of the second century BC. As for the actual reliefs dealt with here, they remained for a long time in a Roman palazzo, near which, under the Church of S. Salvatore in Campo, ancient ruins had been discovered. By dint of piling one unsubstantiated hypothesis on another – a process which even at the time provoked Stendhal to ironic comment – various distinguished archaeologists identified these ruins as part of the Temple of Neptune, assumed that the reliefs had been found there, and in this way manufactured the 'Altar of Domitius Ahenobarbus'. On the death of the owner of the palazzo, his collections were dispersed, and one sequence of reliefs (forming one long and two short sides of a large rectangle) ended up in the Munich Museum, while the other, which covered the second long side, went to the Louvre. What we do know, beyond any doubt, is that these two sequences formed part of the same monument. And that is already something, since the stylistic variations between the various fragments is so great that, had they been dispersed without record, one could hardly have guessed that they once formed part of a whole.

The Munich sequence portrays a procession of marine deities, and is wholly in the late Hellenistic manner. The Louvre sequence deals with the presentation of animals for sacrifice. We see an altar, with a figure that is probably Mars himself standing in front of it. Also visible are some soldiers, wearing breastplates and carrying oval shields, and a group of four civilians in togas, occupied with some business of administrative or electoral registration. Whatever interpretation we place on this scene (perhaps a *lustratio*), both its content and its formal language are totally different from those of the other three sides. Although nearly all the heads on this frieze are heavily restored, one can still recognize a style which, though close to the Mid-Italic style of the second century, nevertheless differs from it in fundamentals. For the first time on any official monument,

53 ROME: ALTAR OF DOMITIUS AHENOBARBUS (DETAIL). ADMINISTRATIVE AND RELIGIOUS CEREMONY. PARIS, LOUVRE

54 ALTAR OF DOMITIUS AHENOBARBUS: ADMINISTRATIVE AND RELIGIOUS CEREMONY (DETAIL)

55

54

51 ROME: ALTAR OF DOMITIUS AHENOBARBUS (DETAIL). PROCESSION OF POSEIDON AND AMPHITRITE. MUNICH, STAATLICHE ANTIKENSAMMLUNGEN

52 ROME: ALTAR OF DOMITIUS AHENOBARBUS. PROCESSION OF POSEIDON AND AMPHITRITE (DETAIL)

53

55 ALTAR OF DOMITIUS AHENOBARBUS: ADMINISTRATIVE AND RELIGIOUS CEREMONY (DETAIL)

56

we can speak of a specifically *Roman* style. The most likely hypotheses as regards date range between 115 and 70 BC.

Two features regarding this monument are of particular note: first, the eclectic combination of two styles, Hellenistic for a mythological theme, and 'Roman' for one that is purely civic; and, second, the way in which the sacrificial animals are represented – that is, patently larger than lifesize. Why this infringement of the naturalistic rules laid down by Hellenistic art, universally accepted at this period by all 'civilized' countries, and perfectly familiar in the cultural context of Rome?

The same question might be asked with regard to the frieze on the arch of Augustus at Susa, in Piedmont, where the sacrificial process is dominated by a gigantic pig, behind which follow other outsize animals – a bull, a sheep, a ram. This arch commemorates the political treaty signed between Rome and Cottius, king of the region round Segusio, about 9-8 BC. Though their setting was provincial, these reliefs were executed right in the middle of the Augustan period, the era *par excellence* of elegant neo-Attic refinement. However, it was not merely the clumsiness of provincial craftsmen which was responsible for thus inflating the proportions of sacrificial animals. Rather it was the desire to give a central position to the victim, by way of underlining the importance of the solemnly accomplished religious act which sanctioned the political treaty – and also, perhaps, to indicate the large number of beasts sacrificed. In other words, this is a representation whose point of departure is no longer naturalistic, but symbolic.

On certain other altars which show magistrates in the act of sacrificing, we see the same symbolism in reverse: here the proportions of the sacrificial animal are greatly reduced, as on the 'altar of the four street-commissioners' (*vicomagistri*) from the Aesculetum quarter in Rome, datable to about AD 2. This example, and many others like it, can be explained by the fact that the animal is represented solely to characterize the action which is being performed. Once again, it is a symbol and nothing else. By reducing its

56 SUSA: ARCH OF AUGUSTUS (DETAIL FROM THE FRIEZE)

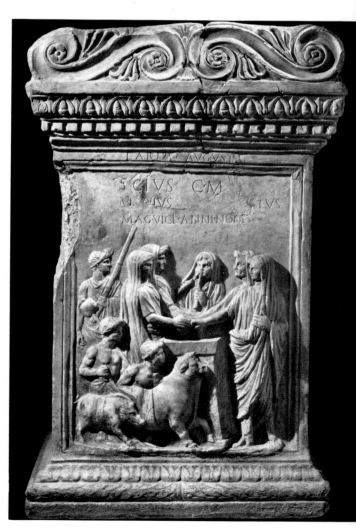

57 ROME: 'ALTAR OF THE STREET-COMMISSIONERS'. ROME

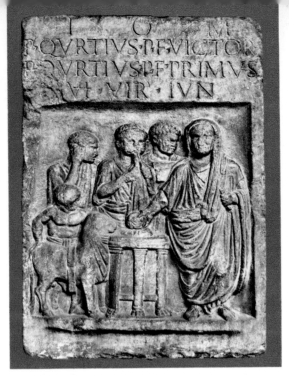

58 ANGERA: ALTAR DEDICATED BY TWO SEVIRI   59 SAN GUGLIELMO AL GOLETO: RELIEF FROM FUNERARY MONUMENT

dimensions, extra space is gained to make a prominent display of the magistrates going about their official duties; since they commissioned the monument, they naturally take pride of place on it. Those Roman funerary monuments set up, between the end of the Republic and the beginning of the Flavian era, by minor magistrates such as the *seviri,* who were enfranchised slaves, bear ample witness to the frequency with which Hellenistic rules of naturalism were jettisoned in order to emphasize the action, and enhance the figure of the donor. These monuments show that the Mid-Italic tradition still survived, reinforcing what it had absorbed from Hellenism with new borrowings from the tradition of official art.

It is natural enough that the evidence for this plebeian trend in art should have been especially preserved in the municipalities rather than the capital. Even so, everything we learn from such sources is of great importance for the history of Roman art. Above all, they show that the refinement of Augustan neo-Atticism never reached beyond a small cultural *élite*. It did not penetrate, much less modify, the living core of Rome's artistic evolution, but remained an urban phenomenon, confined by and large to the capital. Further, they show that, from the first century, this plebeian tradition of art embodies definite iconographic conventions, together with other formal rules, such as the symbolic value attached to non-naturalistic proportions. Other recurrent devices are those of presenting the most important figures in the action full-face to the viewer (e.g. on the Angera altar), and of arranging figures on a uniform plane, side by side, which avoids foreshortening and the illusions of perspective (less easily understood, of course, by an untrained eye). These factors are important, since they embody the recognizable germ of certain artistic concepts which gained ground only in late antiquity, after Hellenism had run its course – from the time, that is, during the third century A D, when a new ruling class of plebeian origin emerged in the Roman Empire.

58

60 SAN VITTORINO (AMITERNUM): RELIEF SHOWING A FUNERAL CORTEGE. L'AQUILA, MUSEO NAZIONALE D'ABRUZZO

Among numerous other examples of a style deriving from the Mid-Italic tradition, one may mention the remains of a funerary monument from San Guglielmo al Goleto, in the province of Avellino. Though this can be dated to the end of the Republican era, or the beginning of the first century AD, the female figure represented on it, so austere in its formal design, shows striking affinities with medieval European sculpture of the twelfth century. Another relief, from Amiternum (S. Vittorino) in the Abruzzi, shows a funeral cortege in considerable detail, and makes it clear that this is a very high-class ceremony, definitely superior to the ordinary funeral with six pall-bearers – but nevertheless inferior to that with ten (though it has, even so, borrowed the latter's musicians and professional mourners). The way in which this composition abandons perspective altogether, leaving the figures standing on conventional base-lines, emphasizes that its prime object is representative and expository. Furthermore, the way the corpse is portrayed, lying on one side on a litter – which suggests either an embalming process or else the substitution of an effigy – at once draws our attention to the numerous stars and moons in the background. (The artist here meant to represent some kind of material, probably spread out as a canopy.) These astral signs undoubtedly allude to the astrological beliefs which had become widespread in Rome during Cicero's

61 RELIEF SHOWING A FUNERAL CORTEGE (DETAIL)

59

lifetime, and were propagated by his friend Nigidius Figulus, himself a native of Amiternum.

Such art had, above all, to make itself a vehicle for the expression of that individual urge for self-assertion apparent throughout the entire ancient world, and given explicit endorsement, as far as Roman society was concerned, by Cicero. He concluded that the idea of *gloria* formed the prime impulse behind all human activity, practical no less than artistic (*Tusc. Disp.* 1.1.4). This, basically, was antiquity's version of the 'efficiency myth' produced by our modern affluent society; nowhere did this trend find more marked expression than at Rome.

Clearly, this urge for self-assertion was particularly strong among ex-slaves. Once freed, by enfranchisement, from their wretched status, the freedmen (*liberti*) soon found openings in trade, and frequently amassed considerable fortunes. From here they could aspire to certain minor magistracies, some of which (e.g. the sevirate) were purely honorific. This collegial office carried a certain amount of prestige in the *municipia*, and involved the organization of public festivals, including gladiatorial shows; the high cost of such spectacles was a tangible proof of the impresario's social position.

The *Satiricon* of Petronius, a picaresque novel probably composed in Nero's reign, strikingly illustrates the mentality behind these manifestations. One celebrated chapter introduces a wealthy freedman – and *sevir* – named Trimalchio, who boasts of never having attended a philosophy lecture in his life, but claims to be a good citizen, rich, generous, and favoured by Fortune. The instructions which he gives (*Satir.* 71) on how his tomb is to be built and decorated find their precise fulfilment in a number of funerary monuments from the *municipia*.

Perhaps the closest illustration of this passage from Trimalchio's Feast is to be found in the tomb of a *sevir* from Teate, fragments of which are preserved in the Chieti Museum (Abruzzi). The *sevir* – his name is given as Lusius Storax by the inscription on the monument – is shown seated on a dais, surrounded by other magistrates (*me sedentem in tribunali*, just as Trimalchio specified for himself). A frieze with gladiators commemorates his munificence in providing entertainment for his fellow-citizens. It is typical of such art that the figures of the gladiators reveal a sophisticated iconography, Hellenistic in origin, whereas the assembly of magistrates (for which parallels are not lacking in Italo-Etruscan art) is completely Roman.

63 CHIETI (TEATE MARRUCINORUM): FUNERARY MONUMENT OF LUSIUS STORAX (DETAIL). ASSEMBLY OF MAGISTRATES. CHIETI MUSEUM

64 CHIETI (TEATE MARRUCINORUM): FUNERARY MONUMENT OF LUSIUS STORAX (DETAIL OF FRIEZE). GLADIATORS

65 ESTE: VOTIVE RELIEF OFFERED BY A TINSMITH. ESTE MUSEUM

66 OSTIA: RELIEF SHOWING A MILL. OSTIA MUSEUM

67 SAN VITTORINO (AMITERNUM) [?]: PEDIMENT. L'AQUILA MUSEUM

68 SAN VITTORINO (AMITERNUM) [?]: PEDIMENT. L'AQUILA MUSEUM

One special characteristic of Roman art is its close connection with the realities of daily life. Freed at last from the aesthetic prejudices imposed by classicism, which refused to admit that anything in Rome was worthy of study apart from her continuation of Greek culture, the archaeologists themselves are beginning to recognize that Roman art strikes its most authentic vein when portraying mundane details.

Its close links with daily life and reality appear in a number of ways: for instance, in decorating the sides and pediments of funerary monuments, not with scenes from mythology, but with the tools of the dead man's trade, be he soldier or craftsman (Ostia, L'Aquila); in using arms and armour on reliefs for purposes of decoration or symbolism. We find instances even at Rome, on friezes found in the neighbourhood of the Capitol (attributed on somewhat flimsy grounds to certain monuments dedicated, about 150 BC, by the cities of the Hellenistic West, and apparently part of a trophy). These motifs placed on tombs do not differ essentially from analogous reliefs of a votive character (Este), or from others which, though found in the same environment, were used for a very different purpose, as signs above shops

69 OSTIA: GREENGROCER-POULTERER'S SHOP-SIGN. OSTIA MUSEUM

and studios. At Ostia, then the port of Rome, just such shop-signs have been found, including one belonging to a greengrocer-poulterer (rabbits and chickens, the latter with only their heads visible, are shown shut in hutches under the counter). The apartment block in which this relief was discovered dates it to the Antonine period (second half of the second century AD); but stylistically it differs little from reliefs of the first century. This is not surprising. Where no emphasis is placed on problems of form, and the chief aim is to achieve a lively, easily comprehended narrative line, the evolution of style (unless accelerated by external influences) is a slow, almost insensible process. The same is true of any human figures portrayed: they are eternal, outside time, neither of today nor of yesterday. Because of its connections with everyday life, and its predilection for humble subjects, this art is commonly referred to as 'popular art'. Such a definition is questionable, for two reasons. First, a slave-owning society's concept of 'people' differs from modern ideas on the subject. Roman society, in particular, maintained a judicial distinction (*Inst.* 1.3-4) according to which 'people' could be defined as 'all citizens, patricians and senators included'; if one wanted to exclude the patrician class and those citizens of senatorial rank, the proper term was *plebs*. Second, the whole idea of 'popular art' was introduced by critics of the Romantic Age. Arguing from literature, they posited the existence of a spontaneous instinct (whether collective or individual) through which the 'soul of the people' (*Volksgeist*) could find genuine expression. This 'soul' was, in fact, a mere critical abstraction; it had no historical reality. Later critics challenged the concept, and redefined popular art at a much lower level. For them it was no more than a collection of 'debased cultural elements' (the *gesunkenes Kulturgut* of historicist criticism) which had filtered down among the working classes, but always derived from models belonging to a higher culture. This definition simply does not fit the particular trend in Roman art which we are examining.

63

70 POMPEII: THE BRAWL IN THE AMPHITHEATRE. NAPLES, MUSEO ARCHEOLOGICO NAZIONALE

Even if we can isolate elements that have been transferred, in an impoverished form, from the art of the cultivated classes (which means, in effect, from the Hellenistic tradition), the main point is that we are here confronted with a wholly distinct concept of art, and one which leads to quite different conclusions in matters of style, expression and iconography. It is preferable, therefore, to call this trend *plebeian*, rather than popular – and even this is no more than a label. It certainly does not imply conscious social opposition to official, or what one might term 'senatorial', art. Indeed, as we shall see later, the two traditions quite often overlap and borrow formal devices from one another.

The trend is very apparent in painting, and Pompeii offers us numerous examples of it: market-scenes, processions, all manner of subjects handled in a way which reveals the determination to achieve maximum clarity. In pursuit of this all-important goal the artist may distort perspective, as we can see from a picture recording a notorious brawl in the amphitheatre, between citizens of Pompeii and Nocera in AD 59. (As a result of the riot, Pompeii's amphitheatre was closed down for ten years, a stern reprisal duly recorded by Tacitus.) In this little picture the façade of the amphitheatre, together with its two entry-ramps, is shown in correct perspective; but immediately behind it we have

64

71 OSTIA: VIA DIANA. SIGN OF A PUBLIC SNACK-BAR (THERMOPOLIUM)

72 ROME: TOMB ON THE VIA PORTUENSE. BASKET OF FLOWERS. ROME, MUSEO NAZIONALE

65

an artificially distorted representation of the interior. Furthermore, the awning (*velarium*), which partially covered the building to shade spectators from the sun, has been lifted up and detached by the artist: all characteristic local features must be portrayed, but in such a way that they do not detract from the scene's legibility. This is the same convention used in the Amiternum relief showing the funeral cortege, where the star-spangled material which in reality formed a canopy over the dead man's head becomes a backcloth behind him. The same fresh, natural approach, without much concern for composition, is apparent in the sign of a 'snack-bar' from Ostia (Via Diana), and likewise in the execution of a basket of flowers at the entrance to a tomb (Rome, Via Portuense). This manner is already looking ahead to the second century, and later we shall observe its influence on certain portraits and children's games.

Many plebeians, such as the baker Marcus Vergilius Eurysaces, amassed great wealth, during the civil wars at the end of the Republic, by securing lucrative army contracts, and built themselves sumptuous tombs on the proceeds. The frieze which portrays various stages in commercial bread-making belongs to this tradition, and has no truck with

75 SAN VITTORINO (AMITERNUM): RELIEF FROM A FUNERARY MONUMENT. BANQUETING SCENE. PIZZOLI, CHURCH OF S. STEFANO

Hellenistic airs and graces – unlike the mosaic-and-cockleshell inscription which (somewhat later, in the first century) a certain Pomponius Hylas had put on his tomb, an elegant columbarium near the Porta Latina.

It is through familiarity with this artistic trend, previously too little studied, that we can best understand the origin of those forms whose symbolism pushed them towards the abstract – forms which were to become common currency during the third and fourth centuries, under the Late Empire. Let us consider three reliefs representing banqueting scenes, connected – or so scholars believe, in view of the number of guests – with the official activities of the *seviri*, already discussed. After enjoying a great vogue under Augustus, the sevirate declined in popularity towards the end of the first century; by then it had become far more difficult to find wealthy plebeians willing to accept an honour that cost them a fortune and carried relatively little prestige. After the first half of the second century, monuments commemorating *seviri* virtually disappear. For this reason, the three reliefs – one from Amiternum (Pizzoli, in a presbytery), the others in the museums of Este (Padua) and Ancona – should probably be assigned

76 ESTE: FUNERARY MONUMENT. ESTE, MUSEO NAZIONALE

77 SEPINO (SAEPINUM): FUNERARY MONUMENT. ANCONA MUSEUM ▶

78 ROME: TEMPLE OF APOLLO SOSIANUS (DETAIL FROM FRIEZE). TRIUMPHAL PROCESSION. ROME, PALAZZO DEI CONSERVATORI

79 ROME: ALTAR-BASE SHOWING SACRIFICIAL PROCESSION. VATICAN, MUSEO PIO CLEMENTINO

to the first century. There is no possible doubt about this date as regards the first example; but the second, with its heavy ornamental draperies, puts one in mind of certain fourth-century mosaics, while the third recalls iconographic motifs that have become familiar to us through the art of the Christian catacombs. Here, then, are further clear examples of what Rodenwaldt calls the 'premonitory signs of Late Empire style' in the development of plebeian art.

68

The existence of this artistic trend (whether linked, in its forms, with Mid-Italic art or with the distinctive civic and religious patterns of Roman society) had one immediate consequence. From its formal and objective fusion with Hellenistic naturalism there sprang a narrative, historical style which constitutes the first real evidence for the emergence of a 'Roman' style in ancient art. Among the known examples of this style (though here transferred to a more refined cultural context) are several reliefs from the first century A D. One, a frieze from the temple of Apollo Sosianus, portrays preparations for a triumphal procession. Another, a frieze forming part of a huge altar-base (which was discovered beneath the Cancelleria and is now in the Museo Pio Clementino), illustrates a similar procession, this time of a sacrificial nature.

The frieze from Apollo's temple was originally set high up inside the building; yet despite the smallness of the figures it must have been clearly visible, for the relief-work is simple and incisive. The possibility of its having been in polychrome cannot be ruled out. Its subject-matter connects it with the triumph which Sosius celebrated in 34 B C, but various considerations combine to suggest that its execution should be dated between 20 and 17 B C. Remarkably similar in style is the relief (again illustrating a procession) which decorates the altar in the centre of the *Ara Pacis*, inaugurated in 9 B C (*pl. 204*). The same style, with certain minor variations, turns up in those rather smaller friezes of religious processions which can be seen, immediately over the archway, on the Arch of Titus in Rome, and that of Trajan at Beneventum.

This constant element in work which otherwise reveals widely differing characteristics is parallelled in the history of ancient literature. Every poetic *genre* in antiquity had its own appropriate metre, and (at least in classical Greek literature) very often its own particular dialect as well. Similarly with figurative art: there was a special style corresponding to every *genre*. The rules governing such categories served as an especially handy guide when art (sculpture in particular) came, as it most often did, within the province of the huge craft-factories: here traditional usage and 'the done thing' constituted a basic point of departure, a vital factor in the organization of production methods.

The relief from the Cancelleria must have adorned a large reactangular altar. Its length, about sixteen ft., corresponded roughly to that of the *Ara Pacis* or the so-called 'Altar of Domitius'. In the procession, we see sacrificial animals, priests and acolytes, musicians with their long trumpets, and, to the right, the four street-commissioners (*vicomagistri*), with attendants behind them, each of whom carries a little image of the Lares, divine guardians of streets and houses. One odd feature is that two of the musicians are shown from behind. Since the relief as a whole shows no particular concern with rendering the composition more varied, this may simply have been an expedient to gain space for the long trumpets. Yet the foreshortened position of the trumpets, and that of the figures turned towards the background of the relief, show that in the sculptor's conception this background was non-existent: it consisted of an empty space through which the figures moved. This conception of space is further confirmed by the fact that the figures do not reach to the top of the frieze, but leave a gap above their heads – a feature which distinguishes this relief from any based on neo-classical principles. In the latter – the *Ara Pacis*, for instance – the figures fill the frieze entirely.

This relief offers one of the very few examples of spatial freedom and concern with

perspective to be found in the initial centuries of Roman art. Its date is still in dispute, since a number of different hypotheses have been advanced concerning the altar to which it belonged. Stylistic considerations suggest that it should be assigned to the Julio-Claudian period, somewhere between AD 30 and 50.

THE PORTRAIT

Isolating a specifically 'plebeian' trend in art has made it easier for us to understand the genesis of certain features common to reliefs with a historical theme. The moment of Roman social life which these reliefs represent may be either private or public, civic or religious; very often it involves all these spheres simultaneously. The 'historical relief' enjoyed a great vogue in Egyptian and Assyrian art, as a means of glorifying the sovereign's exploits. Thus it was not, strictly, a Roman invention – even if Hellenistic monarchs preferred to camouflage the celebration of their various campaigns with stock mythological parallels, commissioning a 'Battle of the Amazons' or even a 'Giganto-machy' (Battle of Giants) to recall their victories over 'barbarian' peoples. Nevertheless, the historical relief is a fundamental element in the development of Roman art.

Another typically Roman form of artistic production is the portrait. Both the historical relief and the portrait are art-forms with a strong down-to-earth quality, an objective attitude devoid of any metaphysical speculation. A great deal has been written about the Roman portrait, not all of it correct. To avoid bogging down in endless polemic, I shall simply state my own opinions, and refer to those with which I disagree only when necessary.

One point must be made clear right at the outset. The historical relief is rooted – conceptually, and to some extent formally, artistically – in plebeian art, which derived from the Mid-Italic tradition. The Roman portrait, by contrast, originated in a patrician milieu; it is, indeed, the art-form which best typifies the mentality and *mores* of the Roman aristocracy. In my opinion, it is also a virtual certainty that those who created the Roman portrait in its characteristic Republican form were artists of Greek education, employed to promote a typically Roman and patrician ideology. Portraiture is always an ambiguous *genre*. It comes into being as the result of some strong sentimental or ideological impulse, but its final realization depends on technique rather than intuition. It does not flourish in all civilizations, nor in every period of any one civilization. In general, the realistic portrait, which relies on details of physiognomy and represents some specific individual, has appeared only in a highly sophisticated urban society, where the ruling social class possesses ample means, and is set in its own traditional ways.

In Greece, the life-like portrait appears comparatively late, unable to develop until the rationalist influence of the Sophists broke down certain moral and political taboos which stood in its way. The first example was probably a likeness of Plato, set up in his honour in a public place dedicated to the Muses – by a man who was not himself Greek, and after Plato's death (i.e. in the second half of the fourth century BC). It was still a public portrait, and in any period such portraits always remain to a large degree invention; the genuine 'likeness', the physiognomical portrait, has purely private origins. This is why the Greek portrait did not develop physiognomical characteristics until the Hellenistic era. Since the majority of Greek portraits were in bronze, very few of them have survived. However, the coins struck by Hellenistic monarchs reflect, in miniature, the great tradition of Greek portraiture, which strove to express every nuance of facial detail and expression (*pl. 386, 387*). These range from the sharp realism displayed in the portrait of Antiochus I of Syria (281-261 BC) to the cool objectivity which characterizes that of Mithridates IV, King of Pontus (169-150? BC), or the air of lofty inspiration – lips parted, eyes staring, hair in disarray – attributed to Mithridates VI (121-63 BC). Confronted by the vast mass of mediocre replicas and bad-quality copies which we still possess, turned out during the Roman period as decoration for libraries, theatres and private houses, one tends to overlook the few examples of Greek portraiture which have survived. This is partly because – in contrast with this flood of mass-produced material – the original portraits in the Roman tradition which we possess reveal a welcome freshness and incisiveness of character, so that students of the subject have taken to referring to a 'Roman art of portraiture', as though this particular culture had enjoyed an absolute monopoly over the private portrait.

On the other hand, a growing interest in Etruscan art has led some people to assume that the immediate forerunner of the Roman portrait was to be found in this quarter. In fact, no realistic, life-like portrait appears in Etruscan or Italic art before the middle of the fourth century – in other words, prior to the evolution of the *genre* in Greece. The features of such earlier figures as survive, reclining on sarcophagi or painted tombs, are completely generalized: rather more so, in fact, than those conventional or restored portraits which we find in Greece during the same period. One somewhat late development in Etruscan art is a tendency towards vigorous expression. This will often impart apparent individuality to some head that is, in fact, purely conventional – as comparison with a number of analogous examples soon makes clear. These portraits do not so much represent individuals as various stock types of humanity – the youth, the old man, the girl, the matron. In those extremely rare cases classifiable as genuine individual likenesses, we have an obvious reflection of the Hellenistic portrait.

81 SAN GIOVANNI SCIPIONI: FRAGMENT OF STATUE. PARIS, BIBLIOTHÈQUE NATIONALE, CABINET DES MÉDAILLES

We have already seen how Rome made use of Etruscan and Mid-Italic artistic traditions prior to the development of a specifically Roman mode of artistic expression. As noted, it is to this Mid-Italic tradition that we must assign the impressive head, supposedly of Brutus, from the Palazzo dei Conservatori on the Capitol (frontispiece). Another head, likewise in bronze, which came from the Abruzzi and is preserved in the Cabinet des Antiques of the Bibliothèque Nationale in Paris, belongs to the same source. (Its provenance is generally given as Bovianum, but in fact it was found at San Giovanni Scipioni, eleven miles from Bovianum as the crow flies.) This head derives directly from the Hellenistic tradition of portraiture, perhaps from that branch of it most common in the Macedonian area. Its provincial variants are notable for a special intensity of expression, and the employment of such 'Impressionist' devices as *pointilliste* dots to represent the beard, a technique inherited from artists working in terracotta.

This surviving bronze, like the 'Brutus', was without doubt a public memorial portrait. As such it must be distinguished from the Roman portrait of the Republican era, which originated in a private, domestic context: more specifically, in the cult of the family – living rather than dead, though later this was extended to include tomb-portraits. At least until the period of the Flavian emperors, public and private portraits remained fundamentally distinct art-forms, each with a style of its own. Even at a comparatively late date in the Roman period (first century BC to first century AD), people were often satisfied with a very simple representation of the human face, as numerous cippi from the Roman necropolis at Tarentum (now preserved in the museum there) bear witness. A single specimen will suffice as illustration. These are generic heads, crudely worked into a geometric form.

On the other hand, the cult of the dead assumed a very special form, at Rome, among the patrician families. We possess a highly interesting literary document on this topic, which acquires particular value from its author's personal circumstances. Before finally invading Greece with an army, Rome had attempted to get a foothold there by diplomatic means. While granting Athens several advantageous concessions, she nevertheless also required the surrender of one thousand Athenian citizens. Though these men were treated as guests, they were in fact hostages; and as such they remained in Rome for a period of seventeen years. Among those who reached Rome in 166 BC was Polybius, the future historian. The son of a prominent member of the Achaean League, he had received a first-class education, and subsequently embarked on a career in the army. When he came to Rome he was forty years old. The record which this open-minded, liberal intellectual has left us of Roman civilization in his day is not only one of the earliest and most important documents we have on the subject, but also one of great honesty. The pages in which Polybius describes the birth of his friendship with Scipio Aemilianus – with whose family he stayed as a guest – must count among the finest literary achievements of all time. He was responsible for the younger man's education, and twenty years later accompanied him, as his adviser, to the siege of Carthage. Clear-sighted and prescient, Polybius saw that time was on the side of the Romans, that their conquest of the Mediterranean, Greece included, was a foregone conclusion. While remaining favourably disposed to Roman institutions, he made careful notes of anything which seemed to him markedly divergent from Greek usage; and what struck him in particular was the funerary ritual practised by Roman patricians. His own words on the subject (*Hist.* 6.53) are worth quoting:

'Whenever any illustrious man dies, he is carried at his funeral into the Forum, to the platform known as the Rostra, where his body is put on display – sometimes in an upright position, and more rarely lying down. Here, with all the people standing round, a grown-up son of the deceased – if he happens to have one who is present, and if not some other relative – mounts the Rostra and makes a speech recalling the dead man's virtues and achievements. As a result, the members of the audience – and not only those who had a part in these achievements, but also those who had none – when the facts are recalled to their minds and brought before their eyes, are moved to such sympathy that the sense of loss, far from being restricted to those actually in mourning, extends to the people as a whole.

'Next, after the interment and the performance of the usual ceremonies, the image of the departed is placed in the most prominent position in his house, enclosed in a wooden shrine. This image is a wax mask, reproducing with remarkable fidelity both the features and the complexion of the deceased. On the occasion of any public sacrifice, these images are put on display and decorated with much care; and when any distinguished member of the family dies, the images are taken to the funeral, and worn by men who bear the closest resemblance to the original in height and general appearance. These men wear togas, with a purple border if the person they represent was a consul or a praetor, whole purple if he was a censor, and embroidered with gold if he celebrated a triumph or achieved a similar distinction.

'All these persons ride in chariots, preceded by lictors bearing the *fasces* (rods and axes), and such other marks of honour as each may be entitled to, according to the offices the dead man held during his lifetime. When they reach the Rostra, they all seat themselves in a row, on ivory chairs. There could hardly be a more ennobling spectacle for any young man aspiring to fame and virtue. For who could fail to be inspired by the sight of these images, so lifelike in appearance, so evocative of justly famous men? What spectacle could be finer than this?

'When he has finished speaking of the dead man, the orator chosen to deliver the funeral encomium recalls the great deeds and achievements of the ancestors, whose images, beginning with the most ancient, are now paraded. By this means, by this constant renewal of the good report of brave men, the celebrity of those who performed noble deeds is rendered immortal, while at the same time the fame of those who did good service to their country becomes known to the people and a heritage for future generations. But the most important result is that young men are thus inspired to endure every suffering for the public welfare in hope of winning the glory that attends on brave men.'

This extraordinary ritual, as here described by Polybius, reveals marked features of ancestor-worship, but is aimed, above all, at the enhancement of the patrician image. It seems to have remained totally unaffected by contacts with the Greek world. It does not in any way foreshadow the practice of putting a portrait of the deceased on his tomb, but is, rather, closely affiliated to a primarily political concept, the *ius imaginum*, which was governed by very special religious and judicial obligations. In essence, it gave legal expression to a right of which the concrete symbol was the privilege of keeping one's ancestral images in the inner court of the house, the *atrium*.

Each of these images had to be preserved in its own little shuttered cupboard, which the head of the family could open only on certain prescribed occasions. Every cupboard bore an inscription recording the name and titles of the deceased; taken in combination, they made up a complete genealogical tree (Pliny, *NH* 35.2,6). This *ius imaginum* was reserved exclusively for the nobility, a privilege which their descendants and relatives by marriage also inherited. A bride would bring with her the images of her own ancestors, which were then added to the series already on display in her husband's house. We hear of incidents and protests occasioned by the insertion of some stranger's mask in a genuine family pedigree (Pliny, 35.2,8). One consequence of all this was the need to execute numerous copies of each *imago*, for the use of relatives belonging to widely scattered branches of the same family. When wax masks came to be replaced by sculptured busts, numerous copies were still essential, some being made at the time and others later. The conclusion to be drawn from this is that only a limited number of 'Republican-style' portraits which still survive were actually executed under the Republic. Most of them, especially those that can be identified as representing members of great patrician families, have reached us only in the guise of late copies, dating from the Imperial era. Here the original concept tends to be overlaid with elements of a different style, that in fashion at the time the copy was made – which often casts serious doubts on dating by stylistic analysis alone.

The *ius imaginum* remained exclusively patrician inasmuch as patricians alone were eligible for the various ordinary magistracies; subsequently this right was extended to such plebeian families as were deemed to come of patrician stock, and finally to the descendants of all those who had held higher (curule) magistracies.

The Senate – that emblem of the patrician class – was hereditary; but any person of free birth, who also possessed the million sesterces (250,000 denarii) that was a condition of membership, could win entry by means of the *cursus honorum*, securing office first as

 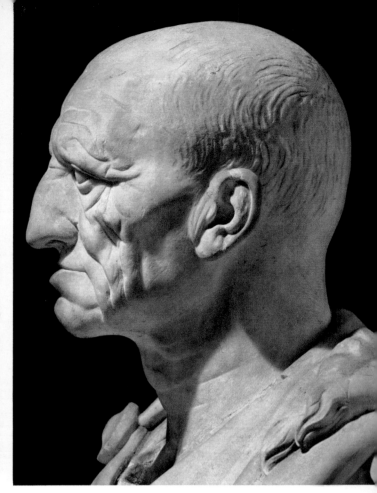

83 ROME: SUPPOSED PORTRAIT OF SULLA. VENICE, MUSEO ARCHEOLOGICO   84 ROME: PORTRAIT OF A PATRICIAN. ROME, MUSEO TORLONIA

quaestor, then as aedile or tribune of the people, and finally attaining the praetorship or consulate. The new Senator did not thereby acquire patrician status, though his descendants thereafter formed part of the *nobilitas*. At this period only members of the Senate could be proconsuls in the provinces or commanders of legions. We see, then, how the concept of *nobilitas* was always closely linked with the family portrait. Sallust (*Bell. Jug.* 85.25) makes Marius say some very harsh things about those Roman patricians who despise him 'as a man of no [ancestral] images and recent ennoblement'. To have the *atrium* of one's house 'crammed with smoke-blackened images' (Seneca, *Epist.* 44.5) was a mark of the old nobility. The masks of condemned criminals were not brought out at the funeral of another member of the family; nor were ancestral images paraded at the funeral of anyone who had suffered such condemnation himself (Tacitus, *Ann.* 3.76).

Thus the portrait enjoyed a position of very special importance in Roman life, though this importance was not so much artistic as political, a matter of caste. It is plain that such emphasis on the portrait as a symbol of senatorial aristocracy must have been especially apparent in any period when the patrician class was recovering power and re-establishing its old perogatives. Just such a period of aristocratic reaction took place in Sulla's day, one consequence of the great alarm aroused by the reforms of the Gracchi. The first laws against these reforms were passed in 121 BC, and the period of reaction lasted until the year 111. After this, the war against the slaves who had rebelled in Sicily (104-100), and

77

the struggle against piracy, led to a second, more decisive period of patrician reaction, beginning in 98 – which must, however, have abated somewhat with the outbreak of open revolt among the Latin Allies, the so-called 'Social War' of 91-88 B C, and the subsequent concession of citizen-rights to all Italians.

During these bitter domestic quarrels, the most reactionary faction in the Senate found its ideal leader in Sulla, who had no scruples about marching on Rome, or, later, destroying Samnite and Etruscan opposition through wholesale massacres. Rival politicians and their supporters were wiped out by means of proscriptions, confiscation of property and the assassin's knife. Sulla's dictatorship (82-79 B C) saw a great increase in the powers of the Senate. Its membership was increased, while various limitations were imposed on the tribunate. The new constitution which Sulla drafted remained in force after his death, indeed until Pompey's consulship in 70 B C, an overall period of twelve years. It was this half-century of resurgent patrician domination and self-confidence, particularly under Sulla, that saw the beginning of the typically 'Republican' Roman portrait, a special variant on Hellenistic realism, and one which continued to evolve until the Second Triumvirate of Antony, Octavian and Lepidus (43-32 B C).

We can get a cross-check on its early stages by examining various numismatic portraits. Until Julius Caesar broke with tradition, it was illegal to put the image of any living person on coins; subsequently the Senate granted a similar concession to Octavian. Because of the ban, magistrates in charge of the mint often adorned new issues with the portraits of their illustrious ancestors. Research on this subject (notably that of Bernhard Schweitzer) shows that such coin-portraits almost always reproduced, more or less faithfully, some likeness taken during the lifetime of the person concerned. All these men had held office between 90 and 70 B C, just when the great patrician revival was taking place. Another event which took place during the same period was the brutal disruption of the economy in the province of Asia Minor; amongst other consequences, this brought about a mass emigration to Rome of artists and craftsmen – silversmiths, sculptors, engravers of precious stones – who worked for a luxury clientele.

The highly specialized type of portraiture which developed at Rome during this period is characterized by a meticulous realism – of the kind that takes pleasure in recording irregularities of skin-texture, as in a relief-map. More attention is paid to analysing detail than to the overall effect. But the main aim is to emphasize, by means of a deliberate contrast with the Hellenistic citizen's worldly and intellectual elegance, the austerity and will-power displayed by a peasant breed, inured to fatigue, used to political argument, and full of pride in their past. Never before had there been a type of portraiture which adhered so completely to objective reality, or was so wholly deficient in aesthetic artifice and all the fashionable graces; and it is precisely these characteristics which demonstrate that the typical Republican portrait is restricted to one class or category of persons. In fact we also find traces of very different styles at Rome during this period: there is the emotional Hellenistic portrait, its expression somewhat theatrical and over-emphatic, and the objective, naturalistic likeness, with just a dash of sober elegance about it – enough to make it smart, and thus acceptable in aristocratic circles.

There is one statue (now transferred from the Palazzo Barberini to the Museo Nuovo on the Capitol) which sums up all I have been saying about the specialized origins of the typically Roman portrait. We see a toga-clad man, carrying two busts. The portrait-bust was unknown to Greek art, which refused to countenance such artificial amputations, seeing in them the destruction of the human form as an organic whole; whereas in an Etruscan, Roman or Celtic context an isolated head was already used to express the entire personality. Typologically speaking, if not as a mode of artistic expression, the formal bust of the Republican era, terminating a little way below the neck, is closely akin to the ancestral mask. However, it would be a mistake to infer (as has in fact been done) that the Republican portrait's style derives directly from the plaster-cast death-mask. Certain features – e.g. an emaciated face with cheekbones so prominent that the taut skin barely covers them (visible in one or two portraits of this period) – may indeed represent physiognomical elements taken from death-masks; but it is just such elements that illustrate the relationship to the Republican ethos. In any case, the Barberini statue's two busts are not examples of that special style peculiar to the patrician portrait in Sulla's day; where they belong is in the Hellenistic and Mid-Italic tradition of objective naturalism. A close comparative study, with particular reference to sculptural technique and the treatment of the features, shows that the bust held in the statue's right hand is a copy of a portrait first made about 50-40 BC, whereas that in the left (which presents undeniable similarities of feature to the first, a genuine 'family likeness') would seem to derive from an original of the period 20-15 BC: that is, about a generation later. Unfortunately, the statue's head is not its original one, which has been lost, but an antique head adapted to modern requirements. Its date is about 30 BC, whereas the type and treatment of the statue's toga clearly belong to the Augustan period. In its original form, then, this statue must have presented a sequence of family portraits covering three generations, from 50 BC to AD 15.

The head placed on the Barberini statue is a typical portrait from the era of the Second Triumvirate (43-32 BC), when a compromise was achieved between Hellenistic form and the trend towards documentary naturalism. Also from this period is the copy of a fine portrait, long identified – though without any real justification – as Sulla (Venice, Museo Archeologico: Roman provenance). But the best example of this type of portrait is an original bust in bronze, now held by the Hermitage Museum of Leningrad – which took it over from the old State collection in 1928, unfortunately without indication of provenance. The portrait of Marcus Brutus, Caesar's murderer, as we see it on gold coins of 43 BC (*pl. 395*), must have been based on a similar sculpture.

The crudely realistic, objective type of portrait had its origins in Mid-Italic Hellenism – which is why we find both humble precursors and modest contemporary examples of the *genre* in those formalized votive heads from the sanctuaries of Latium and southern Etruria. Sometimes this tradition throws up a piece of quite exceptional quality, such as the man's head from Tarquinia in the Tarquinia Museum, the charming woman's head in the Berlin Museum, or the female bust on display at the Vatican's Museo Gregoriano. During the Augustan period, this objectivism absorbed certain neo-classical elements from the Atticizing tradition – so much so that latterly even common-or-garden terracotta votive offerings were barely distinguishable from the earliest portraits produced in Octavian's day.

Thus it becomes quite impossible to find a single, all-embracing definition for the

86-87 'BARBERINI STATUE' (DETAILS): THE TWO PORTRAIT-BUSTS. ROME, PALAZZO DEI CONSERVATORI

Roman portrait of the first century BC. It is true that the portraits produced during this period share one fundamental characteristic, the search for realism; yet the starting-point is ideological rather than artistic, and manifests itself in widely contrasting ways. Any of the four basic formal trends, each from a different source, which met and mingled in Rome could, and did, provide the point of departure. Side by side with the trends we have already examined – the simple, objective portrait of Mid-Italic origin, and the patrician-style portrait which developed under Sulla – there also exist a number of purely Hellenistic portraits, exuberant (even a trifle baroque) in execution: a good example is the head of Flamininus, on the coins which he struck in Greece. There are other portraits which still reveal their debt to the Mid-Italic tradition, but have also

81

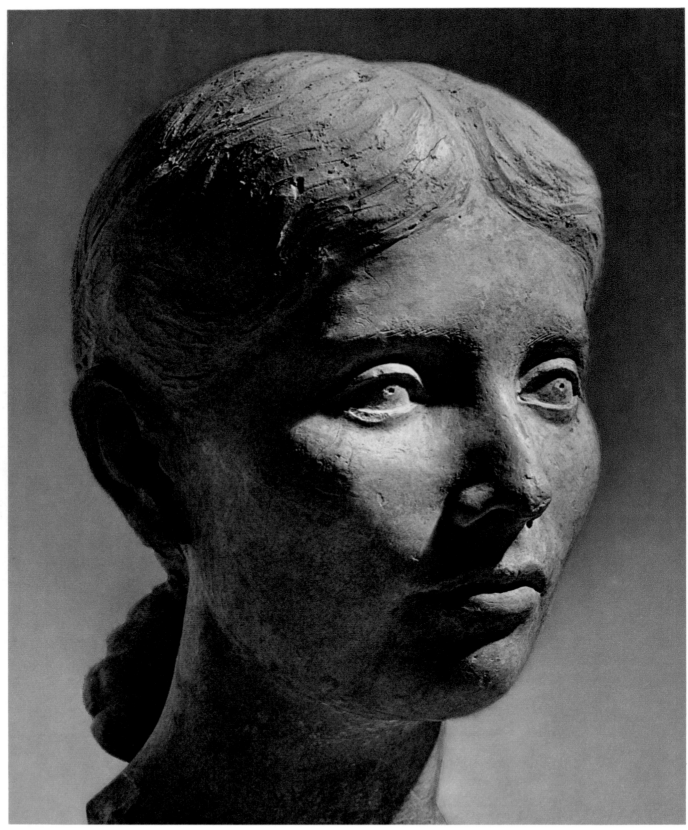

88 LATIUM: PORTRAIT OF A GIRL. BERLIN, STAATLICHE MUSEEN, ANTIKENSAMMLUNGEN

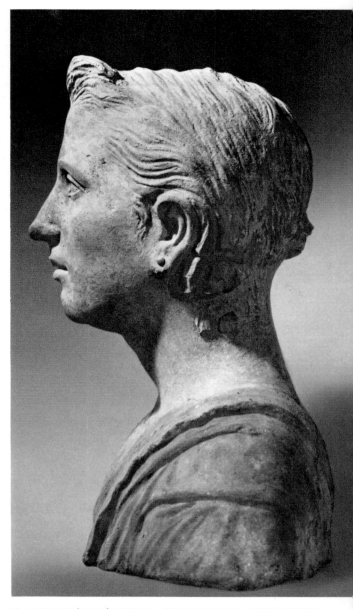

89 PALESTRINA (PRAENESTE): FUNERARY BUST. PALESTRINA MUSEUM

90 CERVETERI (CAERE): BUST OF A WOMAN. VATICAN, MUSEO ETRUSCO

absorbed the latest Hellenistic techniques. In the two latter categories we may place some of the most characteristic examples of this aspect of Roman art. From the Italic tradition, which customarily worked in terracotta, they retained certain formal techniques which – even when the works are executed in stone or marble – still suggest the texture and modelling appropriate to clay.

Among the most typical examples of this mixed tradition, containing both Hellenistic and Roman elements, is the statue of a general (so-called) found at Tivoli, and now in Rome (Museo Nazionale). One must remember that, despite their record of conquest

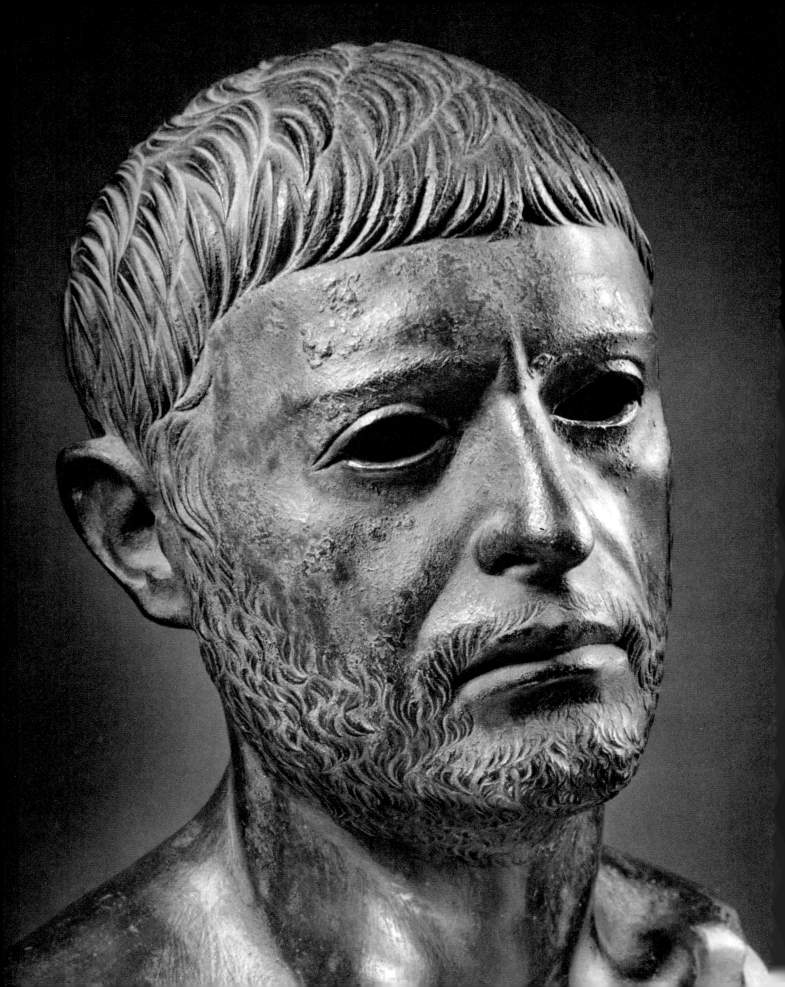

92 TARQUINIA: PORTRAIT OF A MAN. TARQUINIA, MUSEO NAZIONALE

and expansion, the Romans did not possess – either now or during the centuries which followed – anything resembling a corps of professional officers; on entering the *Urbs*, a victorious general had to doff his military garb and appear before the Senate dressed as an ordinary citizen. This statue shows us a naked figure, draped in the 'heroic style', as heroes of Greek legend were represented; but in the present case the drapery is more abundant, and disposed with greater regard for personal modesty. The cuirass, which indicates the subject's military status, is placed beside him, as an attribute (and also to serve as a support for the statue).

Pliny (*NH* 35.18) says quite explicitly that it was a 'Greek custom not to cover the body, whereas the Romans, as soldiers, add the cuirass'. However, Pliny was writing in the time of the Emperor Vespasian, more than a century after the likeliest date for the Tivoli statue, when statues representing the Roman emperors in armour had become the norm. Here, on the other hand, we are still in the initial stage of the 'portrait with cuirass', before it has been fully formulated. The strongly sculptured features owe their exuberant modelling and lightly parted lips to the Hellenistic tradition of portraiture; but the touch of pathos they convey is modified by an excessive attention to detail, characteristic of

patrician portrait-art under Sulla. Hence the formal contradiction apparent in this face, symbolized by the uncertain, hesitant expression – a striking contrast with the 'heroic' pose of the statue as a whole. Thus the work's overall iconography, no less than its detailed portraiture, shows us a still unresolved duality of style and central theme, which is highly typical of Roman culture in the early first century BC. The date of the statue is the subject of much controversy, but the most plausible arguments suggest a period very soon after Sulla's dictatorship, between 78 and 68 BC, which also saw the reorganization of the province of Asia by Lucullus. The officer portrayed could, in that case, have been one of Lucullus's generals. This major political and military undertaking has left at least one enduring legacy behind it: the cherry-tree, with its succulent fruit, which Lucullus introduced into Italy.

During the Augustan age neo-Atticism was the fashion in all upper-class artistic circles. This did much to weaken the impetus of Hellenistic-type sculptural portraiture, besides introducing certain refinements borrowed from Alexandria; the result was a series of portraits such as that of Augustus's sister Octavia (see Ch. 4), and the fresh, charming bust of a young girl in the Torlonia collection. The old patrician-style portrait, austere and disdainful, no longer found favour with a society bent on proving itself more cultured and adaptable than its predecessors, and dazzled by Hellenistic elegance. Yet the type of patrician portrait developed in Sulla's day went on for some time; it turns up, much later, on the gravestones of freedmen and small tradespeople. From Rome it spread out into the Italian provinces, where it became, stylistically speaking, the typical 'Roman portrait'. It has left us statues of both men and women (the Museo Nazionale in Naples has some examples from Campania), besides numerous grave-stelae at Ravenna and in the towns of the Po Valley, where it long flourished. These were the funerary monuments of ordinary lower-class people, who had themselves commemorated in the same style as the *grands seigneurs* once used to do – a fact which suggests that what endured was more often a typology

93 TIVOLI (TIBUR): STATUE OF A GENERAL. ROME, M. NAZIONALE

94 ROME: PORTRAIT OF A YOUNG GIRL. ROME, VILLA ALBANI

than any kind of portrait as such. For this reason the chronological sequence deduced from them (mainly based on Augustan hair-styles) must be regarded as highly dubious.

There is yet another type of portrait which deserves consideration, at least in respect of its iconography and original significance: what the Romans called *imago clipeata*, or the 'portrait on a shield'. The origin of this type of portrait was Greek, as the ancient literary sources specifically confirm. For the Greeks this was the one legitimate form of sculptured portrait that was *not* a full-length statue. For the person thus represented it constituted a special kind of homage, equivalent to being raised aloft on his men's shields – almost, indeed, a first step towards apotheosis. Originally the portrait on the clipeus had to be in some more or less precious metal. Even after the original shield-shape became a mere enclosing frame, it often retained the curving lines appropriate for metal, even when executed in stone or set within the square outline of a painting. For the *imago clipeata* became very popular with painters; it also appears in the tradition of funerary art. Typologically, it persists right through the Empire, on sarcophagi, monumental tombs, and other monuments of a commemorative character.

95 CAMPANIA: FUNERARY STATUE. NAPLES, M. NAZIONALE

96 RAVENNA: FUNERARY STELE OF FAMILY OF P. LONGIDIENUS. RAVENNA MUSEUM

97 CAMPANIA: FUNERARY STATUE (DETAIL). NAPLES, MUSEO ARCHEOLOGICO NAZIONALE

In Greece, the clipeus is mentioned about the year 100 BC, in connection with the sanctuary of the gods on Samothrace. In Rome, if we can rely on the testimony of Pliny (complicated by the fact that he obviously got his characters muddled up while taking notes), the first shield-portraits representing known individuals were placed in Bellona's temple by an Appius Claudius, probably Claudius Pulcher, about 80; soon afterwards, in 78, M. Aemilius used these clipeus-portraits to decorate his own private house. Pompeian paintings of the Flavian era (House of the Vettii, House of the Impluvium)

98 OSTIA: PORTRAIT ON A SHIELD (IMAGO CLIPEATA). OSTIA MUSEUM

show us how metal clipei adorned with heads in high relief were suspended between the columns.

From all this it seems fair to conclude that the Republican period witnessed the gradual development of the Roman portrait as it was to continue for the whole Imperial era. In Rome, the first century BC constituted a kind of melting-pot, in which the most variegated cultural elements met and blended. The process of development consisted in striking a balance between some fundamentally Roman concept, and the habit of using traditional Hellenistic forms to express it artistically. What we have here is not so much a case of individual artistic will, or the search for some new form through the formulation of genuinely Roman artistic principles, but rather a solid background of accepted fact, a well-defined ideology, on to which attempts were made to graft the various principles then in cultural vogue. Various references in our literary sources suggest that, apart from the wax death-mask, the most ancient type of portrait was that painted on a wooden board: *cera* and *tabula* (Martial, 11.102). In any case, even the most casual student of art will be aware that the transformation of the material for a mask into the finished portrait (which recreates, in formal and expressive terms, its subject's living appearance) is by no means merely a mechanical process. Its achievement has the same ambiguous quality that is found whenever an image is transmuted from the world of natural to that of artistic reality. Thus the mask is not so much a formal matrix as an ideological mould for the Roman portrait.

Little wax heads, mounted directly on plinths, have been found in a *lararium* at Pompeii (House of Menander). These were in all likelihood completely generalized

100 POMPEII, 'HOUSE OF THE IMPLUVIUM': POTRAITS ON SHIELDS HUNG IN A BUILDING ▶

99 ROME: TOMB ON THE VIA PORTUENSE. PAINTED PORTRAIT. ROME, MUSEO NAZIONALE

101 ROME OR LATIUM: PORTRAIT BASED ON A FUNERAL MASK. PARIS, LOUVRE

representations, and certainly not derived from death-masks. Their discovery reinforces the theory that the use of masks (unattested by any evidence prior to that of Polybius) was of no great antiquity, and was already one means of satisfying the urge to preserve one's ancestors' features. This desire must have been especially marked among the patrician families, since, as we have seen, the privilege of indulging it was defined and restricted by law. The invention of the plaster cast as a preliminary stage in executing a wax mask was ascribed by the Greeks to the sculptor Lysippus's brother, which implies a date in the second half of the fourth century BC. Although, in fact, plaster masks had been commonplace in Egypt since remote times, this evidence enables us to establish a *terminus post quem* for the application of such a technique to portraiture amongst the ancient Romans.

The best piece of evidence for a direct connection between the mask and the portrait is a terracotta head from the Louvre (Campana Collection), which has its neck resting on a tiny plinth. Its provenance is undoubtedly Latium, perhaps even Rome; but it already shows signs of artistic development towards the typical 'Republican' portrait.

The *imago*, the ancestral likeness, expressed by a mask whose basis was a plaster cast, could not *per se* be termed an artistic achievement, and embodied no sort of plastic concept. Thus it was only through contact with a highly sophisticated tradition of plastic form (as exemplified by the Hellenistic portrait) that Roman civilization, at a certain point in time, found its own individual mode of expression in portraiture. The portrait as such came to be closely identified with the official party line in art, with public display and propaganda. In Rome alone, about eighty silver statues were erected in honour of Augustus during his lifetime, over and above all the rest (*Res Gestae* 2.24). Thus the portrait was always a typical expression of Roman art, one of its show-pieces. Yet the history of its development remains extremely complicated, being dominated by two contrasting trends: on the one hand, an attempt to satisfy the various formal requirements of a flexible glyptic style, sensitive to nuances of skin-texture and the expressive potential of contrast in all its aspects; on the other, a desire to achieve the most accurate possible representation, down to the tiniest detail – a precise if stiff pattern which formed an essential preliminary to the patrician family's domestic cult of ancestral images.

It was not until very near the end of the Republican era that these different (and to some extent conflicting) demands could be reconciled, and the Roman portrait develop in its own right. Yet it did not spring from any novel concept of art; there was no aesthetic problem involved. At this point, the realistic portrait of the Second Triumvirate invaded the funerary monuments also of the lower middle classes, as can be seen from the stele of the Via Statilia (Rome, Museo Nuovo dei Conservatori); while another stele, found quite close to the first, portrays a couple in a way which reveals traces of the new Augustan style – above all, of the refinement and elegance which distinguish the generation at the end of the first century BC from the preceding one, which was the last to live under the Republic. If the inscription recovered nearby did, in fact, form part of the tomb, this second stele may well be a portrait of the big industrial baker Marcus Vergilius Eurysaces and his wife Atistia. The gap between the two generations could hardly be clearer. From now on each new artistic phase, every changing whim of Roman society as regards taste and style, found due reflection in the art of portraiture.

A remarkable collection of characters thus passes before our eyes: such figures as the elderly lady from a distinguished country family (portrait of Palombara Sabina: Rome, Museo Nazionale), or the group portraying a merchant's family from Ostia, both of the late first century BC; or, in the period between Caligula and Nero, the lean and etiolated portrait of a priest of Isis (Rome, Museo Nazionale), and the delicate high-relief representation on a memorial stele from the Porta Laurentina at Ostia (see *pl. 105, 106, 107*).

Between the reign of Titus and that of Trajan we can find portraits in which no trace remains of that sober manner which characterized the Roman portrait during its earliest

94

103 ROME: FUNERARY STELE OF M. V. EURYSACES AND HIS WIFE (?). ROME, GIARDINI PANTANELLA

stages: a famous portrait such as that in the Museo Capitolino, of a lady with her hair swept up in a pile of high, tight curls (perhaps Vibia Matidia, the sister of Hadrian's wife-to-be), provides an example of perfect harmony between stylistic method and the characterization of a brilliant, fashionable personality. The head of an elderly woman (Lateran Museum), assignable to roughly the same date, gives some idea of the range of artistic expression possible within the context of a single culture, and also shows the way in which two requirements basic to all sculptural portraiture – realistic representation and coherence of three-dimensional form – could be blended into one, as the artists working in Rome throughout this period proved.

104 ROME (?): FRAGMENT OF ALTO-RELIEVO. PORTRAIT OF A WOMAN. ANTIQUITIES MARKET

105 PALOMBARA SABINA: PORTRAIT OF AN ELDERLY LADY. ROME, MUSEO NAZIONALE ▶

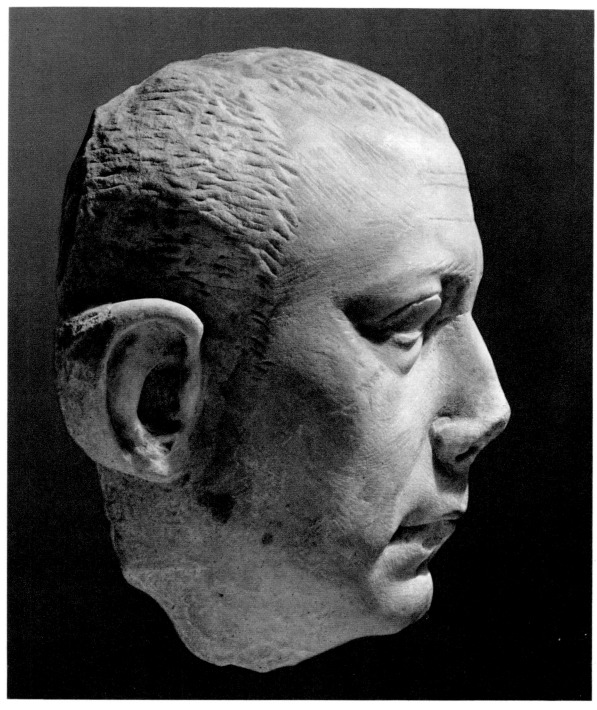

107 OSTIA: FRAGMENT OF ALTO-RELIEVO. PORTRAIT OF A MAN. OSTIA MUSEUM

108 POMPEII: PORTRAIT OF A MUNICIPAL MAGISTRATE AND HIS WIFE. NAPLES, ARCHEOLOGICO NAZIONALE

Also to this period must be assigned the great efflorescence of portrait-painting mentioned by Pliny. When he begins his chapter on the portrait, he speaks above all of *painted* portraits, as being the most common sort. Few examples of this *genre* have been preserved apart from those on frescoes, such as the portrait of a minor Pompeii magistrate and his wife. Yet the series of portraits which form the glory of the art of Roman Egypt was not by any means restricted to the Fayum area. It is only because of specially favourable climatic conditions that these works have survived, whereas similar examples throughout the rest of the Roman world have perished.

Until the crisis in art which began during the reign of Commodus, Roman portrait-art continued to be dominated by the balance struck between these two requirements.

109 FAYYUM: PORTRAIT OF MIDDLE-AGED WOMAN. BERLIN, STAATLICHE MUSEEN, ANTIKENSAMMLUNGEN ▶

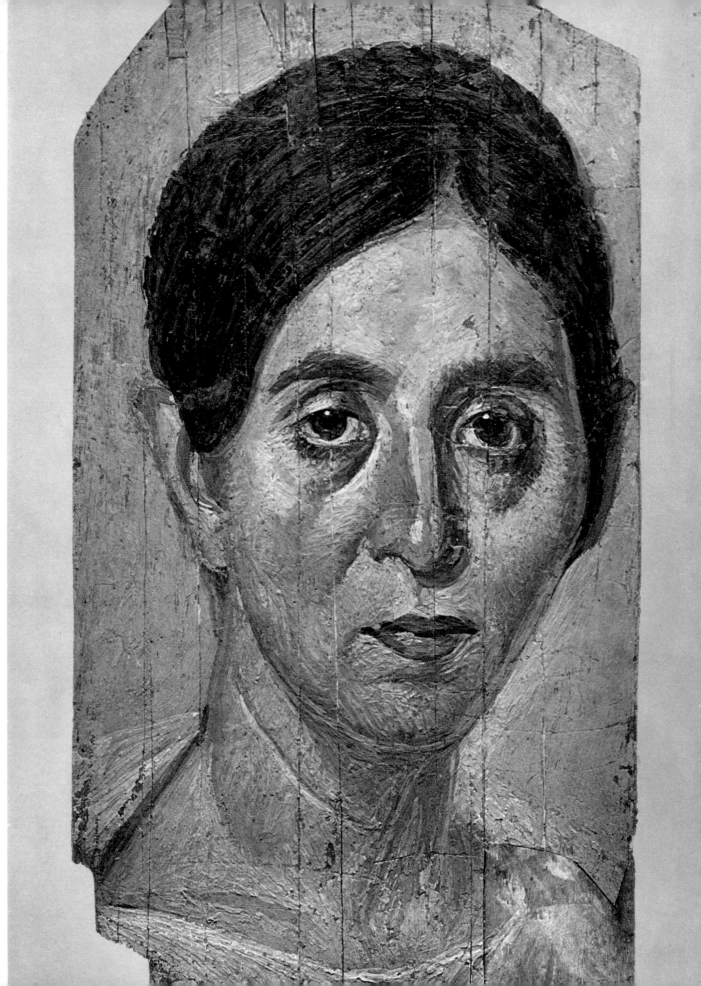

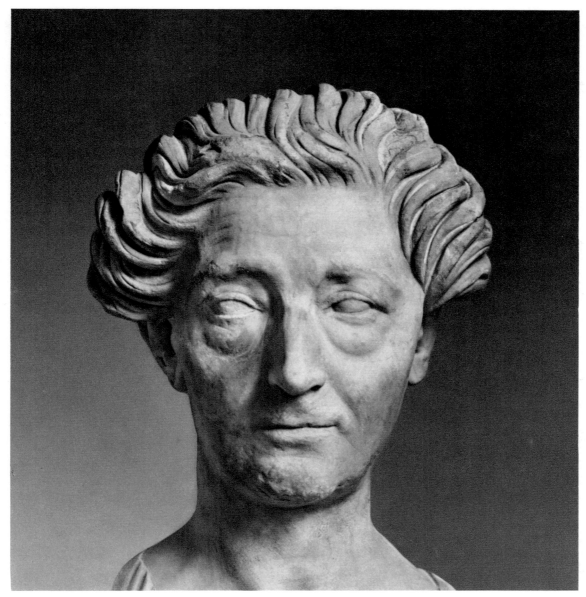

111 ROME: PORTRAIT OF ELDERLY LADY. VATICAN (LATERAN MUSEUM)

Yet its development covered a wide field: busts in the familial or funerary tradition, figures on grave-stelae or tomb-altars, and lastly commemorative statues, where gradual adaptation to the 'official' style then generally current somehow failed to curb its independence.

Those who lacked the capital to immortalize themselves by means of a large artistic monument would join 'funeral clubs', which, in return for an annual subscription, would guarantee their ashes a decent resting-place. Several of these large burial-places still exist, in a fine state of preservation. Because of the numerous niches, most often semi-circular in shape, with which their walls are dotted, like entries for pigeons (*columbae*) in a dovecote, they were known as *columbaria*. One or two particularly impressive

specimens are still extant in Rome, near the beginning of the Via Appia and the Via Latina; one belonging to the freedmen of Augustus's Imperial household (Vigna Codini), and another to the freedmen of Marcella, Marcus Vipsania Agrippa's second wife.

All these different forms of 'exalting an individual above the rest of mankind', as Pliny puts it (*NH* 34.27), offer us – over and above their purely artistic interest – an opportunity to survey one very idiosyncratic feature of Roman society. Profoundly attached to the realities of life, the Romans hoped to achieve survival in men's memories through the medium of personal effigies. They therefore built themselves grandiose tombs, which often bore a close resemblance to fortresses, and were in fact so used during the Middle Ages. When their means did not go so far, they still managed some sort of a shrine or stele. These tombs, whether imposing or humble, were not collected in cemeteries, but were dotted along the roadside, where passers-by could see them and read the inscriptions they bore. In this way they kept in communication with the dead, perpetuating their relationship for all eternity: *non omnis moriar*, 'I shall not die altogether'.

This obsession with personal immortality goes a long way towards explaining the manner in which, later, Romans took refuge from troubles afflicting Imperial society in cults which promised them rewards and happiness after death.

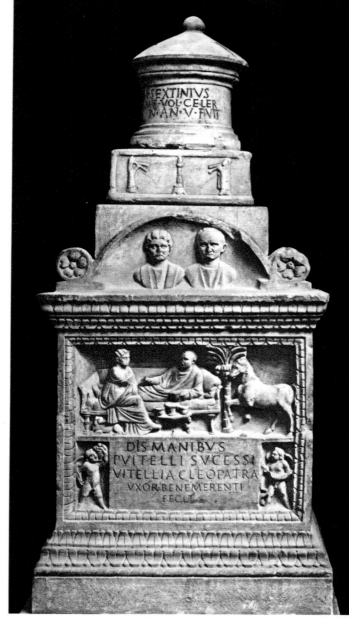

113 ROME: FUNERARY ALTAR OF VITELLIUS SUCCESSUS. VATICAN

3 Problems of Pictorial and Architectural Space

From the thirteenth to the twentieth century – up to the moment of Paul Klee's statement 'Art does not reproduce the visible; rather, it makes visible' – Western art, through its multifarious changes of time, place and personality, has continued to posit the imitation of reality as an explicit and admitted standard. Yet time and again, each artist's natural genius has striven to give it a different appearance, in a personal attempt to penetrate beyond this visible and sensible reality, and to create a new reality: the reality achieved by art in a specific time and place. Realism has been one way of taking mental possession of the world: that is why this artistic exploration has so often gone hand in hand with research of a scientific nature – on the geometry of space, or the properties of light, or anatomy, every functional aspect of life and nature. In the West, during antiquity, this passion for investigation, for getting a rational grasp on the world, was displayed above all by the Greeks.

It was this desire which, centuries later, led Europe to regard the art of antiquity as a second nature, long perfected and clarified, from which all manner of lessons could be learnt. The antiquity which Western Europe thus discovered, and took as its pattern, was in fact that of Rome. When people read Greek and Latin authors they made no distinction between Greece and Rome: the whole lot were lumped together as 'the Ancients'. They fancied they were in the presence of Greek art, and even tried their hand at some attributions. Under the Dioscuri from the Baths of Constantine on the Quirinal someone wrote: *Opus Phidiae, opus Praxitelis*. This was by no means an isolated occurrence.

The first translation into a modern tongue – Italian – of those chapters in Pliny the Elder's *Natural History* which dealt with works of art was undertaken by an artist, and the result inserted in a history of art. Entitled *Commentarii*, this history began with ancient Greece, and went right through to the author himself – Lorenzo Ghiberti, who created the famous doors of the Baptistery in Florence – and his contemporaries. Its date was between 1448 and 1455. The rediscovery of Greece, and the distinction between

Greek and Roman art, took place only well after the Renaissance. Even J. J. Winckelmann, who published his *History of Ancient Art* in 1764, and is regarded as the father of modern art-historiography, never suspected that a fair proportion of the statues he admired as Greek works were not, in fact, originals, but copies from the Roman period, very often cheap, mass-produced stuff.

The history of ancient art began as a mere adjunct to philology: that is, its original function was to gloss and illustrate literary texts. Though Winckelmann set himself the task of studying ancient works of art in order to learn the 'essence of art' – an aesthetic programme – he took as his guide Pliny's text. He completely failed to evaluate the *Natural History* at its proper worth; it never occurred to him that Pliny was as far removed from the times of Pheidias as he, Winckelmann, was from the art of the twelfth century, which he regarded with a mixture of bafflement and disgust. While busily extracting a neo-classical aesthetic pattern from his study of Greek sculpture, he never noticed that Pliny's work was based entirely on information provided by writers of the late Hellenistic period, all of whom belonged to a neo-classical movement that got going about 150 BC in Athens and Alexandria. Pliny follows his sources so slavishly, indeed, that he reports art as 'dead' by the beginning of the third century, and 'resuscitated' towards the middle of the second (*NH* 34.52). In this way, by linking the 'classicizing' art of the second century directly to the classical art of the fourth, without a gap, he chopped out the whole Hellenistic period, and made it look as though Greek art was frozen into a kind of eternal changelessness.

It took a century and a half of archaeological discovery and exploration to fill this lacuna and produce a balanced historical estimate of Greek art. Only then did it become apparent that (contrary to the picture bequeathed us by the neo-classical period) the pioneering art in Greece had been, not sculpture, but painting; and that the formal innovations associated with Hellenism, far from being a digression in the homogeneous development of Greek art, constituted the climax to a process of formal exploration which had begun very early, soon after Greek art as such came into being, about the middle of the eighth century BC. It is this obsession with form which distinguishes Greek art from all earlier artistic civilizations around the Mediterranean basin. We may define it as a determination to render the sense of space, and a manner of representing objects, in their spatial context, as we actually see them.

This search for pictorial space underlies the whole phenomenon of 'grand realism' in Greek art, as well as the naturalism which attained its highest expression during the Hellenistic era. It was directly responsible for the discovery of perspective in drawing (by trial and error to begin with, about the end of the sixth century, and later on a mathematical basis, at the beginning of the fourth), not to mention chiaroscuro, the cast shadow and tonal painting: all things which, at a certain point in time, came to seem natural attributes of sophisticated artistic expression, and as such were basic to the whole great European movement in figurative art, from the thirteenth to the twentieth century.

None of these technical advances, however, from perspective to local colour, which help to suggest the movement of a figure in space could achieve real or lasting results through artistic intuition alone. Such devices can be absorbed into the formal vocabulary of art only by a highly complex society, in which generations of artists deliberately and consciously set themselves the same problem. Such, *par excellence*, was the world of Greek art, where formal progress is invariably accompanied by theoretical speculation (as subsequently during the European Renaissance), and a work of art results from the balance between irrational inspiration and rational theory.

The neo-classical interpretation of art in antiquity had relegated the whole Roman period to limbo. Roman art up to the age of the Antonines was regarded as a degenerate extension of Greek art, unhappily fallen into the hands of an uncivilized people who aspired no higher than clumsy imitation. After the end of the second century A D (according to this view), it lapsed into centuries of barbarism and 'decadence'. Classical archaeologists accepted the theory without even discussing it. It was not until the turn of the present century that two art-historians, Franz Wickhoff and Alois Riegl, opposed this interpretation. Wickhoff's interest in the then highly modern work of the Impressionists led him to make a special study of 'Pompeian' painting, which meant, in effect, of art in the Roman period. Here, to his great surprise, he found just that technical freedom and sense of spatial atmosphere which contemporary painting seemed to be finding in its long battle against academicism. During the nineteenth century, the Academy had been in the habit of setting its pupils to work on historical Roman themes. The Academy's more irreverent critics referred to the helmeted Roman figures in these pictures as *pompiers*, or firemen; now it transpired that art of the Roman period had itself served as a weapon against *pompiérisme*.

Wickhoff was so enchanted by this revelation that he, too, fell straight into the historical trap set for him by Pliny's fable on the death of art (and the interpretation of Greek art to which it gave rise). This was why he interpreted any deviation from the neo-classical pattern in art of the Roman period as a Roman novelty, an original element of Roman art. Such was the genesis of an error in historical judgment which has lain heavily on subsequent studies, and has for long prevented a true appreciation of either Roman or Hellenistic art. Here, too, was the source of that mistaken (if brilliantly argued) theory according to which the accurate representation of space in painting and sculpture was a Roman invention – or at least one made during the Roman period. Some even went so far as to locate its birthplace in Campania; others sought antecedents for it in Etruscan or Italic art. There are those who are searching still.

Let us now turn to the central issue of this chapter: the relationship between artists of the Roman period and the idea of space. Throughout, the way in which the artist visualizes space (that is, the way in which he treats or ignores it) is a fundamental problem of art. Spatial relationships establish themselves most demonstrably in two artistic media: painting and architecture. With painting, space is suggested by a number of technical devices employing both line and colour. In architecture, space can be actually individualized. The two disciplines follow totally different lines of development, and are not directly linked in any way.

PAINTING

The chief archives of painting from the Roman period are to be found in the Campanian towns buried under the ashes and mud of Vesuvius following the eruption of AD 79. Here, however, I shall deal exclusively with the art of Rome herself, the centre of political and economic power – and of culture too, at any rate after the second part of the second century BC, and through the centuries with which we are concerned. Since Rome was neither destroyed nor abandoned, but remained continuously inhabited to the present day, so fragile an art as painting has left comparatively few traces. Yet enough survives to suggest that painting at Rome was not essentially different from that of the cities overwhelmed by Vesuvius, though it seems to have achieved a higher overall standard – as one might expect from a capital city.

Naturally, nothing is left now of all those priceless paintings on wood, the work of Greek masters of the fourth and third centuries, which had been carried off to Rome. Several temples were so crammed with them as to become virtual art-galleries; the same was true of Octavia's Portico, built by Augustus in her honour, on a site where, ever since 147, two small Greek temples had stood with a portico round them. Some of these Greek paintings were copied or imitated in still-surviving mural decorations. But Pliny tells us quite explicitly (*NH* 35.118) that the real art of painting was confined to works executed on wooden panels, and that during his lifetime (the reign of Vespasian, AD 69-79) these had largely vanished (*ibid.* 35.28); whereas the mural paintings that adorned private homes betokened their owners' wealth (especially in the choice of precious coloured materials) more than their artistic taste (*ibid.* 35.50).

A typical example of the two contrasting trends – copies straight from a Greek original, and 'Latin translations' – is provided by two versions of the same composition, *Theseus the Liberator*, the one from Herculaneum, the other from Pompeii and somewhat reduced in scale. The first is a faithful copy of a Greek painting, which repeats, in the figure of Theseus, a formula applied by Lysippus to his statues. The brush-work is solid and rich in chiaroscuro, with light cross-hatching. The conception sticks closely to mythic tradition. Theseus seems half-stunned by the success of his exploit; with staring eyes and a rapt expression he moves majestically forward, past the body of the monster he has slain, wholly caught up in the grandeur of the moment, and paying no attention to the young people he has liberated, now crowding round him. At the top left-hand corner, one can just discern the lower part of some figure, perhaps a nymph, sitting on a boulder. The whole composition is steeped in the enchantment of its mythological setting.

In the Pompeian replica, however, all poetic quality has disappeared. Apart from the bad draughtsmanship, especially noticeable in the figures of the children clinging to Theseus, the figure of the hero himself is ill-proportioned and coarse. The old man and little girls on the right are executed with a flat-footed realism that brings to mind a school outing; and the entrance to the Labyrinth has been endowed with an air of harmless familiarity by being turned into a doorway or postern-gate. The slain monster lies there, one tiny human arm folded across his chest, looking anything but fearsome. The composition – clearly a well-known piece – which the Herculaneum artist copied has, undeniably, influenced the wall-decorator of Pompeii; but by jettisoning the mythical atmosphere, and transposing everything into the language of daily life, the Pompeian artist reveals that he belonged to a quite different culture. The Herculaneum painting, found on the wall of a public building (the basilica), belongs to the Hellenistic-Roman tradition; whereas that from Pompeii, which adorned the exedra of a private house (the so-called House of Gavius Rufus, in Region VII), is unquestionably Romano-Campanian. It reveals that preoccupation with daily realities which forms the basis of all commemorative reliefs; the latter, as we have seen, belong in the category of 'plebeian art', and their links with the Italic tradition of Campania are very close indeed.

These two frescoes may serve to illustrate the distinction between Roman-period painting in the direct Hellenistic tradition, and Roman painting proper. Yet this is no more than a primary distinction: the overall picture is far more complex. In Rome, as at Pompeii, there was a school of purely Hellenistic painting, its tradition maintained by Greek artists; there was also a school of Roman painting, which continued the old Mid-Italic tradition. As time went on, direct Hellenistic influence began to disappear, after which Roman painting kept repeating the repertoire it had learnt – though with increasing difficulty – until the end of the second century A D. But from the third century we witness a revival, with the creation of a new pictorial repertoire and culture, for which there is reliable (though indirect) evidence in the mosaics and miniatures of the pre-Byzantine period.

From the third century B C – the battle of Messina, fought against the Carthaginians in 264 B C (Pliny, *NH* 35.22), provides an early example – we have literary evidence for the existence in Rome of a specialized *genre*, the so-called 'triumphal paintings'. These were pictures carried in the triumphal procession, which portrayed episodes from the war that had just been won – or, more often, the towns and regions that had been conquered, a rough map of the various battle-sites. Just such a map was made to illustrate the campaign of Sempronius Gracchus in Sardinia (174 B C; Livy, 41.33). The fullest account of these paintings is that given by Flavius Josephus (*Jewish War* [*Bell. Jud.*] 7.143-52), while describing the triumph celebrated by Vespasian and Titus after the capture of Jerusalem. Andrea Mantegna followed Josephus's text very closely when composing the sequence of panels entitled *The Triumph of Caesar*, now at Hampton Court.

Naturally, nothing is left of these paintings; but it is inconceivable that they had no influence on the composition of historical reliefs, such as those which adorn the Arch of Titus or Trajan's Column. If this hypothesis is sound, as seems likely, landscape played an important part in triumphal painting. Sometimes (as in the case of the map of Sardinia) it even took on the character of a plan in perspective, a bird's-eye view. Something of the sort can also be detected in the bas-reliefs (coloured, beyond a doubt) illustrating various episodes from the *Iliad* (*tabulae Iliacae*) and other epic poems. These were executed at the beginning of the Imperial era, and some of them bear a signature in Greek, Theodoros – though whether this was the name of the artist or of a merchant remains uncertain.

Recent research has shown how deeply Hellenistic painting, with its mastery of chiaroscuro and space, had penetrated the whole Mid-Italic region, from Apulia to Etruria. Apulia seems to have been particularly advanced in this field, and pictures recovered from Etruria similarly reflect (probably through the intermediary of Apulia)

115 HERCULANEUM, BASILICA: THESEUS LIBERATING THE CHILDREN OF ATHENS. NAPLES, MUSEO ARCHEOLOGICO NAZIONALE

116 POMPEII, HOUSE OF GAVIUS RUFUS: THESEUS LIBERATING THE CHILDREN OF ATHENS. NAPLES, MUSEO ARCHEOLOGICO NAZIONALE

the progressive influence of Greek painting. This was the area in which 'triumphal painting' developed: socially a Roman phenomenon, fostered by artistic techniques borrowed from Mid-Italic culture, and under the influence of Hellenistic art.

As time went on, a more 'prosaic' version of this trend, better suited to Roman taste, must have begun to appear, as we have seen in the two versions of *Theseus the Liberator*. The oldest example of painting in Rome is a fragment from a tomb on the Esquiline. This portrays a historical scene, executed against a blank background, in four superposed bands. Certain characters are named, e.g. Marcus Fannius and Marcus Fabius. These are portrayed on a larger scale than the other figures; indeed one of them, in the upper-most band, of whom nothing is left but traces of the right leg and left foot, must have been bigger still. The left-hand side of the second band shows us a town surrounded by crenellated battlements, before which stands a disproportionately large warrior, equipped with an oval buckler and a helmet surmounted by two erect crests, one on either side. Near him is a man in a short toga, carrying a spear. Above these two figures are the remains of an inscription: this repeats the names that are legible in their entirety on the third band, in roughly the same position. Round the two principal figures one can see soldiers, drawn on a reduced scale, wearing short tunics and armed with spears. On the lowest band, a battle is going on. One warrior, wearing a double-crested helmet and equipped with an oval buckler, is drawn on a larger scale than the other figures, whose weapons and armour suggest that they are Italians, probably Samnites. The identification of this historical episode remains uncertain. The most plausible theory connects the painting with Quintus Fabius Maximus Rullianus, who commanded Rome's cavalry force during the Second Samnite War. The war broke out in 326; four years later (322) Fabius was Consul, and also celebrated a triumph.

Certain peculiarities in the letter-forms of inscriptions are no longer found after the end of the third century BC, and the style of this work is remarkably akin to that of certain tomb-paintings from Paestum, which can be classified as Campanian. But the practice of portraying the protagonists on a larger scale than the rest is peculiarly Roman; we have already observed it in plebeian-style reliefs, where it continues well into the Imperial period. Thus this painting is what might be termed an *incunabulum* of Roman painting, and in particular of 'triumphal painting' on a historical theme. Among the few known names of Roman painters, we find a Fabius Pictor, who belonged to the great Fabian *gens*, and in or about 304 BC decorated the walls of the Temple of Salus (Safety). However, this in itself does not prove that he painted the work of which we still possess a fragment. It is also possible that the fragment does not belong to an early third-century painting at all, but to a faithful copy executed at a later date to decorate the tomb of some descendant of Quintus Fabius.

This fragment from the Esquiline shows us that Roman painting in its earliest stages had not as yet embarked on experiments with chiaroscuro, light-effects and the representation of space – the stock-in-trade of Hellenistic painting. Yet some touch of Hellenistic elegance and pictorial fluidity had nevertheless affected the decoration of pottery manufactured in Latium (and perhaps even in Rome), as we can see from a little bowl (Tarquinia, Museo Nazionale) which belongs to a type of vessel well-known as far back as the first half of the third century BC. Clearly, then, Hellenistic craftsmanship was

118 LATIUM, ROME (?): SMALL BOWL. TARQUINIA, MUSEO NAZIONALE

conditioned by fashion and fluctuations in trade, whereas wall-painting adhered to its own tradition.

One painter whom we can, it would seem, date at the beginning of the second century BC is Lycon, who was a native of Asia Minor, had worked on a temple in Ardea, near Rome, and upon obtaining citizen-rights changed his name to Marcus Plautius – a name which recalls that of the artist responsible for the Ficoroni Cist.

Very soon reflections of Hellenistic painting began to appear upon the walls of Rome. Among the most remarkable instances of this trend is a series of landscapes representing episodes from the *Odyssey* (now in the Vatican Library), originally found in a house on the Esquiline. Wickhoff used this material to support his thesis that landscape painting, with its perspective in depth and resultant atmosphere, had been pioneered by Roman artists. Yet paintings of just this type ('the wanderings of Ulysses from one country to another') are mentioned by Vitruvius (7.5) in a *résumé* of how mural art developed; what is more, they take their place among those subjects handled by the people whom Vitruvius – writing about 30-25 BC – referred to as 'the Ancients'. As early as the first half of the fourth century BC, Plato (*Critias* 107b-d) was writing of 'artists ... reproducing the earth, mountains, rivers, forests, sky and all that encompasses them'. Today all scholars are agreed that the Esquiline paintings are copies, and that the originals are likely to have been Alexandrian work, executed about 150 BC. The copying, it is thought, was done in Rome between 50 and 40 BC, by an artist who may well not have been Greek,

116

119 ROME, HOUSE ON THE ESQUILINE: EPISODE FROM THE ODYSSEY. ARRIVING IN THE LAND OF THE LAESTRYGONIANS. VATICAN, BIBLIOTECA APOSTOLICA

since the Greek inscriptions in the paintings contain one or two errors. Be that as it may, they more properly belong to the history of Hellenistic art, and are mentioned here as evidence for the kind of artistic climate existing at Rome towards the end of the Republic.

On the other hand, the practice of decorating every wall in the house with a sequence of ornamental paintings was a more recent phenomenon (Pliny, *NH* 35.118). Important evidence for determining the chronology of the various types (*not* styles, as they are sometimes termed) of wall-decoration is provided by the paintings in a house on the Palatine. These undoubtedly date from about the year 100, since the house was largely demolished to make way for later buildings, which can themselves be firmly dated. This house, known as the 'House of the Griffins' because of a detail of the ornamentation, has preserved the oldest known example of that mural decoration now labelled 'Second Style': false columns painted on the walls, with a rough attempt at perspective in depth. The same type of column recurs on a mosaic from Palestrina, which formed part of a group of public buildings constructed in Sulla's day. Moreover, it is to Sulla that Pliny

117

120 ROME, 'HOUSE OF THE GRIFFINS': TROMPE-L'ŒIL MURAL DECORATION. ROME, ANTIQUARIUM DEL PALATINO

attributes the introduction of figured mosaic pavements. (The relevant passage, *NH* 36.189, has caused much scholarly debate; but this interpretation, which is supported by archaeological evidence, seems the most plausible.) In Pompeii, the earliest Second Style walls can, similarly, be dated to Sulla's time. Rome, then, will have been slightly ahead of the field, which is what one might expect. The floor of this same room in the 'House of the Griffins' is laid with non-figurative mosaic-work, and has as its centre-piece a pattern of squares, in perspective and chiaroscuro, which is repeated in the painting along the lower part of the wall, and finds its counterpart at Pergamum during the second half of the second century BC.

Yet as late as the close of the first century, by which time wall-painting abounds in Hellenistic motifs, Rome provides us with at least one remarkable example of genuinely Roman 'historical' painting – even though it also embodies formal motifs and figures which are Hellenistic in style. This is the frieze that ran all round an important tomb on the Esquiline, belonging to the family of the Statilii. Today, unfortunately, the frieze is in a bad state of preservation, which makes it hard to interpret. What does seem certain is that it depicted various events connected with Rome's early legendary history. On the south panel, we find the construction of the walls of Lavinium (the city associated with

118

121 ROME: TOMB ON THE ESQUILINE, KNOWN AS THE 'TOMB OF THE STATILII'. HISTORICAL SCENE (DETAIL). ROME, M. NAZIONALE

Aeneas's disembarkation, and, as noted, with religious cults of extreme antiquity), and scenes of fighting (probably the battle near the Numicus River). The north panel shows the discovery, in a rectangular box, of Romulus and Remus; this scene is flanked by the personified figures of a river (the Tiber) and a nymph, both directly borrowed from Hellenistic types. We also see a winged Victory, holding a palm-branch and offering a crown to a warrior on the far end of the south panel.

These paintings reveal both vigorous draughtsmanship and a strongly naturalistic sense of colour. Once again, it seems unlikely that this complex sequence of compositions was created merely to adorn a tomb. In view of the fact that this is not a specifically funerary painting, it is far more probable that the artist employed motifs borrowed from paintings used to decorate some temple or other public building. Here, again, all the scenes unfold on the same level, and there is no discernible interest either in landscape or in conveying an impression of pictorial space. Narration is all.

The decoration of a house found near the Farnesina (the Renaissance palace built by Peruzzi and decorated by Raphael for Agostino Chigi) is of a different type, and

122 ROME, 'TOMB OF THE STATILII': LEGEND OF AENEAS. ROME, M. NAZIONALE

123 ROME, HOUSE NEAR THE FARNESINA. WALL DECORATED WITH TROMPE-L'ŒIL ARCHITECTURAL MOTIFS. ROME, M. NAZIONALE

highly sophisticated in quality. This house, situated near the right bank of the Tiber, must once have been a villa, constructed between 30 and 25 BC. It offers us the best extant example of upper-class taste at the end of the Republic and the beginning of the Augustan period.

One wall was decorated with a scheme of *trompe-l'œil* architecture (advanced Second Style) in over-vivid colours, which lend point to Pliny's critical comment, mentioned above. But of particular interest are the small imitation pictures that form part of this scheme. Here, on a white ground, we find genuine imitations of paintings in the 'Severe Style' – that is, the style of Greek art practised about 460 BC. The taste which this reveals, not merely for classical art, but for a still older period (and which, more often than not, extends to an imitation of the archaic style) is typical of the Augustan cultural elite. The fact that they sought to recapture the Severe Style – the moment of transition between Archaic and Classical, a brief and very pure period of maturation – indicates unusually refined judgment.

On this wall a Greek signature is cut: *Seleukos epoiei*, 'Seleukos made it', which has been taken as an almost clandestine declaration by the artist responsible. This may well be true, and possibly applies equally to the paintings and stucco-work that cover the arches. Such a name might well have originated in Asia Minor, though it could also be Alexandrian.

Even more interesting are the paintings of two other rooms in the house. One room has a high skirting-board, painted black: against this background a series of landscapes had been sketched in, which have now almost disappeared. Along the top of the skirting-board a fragile leafy branch appears, the stylized garland-motif; above this runs a dado with small figures, very lively in design and of unusual subject-matter, depicting several incidents which all centre on a figure in the process of dispensing justice. What we seem to have here are illustrations for a series of anecdotes about some legendary character, in the literary tradition established by the fabulists. A possible candidate in this context is Bocchoris, an eighth-century Pharaoh who had come to symbolize,

124 HOUSE NEAR THE FARNESINA: PICTURE ON WHITE GROUND. ROME

125 HOUSE NEAR THE FARNESINA: A GARLAND (DETAIL). ROME

121

126 ROME: HOUSE NEAR THE FARNESINA. MARITIME SCENE. ROME, MUSEO NAZIONALE

127 ROME: HOUSE NEAR THE FARNESINA. MASKS (DETAIL). ROME, MUSEO NAZIONALE

for the man in the street, the idea of the Good Judge. Whether or not this frieze has such a theme, and apart from its intrinsic interest as a work of art, it also raises the possibility of illustrations on ancient papyrus texts, at a period before the introduction of parchment as writing material.

The other complex of paintings (a corridor and several rooms with a white ground) reveals the presence of a highly original artistic personality. Though this particular *genre* – scenes of rural or marine life enlivened with small figures – must have been extremely widespread, what we have here is no mere copy. Both landscapes and seascapes are sketched in monochrome with a freshness and rapidity that show an immediate link between invention and execution. These figures could have come from the brush of a Magnasco or a Jacques Callot. The same brush was responsible for the masks – so lightly rendered as to look like watercolour work – that adorn the frieze surrounding the scenes in monochrome. There is no point in dreaming up 'Masters' if their work remains an isolated phenomenon, with no body of similar works to assemble round their names. But this painter really does deserve to go down in the history of art as the 'Farnesina Master'. Some have proposed identifying him with the Ludius (or Studius, as some MSS have it) who was one of the few painters in the Roman period whom Pliny thought worthy of mention (*NH* 35.116). He lived during Augustus's reign, and specialized in landscapes depicting pleasant rural scenes. But even though Pliny claims that Ludius invented this *genre*, he can scarcely have been its sole exponent. Admittedly, almost all the subjects catalogued by Pliny find a place somewhere in these paintings.

One fine and unusual example of pictorial decoration, whose date has given rise to much argument, is that in the so-called Hall of Isis (*Aula Isiaca*). This was a spacious chamber on the Palatine, built over during Nero's reign, and afterwards buried under the foundations of the Flavian palace's basilica. Its walls were decorated with landscapes containing scenes associated with the legends of Isis, and on the frieze (*pl. 129*) which runs along their upper level, we find objects belonging to the goddess's cult, including long-spouted jugs, lotus-flowers and cobras. In 21 BC, Agrippa banned the worship of Isis in the neighbourhood of Rome; a year later Augustus banned it within the *pomerium*; in AD 19, Tiberius shut down the sanctuaries and executed the priests. Caligula (AD 37-41) reinstated the cult, and subscribed to it in person. That is why the scholar G. E. Rizzo assigned the decoration of this hall to Caligula's reign. However, subsequent research by H. G. Beyen, carried out in the context of the development of the Second Style, pointed to a date between 30 and 20 BC. This dating was confirmed by observations made during the removal of the paintings, which are now housed in the Palace of Domitian. (The fresco technique is also confirmed by the fact that investigators were able to detect the divisions between different 'working days' behind the backing.) Unfortunately, the landscapes and mythological scenes are now all but obliterated; we have some eighteenth-century engravings of them, but these are inaccurate as regards detail. The ceiling, however, which is in a better state of preservation, constitutes a unique example of decorative work, as we can see both from its general pattern, and from the remains of gilding that have been found on the motif of a ribbon floating against its blue background. The unusual character of this decoration is another argument in favour of up-dating. We must look back to a time when Hellenistic motifs – in this case from

128 ROME: 'HALL OF ISIS' (AULA ISIACA): DECORATION ON WALLS AND CEILING (DETAIL). ROME, PALATINE

130 PRIMA PORTA, LIVIA'S VILLA: MAIN SALON WITH MURAL FRESCO OF GARDEN AND BIRDS. ROME, MUSEO NAZIONALE

Alexandria, for the cult of Isis – were still being imported direct, and ornamentation had not yet been schematized into industrial clichés.

The superiority of the capital over the small towns near Vesuvius is also attested by the great hall, painted to resemble a garden, which is all that survives of the villa that Livia, Augustus's wife, once owned at Prima Porta. It stood on the steep crags of volcanic tufa that rise above the Via Flaminia, and was known as White Hen Villa – *ad gallinas albas*.

The 'garden' in Livia's villa is a painting without parallel. Behind two low fences, of the sort commonly put round flower-beds, there rises a dense wood, lush with every sort of vegetation. Birds perch in the branches, outlined against a blue sky whose variations of tone and colour produce a most realistic effect. That this is the fruit of a Roman conception seems highly unlikely; but we do not possess enough evidence to determine its real origin. The fenced garden, composed of various elements – carefully selected, yet looking wild – is an Iranian invention. The Greek name for it was *paradeisos*, but we have no comparable representation in art from so early a date. One somewhat impoverished painting on a tomb in the Anfouchi necropolis, at Alexandria, reveals much the same general concept, but reduced to a single row of trees. This hardly establishes the existence of a *genre* of 'garden paintings'. The nearest thing to Livia's garden – in Pompeii, from the House of Menander – reveals marked differences.

131 PRIMA PORTA, LIVIA'S VILLA: MAIN SALON WITH MURAL FRESCO OF GARDEN AND BIRDS (DETAIL). ROME, MUSEO NAZIONALE

It is not even certain that this work was executed during Livia's lifetime (she died in AD 29). Up till now no one seems to have noticed that identical pictures, obviously by the same hand, were once to be seen as background to *trompe-l'œil* windows in the hall (also at Rome) known as 'Maecenas's recital-room'. Its construction has not yet been studied in sufficient detail to establish its date, though most scholars place it between 40 and 35 BC. Today these paintings no longer exist: the ravages of time have destroyed them, and there does not even appear to be a photographic record of them.

132 ROME: NYMPHAEUM, KNOWN AS 'MAECENAS'S RECITAL-ROOM'

133 PRIMA PORTA, LIVIA'S VILLA (DETAIL OF MURAL DECORATION) ▶

134 ROME, HOUSE ON THE PALATINE, KNOWN AS 'HOUSE OF LIVIA': MURAL DECORATION (DETAIL). IO WATCHED OVER BY ARGUS

On the other hand, the paintings in another house on the Palatine, conventionally known as the 'House of Livia' (it may in fact have formed part of Augustus's private residence), can be fitted without difficulty into the general development of wall-decoration. The only value of the name is to indicate its approximate date. One wall in this house can be taken as an example of Second Style decoration in its final phase, which lasted from the beginning of the Augustan period to the end of the first century BC. This phase is characterized by *trompe-l'œil* architectural effects, which open up the walls, and in a sense make them disappear. Over and above this, it establishes its own decorative syntax, by placing one large opening at the centre, and a smaller one on each side, the pattern being clearly derived from that of stage decor.

It is not yet possible to give a precise account of the origins and development of the typical wall-decoration of Roman houses. Its constituent elements have been unanimously recognized as Hellenistic; but the destruction of wall-decorations in Hellenistic towns has been so complete that we cannot tell how far the painters who introduced this fashion into Rome were breaking new ground, nor from which Hellenistic centres they came. Whatever the truth of the matter, it is clear that, once introduced, these decorative patterns developed within the context of Roman culture.

This development is characterized by an ever-increasing preoccupation with *trompe-l'œil* perspective, the 'breaking-up' of walls by means of false architecture and vistas, a practice which becomes still more pronounced after about AD 60-63 with the appearance of what is known as the Fourth, or Fantastic, Style. We can cross-check this date for Pompeii, since almost all the decorations of the 'Fantastic' phase are found on walls that were built (or rebuilt) after the earthquake of 62/63. This general tendency towards *trompe-l'œil* is counterbalanced, during the same period, by the development of a primarily ornamental trend known as the 'Third Style', which is found between AD 15 and 40 at Rome, and about AD 60 for the area round Pompeii; its most marked characteristic is great delicacy of execution.

When, about 60, the *trompe-l'œil* style really takes over again, it is with a kind of frenzy: fantasy reigns supreme, ornamentation runs riot. Typical of this phase is the use of figures, which are removed from the context of a well-known pictorial composition and transferred to some architectural schema derived from stage decor. The most

135 ROME, 'HOUSE OF LIVIA': MURAL DECORATION (DETAIL). A GARLAND

important feature, however, is that from now on no more Hellenistic-type innovations appear, either in the architectonic decorations or in the stock range of themes represented. Hellenistic influence has run its course. This was the time, in the years before and after 60, at which a revolution in Roman architecture began to take place, characterized by a new concern with the creation of interior space, on a large scale.

After 79, unfortunately, we no longer possess – for painting at least – that wide range of supporting evidence which the towns from the region round Vesuvius might have supplied, and we have to make do with occasional isolated survivals. But, in any case, it can be asserted that the creative drive ebbed away to nothing during the course of the next generation. Once Hellenistic influence had exhausted itself, no fresh advances were made in *trompe-l'œil* painting. At the same time architecture picked up and developed those themes which Rome's first contact with Asiatic Hellenism had introduced in Sulla's day.

The basic pattern of pictorial decoration (a large central aedicule flanked by two smaller openings) still had a long life ahead of it; the same schema, reduced to a pattern of abstract lines, turns up in the wall-decoration of Commodus's times. It can still be seen in that interlacement of red and green lines on a white base which formed a popular motif in AD 230-40, and later found its way into the Christian catacombs. This seems to me a basic confirmation of our other evidence, all of which indicates, very strongly, that the *trompe-l'œil* style was not Roman but purely Hellenistic, since it disappeared from wall-decoration as soon as Hellenistic influence faded out. This holds good for Nero's reign, which also saw the architectural revolution pushed through by Severus and Celer – though we have to recognize, at the same time, that the last desperate phase of architectonic fantasy originated in Rome itself.

After the great fire of Rome in 64, Nero confiscated for his personal use a vast tract of land between the Caelian and Esquiline Hills, and on it built the *Domus Aurea* or Golden House, in the lobby of which stood a colossal statue of Nero himself, portrayed as Helios-Sol. This bronze statue, some hundred feet high, was the work of a Greek sculptor named Zenodorus, who seems to have come from Asia Minor. (This artist drew his inspiration from classical models, and specialized in colossi. He had already executed a gigantic statue of the Gallic divinity identified with Mercury, which stood in the sanctuary of the Arverni, at the summit of the Puy de Dôme.) After Nero's suicide in 68, and the *damnatio memoriae* later decreed by the Senate, this whole area was taken over as a public pleasure-ground: the Flavian amphitheatre (i.e. the Coliseum) and the Baths of Titus were later erected on it. Nevertheless, a portion of the *Domus Aurea* was left encapsulated in the new buildings, and survives to this day.

It was into these halls, now become underground grottoes, that the artists of the Renaissance found their way. The copies they made of what they saw there were used primarily as decoration, and these works, in view of their origin, came to be termed 'grotesques'. It is one of the curious inconsistencies of archaeological research that, even to this day, the ruins of the *Domus Aurea* have not been completely explored – let alone surveyed, photographed or subjected to proper scrutiny. Yet here one could undoubtedly rediscover – among others – one of the rare individual painters who are mentioned in the literary sources: that Fabullus who liked to give himself airs by painting in a toga, and of whom Pliny said (*NH* 35.121) that the *Domus Aurea* was the prison for his art

136 ROME, 'HOUSE OF LIVIA'. FRIEZE WITH LANDSCAPE

137 ROME, HOUSE ON THE PALATINE, KNOWN AS THE 'HOUSE OF THE MASKS'. MURAL DECORATION (DETAIL)

138 ROME, NERO'S 'DOMUS TRANSITORIA'. DECORATION ON VAULT IN A NYMPHAEUM. ROME, ANTIQUARIUM DEL PALATINO

because he had no chance of working elsewhere. Unfortunately, the present state of research does not permit us to extrapolate, from the *Domus Aurea*'s surviving decorations, the unfolding of a personality which we can identify as Fabullus. Nor do we know – as is possible – whether we should see in him the founder of the Pompeian Fourth, or Fantastic, Style. All we can do is suggest that certain fragments from the *Domus Transitoria* (Nero's first residence between the Palatine and Caelian Hills, also partially destroyed by the fire in 64) should be accepted as forerunners of a type of decoration which is quite different from the usual ornamental patterns, and which turns up again, in a more developed form, in the *Domus Aurea*.

The pictorial decoration of the *Domus Aurea* displays two distinct trends, and is clearly the work of at least two hands. One of them covers the long corridors and their high tunnel-vaulting with a decorative pattern close to those in traditional use. At the same time it is more linear, to a point at which the architectonic elements composing it become wholly inconsistent and fantastic. Furthermore, in the little scenes set into the decoration, the sacred or lacustrine motifs of Hellenistic tradition, widespread in painting ever since the end of the first century BC, are sketched in with a few swift brushstrokes, and have a mellowness of tone far beyond anything achieved by the Impressionist-style painting hitherto in fashion.

The other type of decoration to be found in the *Domus Aurea* radically revises the whole pattern of ornamentation, especially in the vaulting. The walls reveal architectonic composition, with figures inserted at different levels. Here we have a prime example of the Fourth Style, but so rigorously articulated, and in so grand a manner, that it far surpasses in quality all the known Pompeian variants, which, compared to these walls, look thoroughly provincial.

The paintings on the ceiling of the room (no. 85 of the plan on p. 360) situated west of the great octagonal hall have as their main subject Achilles on Scyros (hidden among the daughters of King Lycomedes, Achilles is revealed as a man when he sees arms). This composition seems to be original, and independent of the famous Greek models which turn up – as straight copies or adaptations – among the Pompeian decorators' stock-in-trade. But what, above all, confirms its originality is its obvious deviation from

139 ROME, NERO'S 'DOMUS AUREA': VAULTING DECORATION ▶

140 ROME, NERO'S 'DOMUS TRANSITORIA': DECORATION ON VAULT IN A NYMPHAEUM (DETAIL). ROME, ANTIQUARIUM DEL PALATINO

141 ROME, NERO'S 'DOMUS AUREA'. CRUCIFORM ROOM, VAULTING DECORATION (DETAIL)

142 ROME, NERO'S DOMUS AUREA. NICHE WITH TROMPE-L'ŒIL WINDOW ▶

143-4 ROME, NERO'S 'DOMUS AUREA'. CHAMBER OF ACHILLES ON SCYROS, MURAL DECORATION (DETAILS)

145 ROME, NERO'S 'DOMUS AUREA'. CEILING IN THE CHAMBER OF ACHILLES ON SCYROS

the norms which we can reconstruct as valid for classical Greek painting. This may perhaps allow us, in the present case, to put forward the name of Fabullus. We may also note that such painting finds unmistakable echoes in the sixteenth century; as it happens, it lay precisely on the path by which the artists of the Renaissance found a way into the *Domus Aurea*.

At Ostia, in the 'House of the Painted Ceiling' – which was probably a small inn of somewhat dubious reputation – we have an example of what a more modest dwelling ran to by way of decoration during the same period.

Thus in painting, no less than sculpture, we can confirm the existence of two separate trends. One is connected with the Mid-Italic tradition, which produces (with commemorative intent, and in honour of some distinguished person) scenes relating to local historical events, and which can properly be described as Roman. The other, more

137

146 OSTIA, 'HOUSE OF THE PAINTED CEILINGS'. MURAL DECORATION (DETAIL)

purely decorative in function, utilizes the legacy of great Greek painting, but reduces
and transforms it into mere ornament. It also – following certain Hellenistic innovations
– develops schemes of wall-decoration. In the decade after AD 60, these schemes of
decoration underwent a crisis which completely transformed them. Hellenistic influence
came to an end, and from that moment a genuine tradition of Roman painting came into
being. This did not turn out masterpieces, as Greek painting had done, but concentrated
on historical painting for public buildings, and its by-product, 'triumphal' painting; on
wall-decoration, the *genre* which has survived in the largest quantity, and which becomes
increasingly simplified and at times even negligent; and, finally, on the portrait, of which
magnificent specimens have been preserved outside Rome, in the province of Egypt, but
which undoubtedly were to be found also in Rome itself (as a few survivals and the
literary sources confirm).

138

147 POMPEII: 'HOUSE OF THE QUADRIGAE'. THE FORGE OF HEPHAESTUS

As already noted, among the decorations in the *Domus Aurea* there are to be found certain landscape scenes of easy, fluid form, little more than rapid sketches. Here we see a phenomenon which afterwards becomes highly characteristic of painting in the late Roman period, and indeed of early Christian art: that is, the blocking-out technique, which led to the abandonment of half-tones, areas of chiaroscuro obtained by scumbling or cross-hatching, and produced a direct juxtaposition between highlights (i.e. the lightest tones) and shadow. This technique, which appears for the first time in scenes from the *Domus Aurea*, stems beyond any doubt from the rich pictorial legacy of Hellenistic paintings on wood, which also reappeared in Pompeian mural art. In this connection, consider the detail (reproduced above) from a replica of a painting which portrayed Hephaestus forging the arms of Achilles – found in the 'House of the Quadrigas' and datable to about AD 70 – or, again, any of the numerous fantasy landscapes dating from the close of the Pompeian period. Hellenistic Roman 'Impressionism' was one aspect of the naturalistic tradition in Hellenistic art, just as nineteenth-century Impressionism was a means of breaking away from academicism and renewing contact

139

148 BOSCOTRECASE, HOUSE OF AGRIPPA POSTUMUS. FANTASY LANDSCAPE. NAPLES, MUSEO ARCHEOLOGICO NAZIONALE

149 ROME, TOMB ON THE VIA PORTUENSE: MURAL DECORATION SHOWING CHILDREN AT PLAY. ROME, MUSEO NAZIONALE

with reality and nature. But the blocking-out technique which followed brought about the destruction of naturalism, for which it substituted a wholly cerebral impulse, increasing the already marked intellectualism of the Pompeian fantasy-landscapes and, in the end, losing all contact with the objective reality of nature. Here we have a point of crucial importance for the understanding of subsequent developments in Roman art. Contrary to what is generally asserted (following the line adopted by Wickhoff), Roman art invented neither Impressionism nor landscape-painting. In fact it borrowed both from the Hellenistic tradition, and then proceeded to destroy their naturalism by means of the blocking-out process, which strained the Impressionistic technique to its utmost limits.

This destruction was by no means aimed at the achievement of greater spatiality; on the contrary, it produced the sort of painting which, after the third century, attained a condition of abstract transcendence. Yet during the second century the paintings that one most commonly finds in Rome – e.g. those from a tomb on the Via Portuense – display a narrative, almost popular character, without any attempt at perspective, very much like the old Mid-Italic tradition.

150 ROME, TOMB ON THE VIA PORTUENSE: MURAL DECORATION (DETAIL). ROME, MUSEO NAZIONALE

142

151 ROME, TOMB ON THE VIA PORTUENSE. CHILDREN AT PLAY (DETAIL). ROME, MUSEO NAZIONALE ▶

ARCHITECTURE

The figurative arts – painting and sculpture – are far more subject to the changes of fashion and to intellectual improvisation than is architecture, which expresses the needs of any given society in a much more direct manner, and – through the construction of public buildings – is more closely linked with the ruling class and the economic resources at its disposal. In the other arts, Roman culture did not express its own formal vision from the outset, but for a long time made use of borrowed forms; thus architecture provides a somewhat more reliable guide to its development as a whole. On the other hand, architecture involves technical problems which make it less easy to give an outline of its history that will be not only concrete and objective, but also readily understood by the general reader. For this reason I shall limit myself to describing the development of Roman architecture in broad outline, using only one or two of the most characteristic buildings as illustrative material.

The problem of interior space, within the bounds of any given building, and the significance which the human figure acquires when set in this space (circumscribed as it is by architectonic structures), are fundamental to the understanding of any architectural tradition. Here we come up against an initial fact of some importance. While in painting the Romans showed no particular sign of spatial sensibility (in works derived from a local tradition they even tended to limit the Hellenistic structure of space), in architecture it was quite another matter. Externally, their buildings were constructed in accordance with the Hellenistic concept of linear form; but internally they created rooms that became increasingly rich in spatial relationships. Whereas in Hellenistic architecture space was activated through the external relationships between different buildings or their parts, here the same phenomenon is transferred to the interior. Thus as early as the first century AD we find Roman architecture anticipating that of medieval Europe. The vaulted roof (from which the cupola subsequently developed) is a basic element in this trend; and the vault itself is based on the structure of the arch. The first arches developed were those of small bridges and other such utilitarian structures, about the beginning of the third century BC. There are not, as has often been asserted, earlier examples in Etruria, and it seems likely that the technique was brought to Italy by Hellenistic builders from Asia Minor.

The first instance, in Rome, of a large-scale utilitarian construction employing the arch was the row of storehouses known as the *porticus Aemilia*, built at the southern end of the Insula Tiberina during the first half of the second century BC, and consisting of two hundred rooms with tunnel-vaulting, supported on pillars. In 174 BC another vast store, the *emporium*, was built further downstream, along the left bank. These utilitarian constructions are the earliest evidence we have in Rome for large-scale architecture; for another century and a half the temples remained tied to their original modest proportions – a very characteristic trait.

With the introduction of the arch, and the discovery of strong forms of mortar, tunnel-vaulting developed rapidly, as is seen in various buildings dating from the late third and second centuries BC. By the end of the Republic it had passed into general use, and under Nero and the Flavians the hemispherical cupola likewise became widespread. The most ancient examples are to be found in public baths along the Campanian coast, at Baiae and elsewhere; in terms both of size and of abundance of water, these baths were quite different from those available throughout the Hellenistic world. The use of agglomerates – that is, cement strengthened by mixing fragments of rubble or broken brick into the mortar – would also appear to have originated in Campania. Arches and vaults were built by pouring this material into forms made of wooden shuttering. This process made it possible to obtain extremely solid bearing structures in a very short space of time. During their initial phase these structures were, to some extent, masked by external Hellenistic-type ornamentation, applied almost in the manner of a bas-relief. They then passed through a process of development very much like that which ferro-concrete has undergone in our own day. To begin with it was employed simply as a technical device, which the builders then attempted to overlay with a formally traditional exterior; it was only later that it came to be envisaged as a formal element in its own right – after which the road was open for the introduction of a new architectural style.

During the Roman conquest of Macedonia, some direct examples of Hellenistic architecture (on a comparatively modest scale) became available in Rome. After his triumph in 146 BC, Caecilius Metellus Macedonicus commissioned the architect Hermodorus of Salamis to build a small temple for Jupiter Stator, which contained six columns in its façade, and a colonnade down both sides, but not at the back. This closing off of the back was an adaptation of Hellenistic form to the traditional Italic-style temple. The edifice was modest enough in size, but was nevertheless Rome's first temple in marble. Not far from it was a temple to Juno, also of marble and built on the same hexastyle plan, except that it had no colonnade on its longer sides. The area in which these two small temples stood was surrounded by a portico, in Hellenistic fashion. (Augustus afterwards rebuilt it and dedicated it to Octavia.) Hermodorus built other temples besides, not to mention an arsenal (*navalia*) on the Campus Martius. Nevertheless, later architects continued to build in tufa (partially stucco-faced), as we can see from the temples of Largo Argentina.

Roman architecture experienced its first great independent impulse during Sulla's period, roughly between 120 and 80 BC. At this time columns and revetments were mostly made of a calcareous limestone which derived its name – *lapis tiburtinus*, or travertine – from the open quarries near Tibur, now Tivoli. This is a near-white stone admirably suited for imitating the marble used in Greek buildings; it takes on a fine brownish patina. Under Sulla a quite exceptional generation of architects arose and flourished. It is to them that we owe such buildings as the *Tabularium* in Rome, completed in 78 BC and used to house the State archives. This symbol of the authoritarianism of the senatorial order still stands on the Capitoline Hill, dominating the Roman Forum, which lies spread out immediately below it. In Latium we may mention the sanctuary of Fortuna Primigenia at Praeneste, the temple of Hercules at Tibur and the sanctuary of Jupiter Anxur

153 ROME, ARCADE OF THE TABULARIUM (RECORD OFFICE)

147

154 ROME, BRIDGE OF NONA (DETAIL)

at Terracina. It was now that the technical and artistic foundations of Roman architecture were established; yet neither the late Republic nor the Augustan Age which
followed it saw any fresh advances made. The pioneering work done in Sulla's lifetime
was not carried any further until the end of Claudius's reign, about AD 50, to be followed
by further advances under Nero and the Flavians.

Under Sulla, builders were still employing tufa and peperino in addition to travertine.
By the close of the Republic, brick revetments had passed into widespread use; and from
the last quarter of the first century AD a number of artisans (sometimes banded together
in corporations, and very often freedmen belonging to great families, including the
Imperial household) set up large factories for the mass-production of bricks and tiles.
The trade-marks stamped on bricks turned out by these firms are of great help in dating
buildings. Thus, for example, these brick-stampings alone proved that the present
Pantheon, which still bears on its pediment an inscription of Agrippa (who died in 12
BC), is a reconstruction carried out during Hadrian's reign (AD 117-38) – a period which
also witnessed an unparalleled expansion in the brick industry. Thereafter the produc-
tion of building materials came more and more under the control of the Imperial
Treasury, until by Caracalla's day the State had acquired a complete monopoly.

The most impressive example of architecture from Sulla's period is the Temple of
Fortune at Praeneste. This stands on a series of rising terraces, stretching right up from

148

155 ROME, FORUM ROMANUM: THE TEMPLE OF SATURN

157 PALESTRINA (PRAENESTE): TEMPLE OF FORTUNE. THE FOURTH LEVEL

the public buildings in the colony's urban centre to the sanctuary itself, nearly 300 feet higher. The dating of the complex, formerly controversial, now seems fairly clear. A recent study by Attilio Degrassi ('Epigraphia IV', *Mem. Accad. Lincei*, IV, 2, 1969, pp. 111-41) has shown that many family names which appear in inscriptions in the temple do not appear in inscriptions in the colony of Praeneste itself, set up by Sulla. This reflects Sulla's treacherous massacre of all the male citizens of Praeneste (Val. Max., 12.2.1). Moreover, some of these texts mention guilds and associations of freedmen which are known not to have existed before 112-111 BC or later that 71 BC.

The sanctuary has been planned like a piece of stage decor, ingeniously divided into five levels (see p. 354). Two arcaded ramps led up from the lowest levels (which were free of architectural elements) as far as the second terrace, which already marked a considerable ascent from the point of departure. These ramps were closed in on the valley side. Thus, when one reached the top of them, the view was suddenly revealed in all its splendour. Another basic feature is that all the arcades and exedrae on the fourth and fifth terraces are constructed of agglomerate and include vaulting – yet their façade was decorated in traditional Hellenistic style, with straight entablatures. The arcades of the fourth terrace enclose a large square which was used as a market-place on feast-days.

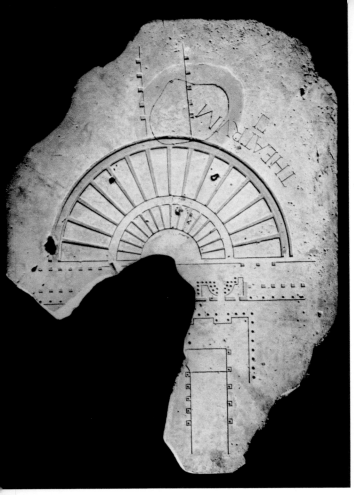

158 PLAN OF POMPEY'S THEATRE. ROME, MUSEO CAPITOLINO

A third characteristic is the juxtaposition of a cult site (in this case the little circular temple on the summit) with an area shaped like the *cavea* of a theatre. Such a juxtaposition occurs at other sanctuaries of this period in Latium; at Rome we find it in Pompey's Theatre, built between 55 and 52 BC, to which the temple of Venus forms a kind of annexe. This was the first stone-built theatre in Rome; it was followed by that which Augustus erected in memory of his nephew Marcellus, dedicated about the year 13 BC.

One remarkable type of building which gradually evolved during the Republican era, after the end of the Second Punic War and Flaminius's victory over Philip V of Macedon (197 BC) was the basilica. Its ground-plan was normally rectangular, with or without an external portico on one of its longer sides. Internally, it was divided into three aisles, and often equipped with a semi-circular apse at the back, on one of its two shorter sides. These buildings served for the administration of justice, and for various meetings connected with civic life. Argument still continues as to where the form of the basilica originated; but here, too, it would seem logical to assume that a type of public building known in the cities of Magna Graecia was adapted to Rome's special requirements – just as in other Hellenistic towns a similar part was played by the long arcades flanking the main square (*agora*). The basilica of Pompeii is earlier than the date at which Rome colonized the town, and was certainly in existence before the three basilicas put up in the Roman Forum (between 184 and 170 BC). One of these, the Basilica Fulvia, was afterwards rebuilt by the Aemilian family, and subsequently restored several times – always under the same name – even during the Imperial era. A coin of 65 BC shows us its two-storey interior, adorned with shields of gilded bronze, which bore the *imagines* of the Aemilian family's ancestors, and had been placed there by the Consul of 78 BC. This basilica remained the most sumptuous as regards its ornamentation, to which Julius Caesar contributed from the profits of booty amassed during his conquest of Gaul. Since the year 159 BC a water-clock had been in operation there, presented by one of the Scipios.

159 COIN: INTERIOR OF BASILICA AEMILIA. ROME, M. NAZIONALE

160 ROME: MARCELLUS'S THEATRE

The basilica was also of prime importance for the evolution of an architectural style that proved fundamental to the construction of Christian places of worship; but this topic lies outside the scope of the present work.

Thus we see that the architecture of the Republican period scored up some real and fundamental achievements. Yet Vitruvius (who wrote in the early years of Augustus's reign, and whose text offers us the only complete architectural treatise to survive from antiquity) employs a Greek-derived nomenclature, stating explicitly that he had no option in the matter, since there was no corresponding Latin terminology available. One feels inclined to endorse the verdict of that great Renaissance architect Leon Battista Alberti, who placed very little trust in Vitruvius, criticizing him on the grounds that he was 'neither Latin nor Greek' (*De re aedificatoria* Bk VI, 1485); nevertheless, the absence of an acceptable Latin nomenclature does indicate that in the period between Sulla and Augustus Roman architecture had not evolved a traditional pattern, let alone any kind of systematic theory. Despite its pioneering of new architectonic types, it was still a purely practical skill.

Another innovation which goes back to this period is the large-scale funerary monument, which we find beside all the main consular highways. The most ambitious sort has a circular ground-plan, and contains one or more vaulted burial-chambers. Above

153

161 ROME: FORUM CAESARIS. LARGE SHOPS

the latter an earthen tumulus was heaped up, with vegetation growing on it – as on the Etruscan tumuli from which this type derives. However, it was given a much more clear-cut vertical structure, in the architectonic sense, and also contrived to be more imposing; Etruscan tumuli were often obtained by digging out the soft and friable tufa *in situ*. One of the best-known examples is the tomb of Caecilia Metella, daughter of the Consul of 69 BC, and married to a Crassus. This tomb stands not far outside Rome, on the Via Appia; it is a large cylindrical structure set on a quadrangular base, and entirely covered with travertine. We do not know the dead woman's exact relationship with Marcus Licinius Crassus, the great banker who backed Julius Caesar in his rise to power, and who, in 60 BC, joined with Caesar and Pompey to form the First Triumvirate, and take over the government of the State; she was probably his daughter-in-law. His wealth and power permitted him to erect a far more elaborate tomb than any other then in existence (e.g. that of the Plautii); and indeed it was never outdone, even in after times, except by the Imperial mausoleums, which were built to the same plan.

Julius Caesar recognized the need to enlarge the old Roman Forum, which by his day was wholly inadequate for the purpose it served (see p. 355). The construction of a new Forum began in 51 BC, beside its predecessor, at the foot of the Capitol. A large

154

square was cleared, and surrounded by imposing shops, built from blocks of peperino and vaulted overhead. In the middle stood the temple of Venus Genetrix. legendary ancestress of the Gens Julia: a Greek-style building in marble, its columns very close to one another. This temple contained the goddess's cult-statue, executed by the neo-Attic sculptor Arce-silaus, and some paintings by Timomachus of Byzantium. Before he could construct this Forum, Caesar had to buy up and demolish all the houses in this area – mostly belonging to the nobility. The negotiations alone went on for three years, and the overall sum needed to acquire the site was either sixty or one hundred million sesterces (our sources vary as to the exact figure). The latter would be about the equivalent of £2,000,000 in gold sovereigns – which gives one some idea of the high prices commanded by building sites in central Rome. Excavation has recovered a few fragments: not, however, of the temple erected in Caesar's day, but of the restored and enlarged edifice commissioned by Trajan.

Nearly half a century elapsed between the construction of the Forum Caesaris and that of the Forum Augusti. The latter was not designed for any practical purpose (e.g. as a trading-centre), and remained primarily commemorative and monumental in character. Here were set up statues of all Rome's most famous leaders, beginning with Aeneas and the kings of Alba Longa, and leading up to Caesar. Each image had a panegyric inscribed beneath it. The decision to erect a temple to Mars Ultor (Mars the Avenger) was taken after Octavian's decisive victory, at Philippi (42 BC), over the faction led by Caesar's murderers – he himself being Caesar's heir and adopted son, subsequently changing his name from Octavian to Augustus (27 BC). The temple, of majestic proportions, was executed in white marble, and flanked by two sumptuous apses, faced with coloured marble of the sort long referred to as 'African' (though the quarries have recently been located at Teos, near Izmir). This precinct was closed off, on the side facing the teeming quarter of the Suburra, by a high wall made of Gabii stone and peperino. The line of this wall had to be adapted to the existing urban

162 ROME: FORUM CAESARIS. ENTABLATURE OF TEMPLE (DETAIL)

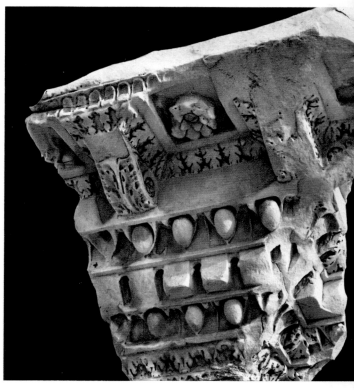

163 ROME, DOMITIAN'S PALACE. ENTABLATURE (DETAIL)

155

164 ROME, PORTA MAGGIORE. TOMB OF THE BAKER M. VERGILIUS EURYSACES

165 COIN: TEMPLE OF NEPTUNE. LONDON

166 COIN: ALTAR OF JULIUS CAESAR. LONDON

167 COIN: ARCH OF AUGUSTUS. ROME

168 COIN: PALACE OF TIBERIUS. ROME

169 ROME, PORTA MAGGIORE. CLAUDIAN AQUEDUCT AND TOMB OF M. VERGILIUS EURYSACES

topography; the acquisition of such a region – involving as it did the demolition of a heavily populated district – was an even more difficult proposition than it had been in Caesar's day. When the Forum was officially opened, in 2 BC, the temple was not yet finished. It, too, underwent restoration during Hadrian's reign.

Coins provide us with some sort of record (though not always a very clear one) for buildings erected under Augustus and Tiberius. In any case, no real innovations appear until the time of Claudius (AD 41-54). It was this period that first witnessed the practice of building with large rough-quarried blocks, sometimes even with irregular protuberances left visible on their surface. One notable instance is the double archway commonly known as the Porta Maggiore. This was originally built to carry the Claudian aqueduct (finished in AD 52) over the Via Praenestina; the architect was at some pains to leave the existing tomb of the master-baker Marcus Vergilius Eurysaces intact when planning his structure.

It was not until Nero's reign that Roman architecture reached a decisive turning-point, and one which had repercussions throughout the Empire. We find initial hints of this in the *Domus Transitoria* (AD 54-64), already referred to, and afterwards, more especially, in the *Domus Aurea* (AD 64-68). The trend developed and crystallized still

157

170 RUINS OF THE CLAUDIAN AQUEDUCT, NEAR ROME

171 ROME: PRECINCT-WALL OF THE FORUM AUGUSTI (DETAIL)

172 TIVOLI (TIBUR): TOMB OF THE PLAUTII AND BRIDGE ACROSS THE ANIO

further with the palace of the Flavians on the Palatine, begun by Domitian between 87 and 96 and subsequently enlarged (the *Domus Augustana*); and, lastly, with the markets Trajan built during the first decade of the second century. Under Hadrian, who took a personal interest in architecture, a number of daring innovations were introduced, which continued to bear fruit even after the decline of the ancient world.

All original development during this period of Roman architecture took place in Rome itself, and was closely bound up with constructions commissioned by the Emperors in person, for other than strictly utilitarian or functional purposes. It marks a creative apogee in the art of antiquity; and one which, by developing the themes and traditions of pre-Imperial architecture in Campania and Latium, laid the foundations for some of the fundamental architectural forms which dominated late antiquity and the Middle Ages. This is what gives the architecture of the period its historic, European significance. Though it originated in Rome, it did not remain limited either to one specific era, or to any particular geographical region.

174 ROME, 'DOMUS AUREA': RECONSTRUCTION OF 'CHAMBER WITH GILDED VAULTING'. LIBRARY OF THE ESCORIAL

Thus we are entitled to regard the architecture of late antiquity, and indeed some medieval architecture, as a direct derivation of work carried out between the middle of the first century and the middle of the second; and we should also bear in mind how valuable this architecture proved in the Renaissance. Leon Battista Alberti, in the passage cited above, also has this to say: 'Every edifice of Antiquity which could, for whatever reason, be of any importance, I have examined, with a view to extracting some advantageous knowledge therefrom. I have, with unremitting diligence, excavated, scrutinized, measured and sketched all that lay within my power, that I might master, and put to good use, every aid which the intelligence and achievement of bygone ages

175 ROME, NERO'S 'DOMUS AUREA': THE OCTAGONAL HALL (DETAIL)

162

might afford me.' This work continued throughout the sixteenth and seventeenth centuries, especially in and around Rome.

It can confidently be asserted that the architect of the *Domus Aurea*, Severus, and his collaborator Celer, were the first actually to construct a building in accordance with the new principles, and to apply with profit – for the realization of new architectonic patterns – techniques that had hitherto been experimented with in a purely structural sense.

In Greece, architecture had kept its character wholly unitary through treating the pattern of the peripteral temple as a norm for every type of building whatsoever. At Rome, on the other hand, while the temples continued to follow the Greek pattern, various other kinds of building developed, each corresponding to the function for which it was destined – though Greek elements were still employed by way of external ornamentation.

Another basic difference between Greek and Roman architecture lies in their wall-building techniques. The Greeks continued to make their walls out of quarried stone blocks, which, while giving them a massive structural consistency, still preserved a certain life and sensitivity. A Roman wall, on the other hand, being built of bricks or other small units bound together with mortar, is envisaged as an inert element designed to enclose space – a kind of shell dividing one room from another – rather than as a bearing structure. Areas of interior space, covered by concave surfaces that were often far above them, created their own volume, or mass, with its focal point *inside* the building. Any human being located in such a spatial mass feels overawed and even bewildered (a sensation which we can still experience today inside the Pantheon). The eye, being unable to find any articulate *point d'appui* on a surface of this nature, receives a wholly new kind of dynamic stimulus in consequence. At the same time, any person who places himself on an even moderately raised surface, such as a dais or rostrum, is endowed with a quite extraordinary appearance of elevation, both by the space around him and by the vaulting high overhead: he appears somehow remote and numinous. Pure Greek rationalism here gives way to mystery and symbol.

The monument known as the Tower of the Winds (built at Athens in the first century BC by the Syrian architect Andronikos Kyrrhestes, with a sundial on each face and a water-clock inside) has an internal octagonal design 26 ft. 6 in. (7·95 metres) in diameter. Yet one can grasp its architectonic significance only from the outside, which is why it gives the impression of being a tower. By way of contrast, the octagonal hall in the *Domus Aurea* – almost double the diameter, and enclosed within a massive rectilinear structure – impresses only by reason of its interior space. Since the outer shape of the building does not hint at this space in any way, anyone who walks into it experiences both surprise and a feeling of transcendance. The reaction remains valid even though it is not possible to be sure whether this was the room with a dome, mentioned by our literary sources, which 'revolved day and night like the firmament' (Suet., *Nero* 31·2) – and even if one rejects the cosmogonic interpretation of it, based on Iranian concepts, though this, too, could be convincingly argued. (The Oriental ideology of a sovereign creator of the Cosmos did, in fact, play a part in Nero's madness.) Some coins of Nero's reign portray a building with arcades, crowned by a very solid-looking cupola; but this is more likely to be the great public market (*macellum*) which he had put up.

176 ROME, THE COLISEUM: EXTERIOR VIEW

177 ROME, THE CENTRAL MARKET. ROME, MUSEO NAZIONALE

178 ROME, THE COLISEUM. ROME, MUSEO NAZIONALE

179 ROME, THE COLISEUM. FIRST-FLOOR CORRIDOR

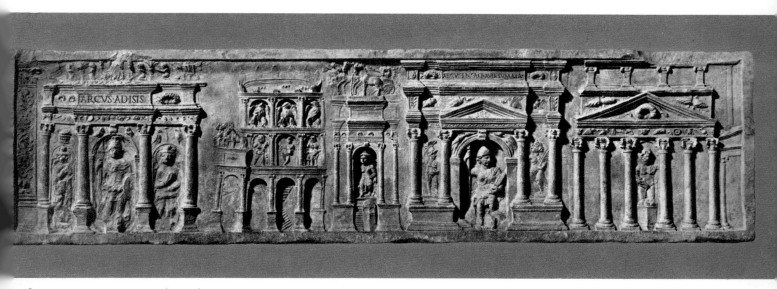

180 ROME, TOMB OF THE HATERII (DETAIL): BUILDINGS ERECTED IN ROME UNDER THE FLAVIAN EMPERORS. VATICAN (LATERAN MUSEUM)

181 ROME: THE COLISEUM. VAULTING DECORATED WITH STUCCO (DETAIL)

182 ROME: THE COLISEUM. RECONSTRUCTION OF STUCCOES

166

183 ROME: THE COLISEUM. VIEW OF THE INTERIOR

When an exhaustive analysis of the *Domus Aurea* is eventually undertaken, it should be carried out simultaneously with an investigation of the vast baths constructed between the reigns of Titus and Trajan, which formed part of the scheme to develop the vast area which Nero had commandeered in order to feel 'lodged in a manner befitting a man', for the benefit of the public at large. The same scheme included, immediately opposite, the Flavian amphitheatre, better known as the Coliseum.

The Coliseum was begun by Vespasian, continued by Titus and completed by Domitian. How long its vast fabric took to build is uncertain: estimates range between five years and ten. On one coin of Titus the project is shown as already complete, although a relief from the following reign, that of Domitian, shows it still unfinished. The arcades which compose its external façade are arranged in three rows of eighty, flanked by engaged columns: Doric for the lowest level, Ionic for the second and Corinthian for the third. The arches themselves have a span of 13 ft. 8 in. (4·20 metres); those in the lowest course are 23 ft. 9 in. (7·05 metres) high, those in the higher two 21 ft.

184 ROME: PALACE OF THE FLAVIANS ON THE PALATINE. AERIAL VIEW

6 in. (6·45 metres). There is an Attic storey, minus arches but pierced by windows, the latter formerly alternating with shields of gilded bronze. None of this presents any new architectonic features, but the building's vast proportions posed special technical problems. These included questions of stress in the material, and the need to organize the movement, in and out, of some fifty thousand spectators.

The material employed was travertine, with stucco decorations on the inner surface of the vaults. Little of the stucco now survives, but it was still visible during the Renaissance, and we possess some sketches made at the time. The architect of the Coliseum is unknown; there are strong arguments against the identification with Rabirius, who built the Palace of the Flavians for Domitian on the Palatine.

The central section of this palace was completed before AD 92, whereas those parts beside the Roman Forum and the Hippodrome remained unfinished until some point between 93 and 96. Most of the rooms in it were public: audience-chambers and the like. With later additions to its domestic quarters, it became the Emperor's official residence (*Domus Augustana*) until the end of antiquity. We see here a development of those architectural innovations originally pioneered during Nero's reign, together with a greater formal coherence. Full advantage is taken of the possibilities opened up by vaulting: the arrangement of rooms on the upper floors need no longer be tied to the ground-level plan, which leaves the architect far wider scope for originality. What most astonished people at the time about Domitian's palace was the height of the rooms from floor to ceiling. They really felt that 'a *dominus et deus* must dwell there', a god invested with

185 ROME: APPROACH TO THE PALACE OF THE FLAVIANS ON THE PALATINE ▶

186 ROME: PALACE OF THE FLAVIANS ON THE PALATINE. DETAIL OF THE VAULTING

187 ROME: PALACE OF THE FLAVIANS ON THE PALATINE. FAÇADE OVERLOOKING THE GARDENS ▶

189 ROME: ENTABLATURE OF THE TEMPLE OF VESPASIAN (DETAIL). ROME, TABULARIUM (RECORD OFFICE)

terrestrial authority. This was the period when the concept of divine sovereignty began to gain ground; the new Roman-style architecture employed in the palaces was an attempt at expressing it. Once established, these new forms continued to develop even under those second-century Emperors who rejected the ideology behind them. From the time of Commodus, however, divine sovereignty rapidly re-established itself, and became even more popular as time went on. Finally, in the third century, it imposed permanent rules and standards, not only on etiquette and protocol, but on artistic and architectural modes of expression.

Nero's reign, then, formed an important turning-point in the history of Roman art. It is at this point that we can observe the first appearance of a wholly novel concept of space. In painting, it produced those fantastic mural decorations which characterize the final Pompeian phase; but it was also responsible for that disintegration of pictorial form and substance which later led artists to abandon spatial perspective altogether. In architecture, on the other hand, the idea of interior space continued to assume impressive and enduring forms.

190 RELIEF SHOWING A VIEW OF A TOWN, IN PERSPECTIVE (DETAIL). AVEZZANO, PALAZZO TORLONIA

191 ROME: FORUM NERVAE. FRIEZE (DETAIL)

At Rome, the imposing remains of a large edifice situated between the Quirinal and the Pincio, in the Gardens of Sallust, built during either Trajan's or Hadrian's reign, shows that this new-style architecture also produced sumptuous private houses, palaces consisting of several storeys with a central domed hall, and that these were not restricted to the Palatine area.

Houses put up during this period by wealthy middle-class merchants reveal the same trend towards architectural innovation. We have better evidence for this at Ostia than Rome; but such vestiges as do survive in the capital make it clear that the same type of mansion existed there. The house with an atrium and a central cloistered peristyle is replaced by a brick-built edifice with a vast, arcaded courtyard. This type of house – still designed for a single family – soon evolved into something much larger. The court-yards and interconnecting groups of rooms multiplied. The building rose to three (some-times perhaps even four) storeys, with external balconies. It was, in fact, a high-density housing unit, of a kind previously unknown, which opened on to the street rather than the inner courtyard, and contained flats for several families. Such a structure partly anticipated (and in some ways improved on) the type of house occupied by rich burghers in medieval Europe. Most important of all, it testifies to the existence of rational town-planning, with uniformly designed houses, like those erected in Ostia under Trajan and Hadrian. One remarkable relief, now in a private collection at Avezzano (Abruzzi), gives us a very clear idea of what a town of this period looked like.

4 From Neo-Atticism to Neo-Hellenism

'CONSIDER as wise men those who drink old wine and prefer to watch old comedies; ... new comedies are even worse than the new currency.' It was with these words that the prologue to Plautus's *Casina* presented what it termed 'an old comedy of Plautus which greybeards have already had occasion to appreciate, but which the young have not yet seen.' Much discussion as to which period such a speech could best represent led to the conclusion that it must be about 150-130 BC. Cicero (106-43 BC) was still an admirer of Plautus, whereas Horace (65-8 BC) disliked him intensely. It was during this period, covering some four generations – from the conquest of Africa and Greece and the establishment of Asia and Syria as provinces, up to Caesar's return from Spain and his consulate in 59 BC – that a number of major changes took place in Roman society. Rome's internal history, after a century of bitter strife, now took a new turn.

We have already observed how, during this period, a wide variety of creative influences converged on Rome, to produce an eclectic artistic culture. This eclecticism was most marked in the sphere of sculpture; it was only through architecture that Rome, as a new and rapidly expanding power, found it possible to express her individuality and to produce technical innovations.

The great artistic civilization of Oriental Hellenism (which was the true and authentic Hellenism) had a strong influence on Rome, first through Asia and Syria, then by way of Alexandria and Cyrene (the latter was bequeathed to Rome in 96 BC by the will of its legitimate sovereign). From Athens, on the other hand, Romans borrowed the Athenian passion for their classical epoch (the fifth and fourth centuries BC) and the periods which had preceded it, the Severe Style and the Archaic Period. The Athenian intelligentsia, however, were living in an age when all hope of freedom and independence was lost to them for ever; thus when they exalted Pheidias above all other artists, they were also commemorating the great period of their power and glory. The classicizing tendency (apparent in every centre of the Greek world) developed, at Athens, into the phenomenon known as 'neo-Atticism', which expressed itself both in the figurative arts and in Athenian culture generally. This culture held a very considerable attraction for young

192 ROME: THE PORTLAND VASE. LONDON, BRITISH MUSEUM

177

Romans of good family, who went to Athens to lose their provincial manners – yet never understood that the cultural tradition they were absorbing had lost all its inner vitality, and was now merely ornamental. The neo-Attic style, as a movement, was consciously opposed to just those trends which had shown the greatest liveliness and originality in post-Lysippean Hellenism.

The great vogue for private collections, which had reached its height in the first half of the first century BC, had now subsided. The torrential influx of works of art and new artistic trends had similarly run its course. By now this over-rich mixture was beginning to settle and clarify. Art-collecting on a major scale came to an end for highly practical economic reasons, with the removal of the Roman citizen's immunity to taxation. In 43 BC, by which time the funds confiscated from their enemies by proscription had run out, the Triumvirs (Antony, Octavian and Lepidus) imposed a property and land tax. For rented land the tax was the equivalent of the rent paid; for non-rented land it was half the rental value. In addition, a general 10 per cent levy was now instituted. Dio Cassius (47.16) says that in actual fact the 10 per cent was what remained for the landowner. Tax was assessed on the basis of a declaration by the interested party; but if any falsification came to light, he was liable to have all his property confiscated. It was also possible to renounce one's entire inheritance and get back one-third of it; such property as one decided to sacrifice was put up for auction, but the prices fetched in such cases were very low (see Suetonius, *Aug.* 40). For the majority of propertied men, these taxes meant the loss of their liquid assets. Caesar's avengers were almost the only people left who still had considerable fortunes at their disposal.

Just ten years later, the two surviving Triumvirs, Octavian and Antony, had their final and open break. Two years after that, the long interlude of the civil wars came to a close. For four months the combined fleets of Antony and Cleopatra had been bottled up by Agrippa's squadrons in the Gulf of Preveza, in Epirus, north of the island of Leucas. On 2 September 31 BC they broke the blockade and joined battle. But

194 RHODES (?). OCTAVIAN. FORLI, PIANCASTELLI COLLECTION

this sortie swiftly degenerated into wholesale flight and desertion, by land and sea alike. Antony's galley followed in the wake of the vessel bearing Cleopatra to Egypt: this decided his fate. It was here, in the Gulf of Arta near Actium, that the final issue of the Civil War was determined, though it continued to drag on for almost a year longer.

Despite the large numbers of vessels involved (at least four hundred on either side) the Battle of Actium was in fact an unremarkable engagement, though afterwards it passed into legend, and was duly placed under the sign of Apollo by its victor, Caius Julius Caesar Octavianus. Before long he was having himself addressed as *Imperator Caesar divi filius*; four years later he took the title of Augustus by which all future ages knew him. In fact Actium marked the end of a period of crisis which had begun a century before, in 133 BC, with the reforms carried out by Tiberius Gracchus. Like every epoch which sees the fabric of human society shaken by profound economic and political changes, this had been a violent, tortured age, one in which life was hard and dangerous.

The crisis had broken, violently enough, some twelve years after the destruction of Carthage (146 BC) and the final subjugation of Greece – two events which marked the end of Mediterranean conquest for the benefit of Rome's leading Senatorial families. The reforms of Tiberius Gracchus boil down, essentially, to what we may consider a very moderate law, against usurpation of State domains by private landowners. Little by little – and quite illegally – a number of vast *latifundia* had been built up. Under this law, private property was left intact. The only territory affected was *ager publicus*, common-land, that had been enclosed by private individuals. Even in these cases the law was only invoked where the acreage exceeded a certain figure – which was always double that originally conceded by law. Over and above this (at least in the original draft) provision was made to pay an 'improvement indemnity' for work carried out on this common land. However, the irresponsible opposition of Senators personally affected by Gracchus's scheme turned Tiberius Gracchus himself into a hard-lining revolutionary – and this in spite of the fact that his family was connected with the highest patrician families in Rome (he himself was the nephew of Scipio Africanus). The Senate as a whole at once identified its own private interests with the maintenance of all existing political institutions. Tiberius Gracchus was battered to death with chairs, during a riot led by his cousin Scipio Nasica, the *pontifex*. This episode, in the course of which over two hundred persons lost their lives (autumn 133 BC), was the first of many such bloody brawls – deliberately organized, politically inspired – to disfigure the streets of Rome. Indeed, from then until the Battle of Actium Romans lived continually under the threat of civil war.

The senatorial reaction, which, as we have seen, reached its climax with Sulla, had merely intensified these differences and rivalries. When Sulla, then fifty-six, entered Rome on 6 July 82 BC, he had with him Crassus, Verres, Catiline and Pompey, the last-named still a young man of less than twenty-four. Previously there had been a massacre among the nobility and a fire on the Capitol. Sulla drew up a proscription list, and either auctioned off or confiscated the property of 4,700 citizens who belonged to the opposition party. After his final victory, in November, Rome witnessed the spectacle of six thousand prisoners – political enemies would be a better description – being butchered, in defiance of all promises, on the Campus Martius. The tomb of Marius was desecrated;

his nephew, after being put to the torture, was killed as a kind of expiatory victim. However, on the 27th and 28th of the following January, Sulla celebrated his triumph and was acclaimed 'Saviour and Father of the City'.

If we wish to avoid being carried away by superficial historical analogies, we should never forget that the class-struggle at Rome was fought out, at every stage, by and for a privileged minority of free citizens – a fact which made for even more violence and ruthlessness, while no success could be anything more than provisional. From this inevitably unstable situation there at last emerged the impulse towards an authoritarian solution, something much akin to monarchy. By the time Julius Caesar appeared on the scene, such a scheme had been in the air for quite a while, as a means of coping with the new situation created in Eastern Mediterranean countries after their subjugation by Rome. If we free ourselves from that romantic concept of history which explains everything by the personality and ambition of its protagonists, it is easy enough to understand how, having entered the political arena as a 'man of the people', Caesar subsequently opted for a Hellenistic-style monarchical regime, which best suited the economic interests of his supporters.

'Caesarism' is not a universally valid historical category; we should rather view it as a political movement of clearly identifiable social origins, and closely bound up with the individual development of Roman society. Naturally it also evolved its own special ideology, which was inspired by that of the Eastern-orientated Hellenistic principates, and continued to develop along very similar lines. From the end of the second century BC, various new mystical cults had been imported into Rome, to be followed later by certain Messianic beliefs, clearly alluded to in late Republican literature. As far as we can tell, such eschatological beliefs must have found a favourable soil in which to take root, despite the rationalism promulgated by Greek philosophy. What best favoured them were the old Etruscan concepts, still very much present (and indeed officially practised) throughout Roman society. (See Cicero, *Cat.* 3.8.18;

195 ROME: HOUSE NEAR THE FARNESINA. OCTAVIAN AS HERMES-THOTH

181

196 COPY OF THE 'DORYPHOROS' OF POLYCLETUS. NAPLES

De Resp. Harusp. 19.40) We know, today, how deeply rooted in man's spirit is the need for ritual. Men looked forward to the advent of a New Age – in accordance with the theory of secular cycles – first during the year 83, then again in 63. The predictions remained unfulfilled, which did not dampen the expectations of the faithful. As always in such cases, fresh research produced a brand-new interpretation, and people continued to pin their hopes on the arrival of a man who would bring about this great revolution.

Julius Caesar's house had been adorned with a cupola, that sacred cosmic emblem borrowed from the Achaemenid civilization. As early as 40 BC Mark Antony was dressing up as Dionysus, and Octavian taking the role of Apollo. On the stucco-work of the villa near the Farnesina, amid other religious scenes which display a markedly Hellenistic taste, we find a group of deities including Hermes-Thoth, the Graeco-Egyptian divinity who symbolized mystic wisdom – and who here has been given the features of Octavian, *Novus Mercurius*. It was thus that Horace afterwards celebrated him (*Odes* 1.2); and it was with the same title that, two generations later, the Apostle Paul found himself greeted at Lystra (*Acts* 14.12): 'And they called Barnabus, Jupiter; and Paul, Mercurius, because he was the chief speaker.' This was the context in which Kleomenes the Athenian executed the statue of a prince belonging to Augustus's family, which – idealized portrait apart – is an exact replica of the Hermes as Orator (*Hermes Logios*) created in classical Athens. The expectations of a sovereign who would bring peace and usher in a new era are given clear expression (and openly linked with Augustus) both by Virgil in his Fourth *Eclogue* and by Horace in *Carmen Saeculare* (17 BC). The *Carmen Saeculare* antedates by four years the Senate's decision to build the *Ara Pacis*, which once more raises the hymn to fertile Earth, present in a new world-order.

These beliefs and attitudes (confirmation for which was also sought from astrology), and above all the impression of relaxation and relief obtained at the price of renouncing aspirations which had been fought for, are reflected in the characteristic features

182

197 PRIMA PORTA: PORTRAIT-STATUE OF THE EMPEROR AUGUSTUS. VATICAN, MUSEO CHIARAMONTI

which art of this period reveals. People take refuge in what is pre-established and codified. Thus official Roman art came to acquire – more or less permanently – a retrospective, academic character, together with the taste (often, one must admit, a very bad taste) for camouflaging new work under the literary-cum-rhetorical appearances and modes proper to classicism. Such were to be the salient, and lasting, characteristics of all artistic products commissioned by the ruling class. The Augustus from Prima Porta reveals, lurking beneath his cuirass, the body of Polycletus's *Doryphoros* (Spear-bearer). Two centuries later, under the Antonines, we find ladies and gentlemen following the Emperor's lead and having themselves portrayed as Mars and Venus, with a quite eclectic

198 OSTIA. A COUPLE PORTRAYED AS MARS AND VENUS. ROME, MUSEO NAZIONALE

choice of models: the Borghese Mars, which derives from a fifth-century BC statue, and the third-century BC Venus de Milo. Another lady, probably the mistress of some Herculean character in the third century AD, must have felt flattered when her rather commonplace nude figure was immortalized in the guise of victorious Omphale, bearing the demigod's club and lion-skin as spoils. Alexander the Great's mother had been

184

199 ROME: YOUNG WOMAN PORTRAYED AS OMPHALE. VATICAN, MUSEO PIO CLEMENTINO

portrayed as the seated Venus; so, in due course, was Helen the mother of Constantine, in imitation of a statue-type first created eight centuries before, in Pheidias's circle – the only deviation being the face, for which a portrait was substituted.

This backward-looking quality which was to characterize Roman Imperial art – always erudite and rich in political allusions – established itself very early on, during the

200 ROME: ARA PACIS AUGUSTAE. EXTERIOR VIEW

Augustan period, and in a remarkably lasting manner. We can best appreciate it by studying a typical monument such as the *Ara Pacis Augustae*, which, *inter alia*, has the advantage of all-but-complete documentation: we know the dates of its conception and completion (though not the artist's name). Augustus himself provides written testimony (*Res Gestae* 2.37f.) that, in order to celebrate his victorious return from Spain and Gaul, and the peace that had been so long and ardently desired, the Senate decreed the erection of an altar on the Campus Martius, at which magistrates, priests and Vestals were to celebrate a commemorative ceremony every year. The altar was voted in the year 13, and inaugurated in 9 BC.

Its remains were discovered in 1568, when some slabs decorated with bas-reliefs turned up in the foundations of a palace situated behind S. Lorenzo in Via Lata (the old name for the Corso). Between then and the final excavations of 1937-8, the larger part of this monument was restored, fragment by fragment, to the light of day. Though its reconstruction is something less than felicitous, both technically and as regards the new setting chosen for it, the *Ara Pacis* nevertheless remains one of the surviving examples from Roman sculpture of this period which we can most readily visualize in its original state. This fact, combined with its powerful historical associations, has more often than not falsified scholarly estimates of the monument's aesthetic value. It is not a great work

201 ROME: ARA PACIS AUGUSTAE. VIEW FROM INSIDE THE PRECINCT (DETAIL) ▶

of art, but it is a highly characteristic product of its age. The monument originally consisted of the altar proper, and a surrounding precinct-wall, the latter decorated with ornamental and figural reliefs. There is no harmonious proportional relationship between wall and altar; the two elements are set in frigid juxtaposition, without any genuine connection. The altar fills almost all the space inside the precinct. It consists of a plinth with relief decorations, and a frieze on a ritual theme, portraying a number of small individual figures, vividly carved from the marble, their lines so clear-cut that they might have been embossed in metal. Despite its monotonous composition, this scene is not lacking in freshness. However, its effect in the context of the whole monument is negligible. The interest of the *Ara Pacis* resides chiefly in the decoration of the precinct. This had two doorways in its shorter sides, along the line of its major axis. Inside, the precinct was decorated along its upper surface with a sequence of garlands in high relief, supported at intervals by bulls' skulls (*boukrania*, symbolic remnants of sacrifice) and *paterae*, round metal bowls that were used, by those making an offering, to sprinkle liquid on the altar. Below, the marble is carved to resemble a wooden palisade. These

203 ROME: ARA PACIS AUGUSTAE. PRECINCT (DETAIL): AENEAS

two decorative motifs represent a transposition, into a noble medium and a slightly stylized form, of the kind of temporary precinct that was employed for occasional ceremonies – a structure made of wooden boards and decorated with real garlands.

These decorative and structural motifs inside the precinct have no connection whatsoever with the external decoration; and this, in its turn, is composed of elements which remain structurally independent of one another. Apart from the merely physical juxtaposition, their only relationship is a symbolic one. Even this is frigid in conception, sharing the programmatic conformity which stamps all official art. It has always been the fate of such art to win approval from those who are indifferent to the genuinely artistic element: people whose interest must be caught by symbolism straightforward enough to give the impression that, thanks to them, a great idea has been immortalized in artistic form.

In the *Ara Pacis*, the two doorways of the precinct were decorated on either side with symbolic compositions drawn from the legend of the foundation of Rome. The entrance was flanked by two scenes associated with the city's origin. One was the 'Lupercal', that is the discovery, by the shepherd Faustulus, of the two twins marked out by destiny and suckled by the she-wolf. Mars and perhaps Rhea Silvia would have been included too; but unfortunately no more than a few fragments of the scene survive. On the other side we have pious Aeneas's sacrifice to the Household Gods (*Di penates*), whose shrine is placed high up, in a rocky, wooded landscape; the style here is Hellenistic. Beside the

204 ROME: ARA PACIS AUGUSTAE. PRECINCT: THE PROCESSION (DETAIL, RESTORED)

far entrance there was placed, on one side, the personified figure of Earth (*Tellus*), rich in nourishment for all mankind, and accompanied by other figures symbolizing waters and winds. On the other side of the same doorway was a second personification, Rome in arms, a female figure seated upon a heap of weapons, mistress and guardian of the world. Rome and Earth: the two elements which defined a Roman citizen's position under the peace of Augustus. The two longer sides of the precinct are filled with two rows of figures in procession, portrayed realistically, but at the same time frozen into conventional gestures. They presumably represent the actual procession which took place at the time of the altar's first consecration. There is no connection between the compositions on the short and the long sides, or even between the two halves of the procession.

How do these figured and decorative reliefs function in structural terms? It is very hard to see. The architectonic frame into which they have been inserted cuts through the

205 TARQUINIA; 'TOMB OF THE BULLS'. MURAL DECORATION (DETAIL)

compositional line and has no connection with the spatial arrangement of the figures. Even if we assume – as seems very likely – that the reliefs were originally polychrome, their modelling is so sharp and detailed that we cannot conceive of them as painted panels, pictures in frames, like the reliefs on the mausoleum of Saint-Rémy-de-Provence (*pl. 277*). And what is the significance of the floral decoration beneath the figured frieze? From the purely formal artistic viewpoint, this decoration is perhaps the most vivid feature of the entire monument; yet its functional relationship with either of the friezes remains nil.

Such a lack of structural logic and organic cohesion within a work would have horrified the Greeks of the classical period, when every part of a creative work always had a clear *raison d'être* and a logical no less than a structural function. But in an Italo-Roman context, such juxtapositions were by no means a novelty. As early as the sixth century BC we find Etruscan paintings (in the Tomb of the Bulls at Tarquinia) which display an identical pattern: figural and floral friezes, one above the other, wholly unrelated in any organic sense; the figures are placed above vertical elements which recall the stylized palisade on the inner face of the precinct in the *Ara Pacis*.

206 ROME: RELIEF FROM A FOUNTAIN. VIENNA, KUNSTHISTORISCHES MUSEUM

In this monument, then, we see that such things as the general conception of an altar inside a precinct, the thematic blending of myth and history (as on the so-called Altar of Ahenobarbus), and the indifference to any structural or logical relationship between the component parts, all clearly suggest Roman taste, linked to the Italic tradition. Yet when we come to examine the artistic form in which this conception is embodied, we are forced to conclude that the artists responsible for its adoption and execution were Greeks. Whether they were also able to make use of local sculptors we do not know; in any case, it makes no essential difference.

The relief portraying Aeneas follows the same line as a series of bas-reliefs dealing with idyllic pastoral subjects, in which sculpture seems to be trying to outdo painting in the representation of landscape (rocks and grottoes form the most common motif). This longing for a rustic universe is what underlies Virgil's *Eclogues,* and prompted his famous cry, in the *Georgics* (2.458-9): *O fortunatos nimium, sua si bona norint agricolas!* ('Too happy the farmers, did they but know their own good fortune!'). Such an attitude is typically urban; Cato would have had no time for it. It is directly derived from late Hellenistic literary fashions; it also proved remarkably useful for furthering the political aims of the ruling class in Virgil's day. Later, during Tiberius's reign, it was to find

207 PALESTRINA: RELIEF FROM A FOUNTAIN. PALESTRINA, MUSEO BARBERINIANO

artistic expression through a group of reliefs used to decorate a public fountain; two, formerly part of the Grimani Collection, are now in the Vienna Kunsthistorisches Museum, and a third has recently come to light at Palestrina. The official Roman culture of the period adopted this trend with all its fads, symbols and mannerisms; but the concept which inspired it remained wholly Hellenistic, and alien to genuine Roman sentiments.

A close examination of the decorative pattern employed for the floral frieze on the *Ara Pacis* – its original layout is preserved on a slab at the shorter end, nearest to the south-east corner – has revealed that its motif is typically Pergamene. Yet such a motif had passed out of fashion at Pergamum itself, as Theodor Kraus has shown, as early as the second century BC. That fact tells us something about the artist who planned the decorations for this Roman monument: his attitude was clearly backward-looking, classicist. Yet this classicism does not wholly mask the sense of space and atmosphere (recognizable, by now, as specifically Hellenistic in character) which emanates from this foliated scroll-work; it merely attenuates it, by oblique and evocative touches of the greatest delicacy. The same feeling for space is evident in the handling of the garland-ribbons, on the inner side of the precinct wall: they flutter freely in the air, with a bare minimum of relief. The *paterae*, which today appear inexplicably attached to the wall, must originally have been shown suspended by painted ribbons.

193

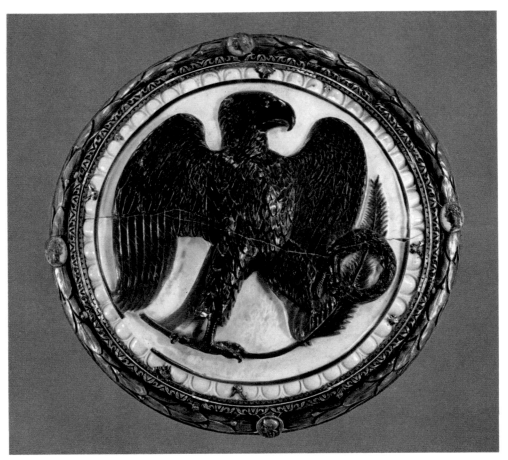

208 ROME (?): CAMEO. EAGLE WITH SYMBOLS OF VICTORY. VIENNA, KUNSTHISTORISCHES MUSEUM

This Hellenistic sense of atmosphere is equally apparent in contemporary toreutic work, reinforced in this case by minute accuracy and quite extraordinary technical skill. This technical virtuosity imbues these ornamental sculptures – like all characteristic sculpture of the Augustan era – with a rare refinement, a touch of perfection. Hellenistic naturalism, still barely curbed by neo-Attic or neo-Asiatic tendencies, here puts itself at the service of a frigidly programmatic type of official art, and turns it into something precious. It is this which compensates for the absence of creative drive or poetic imagination, and renders the work of these supreme craftsmen not merely agreeable but sometimes admirable. Through them Rome glimpsed memories of the old artistic splendour which had characterized court life in the Hellenistic kingdoms: indeed, they produced something very like a Hellenistic renaissance. This reflection meets us at every turn, throughout the Augustan period: in engraved gems and cameos no less than in the statues of distinguished public figures. The great 'Cameo of France', for instance, presents a composition set out on three levels. At the bottom we have a group of barbarian prisoners, in the middle a scene portraying some episode from the history of the Imperial Court, and above, various divinities, one of whom is mounted on a winged horse. In the Middle Ages this cameo was placed among the treasures of the Sainte-Chapelle in Paris, since its subject-matter had been interpreted as Joseph before Pharaoh.

194

209 ROME (?): CAMEO. THE 'GEMMA AUGUSTEA'. VIENNA, KUNSTHISTORISCHES MUSEUM, ANTIKENSAMMLUNGEN

210 ROME (?): THE GREAT 'CAMEO OF FRANCE'. PARIS, BIBLIOTHÈQUE NATIONALE

Even today scholars are by no means unanimous as to its correct historical interpretation. One recent thesis even asserts that the piece has been reworked by someone who wanted to portray members of the court of Charles IX and Catherine De' Medici – its original subject having been the Emperor Hadrian and his entourage. Most people, however, take the two seated persons to be Tiberius and his consort Livia, while the warrior standing before them is variously identified as Germanicus, the Younger Drusus, Caligula, or even Germanicus's son Nero (not the Emperor). The actual execution of this piece is far less delicate than that of the *Gemma Augustea,* a glorification of Tiberius, who is shown seated beside Rome and receiving a crown from a personified *Oikoumene* (the 'inhabited world', i.e. the Mediterranean). The Cameo of France is, nonetheless, the largest sard to have survived from antiquity: its composition probably derives from an official painting. It evokes admiration, but fails to arouse any feeling of pleasure or real emotional sympathy, in the way that a less perfect work can when it is imbued with human passion and conflict; here, subject, expression, technique and style are all

211 ROME (?): THE 'GEMMA AUGUSTEA' (DETAIL). ROME AND TIBERIUS. VIENNA, KUNSTHISTORICHES MUSEUM ▶

212 ROME (?): AMETHYST SIGNED BY PAMPHILOS. PARIS

213 ROME: CAMEO. OCTAVIA, AUGUSTUS'S SISTER. PARIS, BIBL. NAT.

resolved in advance. At long last, it would seem, Rome has found peace under the leadership of one man, and in a culture operating according to a predetermined programme.

In art, a style gradually evolves from the earlier eclectic pattern: basically neo-Atticist as regards sculpture, but nevertheless revealing a new accent in the tradition of ancient art. When we look at the *Ara Pacis*, we see a work in which the artistic legacies of Pergamum, Alexandria and Athens have met and mingled – and which still appears typical of the Augustan age. All these factors help to explain just why Augustan art has invariably been favoured by natural conformists.

What did the *Pax Augusta* mean to the Romans? Not, certainly, the achievement of a long-fought-for goal; rather, the end of a period of agony and danger, of tortured uncertainty, of a perpetually changing situation that had become intolerable to all those not directly involved in the political struggle. Indeed, the *Pax Augusta* itself was based on a polite fiction. Yet this fiction came to be accepted even by those who got no advantage from it, simply because they were weary of fighting. As a slogan, the *Pax Augusta* received an enthusiastic welcome from vast sections of the populace, even among the opposition.

It was, moreover, skilfully promoted by the mild and unctuous atmosphere which Augustus always managed to convey, presenting himself as a sincerely religious and disinterested man. This is the most surprising feature of his character: the fact that he could transform himself from a civil-war commander, decisive and ruthless, to the very model of a discreet and affable prince, prudent, restrained, accepting duties and honours only to please those whom he had put in a position where they could bestow them. He embodied piety, benevolence, respect for tradition: through him traditional morality, centred on the family, was to be shored up and refurbished.

This double personality comes across very well in two of the numerous surviving portraits. That from the Museo Capitolino (formerly Albani), which must be earlier than Actium, is a spirited likeness, very

214 CAMEO: LIVIA, AUGUSTUS'S WIFE. THE HAGUE, KONINLIJK PENNINGKABINET

199

215 ROME: BUST OF OCTAVIAN AT THE TIME OF THE BATTLE OF ACTIUM. ROME, MUSEO CAPITOLINO

much in the Hellenistic manner. It shows us Octavian at about twenty-five, already flattered by the artist, his features set in a resolute expression. At the time when the portrait from the Via Labicana (Rome, Museo Nazionale Romano) was executed, Augustus was in fact quite an old man; yet the artist makes only the barest reference to his age, through a slight hollowing of the cheeks. Absorbed by the sacrifice which he is performing, he wears a gentle, serene expression, impressive in its gravity and simplicity. Yet it also conveys the wisdom and understanding of a man who has passed through the maelstrom of life. This is not only the finest extant portrait of Augustus (far more intense, for instance, than the correct but banal statue from Prima Porta), but one of the most significant and original works produced during the entire century. Here we have the successful realization of something which hitherto had not existed: a new ethical content, the embodiment of a new world that has found a new form. The careful arrangement of the hair clearly reveals a neo-Attic origin and a classical model; but the face is a world away from that always slightly theatrical pathos which characterizes a Hellenistic

216 ROME: AUGUSTUS AS PONTIFEX MAXIMUS (DETAIL) ROME, MUSEO NAZIONALE ▶

217 ROME: BASE OF ALTAR. NYMPH AND SATYR. VENICE

portrait. It reveals a simple, objective realism, a sensitivity to skin texture, for which one finds parallels in the terracottas discovered in the sanctuaries of Latium and southern Etruria. It looks very much as though the work of this unknown sculptor reflects one point in Augustus's programme – the revival of the Italic tradition, with its obvious aim of helping in the general restoration of peace throughout the peninsula.

It is for just this subtlety of execution that the work produced during Augustus's century has been generally acclaimed as marking a creative apogee in the history of Roman art. But it so happens that the ideal of tranquillity, order and well-being which it expressed was also the ideal of the liberal nineteenth-century period during which this verdict gradually evolved: a verdict which I am unable to accept. What the art of the Augustan era does seem to express is something eminently suitable for the official world which it serves, a phenomenon bound up with this society and limited to the centre of political power. Art under Augustus, like his principate, was founded on a fiction: it presumed the simultaneous continuity of two traditions, that of the Hellenistic kingdoms on the one hand, and that of the consular Roman Republic on the other. This art seems afraid to voice an opinion of any sort; it takes refuge behind the conformist camouflage of 'correctness' and technical virtuosity. The fluidity and Protean nature of Hellenistic art, with its constant reformulations, the sense of space and atmosphere – all these things are attenuated, emptied of their substance; and nothing bears a larger share of responsibility for this state of affairs than neo-Atticism.

Neo-Atticism did not originate in Pergamum, as some scholars have supposed, but in Athens itself. There was more to this trend than a mere matter of taste, a preference for forms embodying limpidity, clarity and grace; it also gave expression to a specific situation. When Greece passed under the control of Macedonia, Athens lost her role as an active political centre. While remaining the most elegant, refined, cultivated and intellectual of all Greek cities, politically she became a seething backwater of jealousy and

218 CASTELLAMMARE DI STABIA (STABIAE). BOWL WITH EGYPTIAN MOTIFS. NAPLES   219 AREZZO: FRAGMENT OF BOWL. AREZZO

intrigue. Other towns, flowering and expanding under the new dynasties, attracted the most energetic and original artists; Athens no longer provided serious patronage. Her artistic output was limited to pleasant but small-scale artifacts, decorative in function and commercially produced, but of very high quality. Such were the origins of the popular neo-Attic trend, with its strong flavour of neoclassicism and nostalgia.

But when neo-Atticism was transported to Rome, the nostalgic feeling which had kept it alive swiftly evaporated. All that remained was its exploitation as a formal tradition, which soon sank to mere frigid correctness and commercial imitation. With its taste for clear-cut forms distributed over large areas against a neutral background, neo-Atticism utilized classical, archaic or even Egyptian motifs (for this, see the obsidian cups from Stabiae, with their enamel inlay secured by fine gold wire). It also spread to the workshops of Alexandria.

Such was the genesis of Augustan style. Only rarely did a few non-classical elements, derived from Italic Hellenism, contrive to infuse some warmth into it; for the most part their survival was restricted to local craft tradition. For examples of neo-Atticism during the Augustan era we must turn to the ceramic ware of the Arezzo district. Here we find it applied to a type of craft product which found its technical antecedents partly in Greece (for the reliefs) and partly in Central Italy (for the colour). These potteries had been active as early as Sulla's day; but they reached their artistic apogee under Augustus. The work they produced – pottery decorated with moulded reliefs, applied before glazing and firing (*terra sigillata*, from *sigillum*, a figurine) – were exported from Arezzo to every corner of the Empire. Particularly productive factories were established in Gaul. Pots from the Arezzo workshops have even been found during excavations at Arikamedu,

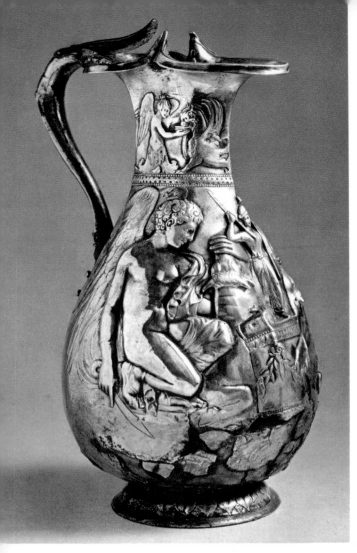

220 BOSCOREALE: CARAFE. PARIS, LOUVRE

221-2 ROME: THE PORTLAND VASE. ORIGINAL AND RECONSTRUCTION

223 BOSCOREALE: CUP (DETAIL). HOMAGE TO AUGUSTUS

south of Pondicherry, on the east coast of India. Yet this is no more extraordinary than the discovery of an Indian ivory statuette at Pompeii. In fact, at least four diplomatic and commercial missions reached Rome from India during Augustus's reign, and one from Ceylon under Claudius.

But it was in craft products employing precious materials, and destined for an aristocratic public which actively disliked innovations, that the art of the Augustan era – often produced by Greek artists – reached its apogee and its most typical expression. Moreover, it was in this field that continual inspiration was provided by treasures from the courts of Pergamum and Syria and Alexandria. What the artists of Augustus's day produced in the arts of silver-embossing, cameo-work, gem-engraving and glassware treated with cameo techniques was to serve as a model for as long as the Roman Empire lasted – so much so, indeed, that from time to time it is discovered that some gem or cameo or silver cup, hitherto labelled 'Augustan', in fact belongs to the age of Constantine.

Apart from treasure-hoards of precious objects brought to light in Italy, such as those at Boscoreale

224 BOSCOREALE: CARAFE (DETAIL). PARIS, LOUVRE ▶

226 POMPEII, HOUSE NEAR THE PORTA MARINA. GLASS PLAQUE CUT TO RESEMBLE A CAMEO. NAPLES, M. ARCHEOLOGICO NAZIONALE

227 BOSCOREALE: VASE AND SALT-CELLARS. PARIS, LOUVRE

◄ 225 POMPEII: GLASS PLAQUE CUT TO RESEMBLE A CAMEO (DETAIL). NAPLES

228 ROME: FRAGMENT OF THE ARA PIETATIS. ROME, VILLA MEDICI

228 ROME: FRAGMENT OF THE ARA PIETATIS. ROME, VILLA MEDICI

229 ROME: FRAGMENT OF THE ARA PIETATIS. ROME, VILLA MEDICI

and the House of Menander in Pompeii (where pieces contemporary with Augustus are mingled with other slightly later work), a collection discovered at Hildesheim in Saxony shows us how valuable silverware of this sort accompanied its owner even when he moved to the provinces. Furthermore, the hoard found at Hoby, in Denmark, proves that even the chiefs of great tribes in northern Europe sometimes acquired such articles.

Official art, then, completely turned its back on those elements which had formed Hellenism's true contribution to Italo-Roman artistic culture – vivid emotionalism of expression, coupled with a quick, perfunctory, often unpredictable treatment of form. As a result, the liveliness and realism which had characterized portraiture under the Republic now vanished altogether. This is one of the factors which make it so difficult to identify certain members of the Julio-Claudian family – especially those princes whom Augustus, anxious to secure a prearranged and dynastic succession for the Principate, named as his heirs one after the other, and every time in vain. All died prematurely – the sons of Tiberius no less than those of Agrippa and Augustus's daughter Julia. Tiberius, born in 42 BC, was the son of Livia, whom Octavian took as his third wife in 38, arranging for her divorce from the Elder Drusus when she was still pregnant by him. Tiberius took Julia as his third wife, and became the successor of Augustus; but when *he* died, it became necessary to call on an even more distant relative, in the person of Caius, the Elder Drusus's nephew, better known as Caligula. Caligula's mental instability ensured a warm (not to say relieved) reception for his uncle Claudius, the next Emperor. Timid and elderly, handicapped by a slight stammer, he showed himself so normal and unaggressive that – in comparison with all these neurotics – he came to be regarded as something of a simpleton.

In the history of the Empire, the reign of Claudius (AD 41-54) represents an interlude of prudent government and close co-operation with the Senate, which came to an abrupt and violent end a few years after his successor and son-in-law Nero ascended the throne. As far as the history of art is concerned, Claudius's

208

reign marks the end of the courtly style which characterized the Augustan period. Neo-Attic inspiration – at least as regards sculpture – is still very noticeable; but surface textures begin to display a richer and livelier style of relief-work, a tonal quality that becomes more pronounced during the second half of the century, preparing the way for the characteristic relationships produced by the next period of art (AD 69-98, the years of the Flavian Emperors, Vespasian, Titus, Domitian and, finally, Nerva).

This vibrant quality emanating from plastic surfaces, which recaptures the sensitivity and sophistication characteristic of Oriental Hellenism, is visible, very early on, in a monument linked both conceptually and formally with the *Ara Pacis*: the *Ara Pietatis Augustae*, voted by the Senate in AD 22, when Tiberius was still alive, and finally dedicated in 43, by Claudius. This monument too consisted of an altar enclosed within a precinct, which was similarly adorned with reliefs portraying scenes of sacrifice; but so few fragments survive that a reconstruction is quite impossible. The best of them found their way into Cardinal Della Valle's collection at the time of the Renaissance, and were subsequently utilized to decorate the Villa Medici on the Pincio (later the Académie de France).

One of the oddest items from the reign of Claudius is the so-called underground basilica near the Porta Maggiore. This is an apsidal chamber with three aisles; according to one theory it was used for secret meetings by a sect which probably included a number of wealthy Roman intellectuals among its members. This sect, it is argued, derived its inspiration from neo-Pythagorean doctrine, which regarded spiritual purification and metempsychosis as the road leading to release and eternal happiness after death. However, the symbolic interpretation of this basilica's decorative scheme remains in doubt (see J. Carcopino, *De Pythagore aux Apôtres*, 1956).

From the artistic viewpoint, this monument offers us the best surviving example of decorative work in white stucco imbued with such grace and spirit as we never find again (or only in the poorest of imitations) until the close of the eighteenth century in Europe;

230 ROME: UNDERGROUND BASILICA NEAR THE PORTA MAGGIORE

231 ROME: UNDERGROUND BASILICA NEAR THE PORTA MAGGIORE. SAPPHO'S LEAP (DETAIL)

the nearest thing to the decoration of this basilica is to be found in some of those small, elegant eighteenth-century apartments known, in Venice, as *ridotti*. We have already come across this Alexandrian technique during the Augustan period when looking at the villa near the Farnesina; but here, in the basilica, the entire tone of the decoration has become lighter. Figures are small and isolated; scenes occupy the centre of large empty spaces, and remain subordinate to the overall grid pattern, which divides up the surfaces into a number of regular panels. Though some scenes could conceivably be interpreted allegorically, they are given no more prominence than the purely decorative ones. All the figures are obviously conceived, first and foremost, as ornamentation; and the impression one gets is that the adepts of this mysterious society, granted that they must have had some sort of ideological pretext for frequenting such a place, did not, nevertheless, take their fashionable mysticism over-seriously.

The tombs of this period (there is a good example found near the Ponte Mammolo) were likewise decorated with stucco reliefs, which drew their inspiration from Greek mythology. This marked a change from those endless paintings in commemoration of glorious ancestral exploits which had been so fashionable a century earlier, when the Republic was controlled by its great patrician families.

The main features of Claudian art showed no appreciable change under Nero – not, that is, in the field of sculpture. On the other hand, we have already seen how the breaking of accepted neo-Attic patterns produced an upsurge of vigour in painting, and something approaching revolutionary violence in architecture. Both then reverted

233 ROME: PONTE MAMMOLO TOMB. DIONYSUS INEBRIATED. ROME, MUSEO NAZIONALE ▶

232 ROME: HOUSE NEAR THE FARNESINA. STUCCO DECORATION ON VAULTING (LANDSCAPE)

234 VESPASIAN (PRIVATE PORTRAIT). COPENHAGEN, NY CARLSBERG GLYPTOTEK

235 VESPASIAN (OFFICIAL PORTRAIT). ROME, MUSEO NAZIONALE

to those first direct contacts which they had established with Hellenism, in Sulla's time or even earlier. In sculpture, similarly, it is not until the era of Domitian, with whose sinister personality (AD 81-96) the first century of the Principate draws to a close, that we find a fresh resurgence of neo-Hellenism.

When we study the portraits of the first Flavian emperor, Vespasian, a reversion to pre-Augustan manners is at once apparent, together with a sharper distinction between private or funerary portraits and those that are officially commissioned, or executed in honour of the Emperor. The bust of Vespasian in the Ny Carlsberg collection quite clearly matches the physical description given us by those historians who narrated his military exploits: an old soldier of plebeian background, looking every inch the peasant, with a leathery tan and a coarse, awkward manner. The portrait in the Museo Nazionale Romano, by contrast, presents him as the *princeps* – distinguished and even intellectual in appearance, and vaguely reminiscent of some Hellenistic sovereign.

The commemorative historical plaques found in Rome, under the Cancelleria in an ancient dump of surplus marble, and dating from Domitian's reign, still show a last faint

212

236 ROME, PALAZZO DELLA CANCELLERIA. RELIEF (DETAIL): THE SENATE AND ROMAN PEOPLE IN PROCESSION. MUSEI VATICANI

flicker of Augustan classicism. But the arch erected in honour of Titus, at the point where the Via Sacra debouches into the Forum, is quite another matter. Its decorations exemplify a wholly new mode of artistic expression. One of the plaques from the Cancelleria shows all its figures still aligned in a single row, the wall against which they are set forming a completely neutral background; on the other, the figures are arranged in a slightly curving line, so that the main ones stand out a little beyond the rest. But in the representation of Titus's triumph, the procession first comes so close to the spectator that it almost seems to brush against him, then curves away and vanishes under an arch (the *porta triumphalis*). The figures, which reveal great variety of relief-work, are set out above a line forming a convex arc, while at the same time the background is made concave.

213

237 ROME: ARCH OF TITUS. THE TRIUMPH OF TITUS. THE EMPEROR

This is not merely a new device on the artist's part designed to give the scene animation. The very fact that he felt the need to employ it shows that some change was taking place in the way people perceived (and, thus, represented) the relationship between man and the realities of his world. This is equally apparent in a change of relationship between the spectator and the reality of art.

Despite its various recent innovations of idiom, Greek art had never made any attempt to alter the relationship between spectator and representation, evolved during earlier stages of artistic development. This relationship was conceived, essentially, as follows. The spectator stood motionless (it was assumed) at some fixed point, and the background to the composition, complete with moving figures, unfolded along a horizontal line. The general plan is still classical in conception; the spectator still stands motionless at a fixed sighting-point. But the spatial relationship has altered. The line along which the background unfolds is no longer horizontal, but convex or concave. Another century, and we find persons in the foreground who are seen from behind, so that the spectator himself becomes a direct participant in the spatial area through which the figures move; he will feel as though he is in a second row, behind those represented. An early attempt in this direction – bold if not wholly successful – was made with the relief inside the arch, at the top of the vault. This shows the apotheosis of Titus, executed

214

238 ROME: ARCH OF TITUS. THE TRIUMPH OF TITUS. SPOILS FROM THE TEMPLE IN JERUSALEM

with a foreshortening technique which places the Emperor's head directly in contact with the body of the eagle bearing him off into the sky. The idea recalls a ceiling by Tiepolo, though without his easy fluency.

A family tomb of the Haterii on the Via Casilina, on the outskirts of Rome, yielded an interesting series of sculptures, typical of unofficial art under Domitian. Unfortunately the excavation, carried out in the mid-nineteenth century, was a very haphazard affair. There is good reason to identify the owner of this tomb as one Q. Haterius Tychicus, by profession a *redemptor*, or public works contractor. This would explain why the reliefs that formerly decorated the fabric of the tomb itself included representations of various public buildings (including the Coliseum, with its Attic storey still unfinished) and a building hoist. Indeed, a large-scale building contractor epitomizes, with uncommon aptness, the triumphant upsurge of the middle classes, in the context of that vast passion for building which manifested itself during Domitian's reign. The artist lays emphasis on any elements which symbolize religious or funerary ritual, executing them in minute detail – but with complete disregard for maintaining a realistic scale of proportions between the different sections and figures. As we have seen, such representation characterizes the 'plebeian' trend in art. Yet at the same time the monument includes some portrait busts of outstanding quality. Roman realism, toned down

215

239 ROME: ARCH OF TITUS. THE TRIUMPH OF TITUS (DETAIL)

241 ROME: ARCH OF TITUS. SUMMIT OF VAULT. TITUS'S APOTHEOSIS

◄ 240 ROME: ARCH OF TITUS. THE TRIUMPH OF TITUS (DETAIL)

242 ROME: TOMB OF THE HATERII (DETAIL). HOIST, BUILDINGS AND VARIOUS FUNERARY EMBLEMS. VATICAN (LATERAN MUSEUM)

244 ROME: TOMB OF THE HATERII (DETAIL). PORTRAIT OF A WOMAN. VATICAN

243 ROME: TOMB OF THE HATERII. PILLAR WREATHED WITH ROSES

245 ROME: TOMB OF THE HATERII (DETAIL). PORTRAIT OF AN INFANT. VATICAN

and refined by Hellenistic influence, here achieves some of its finest work. These are true busts, not, as previously, limited to the head and a small part of the neck, but real half-torsos minus the arms. Two of these portraits are set in little niches, which must originally have stood out from the wall, and vaguely recall those little cupboards in which patrician families formerly kept their ancestral images.

In the niche containing the bust of a lady, we find roses trailing up the pilasters and columns (which, like those in decorative mural frescoes, are inconsistent with the normal architectonic rules). A squared-off rectangular stone, probably one of several which formed the frame for a *transenna*, or tomb-grille, has a column carved on it in relief, and round the column the winding-rose motif is again repeated. These bas-reliefs have a vibrant sense of atmosphere, but one that concentrates on the actual objects portrayed. It is a different phenomenon from that noted in the reliefs devoted to Titus's triumph; yet it stems from the same initial impulse – to convey a sense of space. What this trend reveals is the pursuit of naturalism, here equated with ever greater accuracy in detail. Such a preoccupation, however, is somewhat out of key with the artist's perceptible indifference to overall effect; whatever the general composition may be said to be aiming at, it is certainly not naturalism. Thus, though Hellenistic naturalism is evident in the mode of artistic expression, the content is based on the Italo-Roman tradition. An extraordinary degree of delicacy has been attained in the relief-work: the rose-leaves are no thicker than their real-life counterparts, and however sumptuous the modelling, outlines still remain clear-cut. Similarly with the portrait-heads: every inch of their surface is brought alive by means of minutely detailed and vigorous relief-work, as colourful as it is decorative. The hair becomes an ornamental feature, soft and wind-swept. The sculptor who executed these works handled his chisel as easily as a sketching-pen.

246 ROME: SARCOPHAGUS OF BELLICUS. PISA, CAMPOSANTO

247 ROME: CAPITOL. TROPHY OF DOMITIAN

248 ROME: MURAL RELIEF. PRIAPUS AMONG VINES. VATICAN (LATERAN MUSEUM)

249 POMPEII: HOUSE OF LAOCOON. SKETCH OF BACCHUS AND MERCURY

Another fragment, decorated with ivy-bines and from a different locality, shows yet another advance in the manner of conveying atmosphere. The background is often scooped out round the leaves in order to make them seem still lighter, and parts in the middle ground are barely traced in. We see here the preliminary evolution, in a fine ornamental context, of those techniques and modes of expression which were afterwards exploited to the full by a major artist for the reliefs on Trajan's Column.

250 ANKARA: BUST OF TRAJAN IN OLD AGE. ANKARA, ARCHAEOLOGICAL MUSEUM

5 The Creation of an Imperial Art: Trajan and Hadrian

I N A D 68-69, after the brief but violent civil war during the 'Year of the Four Emperors' (Galba, Otho, Vitellius, Vespasian), Rome's political and administrative system underwent far-reaching changes. These began with Vespasian's principate, and were a decisive factor in the following period, from Nerva (96-98) to Marcus Aurelius (161-80) – which antiquity itself regarded as the happiest era of Imperial rule. In the panegyrics delivered before Constantine (A D 306-37), it was still *de rigueur*, when eulogizing him, to compare his government to those of Trajan, the *Optimus Princeps* (98-117), Hadrian (117-38) and the Antonines (Antoninus Pius, 138-61, Lucius Verus, 161-69, and his adopted brother, father-in-law and co-regent Marcus Aurelius). Furthermore, the years spanned by these emperor's reigns are referred to on coins as *felicia tempora*. In this sense, Imperial propaganda had, for two generations, an effective and practical value, at least for the citizens of Rome. The period of increasingly serious crises which followed shed an ever-brighter lustre, in retrospect, on their lost golden age.

It was an exceptionally solid and united army which carried out the wars of conquest: first Trajan's, mainly in Dacia (modern Rumania) and the East (in Armenia and against the Parthians), and then those of Marcus Aurelius, waged to defend the northernmost provinces (Germany) and the lands beyond the Danube. At the same time, two basic factors guaranteed a long period of prosperity and internal peace, and not only transformed, but came to typify, the Empire during this period. One was the creation of a Romanized aristocracy in the provinces; the other was the solution found to that ever-recurrent problem, the Imperial succession.

Composed of former soldiers, and latterly of civil servants also, the provincial aristocracy gradually brought about a complete transformation of the old senatorial class. Roman senators were still obliged to be domiciled, and have property, in Italy; yet, in reality, the Senate – on a basis of birth and privilege – represented the entire Empire. Furthermore, it was composed of men whose authority rested not so much on wealth as on their experience as soldiers, administrators and provincial governors. One result of the army reforms carried out by Vespasian was that Roman soldiers (a small proportion of the Praetorian Guard excepted) ceased to be recruited from the Italian proletariat. Instead, they were sought among the better educated and more cultivated provincials, farmers and peasants belonging to the newly formed municipalities which stood for a policy of increasing provincial urbanization.

To begin with it was the Western provinces (Spain, Gaul, Illyria, Noricum, Pannonia) which became most directly involved in the political and administrative organization of the Empire. Some Emperors, such as Trajan and Hadrian, were born in Spain; others, like Antoninus Pius and Marcus Aurelius, were descended from the Gallic landed nobility. Even in Vespasian's day, three Orientals had seats in the Senate, one of them a former king; under Trajan, Greek senators began to appear, and under Hadrian their numbers substantially increased. Towards the end of the first century (92 and 93) there were even consuls from Asia Minor. The links between Rome and the provinces grew steadily closer, and the old master-subject relationship gave way to that subsisting between members of an administrative commonwealth. Nationalist opposition to Rome in the provinces did not automatically vanish; yet throughout the Empire there was now greater unity than there had ever been before.

It is no coincidence that there began to develop during this period a new artistic tradition – one that genuinely expresses the Roman Empire and is not to be confused with any earlier trend in art. At long last the legacy of Hellenism loses its alien, borrowed quality, to be fully assimilated and transformed into a new culture. We can see this in the new type of decoration which appears in the tombs of the nobility, and also in private houses – the latter more rarely, since little evidence survives. One good example is provided by certain tombs on the Via Latina, where the groin vaulting carries elegant paintings and stucco-work; freely designed after Hellenistic motifs, these (in their own more modest way) give a wider circulation to patterns used on the ceilings of the *Domus Aurea*.

The second factor (a fundamental one for the creation of the historical conditions peculiar to this period) was the method chosen to settle the problem of the Imperial succession; this directly influenced the manner in which both Imperial power and the person of the Emperor were regarded. As a result, it too had a very definite influence on art, especially on Imperial portraits – the style of which was often adapted to private likenesses. It was now that the succession came to be determined by means of adoption, theoretically without any regard for family ties. This principle represented a victory for the intellectual opposition, since it translated into practical terms a notion widely discussed in contemporary philosophical literature. On this point, the beliefs of the Pythagoreans finally merged with those of the Stoics and the popular philosophers who regarded themselves as representing the Cynics. There is no doubt that these philosophical discussions were politically orientated; if proof were needed, the tyrant Domitian's decree expelling all philosophers from Rome is there to supply it. Among those banished were Dio of Prusa, in Bithynia, afterwards known as Dio Chrysostom, and Musonius the Stoic. The former, in particular, devoted himself to the life of an itinerant philosopher and political speaker, wandering from town to town, often disguised and under an assumed name. From his discourses – in which Domitian figured as the main target – the fundamental ideas held by this opposition group emerge very

251 ROME: TOMB ON THE VIA LATINA. VAULT DECORATED WITH PAINTINGS AND STUCCO-WORK (DETAIL)

clearly. One point they continually harp on is the distinction between the tyrant and the good and legitimate king. The latter receives his authority from God, who chooses him because he is the best of men; it follows that his rule can neither be hereditary, nor founded on tyranny. The adoption of his successor by the Emperor, who chose for this purpose the worthiest member of the Senate available, follows the same principle. Men such as Trajan, Hadrian and Marcus Aurelius fully satisfied the requirements of contemporary philosophic thought, according to which to exercise supreme power was a service, a duty imposed by God and the State. The Emperor, far from being master of the State, was its first servant, and as such was required to possess austere self-discipline, a strong sense of duty, and the will to shoulder duties as incessant as they were laborious. The entire concept was fundamentally liberal and deeply religious, with a tendency towards mysticism that grew steadily more marked in Stoic writings from the time of Musonius's great disciple Epictetus (born at Hierapolis in Phrygia, and died at Nicopolis-Actium between AD 125 and 130). That moving and often tragic document, the *Meditations* of Marcus Aurelius, is the direct product of his teaching. Because of the divine inspiration which was assumed to dictate the choice of an Emperor, the latter's person came to be regarded as sacrosanct, a visible embodiment of the Empire's majesty.

With Trajan's accession in AD 98, the philosophical opposition quietened down. Dio became something very like the Emperor's official spokesman, delivering speeches 'on royalty and tyranny' in all the most important Eastern cities – an effective contribution to the pacification of the provinces. The first of these speeches dates from the year 100, and is thus coeval with the Younger Pliny's *Panegyric* to Trajan. In 108, to celebrate the tenth anniversary of Trajan's reign, there was executed a portrait of the Emperor which marked a new development in iconography. Previously, as we have seen in Vespasian's case, two different types of portrait existed side by side: official portraits, idealized (or even divinized) according to the artistic tradition of classical Greece, and private

252 ROME: BUST OF TRAJAN. LONDON, BRITISH MUSEUM

253 ROME: TRAJAN'S COLUMN. TRAJAN WITH SURA (DETAIL)

227

257 PERGAMUM: THE GREAT ALTAR. FRIEZE OF TELEPHUS (DETAIL). BERLIN, STAATLICHE MUSEEN

THE EMPEROR ON HORSEBACK, ATTACKING THE ENEMY. ROME, ARCH OF CONSTANTINE

likenesses, the realism of which made no concessions or compromises. Now, at last, this double standard vanished, and the result was a unique portrait of the Emperor. It does not convey any hint of divinity; but by enhancing the subject's human qualities, it elevates him to the full height of his power, presenting him in a pose both lifelike and heroic. Here the new Imperial ideal finds its true expression. Never, perhaps, has any artist better conveyed the human relationship (one of fundamental trust and devotion) between a senior minister, also a personal friend, and a leader with the gift of calm decision and sure command, than in this representation of Trajan and a member of his entourage (a *comes*), probably Lucius Licinius Sura. Yet this group is lost among a hundred others on the column commemorating the two wars which the Emperor conducted against the Dacians.

Once we have caught the age's characteristic tone and atmosphere, it becomes easier for us to appreciate the novel content of its art, which at long last can properly be termed *Roman*, in the full sense, since it gives expression to a new and structurally non-Hellenistic society. To this we may add that during Trajan's reign one of the greatest artists in all antiquity had the genius to give this content formal expression. We know nothing about him personally, though various hypotheses have been put forward;

258 'MAESTRO DELLA GESTA DI TRAIANO': THE GREAT FRIEZE (DETAIL). ROME, ARCH OF CONSTANTINE (MOULDING)

232

259 'MAESTRO DELLA GESTA DI TRAIANO': THE GREAT FRIEZE (DETAIL). ROME, ARCH OF CONSTANTINE (MOULDING)

IMP·CAESARI·DIVI·NERVAE·FILIO
NERVAE·TRAIANO·OPTIMO·AVG
GERMANICO·DACICO·PONTIF·MAX·TRIB
POTEST·XVIII·IMP·VII·COS·VI·P·P
FORTISSIMO·PRINCIPI·SENATVS·P·Q·R

that is why he is sometimes referred to as the *Maestro della gesta di Traiano*. Yet his artistic character is very much in evidence. We still have the column which was erected in Trajan's Forum between 110 and 113, with a continuous relief some two hundred yards long spiralling round it. We also have part of a frieze, about ten feet high, portraying life-size figures in alto-relievo; several plaques from this have been set, independently of one another, in the central archway and the Attic storey of the Arch of Constantine. When we relate them to various other fragments surviving in museums, we can deduce that the original frieze must have been over 90 feet long, perhaps as much as 103 feet.

This vast frieze, the scale of which was without precedent in Rome, must have adorned some building in the Forum; but we do not know precisely where or how. All trace of neo-Atticism has now vanished. With remarkable skill the artist has picked up certain modes of expression from the Telephus frieze on the Altar of Pergamum, and some iconographic motifs previously applied to Alexander the Great (the Emperor on horseback attacking and routing the enemy); but these are quickened by a wholly new vigour and majesty in the execution, and more than suffice to express the concept which this work was designed to promote – the matchless and unassailable power of the Roman Empire.

Lastly, we have Trajan's Arch at Beneventum, voted by the Senate in 114 to commemorate the opening of the new Via Appia. (The latter provided a much-improved link with the port of Brundisium [Brindisi], from which all expeditions for the East set out.) This arch was completed in Hadrian's reign, with an obvious change in the style of the reliefs adorning the Attic storey: here we can observe the intervention of a guiding mind very different from that which had presided over the other sculptures, with their close resemblance to those in Trajan's Forum. Inside the main archway is a large relief commemorating a measure taken by Trajan (and one typical of this emperor): the *institutio alimentaria*, which was a State fund for making loans to smallholders. (The interest on these loans was set aside to subsidize the education of the smallholders' children.)

261 BENEVENTUM: TRAJAN'S ARCH. THE 'INSTITUTIO ALIMENTARIA'

262 ROME: TRAJAN'S MARKET (DETAIL)

In the relief, grouped in front of Trajan and various allegoric figures, we see the grateful
settlers with their children, both boys and girls, whom they are holding by the hand or
carrying on their shoulders. Stylistically, there is a close resemblance to the reliefs on
Trajan's Column. Furthermore, quite apart from its artistic achievement, this composition presents a striking thematic innovation. Here, for the very first time, the lower
classes appear on an official monument.

The mode of artistic expression which all these works of sculpture display reveals
such a wealth of new ideas that one is tempted to predicate the existence of a number of
workshops directed by one major creative artist. During this period we find no comparable sculpture in the provinces; but subsequently reflections of the new style begin to
appear over a wide area – something which had not happened with any previous phase

236

of monumental sculpture in the capital, and which confirms the fact that we are at a significant point in the development of Roman-period art.

It is possible that the dominant artistic personality whose existence we are led to postulate can be identified as Apollodorus, described, by the few historical sources surviving for this period, as Trajan's architect and military engineer. One of these sources, Procopius, further states that he was born at Damascus, in Syria. We may note that all the architectural works erected in Trajan's Forum (of which we have representations on coins), and likewise the Beneventum arch, are quite exceptionally rich in decorative sculpture, so much so, indeed, that the architectural structure itself seems a mere support or framework for the sculptures. The same applies to Trajan's Column, a completely new type of monument, of which only the base and the capital display purely

263 ROME: TRAJAN'S MARKET. THE GREAT MARKET-HALL (DETAIL)

architectonic form. We may, then, suppose a close collaboration between a famous architect, Apollodorus, and some great but unnamed sculptor who directed the stone-carvers' workshops – unless, that is, we conclude that architect and sculptor were one and the same person.

Our historical sources are unanimous in attributing Trajan's Forum (see p. 355) to Apollodorus; and it was a work of genius. Attempts have been made to split it up between two different architects, with one responsible for the Forum and basilica, which are particularly rich in Hellenistic elements, and the other for the buildings of the market, which adhere to the typically Roman architecture of Domitian's day. Such theories are doomed to failure. These two groups of buildings formed part of a unique and quite exceptional essay in urban planning. By cutting a section out of the slope of the Quirinal Hill – the Column is a fair index of its height – the architect produced a magnificent public square. To enter it one skirted the Forum Augusti, and passed through a monumental archway, on top of which stood a *quadriga* drawn by elephants. This arrangement finally settled the problem of continual enlargements and additions to the Forums (begun with the Forum Caesaris, continued with the Forum Augusti, and carried still further by means of the Forum Transitorium – a long colonnaded piazza begun in Nerva's day, which provided a fresh approach to the Forum Romanum). The new urban planning scheme was conceived on a generous scale. It included the vast Ulpian Basilica, two libraries, one Greek, the other Latin, with Trajan's Column between them, and a temple (subsequently dedicated to the cult of Trajan). Behind a large circular exedra, and along the escarpment produced by the cutting-away of the hill, there was constructed a vast complex of shops, set out on several terraced levels. These stood beside a W-shaped road (the Via Biberatica), which began down on the level of the Forum, and ended almost at the summit of the Quirinal. At its topmost point this commercial complex (which centralized most of the city's trade) ended in a great vaulted hall with two tiers of shops, very like that somewhat later phenomenon, the Islamic bazaar, and similar in structure to the galleries of large modern department stores.

Till the very end of antiquity, Trajan's Forum remained the greatest wonder of Rome – as we can tell from Ammianus Marcellinus's description (16.10.15) of the visit which the Emperor Constantius II made in the year 356. The buildings in the Forum were covered with marble, stucco, sculpture and paintings. It is hard to visualize, with any precision, just how these works of architecture looked in their complete state, what effect the play and reflection of light had on them. Today nothing but their essential structure survives, crude and unadorned. The public market, on the other hand, was built of unfaced bricks, put together with great precision and expertise by highly skilled workers. In the whole of this complex there were no columns and few cornices: decorations were in terracotta.

As regards the general appearance of the Forum, with its temple and basilica, scholars have noted the existence – at Damascus, oddly enough – of a large arched piazza, Hellenistic in style, and dating from the Julio-Claudian era. Various buildings had found a place inside this piazza – as, later, did the mosque of the Umayyad dynasty, and the Church of St John. As parallels to Trajan's great market-hall, the markets of Ferentino and Tibur have been cited, both dating from the early first century BC. Both already have a spacious rectangular ground-plan, roofed over with tunnel-vaulting and flanked by side-halls. This basic scheme is re-elaborated in Trajan's market, but with novel purpose and results, aesthetic no less than utilitarian. If we compare the excessive thickness of building-walls during the Republican era with the strictly functional dimensions of those – in brick-faced conglomerate – employed for the construction of Trajan's market, we can see, very clearly, just how much technical progress architects had made by his day. Furthermore, the markets of Ferentino and Tibur exist in isolation, whereas Trajan's commercial complex is subtly and harmoniously integrated with its surroundings, on six main levels along the slope of the hill. Both internally and externally the desired effect – an abundance of air and light – is fully achieved; the whole complex is an outstanding example of urban planning.

If Apollodorus was, in fact, responsible for designing both Forum and Market, he scored a remarkable success with them. He reinterpreted, with great originality, principles not only of Hellenistic but also of Roman architecture (as far back, in the latter case, as the building of Domitian's reign and the sanctuary at Praeneste). One special feature which characterizes the bas-reliefs on Trajan's Column is, again, the basic fusion of Hellenistic and 'plebeian-Roman' elements. The result is a completely new style; from now on we can speak of 'Imperial Roman art'.

Our sources refer to other buildings designed by Apollodorus: an *Odeion*, or concert-hall, of which no trace survives, and the Baths (connected with those of Titus) above the *Domus Aurea*. Modern theories, all non-provable, have credited this architect with the artificial harbour between Porto (near Ostia) and Fiumicino, not to mention the port of Civitavecchia and various other undertakings. The great bridge over the Danube and other similar constructions portrayed on Trajan's Column testify to Apollodorus's activities as a military engineer. The Mynas MS of his *Poliorcetica* contains sketches of siege engines which, though made in the Byzantine era, still substantially reproduce their original models

264 ROME: TRAJAN'S COLUMN (RENAISSANCE ENGRAVING)

265 ROME: TRAJAN'S COLUMN. THE BASE ▶

266 ROME: TRAJAN'S COLUMN. INTERIOR STAIRCASE

(ed. R. Lacoste, *Revue des Etudes grecques* 8 [1895], 198ff.).

From the typological viewpoint, Trajan's Column constitutes an entirely new departure. From the Hellenistic age onward, Rome had followed the Greek practice of using free-standing columns to support commemorative statues, while columns decorated with superimposed bands of relief-work had also been dedicated to various divinities in the provinces (e.g. the column at Mainz, sacred to Jupiter). What is absolutely without precedent is the idea of taking a colossal memorial column, surmounted by the Emperor's statue (in the original design, as we can see from some coins, this figure was to have been an eagle), and winding a long figural relief all the way round it in a spiral. According to one theory, which held the field for a long time, the object had been to portray a huge illustrated roll, this being at a time when the roll was still the only form of book in use. It was pointed out that the Column stood directly between the two libraries, and that the relief-work had, without a doubt, been decorated in polychrome. Now that we are better acquainted – thanks mainly to the research of Kurt Weitzmann – with the problems attendant upon textual illustration in antiquity, this theory has fallen out of favour. We do possess rolls filled from end to end with a sequence of illustrated episodes, such as the tenth-century 'Joshua Roll' (Vatican Library); but the inspiration for these, it is now thought, came from Trajan's Column and subsequent columns in Rome and Constantinople.

It follows that the notion of decorating the Column with a continual spiral relief is wholly original; we cannot explain its genesis as anything but invention pure and simple. On the other hand, we must still investigate the composition of the reliefs in these triumphal scenes, and see what we can deduce about its antecedents. The base is decorated with piles of arms: this picks up a motif which had earlier been used, on the balustrades of the sanctuary of Athena Polias at Pergamum. Above the base rises the main shaft of the column, to a height of nearly 27 metres (26·62 m. to be precise; or, if we include torus, shaft and capital, 29·78 m., which comes to exactly 100

◄ 267 ROME: TRAJAN'S COLUMN. ENTRANCE TO BURIAL-CHAMBER

Roman feet; the overall height, taking in plinth and statue-base, is 39·86 m.). The column-shaft is formed from seventeen drums of Parian marble, each one being 3·83 m. in diameter and 1·56 m. high. There is no doubt that the relief carving was done after the erection of the column. It makes twenty-three complete spiral turns, over a distance of 200 metres. As this illustrated band ascends, it becomes steadily wider, in order to correct the optical effect of diminution produced by distance: as a result all the bands look the same. (In actual fact, their height ranges from 0·89 m. at the base to 1·25 m. at the summit, and the figures on the reliefs naturally grow with them, from 60 cm. to 80 cm.) The way in which the project has been carried out, together with these very precise modifications of perspective, clearly presuppose a working sketch-plan. The latter are cut very flat to avoid distorting the architectonic line of the column (an effect all too noticeable on the later Antonine Column of Marcus Aurelius), and employ certain techniques which more properly belong to painting or drawing. The figures are often thrown into prominence by a groove chiselled round them: this not only emphasizes their outline, but, by creating a shadow, highlights the relief itself. Sometimes certain details of the figures retreat into the background, and are expressed in sunk carving rather than relief. Thanks to such methods, and by varying the consistency of the surfaces, the artist obtained a marvel-lously fluent pictorial relief: though its moulding projects no more than a centimetre or two, it still contrives to give an illusion of spacious perspective in depth, through which the figures move and develop without effort. Conventional perspective, as a method of representing buildings and towns, had been in use for centuries; but in this work the buildings shown acquired an unprecedented clarity and great architectonic precision.

The preliminary sketch-plan must have already been in existence when it was decided to make the upper part of the column accessible, by means of an internal staircase cut through the marble drums which formed it. The loop-hole windows that provide this staircase with light were cut at the same time as the reliefs, but they spoil the figures – sometimes very badly – and thus cannot have been allowed for in the original design. (This particular annoyance does not recur in the Antonine Column, even though in general the latter is much less meticulously planned.) Lastly, yet another unprecedented touch: the base of the column served as a last resting-place for the urn containing the Emperor's ashes, while his statue, in bronze, adorned its summit.

What those two hundred metres of relief describe are the two Dacian Wars of 101-2 and 105-7, which took a Roman army (under Trajan's personal command) across the Danube and the Transsylvanian Alps, as far as the Eastern Carpathians. There were two reasons for these expeditions against the Dacians. First, the frontier along the Danube was no longer sufficiently secure; since the days of Vespasian and Domitian it had been attacked, successfully, on numerous occasions, thus encouraging the Dacians to invade the provinces of Moesia; second, these campaigns formed part of a general policy of expansion towards the East, the Black Sea and Armenia. The acquisition of Dacia brought nearly the whole Black Sea region under Roman control, together with its rich deposits of gold and iron.

Can the reliefs of Trajan's Column be used as evidence to reconstruct a connected account of these two expeditions? Here opinion is divided. There can be no doubt that events are portrayed in chronological order, and the armour and weapons of various military units are represented with minute accuracy. From the artistic viewpoint – which is what mainly concerns us here – the frieze on Trajan's Column is not only the most brilliant and original example of Roman historical relief carving in existence, but also one of the most significant works of art from all antiquity. Hitherto an inadequate photographic record has made critics slow to appreciate this fact; but the artists of the Renaissance were conscious enough of it – above all Donatello, as his bronze reliefs in S. Lorenzo (Florence) and in S. Antonio (Padua) prove.

The description of both these expeditions is founded on one or two fixed themes, which had probably already passed into the stock repertory of triumphal pictures: the setting out, the construction of roads and fortifications, religious ceremonial, addresses to the troops, the actual assault or battle, the enemy's surrender. Sometimes, too, we find scenes of savagery and plunder, mute testament to the pitiless destruction of a people. Each of these themes, however, is adapted to individual circumstances and varies a good deal in detail; between them we find episodes such as characterized the general course of the campaign. The astonishing thing is that despite such a crowd of figures – not to mention much thematic repetition – the composition never once, in all its two hundred metres, shows the faintest trace of fatigue.

We are concerned here, it is true, with an occasional work, commissioned as an instrument of Imperial propaganda. But the artist's creative freedom has risen above such limitations: this becomes abundantly clear when we study the way he has represented and composed the various episodes which make up his theme. So untrammelled is his technique that he has virtually created a new formal language. As for the subject-matter, we have already encountered one instance (the scene showing the Emperor in conversation with Sura) of the way Trajan's powers are suggested. This highly representative scene is governed by the new concept of the *princeps* as the State's chief civil servant, whose position absorbs every scrap of personal ability and authority which he possesses. In none of the many portrayals of the Emperor do we sense an attitude of flattery or adulation. Even in the great surrender-scene, which rounds off the second campaign of the earlier war – a vast composition forming a very sizable frieze on its own – the seated Emperor, glimpsed in profile, looks more like a judge than a conqueror. There is a profound difference of concept, ethical no less than political, between these representations and the ones we find on the Antonine Column, where the enemy is massacred and subjected to all manner of outrage. When we turn to some of the scenes portrayed on coins struck by Christian Emperors in the fourth century, the gap is even wider. When these gigantic figures crush the fallen foe beneath their feet they seem to take on all the destructive violence of Yahweh in the Old Testament.

The respect for a beaten foe which finds expression on Trajan's Column reflects an ethical system derived from Greek culture and Stoic philosophy. Marcus Aurelius was to put the matter very clearly in his *Meditations* (10.10) when, speaking of a hard-fought campaign against the barbarians, he compared a soldier who ambushed a Sarmatian and took him prisoner to the spider, exultant over the capture of a fly. Both, in his opinion, were common murderers. But the reliefs on Trajan's Column go further still. The Dacians are portrayed with obvious sympathy. There is great emphasis on the stubborn persistence of their guerrilla operations in the forests, on the splendid courage of their

269 ROME: TRAJAN'S COLUMN. MASS SUICIDE OF THE DACIANS (DETAIL)

244

270 ROME: TRAJAN'S COLUMN. MASS DEPORTATIONS (DETAIL)

271 ROME: TRAJAN'S COLUMN. HECATOMB OF BARBARIANS (DETAIL)

272 ROME: TRAJAN'S COLUMN. PURSUIT THROUGH THE WOODS (DETAIL)

273 ROME: TRAJAN'S COLUMN. BATTLE ON THE DANUBE (DETAIL)

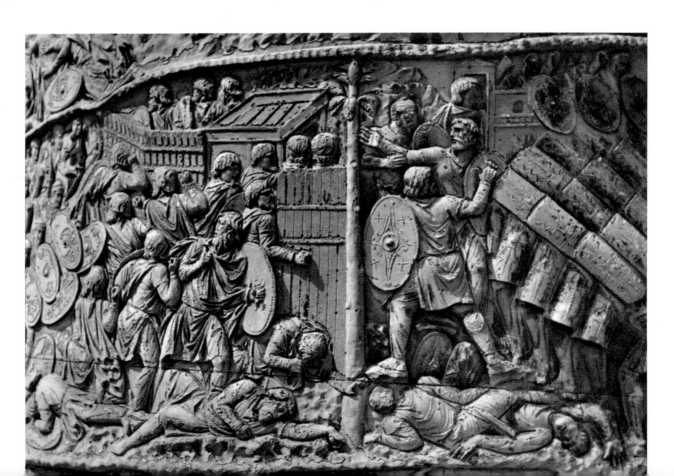

275 ROME: TRAJAN'S COLUMN. THE DACIANS IN BATTLE (DETAIL)

◀ 274 ROME: TRAJAN'S COLUMN. ASSAULT ON A DACIAN FORTRESS (DETAIL)

276 ROME: TRAJAN'S COLUMN. THE FLIGHT OF DECEBALUS, THE DACIAN CHIEFTAIN

277 SAINT-REMY-DE-PROVENCE (GLANUM): FUNERARY MONUMENT OF THE JULII (DETAIL)

248

mass suicides, on the wretched plight of peasant families in retreat before the enemy or forced to abandon their mountain homes. Is this evidence for Trajan's high-minded and deliberate magnaminity, or perhaps rather an expression of the artist's own personal feelings? (Provincial-born, he would know at first-hand the degree of misery which subjection to Rome could bring in its wake.) There can be no doubt that, from the artistic viewpoint, it is the scenes describing Dacian resistance which tend to be the most brilliantly handled. Thus the account of how Decebalus, the Dacian chieftain, met his fate ends by glorifying him as a proud but unfortunate champion of Dacian independence. We see him fleeing through the woods with a small escort, while Roman soldiers lead off horses laden with rich vessels from the royal treasure, the hiding-place of which had been betrayed to them (Dio Cassius, 68.14). Decebalus's route takes him through thick and inaccessible woods not far from the town. We see him talking to his men, some of whom commit suicide. Pursued by the Roman cavalry, he takes off at a wild gallop with a few faithful companions. When finally overtaken, he drops off his horse and kills himself. His head is then borne off on a large platter by the Roman soldiery.

Lehmann-Hartleben, who was the first scholar to study Trajan's Column in detail, claimed that it was a work of art from the beginning of Late Antiquity (the *Spätantike*). To accept this idea would be tantamount to endorsing a misinterpretation which has burdened the history of Roman art for many years: the belief that its apogee must be sought in the Augustan era. I have tried to illustrate the fundamentally artificial nature of Augustan art, to show how frigid and academic it was, shackled by the demands of a clear-cut political ideology, and borrowing all its formal innovations from neo-Atticism – itself by now a wholly artificial phenomenon. The artistic output of the Augustan age camouflages its lack of sincerity and vitality with a dazzling technical refinement. If this interpretation holds good, we must (as I have tried to demonstrate) see in Flavian art the re-establishment of that fruitful contact between Eastern Hellenism and the Mid-Italic creative tradition – a contact first made under the Republic – which resulted in Roman art. But it is in the art of Trajan's reign that this fusion is most fully realized.

We have already had occasion to observe that certain developments in 'plebeian' art anticipated the artistic trends of Late Antiquity. Some of these modes are visible in the language of Trajan's Column, having probably got there via triumphal painting. But there is never a hint of hierarchic or symbolic disproportion, nor any composition in which all the characters stand in a row on the same line, against a neutral background. The substance of what is expressed always adheres to the great tradition of Hellenistic naturalism; indeed, one might say that it has carried the trend to its logical conclusion. It was only by abandoning and rejecting the fundamental principles of Hellenistic naturalism that a new concept of artistic form could be attained, which we associate with Late Antiquity (and Late Antiquity means the beginning of the Middle Ages). The first break, the first sign of crisis in this sphere, did not appear until the age of Commodus. Certainly we get no hint of either from the fluid and graphic relief-work of Trajan's Column, for which a good formal parallel may be found in the reliefs on the funerary monument of the Julii at Glanum (Saint-Rémy-de-Provence). Even as early as the first century BC, Gallia Narbonensis was permeated by Greek cultural influences, and much Hellenistic-style painting went on there; these reliefs translated the trend into stone.

It is therefore wrong to recognize any characteristic features of Late Antiquity in Trajan's Column; it does, however, contain one touch of idiosyncratic self-expression which tends to diminish, if not naturalism generally, at least one of its constituent parts: the organic cohesion of those formal elements which compose the human body. Such diminution enables the 'Master of the Column' to distort and adapt human figures, on occasion, in a far from naturalistic manner; the result is something akin to pure decoration, a geometrical element designed to fill up blank spaces. We may note that, as far as the reliefs on the Column are concerned, this attenuation occurs only in the figures of the dead, which intermingle and crowd together in odd twisted postures, skilfully worked out by the artist so as to fill up the blanks in his composition. Here is yet another detail which we can trace back to the sculpture of Pergamum; but what had there been a mere isolated allusion now emerges as a variously recurrent motif, a theme in the full sense. This theme was soon to find frequent expression in the scenes of battle between Romans and barbarians which figured on sarcophagi towards the end of the second century, and still more in the third. In this sense – and for no other reason – the sculptures on Trajan's Column reveal an affinity with later developments in the same field; but the formal concept remains profoundly different, and the value of the repeated motif is essentially iconographic.

The genius of the *Maestro della gesta di Traiano* is manifested in his seemingly limitless capacity for invention, and the novelty of his iconographic patterns. We know how persistent these patterns were throughout antiquity once they had been introduced: passed on from one workshop to another, codified by the divisions between various artistic *genres*, preserved by that ritual element (symbolic no less than commemorative) which characterized most artistic production in the ancient world. Here, for the first time since the great artists of classical and Hellenistic antiquity, we have a sculptor who is inventing a new language. Yet – and this holds good for the Greek masters too, from the Geometric style to fully Classical art – what he is doing does not constitute a change of direction, a break with the past, so much as a milestone in the progressive evolution of one unbroken artistic culture. As this culture develops, its exponents retain all the traditional modes of expression worked out during its previous history.

At Rome, and in those works of art directly dependent on Rome as an artistic centre, the style created by the *Maestro della gesta di Traiano* was abruptly cut off in mid-development as a result of the personal tastes and preferences evinced by Trajan's successor Hadrian. Our literary sources preserve the memory of Hadrian's precocious disagreements with Apollodorus, while still a mere youth; according to some of these sources, the two men clashed again, and far more violently, after Hadrian's accession to power. Once he became Emperor, it is claimed, this artistic dilettante actually had the great architect banished, and perhaps put to death. Whatever the reliability of this tradition, it is certainly true that (as we saw earlier) the Attic storey of the Beneventum arch reveals a definite shift in orientation. One of the scenes represented on it cannot have been planned earlier than 20 February 116, the date on which Trajan took the title of *Parthicus*; there is a clear allusion to this event in the relief. Now Trajan died, aged sixty-four, in August 117, at Selinus in Cilicia; it follows that the sculptures must have been completed under Hadrian.

279 BUST OF TRAJAN IN OLD AGE. ANKARA, ARCHAEOLOGICAL MUSEUM   280 BUST OF PLOTINA, TRAJAN'S WIFE. ROME, MUSEO CAPITOLINO

We still possess a most moving portrayal of Trajan in old age, which brilliantly conveys the impression both of weariness and of nobility. This is the bronze *clipeatus* portrait now in Ankara, which has its psychological counterpart in the sad and sober portrait bust of his wife Plotina. The Ankara portrait makes a striking contrast both with that commissioned to mark Trajan's tenth anniversary, which portrayed the Emperor in his prime, and with the monumental posthumous portrait found at Ostia, and dating from Hadrian's reign, in which the features have been purified and exalted to heroic status. It is a very plausible assumption that what we have here is a copy of the portrait borne in the posthumous triumph with which Hadrian honoured Trajan.

281 OSTIA: POSTHUMOUS PORTRAIT OF TRAJAN. OSTIA MUSEUM

283 ROME: FORUM ROMANUM. PARAPET SHOWING AN EPISODE FROM TRAJAN'S REIGN

On the other hand, the two *transenne* (parapets) found in the Roman Forum still retain the style of Trajan's age. Inside they are decorated with sacrificial animals, and outside with scenes in which various measures taken by Trajan are shown against the background of the actual buildings in the Forum itself. But the decoration of a room found in an edifice near Rome's Porto Flumentano, on the Tiber, and datable to about AD 131, bears no relation to traditional patterns; the motif of boats and fishes seems to have derived from mosaic flooring, and was in general use only in the next century.

Hadrian went in for building projects on a vast scale and with frenetic energy. The most characteristically grandiose and dramatic specimen of his work in this field is the Temple of Venus and Rome, sited between the Coliseum and the Forum Romanum. If we are to believe the traditional story, the final break between Hadrian and Apollodorus came about directly as a result of the planning for this edifice, on which the Emperor himself is said to have collaborated. The temple was begun about the year 121, after space had been cleared by the demolition of other buildings, some dating from Nero's reign, others from the time of the Republic, and the displacement of the colossal statue of Nero himself as Helios. When Hadrian died, in 138, it was still unfinished. Imposing in bulk and overloaded with ornamentation, this building is constructed according to a most singular plan: it is really *two* temples, with their *cellae* facing one another, and linked by the tangential curves formed by their respective apses (see p. 357). These *cellae* were roofed over with coffered vaulting, which meant that the walls had to be of a great thickness. Their surface was faced with marble, and they contained a number of niches for statues. Those on the long sides (because of the double *cellae* they measured no less than 164·90 metres, or some 541 feet) were flanked by a marble colonnade, while in the

285 ROME: HOUSE NEAR THE PORTO FLUMENTANO. MURAL DECORATION (DETAIL). ROME, MUSEO NAZIONALE

◄ 284 ROME: HOUSE NEAR THE PORTO FLUMENTANO. DECORATION OF A ROOM (DETAIL)

286 ROME: TEMPLE OF VENUS AND ROME. VIEW OF THE APSE

pronaos there stood monolothic columns of grey granite. With ten columns along each of its two facades, this temple was – and remained – the most grandiose in Rome. Its bulk was thrown into extra prominence because of the high foundations – mostly earlier buildings, now pulled down – on which it stood. Coins of Antoninus Pius preserve its original appearance for us – just as some of Hadrian's issues record a temple which he built for his mother-in-law Matidia, who had been largely responsible for his success. This was the first temple ever dedicated to an Empress.

From the critical viewpoint, the sculpture of Hadrian's era poses a special problem. It has even been defined by Jocelyn Toynbee as a chapter – the last – in classical Greek art. Such a definition could be sustained only if one began by assuming that during it there appeared a new, and final, type of athletic statue – that associated with the name of Antinoüs – which followed all the canons of classical sculpture. This young man, a native of Bithynia (on the north coast of Asia Minor) was beloved by Hadrian, and met a mysterious death (which some have even thought ritual) by drowning, in the Nile. Yet although such statues do draw their inspiration from classical forms, they are so permeated, even in the formal sense, with emotionalism and nostalgia that they fall into

258

287 ROME: ANTINOÜS (DETAIL). NAPLES, MUSEO ARCHEOLOGICO NAZIONALE   288 OSTIA: PORTRAIT FROM THE HADRIANIC PERIOD. OSTIA MUSEUM

the romantic category rather than the classical. We may even say that this marks the first appearance of the romantic element in European culture. Its emotional tone, which comes out in that studied contrast between smooth-polished flesh and violent chiaroscuro in the hair (well illustrated by a portrait from Ostia), was subsequently picked up and perpetuated by sculptors under the Antonines.

The type had already begun to appear during Trajan's reign; we find it in southern Asia Minor, where large marble quarries were being worked conveniently near the centres of artistic production. Amongst these centres that of Aphrodisias was exceptionally active: works signed by its artists turn up regularly, in Rome as elsewhere, from Hadrian's day onward. They were sculptors of great technical ability, whose main occupation was copying statues from the classical period. Under their chisels the marble acquired a characteristic delicacy and warmth, which set their work apart from the frigid neo-Atticism of the Augustan age. Even at Athens classicism took on a fresh lease of vitality during this period, as we can see from imported Attic sarcophagi. One particularly charming example was found in the necropolis of Ostia: it was intended for two children, and decorated with infant figures. Another very similar piece of work is the

259

frieze from the Temple of Venus Genetrix, which stood in the Forum Caesaris and was restored by Trajan.

There can be no question that Hadrian was passionately devoted to the pure beauty of Greek art, and his taste favoured any artistic trend which appeared to derive from the traditional canons of antiquity. We should not, however, lose sight of the fact that this preference also had very clear political implications – a point which becomes self-evident when we consider the amount of time Hadrian spent travelling in Greece and the other

260

Eastern provinces. During these journeys he was accompanied by his wife Sabina. He had no great affection for her; she was there to carry out various official duties in her capacity as Empress – the first time such a thing had happened in Rome's history. Hadrian's travels, as we know from the ceremonies accompanying them (on which we have the evidence both of inscriptions and of coin-issues struck by local mints) were dictated by definite political considerations. He was determined to abandon Trajan's most distant conquests: the Parthian provinces beyond the Euphrates, and Armenia (where a vassal king was established with Rome's backing). Arabia and Dacia – the latter after some hesitation – were kept on, and treaties concluded with the chieftains of the Roxolani, Jazyges, Suevi, Quadi and Marcomanni: in other words, all the tribes dwelling along the frontiers of the Empire, that is from the Black Sea to Bohemia.

Although Hadrian claimed to be merely implementing Augustus's own original policy, this series of withdrawals and treaties did not go down at all well with the group of senators who had been closest to Trajan. On the other hand, he accompanied them with a generous remission of outstanding tax-arrears; in the more or less permanent state of war now prevailing, these arrears had mounted up enormously. Hadrian's policy was clear: there were to be no further conquests, and the frontiers were to be stabilized, whether on a military basis (e.g. by Hadrian's Wall in Britain), or by diplomatic means. At the same time he was working to strengthen the cultural and religious ties between Rome and those provinces which had formed part of the old Hellenistic kingdoms, with Greece – and Athens especially – at their head. This programme aimed to achieve a tight-knit ring of defences against the ever-growing pressure of 'barbarian' populations.

At the same time, Hadrian's reign saw a definite advance in the 'sacred' concept of the Emperor's power, and in the Imperial cult. The Stoic philosophy which Hadrian had adopted might give the *princeps* a lofty sense of duty, justice and *humanitas*, but it also incorporated a number of quasi-mystical elements,

291 ROME: ARCH OF CONSTANTINE (DETAIL)

261

292 ROME: ARCH OF CONSTANTINE. HADRIAN AS LION-HUNTER

293 ROME: ARCH OF CONSTANTINE. SACRIFICE TO DIANA (DETAIL)

such as the notion of the wise man as a 'witness to divinity' (Epictetus, *Dissert.* Bk 3).

If we take all this into account, Hadrian's philhellenism can be seen as something more complex than a purely personal predilection, the fruit of his ever-restless intellectual curiosity. Similarly, what are perhaps the most characteristic pieces of sculpture from this period in Rome (those eight reliefs in circular frames which were subsequently added to the Arch of Constantine) take on a more explicit significance. We lack the evidence to determine for what type of building Hadrian originally commissioned these eight reliefs; both formally and typologically they are most unusual. They represent hunting scenes, and the sacrificial offerings made to those deities that were associated with the various beasts slain. Stag, boar, bear and lion are matched by Apollo, Diana, Silvanus and Hercules. Hitherto the Romans had not set any great store by hunting. Among the Eastern nations, however, from Egypt to Assyria, it had long been celebrated as a most noble pursuit, the touchstone of merit (*virtus*), and in all respects worthy of a prince. It had been glorified by Alexander the Great, who had a passion for lion-hunting, and in more recent times by the Parthian monarchs, whose favourite quarry was the stag or the boar. Beginning

294 OSTIA (?): FUNERARY RELIEF OF A MAGISTRATE RESPONSIBLE FOR CIRCUS ENTERTAINMENT. VATICAN (LATERAN MUSEUM)

with these reliefs from Hadrian's reign, hunting-scenes become increasingly popular in Roman art. They turn up on sarcophagi, in mosaics, and (we need not doubt) in painting – though less as a celebration of princely pleasures than for their symbolic value.

Even during the period of refined classicism which marked Hadrian's reign, the 'plebeian' trend in art still clung to its basic principles, regarding thematic detail and the commemoration of the individual as more important than naturalism or correctly proportioned relationships. One example will suffice to demonstrate this point. There is a relief portraying an elderly married couple, still wearing their hair in the way that was fashionable under Trajan, who are set beside a scene of chariot-racing in the circus. The scene itself is shown in conventional proportions and perspective, whereas the couple are made disproportionately large, to indicate (we may assume) the great importance of the husband. Nor are their own bodily proportions consistent: once again we find the head assuming its old predominant role.

Herms portraying racing charioteers, their coarse features ennobled by a smoothly polished style, have been found in a sanctuary on the Aventine. Here circus employees of the day worshipped a recumbent Hercules (*Hercules cubans*), whose gross image

295 ROME: THE RECLINING HERCULES. ROME, MUSEO NAZIONALE

263

296 THE PANTHEON (AS RECONSTRUCTED IN HADRIAN'S REIGN)

297 ROME: THE PANTHEON. AFTER AN ENGRAVING BY ANTONIO SARTI

bears witness to the magico-religious attraction which primitive forms have always exercised.

Of Hadrian's great passion for building there survive two projects in particular which enable us to reach a judgment on the architecture of the period at Rome. One of them is the restored version of Agrippa's Pantheon, formerly linked to Agrippa's Baths. The other is Hadrian's Villa, set at the foot of the Tibur hills, the prematurely aging Emperor's last retreat (he was only sixty-two when he died), the last romantic setting for this great dilettante, who combined the roles of decadent poet, still-life painter, and architectural pioneer.

264

298 BAIAE: BATH-HOUSE, KNOWN AS 'TEMPLE OF DIANA'

299 ROME: HADRIAN'S MAUSOLEUM. FOUNDATION (DETAIL)

This is not the place to make a detailed analysis of the construction of the Pantheon. I shall restrict myself here to considering the effect it produced. The fact that it happens to be the only architectural work of its kind from the Roman period which has survived virtually intact makes it almost impossible to evaluate. Just how does it differ from other similar buildings known to us only as ruins, or by their ground-plans? What gives it its superiority? Because of these circumstances, the Pantheon always remains, for us, the most perfect embodiment of a typically Italo-Roman architectonic concept. The building's peculiar virtue resides in its sense of interior space – a quality we have already noted while discussing the palace architecture of Nero's and Domitian's reigns, not to mention examples from the age of Sulla and even earlier times, which are found in certain coastal resorts of Campania, such as Baia and Pozzuoli. In this connection there is also one fundamental difference we should take note of. Greek civilization abandoned the Minoan-Mycenaean domed tomb long before the advent of the Geometric style (eleventh-tenth centuries BC), preferring to employ a non-accessible type of sepulchre, where ritual could take place only outside. On the other hand, Etruscan and, latterly, Roman civilization always retained the chamber-tomb. At the same time they were quite capable of varying its appearance, both internal and external, while evincing a general preference for forms that allowed the individual to feel himself enclosed within a space which not only surrounded and (in some sense) protected him, but also conveyed an atmosphere of magic and mystery. We find the same impulse (though in a somewhat less extreme form) throughout the area covered by Hellenistic civilization, in Alexandria no less than Anatolia, and all over Asia Minor. But apart from those cult-centres specifically connected with the Mysteries, it is alien to the sentiments of classical Greek culture, and thus plays no part in its architecture, which always remains based on the façade.

Hadrian built a mausoleum for himself and his successors on the right bank of the Tiber, and linked it to the Campus Martius by means of a magnificent bridge. This edifice still retains the basic pattern of a circular tumulus-grave, with its large burial-chamber.

265

300 TIVOLI (TIBUR): HADRIAN'S VILLA. THE RUINS (DETAIL)

During the Republic and under Augustus the tumulus chamber-tomb, as found in large
Etruscan cemeteries, was progressively enlarged and transformed; Hadrian's mausoleum
simply took this process one step further. Its central structure, stripped of the marble
which once faced it, can still be seen in the lower part of the Castel Sant'Angelo, for long
a Papal fortress.

301 TIVOLI (TIBUR): HADRIAN'S VILLA. THE RUINS, AFTER AN ENGRAVING BY G. B. PIRANESI

Hadrian's so-called 'villa' near Tibur was undoubtedly the place he loved best in the whole world. The exceptional character of this vast complex of buildings – all very different from one another, and sited amid hills and valleys that were doubtless tree-clad even in antiquity – reveals the satisfaction he derived from designing them. Their variety is amazing (see p. 356). While some parts have an intimate quality that invites relaxation

267

303 TIVOLI (TIBUR): HADRIAN'S VILLA. THE 'TEATRO MARITTIMO' (DETAIL)

and meditation, elsewhere we find buildings of striking amplitude and solemnity – the former being designed for private use, and the latter for the reception of numerous guests, as libraries and baths, or for the evocation of mythological cult-imagery (this last also serving as a good excuse for parading replicas of well-known works of art). This is what happened when a cultivated introvert was able to realize his most extravagant dreams, and to evoke local atmosphere in a manner wholly consonant with his personal feelings. The result was a most extraordinary complex of buildings, which because of their picturesque nature have always, throughout the ages, continued to charm and fascinate those who visit them. Yet much detailed work (and not only in the architectural sphere) remains to be done on them; we do not even know what purpose some of them served.

The most unusual buildings, architecturally speaking, are those known respectively as the Teatro Marittimo, the Piazza d'Oro and the Canopus. The first might be described as an elegant little villa, totally isolated by a circular moat with a drawbridge. Round the moat there ran a circular vaulted portico. From this the visitor gained access to two large enclosed chambers, one to the north, the other (of apsidal design) to the west. On the east side was a large courtyard. This in turn led to what would appear to have been the actual residential quarters – or, more precisely, one section of the private apartments. From here one reached a wing occupied by a suite of rooms, all opening on to the same wide corridor; these, it has been suggested, were the quarters reserved for guests. Each room is floored with a different mosaic – pleasant black-and-white work such

304 TIVOLI (TIBUR): HADRIAN'S VILLA. PAVEMENT MOSAIC: CENTAUR AND WILD BEASTS. BERLIN, STAATLICHE MUSEEN

305 HADRIAN'S VILLA, GUEST CHAMBER. PAVEMENT MOSAIC

as is typical of both the Hadrianic age and that which followed it. In other parts of the Villa poly-chrome mosaics with figures have come to light, which mark a return to the Hellenistic technique of reproducing paintings. During Hadrian's reign a certain typical kind of decoration in black-and-white became popular for floor mosaics, and heralded the emergence of mosaic work as an independent art. During the third century in particular, it became a characteristic feature of Roman culture.

The title of Piazza d'Oro has been attached to a big arcaded peristyle, located behind the supposedly residential quarter. Access to it was by way of an octagonal room with four circular apses. The longer sides of this peristyle are flanked by cryptoportici; at its bottom end it leads into a suite of rooms, the purpose of which it is impossible to determine. These rooms are connected to a construction of bold design – indeed, in its particular *genre*, unique. The ground-plan is square, with semi-circular apses set in each corner. On this base the architect has inscribed a pattern of curvilinear walls, running either concave or convex in relation to the centre, and giving rise to an array of semi-cupolas and columned openings. The latter provide a series of views in depth, either

306 TIVOLI (TIBUR): HADRIAN'S VILLA. PAVEMENT MOSAIC (DETAIL). BERLIN, STAATLICHE MUSEEN

308 TIVOLI (TIBUR): HADRIAN'S VILLA. INTERIOR VIEW OF THE 'CANOPUS' (DETAIL)

through to the rooms down either side, or else into that directly opposite, which is closed off by the curvilinear façade of a large fountain (*nymphaeum*). In the façade are a number of niches, both round and rectangular. This sequence of rooms can never have been intended for any utilitarian purpose. What it suggests, rather, is the result of picking up the boldest innovations made possible by the new building techniques first brought in under the Flavians, and carrying them, gratuituously, to extremes. Though we may admire its astonishing potential, this architectonic virtuosity (which constitutes an end in itself) is ultimately limited – and condemned – by its own exclusively intellectual character. In point of fact it remained without issue or development, even at the time. To us it appears very much the equivalent of a literary effort such as the *Laudes Fumi et Pulveris* ('In Praise of Smoke and Dust'), on which Fronto the rhetorician, Marcus Aurelius's tutor, expended so much linguistic virtuosity. The feeling behind it, beyond any doubt, was not classical but baroque.

The 'Canopus' (a name attested by our historical sources, and evocative of Egyptian memories) consisted of a narrow valley between two heights (on one of which, today known as Roccabruna, there stood another group of residential buildings). The entrance to this narrow valley was flanked by a series of small rectangular buildings, the rest of its length being taken up by a long canal-like pool. Closing off the pool, at the far end, there rose a high architectural façade, at the centre of which was a large niche with a waterfall cascading down it. The Canopus has yielded numerous excellent copies of classical

309 TIVOLI (TIBUR): HADRIAN'S VILLA. COPY OF THE 'AMAZON' OF PHEIDIAS

statues. Among others recently found there are replicas of the Caryatids from the Erechtheum in Athens, and a marble copy of Pheidias's *Amazon*.

As time went on, burial rather than cremation became increasingly popular among the well-to-do classes. This fact was of special importance for Roman art – and also, indeed, for the pervasive influence which it had on the art of the Middle Ages and the early Renaissance in Europe. The practice led to a growing vogue for marble sarcophagi, decorated with reliefs, and the setting up of specialized workshops, in Athens and Rome as well as throughout Asia Minor. This fashion seems to have developed as a result of close contacts with the Hellenized cities of Asia Minor – now flourishing as never before – which had been using sarcophagi for centuries. At the same time we should not forget the way in which Roman culture was becoming increasingly addicted to philosophical and religious symbolism: both acquired a very special importance in all artistic work connected with funerary monuments.

The most ancient sarcophagus from this period, of Roman provenance, bears the name of G. Bellicus Natalis Tebianus (who had been Consul in 87) and is preserved in the Camposanto at Pisa. It is decorated with garlands, a very common motif in Asia Minor and at Alexandria. Between the garlands are a number of small mythological scenes. Though these too reveal Hellenistic influence, typologically they constitute an innovation. The present state of our knowledge suggests that they should probably be attributed to some workshop in Rome. However, the recent discovery of paintings in the necropolis at Tyre, where we find mythical subjects being used to fill the blank space above the garlands, shows us that during this period the same motif was also widespread in Syria.

In other typologically similar examples from Hadrian's reign the device attains a considerable degree of elegance and subtlety: see, for instance, the sarcophagus from the Louvre which carries a sequence of episodes connected with the legend of Actaeon. Another innovation which marks the products of the Roman workshops is the practice of

310 ROME: SARCOPHAGUS. THE MYTH OF DIANA, WITH GARLANDS (DETAIL). PARIS, LOUVRE

decorating sarcophagi on three sides only. The fourth side, left plain, was set against the wall of the tomb, which always kept, essentially, the shape and dimensions of a room, according to ancient Italic practice. On the other hand, those sarcophagi imported from Greece and Asia Minor have all four sides decorated, which presupposes a type of tomb in the form of a small edifice or shrine (*heroön*), with the sarcophagus at its centre.

The type of Roman sarcophagus most popular in Hadrian's day is well illustrated by the two specimens found in a tomb which (thanks to its brick-marks) can be dated to between AD 132 and 134, together with a garlanded sarcophagus like that described above. The coffin-shells are innocent of any element which might suggest design or structure, such as we always find with Greek sarcophagi – e.g. imitation of a wooden coffin, or an attempt to convey some notion of architectonic cohesion. This indifference as regards logical organic structure is a typical Mid-Italic and Roman phenomenon. Here we have one reason why the reliefs appear to be inspired by Hellenistic graphic compositions on mythological themes, and show a marked preference for compositions with an abundance of figures. These two examples illustrate the myths of Orestes and the children of Niobe. In the latter case, we should note how the artist has represented the protagonists in the massacre, Apollo and Artemis, by relegating them to the panels at the corners of the coffin-lid, and reducing their proportions, as though to suggest their

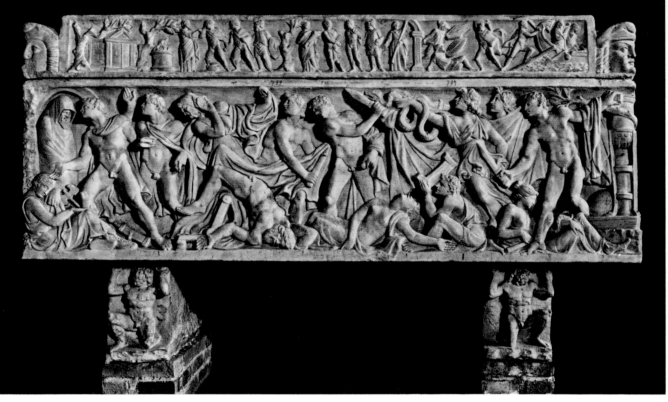

311 ROME: SARCOPHAGUS. THE MYTH OF ORESTES. VATICAN (LATERAN MUSEUM)

312 ROME: SARCOPHAGUS. THE MYTH OF NIOBE'S CHILDREN. VATICAN (LATERAN MUSEUM)

313 ROME: SARCOPHAGUS (DETAIL). THE DEATH OF AEGISTHUS. VATICAN (LATERAN MUSEUM)

315 ROME: SARCOPHAGUS. THE MYTH OF ORESTES. ROME, PALAZZO GIUSTINIANI

remoteness in the sky. It is very easy to imagine them being thus represented in a painting. We can understand the way these workshop artists went about their business if we study another sarcophagus portraying the myth of Orestes (Rome, Palazzo Giustiniani). The same 'cartoon' has been employed for the principal figures, but the characters round them have been simplified. This was mass production, of high quality admittedly, but invariably standardized. The prospective purchaser would choose, from among a number of set themes, that which best suited both the occasion and his pocket. However vast the production of Roman sarcophagi, this factory remained constant, even when (about the end of the second century) mythological subjects went out of fashion and were replaced by scenes connected with the daily life of Rome. Specially commissioned jobs, which mark a breakaway from the stock workshop repertoire, must be regarded as quite exceptional, and always indicative of some very important person. It follows that the sarcophagi can provide us with direct evidence concerning the line of development which Roman-period art took after Trajan and Hadrian. Here, too, we have confirmation for the establishment of a new and authentic Imperial Roman art.

◀ 314 ROME: SARCOPHAGUS (DETAIL). NIOBE. VATICAN (LATERAN MUSEUM)

6 The First Crisis in the Hellenistic Tradition: The Antonines

For almost the whole of the first century AD, certainly until the time of the Flavians, Rome had been able to regard herself as the heir to the Hellenistic kingdoms. Her emperors, together with the Senate, felt that they were still carrying out Alexander the Great's policies as interpreted by his direct successors, even if the centre of power had moved to Rome. Under Trajan, Rome's position as the hub of the Empire was deliberately emphasized, and reinforced by the construction of new monuments. With Hadrian, however, we see an attempt to bind Rome and the culturally Hellenistic provinces into a single whole by encouraging fresh building projects in the ancient cities. In Athens a whole new quarter of monumental edifices arose – 'no longer Theseus' city but Hadrian's', it was said – which was approached through an arch of curious form and undoubtedly Hellenistic inspiration. Beyond it there now stood a library (with one hundred columns of *pavonazzetto* marble), a Pantheon, and temples of Hera and Zeus Panhellenios; the colossal temple of Olympian Zeus, which Antiochus IV Epiphanes of Syria had left unfinished three centuries earlier, was now completed.

Under Trajan and Hadrian, an efficient administration gave the provinces unprecedented economic stability, and a fresh stimulus to development. Yet during the same period in Rome itself, the economic and administrative situation – not to mention military problems – grew progressively more serious. The creation of an Imperial art coincides with a change in the structure of the Empire. This change becomes increasingly obvious under the Antonines, a period which saw the provinces acquiring more and more influence at the expense of Italy. The most active provinces now were the old Hellenistic Eastern kingdoms, which produced a steady stream of writers, doctors, craftsmen, philosophers and magicians, as well as artists and works of art. At the other end of the Mediterranean, the only provinces to show any signs of originality in their literary, philosophical or artistic output were towards the western side of North Africa: Africa Proconsularis, Numidia and Mauretania (corresponding to Tunisia and parts of Libya, Algeria and Morocco). However, nothing which emerged from these provinces, whether Oriental or Occidental, could be characterized as 'provincial'. This term must be kept for the products of territories traversed by the Danube, and for any artifact from an area, embracing Britain, Gaul, and northern Italy as far as the arch of the Apennines, which might be labelled 'European'. The provinces of the Hellenistic East, in particular, had close ties with Rome, and were responsible for the liveliest cultural developments, as well as providing the most active politicians, administrators and military leaders.

This was the situation immediately preceding that which led to the *Constitutio Antoniniana* of Caracalla, in 212, by which the privilege of Roman citizenship was legally extended to almost every provincial, with a view to consolidating the unity of the Empire. The process of interpenetration between Rome and the provinces had gone so far under the Antonines that for any subsequent period it becomes impossible to view Roman art from a standpoint based on Rome. The historical transformation which now began was to culminate, a century and a half later, in the transfer of the centre of power from the old to the new Rome, Constantinople (founded in 324 and inaugurated in 330).

As stated earlier, the problem of the succession – a formidable one, since those concerned would never openly admit the monarchic nature of their power – had been solved by the device of adoption. This was applied in all cases from Nerva to Marcus Aurelius. The lines of descent are complicated, to say the least of it. Before his death, Trajan adopted Hadrian, a distant relative of his; the adoption did not go unchallenged. Matidia (to whom, as we have seen, Hadrian later dedicated a temple) had been married twice. By her first husband she bore Vibia Sabina, who afterwards became Hadrian's wife; by her second, Rupilia Faustina. The latter married Annius Verus, three times consul, to whom she bore a son of the same name, and a daughter, the Elder Faustina, who married Hadrian's adoptive son and successor, Antoninus Pius. The younger Annius Verus died in 130, having nine years previously begotten a son whom we know by the name of Marcus Aurelius, and who – once more at Hadrian's command – was adopted by Antoninus Pius. In 145 he married the latter's daughter, the Younger Faustina. Hadrian, meanwhile, had carried out a second adoption, that of L. Aelius Caesar; but this came to nothing, since the young man died before the Emperor himself. However, Aelius had left a son, Lucius Verus, whom Marcus Aurelius created joint-Emperor and married to his daughter Lucilla. On Marcus Aurelius's death in 180, the succession, unfortunately, went to his son, L. Aurelius Commodus, whose faults the philosopher Emperor knew all too well, but whom he had created his Imperial associate at a very early age. Born in 161, he was the sole surviving male heir from a family of thirteen children, most of whom were girls. It was this genealogically complex family (see p. 386) which governed the Empire between 138 and 192: a time which saw the first crisis of the Empire and the first break with Hellenistic-style Roman art.

Of particular note among the few surviving monuments from the reign of Antoninus Pius is a group of reliefs (from the temple of the deified Hadrian, dedicated in 145) in which the provinces are personified: for this, in a way, symbolizes the new links which had developed between Rome and the whole provincial world. In the Piazza di Pietra, at the very heart of Rome, we can still see eleven of the thirteen columns which formed one side of this temple. The figures representing provinces were probably ornamental additions to a plinth, which supported the engaged columns used to decorate the inner face of the temple walls. The whole edifice was roofed with vaulting which, at its highest point, was nearly sixty feet clear of the ground. In their close association with the plinths,

317 ROME: HADRIAN'S TEMPLE. FRAGMENT OF RELIEF PORTRAYING TWO ROMAN PROVINCES. ROME, PALAZZO DEI CONSERVATORI

these figures acquired a symbolic value: they were, so to speak, the foundation on which the Imperial structure rested. This symbolism is in line with the climate of thought current at the time, and is further expressed by the stance of the figures, which shows no signs of submissiveness. Stylistically, a vague classicism still prevails, and one cannot detect any attempt to distinguish these personified figures by giving them the physical features associated with various ethnic groups. But that striving after visual effect which is so typical of the Hadrianic period comes out strongly in the deep chisel-strokes used to make the figures stand out against their background; it is also seen in the use of the running ground-auger (see p. 316). Some twenty of these figures have now come to light: three are in Naples, two in the Villa Doria-Pamphili, two more in the Palazzo Odescalchi, one in the Palazzo Farnese and one in the Lateran – apart from the seven rather better-known examples in the Palazzo dei Conservatori, and four others which are now lost.

Further developments in the new style of Roman architecture, pioneered under Nero (though it later reverted to the ornamental airs and graces of Hellenism), are confirmed by the buildings which we find reproduced on coins, e.g. the round temples of Cybele and Bacchus in the Forum Romanum (see p. 352).

318 ROME: PORTRAIT OF LUCIUS VERUS. ROME, MUSEO NAZIONALE

The portraits from this period, such as those of Lucius Verus or the young Marcus Aurelius, accentuate the velvet-smooth texture which sculptors had already begun to bestow on flesh in Hadrian's reign, and which is typical of certain workshops in Asia Minor. They also show further effort to achieve striking effects with hair, beard, and drapery. On the other hand, the relief portraying the apotheosis of Sabina (despite extensive restoration, including almost all of Hadrian's head as well as that of the person next to him) adheres strictly to the traditional classicism of the Attic studios. Even its

319 ROME: PORTRAIT OF MARCUS AURELIUS AS A YOUTH. ROME, ANTIQUARIUM DI FORO

320 ROME: THE APOTHEOSIS OF SABINA. ROME, PALAZZO DEI CONSERVATORI

iconography follows the Greek pattern, and this despite the fact that apotheosis as a concept had long been deep embedded in Roman culture. Above the funeral pyre, and the young man who personifies the Campus Martius, we see the dead Sabina being borne away by a winged figure somewhat like a Victory; the diagonal break in the composition likewise reveals a rhythm which imitates classical style. However, the decision to make a relief portraying this wholly unreal and symbolic event marked a real conceptual innovation. It was something quite different from the accurately delineated historical scenes which Roman commemorative art had hitherto preferred, and the vogue for metaphysical symbolism which it introduced grew steadily more pronounced. About twenty-five years later we encounter another scene of apotheosis, this time on the base of the column erected in commemoration of Antoninus Pius by his successors Marcus Aurelius and Lucius Verus.

This column stood in the Campus Martius (roughly on the present site of the Montecitorio obelisk, originally set up by Augustus as the *gnomon* of a huge sundial). It was a pink granite monolith, undecorated, and topped by a statue of the Emperor with Jupiter's attributes. The dedicatory inscription refers to Antoninus alone; but in the relief, an apotheosis reunites the Emperor with his wife Faustina, who had died twenty years earlier. The symbolic element, then, is becoming more marked. The winged figure, interpreted as *Aeternitas* in the Sabina relief, where it is feminine, here becomes male, and must accordingly be seen as *Aiôn*. This is the personification of absolute time, as

286

321 ROME: BASE OF ANTONINUS PIUS'S COLUMN. APOTHEOSIS OF ANTONINUS AND FAUSTINA. VATICAN, CORTILE DELLA PIGNA

opposed to *Chronos*, time conceived in relation to human life, and long since characterized in classical thought (as in Plato, *Timaeus* 37). But here *Aiôn* was probably portrayed
– in accordance with the Oriental mystery-cults – as embodying the attributes of supreme
godhead, or even as the Supreme Being, primordial and eternal, Time perpetually
renewed. Though the style bears a superficial resemblance to that of the Sabina relief,
there are significant differences. In contrast to that immobility which reduces the
symbolic seated figures down below (Rome and the Campus Martius) to the level of
mere objects, the great winged daemon embodies a sense of dynamic upward movement;
we can almost *see* its silent ascent, the wide beat and thrust of its gigantic wings. Clever
little touches lift the work out of its apparent classicism: the left wing extends beyond
the corner of the background; the shield held by the figure personifying Rome breaks
the outline of the composition; and a fold of drapery hangs down over the base of the
column. These all hint at a transition towards a form of expression that is richer in colour
and movement, that breaks the restricting classical moulds. The shorter sides of the base
allow greater scope to these new trends, as in the relief which shows a 'merry-go-round'

287

322 ROME: BASE OF ANTONINUS PIUS'S COLUMN. CAVALCADE. VATICAN, CORTILE DELLA PIGNA

of horsemen. What, in fact, is being performed here is the *decursio*, an ancient ritual in honour of the dead. A group of mounted soldiers (in this case Praetorians) would ride three times round the funeral pyre or the tumulus covering the grave. This ceremony was followed by parades, races, or mock-fights between dismounted cavalrymen. The figures on foot at the centre of the 'merry-go-round' must have to do with this second part of the programme. The whole scene looks almost like a transposition into alto-relievo of that unassuming relief (chariot-race watched by husband and wife) examined in the last chapter. Another parallel is a relief preserved at Foligno, again with a racing theme. Both stem from the 'plebeian' tradition, which was basic to the Roman historical relief. What we have here is the old 'plebeian' approach, dressed up in a new and formally elaborate

323 ROME: BASE OF ANTONINUS PIUS'S COLUMN. CAVALCADE (DETAIL) ▶

324 RELIEF: RACES IN THE CIRCUS. FOLIGNO, MUSEO ARCHEOLOGICO

325 RELIEF: RACES IN THE CIRCUS (DETAIL). FOLIGNO, MUSEO ARCHEOLOGICO

326 ROME: FORUM ROMANUM. TEMPLE OF ANTONINUS AND FAUSTINA

manner, with much violent chiaroscuro and a general flavour of the baroque. On the base of the monument we can observe a phenomenon which was to be a commonplace in early Renaissance painting, especially associated with the predellas of large altarpieces. It is here, on a less prominent part – the exact equivalent of the predella – that the artist gives freest expression to thematic novelties and changing modes: for such innovations could still offend a conformist official patron. The same Imperial couple were the dedicatees of a temple in the Forum Romanum, still preserved in part, and originally consecrated by Antoninus to Faustina alone.

The taste for violent contrasts of light and shade – worked out by means of a technical virtuosity which

327 ROME: TEMPLE OF FAUSTINA. ROME, MUSEO NAZIONALE

328 OSTIA, ISOLA SACRA: PORTRAIT OF VOLCACIUS MYROPNOUS. OSTIA MUSEUM

treated marble as though it were clay – found expression in numerous portraits. We may cite that of a young man called Volcacius Myropnous, from Ostia, which can be dated before the death of Antoninus Pius, and several studies of Commodus – the first as a youth, the second made about the time of his accession (where he looks like a contemporary of Louis-Philippe), and the third from the end of his life, when he had taken to dressing up as Hercules and was completely in the grip of his politico-religious mania.

329 LATIUM: OFFICIAL BUST OF THE YOUNG COMMODUS. ROME, MUSEO CAPITOLINO

330 ROME: PORTRAIT-BUST OF COMMODUS, AGED 20. VATICAN, MUSEO PIO CLEMENTINO

331 ROME: BUST OF COMMODUS AS HERCULES. ROME, PALAZZO DEI CONSERVATORI ▶

332 THE VATICAN (GROTTE VATICANE): TOMB OF THE VALERII. STUCCO HEAD

Decorations in stucco were especially popular in this period, and embodied all the new artistic features we have been discussing. The treatment of the medium shows great lightness and fluidity, as though it had been laid on with a brush. Indeed, it may have been. What points in this direction is the probable use, as an ingredient for preparing stucco, of what was known as 'Punic wax'. This served as a binder in mural painting, and enabled the fresco to achieve great variety of texture, ranging from the fluidity of water-colour to a thick impasto effect (see E. Schiavi, *Il sale della terra*, Milan 1961).

In painting, the traditional schemes of mural decoration were now abandoned. Nevertheless, some of the old motifs – such as that of seaside villas – continued to be repeated (one example can be seen in a house under S. Sebastiano, on the Via Appia). These motifs now reveal a new experimentation with perspective, which accentuates their quality of airy depth. In general, however, we find a trend towards simplicity in

334 ROME: HOUSE UNDER S. SEBASTIANO. PAINTING OF SEASIDE VILLAS ▶

333 THE VATICAN (GROTTE VATICANE): TOMB OF THE VALERII. DECORATED NICHE

335 OSTIA: 'HOUSE OF THE PAINTED CEILINGS'. CEILING OF A ROOM

ornamental motifs, and often also a certain untutored roughness of manner, which tends to isolate the motifs from their surroundings. This facilitates the artist's work, and makes it easier for him to employ a wide range of subject-matter; but it also increases the decorative value of the motif itself, by giving it immediate impact. To isolate any motif increases its effectiveness, as modern designers, nurtured on advertising techniques, know very well. Mosaic pavements now reveal similar tendencies: cartoons based on the requirements of painting are deliberately jettisoned, to be replaced by a new and idiosyncratic style which belongs to pavement-mosaics alone.

336 OSTIA, ISOLA SACRA: CEILING OF A TOMB (DETAIL). MERCURY. OSTIA MUSEUM

337 ROME: A MAENAD. ROME, MUSEO NAZIONALE

338 OSTIA, PORTA LAURENTINA: NECROPOLIS, TOMBS

339 ROME, VIA APPIA: TOMB OF ANNIA REGILLA

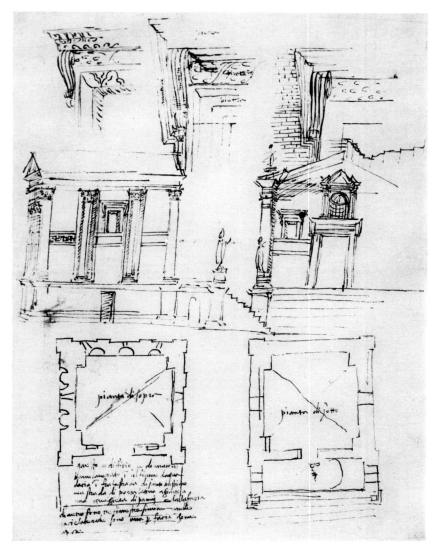

340 ROME: TOMB OF ANNIA REGILLA, AFTER A SKETCH BY A. DA SANGALLO

Architecture in unfaced brick, which had come to the fore under Trajan and Hadrian, continued to be used for a variety of buildings: funerary monuments, apartment blocks, warehouses, and large commercial emporia, of which there are magnificent examples at Ostia. Sometimes the architect obtained a sober particoloured effect by using alternate courses of brick and pumice. In such basically unpretentious buildings the design was kept simple, and the effect is achieved by the beautifully calculated proportional relationship between the design as a whole and the solid and hollow parts of the outer walls. The techniques employed were still of great interest to the architects of the Renaissance, as we can tell from the countless surviving sketches they made of them – some of these being proper plans drawn to scale. These architects range from Baldassarre Peruzzi (1481-1536) to the Sangallo family – Giuliano (1445-1516), his brother Antonio (1455-1534), and Antonio the Younger (1483-1546). Even the Appian Way tomb of Annia Regilla, who was married to the immensely wealthy Herodes Atticus, bears witness to the same formal moderation and sobriety of taste.

341 ROME: SARCOPHAGUS. BATTLE AGAINST THE GALATIANS. ROME, MUSEO CAPITOLINO

342 OSTIA: SARCOPHAGUS. THE MYTH OF ALCESTIS. VATICAN, MUSEO CHIARAMONTI

The sarcophagi, by contrast, evolve an extremely lively type of high-relief sculpture, partly based on Hellenistic models, and in particular on the art of Pergamum. These models predominate in scenes portraying battles against barbarians, who are generally represented as Galatians. When the artist adapted an older design, he tended to keep the original fashions, as we can see in the treatment of the hair and other such details. A good example is provided by a sarcophagus now in the Vatican, which illustrates the story of Alcestis. Euripides' version of the myth of Alcestis – the wife who volunteered to die in her husband's stead, and who was brought back to the world of the living by Heracles – was widely known. It was especially well suited to funerary symbolism, as an emblem

343 ROME: SARCOPHAGUS. BATTLE AGAINST THE GALATIANS (DETAIL). ROME, MUSEO CAPITOLINO ▶

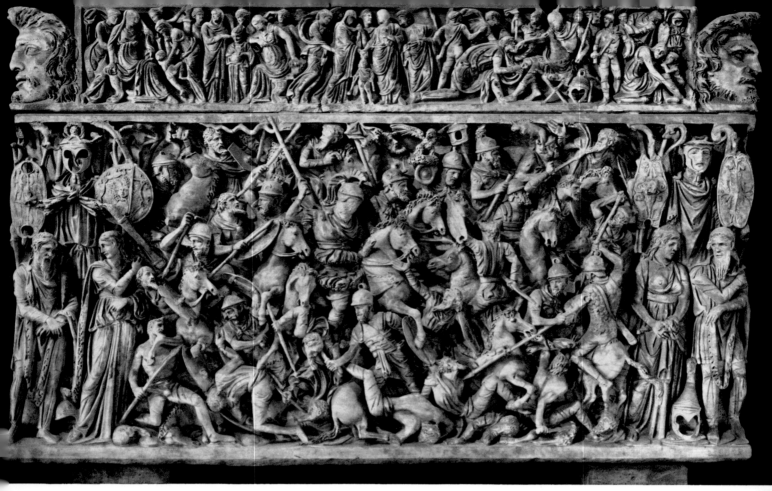

both of conjugal fidelity, and of that life after death which devotees of the mystery cults looked to as their ultimate reward. In one tomb on the Via Latina this myth recurs in the mid-fourth century AD in a Christian context (see A. Grabar, *The Beginnings of Christian Art*, 'Arts of Mankind' series, pl. 251).

During the period 180-200, side by side with the generalized iconography of battle against the barbarians, there also developed a new and specifically Roman type of monumental sarcophagus. We find battle scenes here too, with one side explicitly identified as Romans, and their opponents as barbarians from the tribes on Rome's northern frontiers, though whether Marcomanni, Celts, Quadi or Roxolani is not made clear. One of the most important examples of this *genre* is the sarcophagus from Portonaccio on the Via Casilina (now in the Museo Nazionale Romano), which, we may assume, contained the body of some general who served under Marcus Aurelius. The head of the central figure is left blank, which shows that even so finely wrought a piece of work as this was based on a stock pattern, and would be completed by inserting the portrait of the dead man for whom it had been ordered.

The workshop responsible for this sarcophagus – along with several others, now variously in Rome (Palazzo Giustiniani), Frascati (the Villa Taverna) and Perugia

346-7 ROME: SARCOPHAGUS OF ONE OF MARCUS AURELIUS'S GENERALS (DETAILS). CAPTIVE BARBARIANS. ROME, MUSEO NAZIONALE

(Museo Nazionale) – was also, it seems certain, at work during the same period on the Antonine Column. Nevertheless, the sarcophagus shows greater subtlety of execution, and a surer sense of composition in the scenes themselves, which alternate and interweave with an elegant striving after spatial effect that cheerfully meets and surmounts all technical difficulties. The figures of the barbarian prisoners, shown in miserably dejected attitudes, are a legacy from Trajan's reign, it is true; but the increased sense of pathos which they convey is in line with a general growing tendency to strive after emotional effect. In this connection, we may note a phenomenon which has not, as yet, been the subject of systematic study. In Roman sculpture, that special pathos in the expression which denotes, not physical pain but agony of spirit, first appears in the 'plebeian' sculpture of Northern Italy, and in Romano-Gallic art; subsequently it spread into Pannonia. This observation has a certain general interest when one considers how often the same expression of spiritual suffering turns up in third-century portraits, even those of children.

Hadrian and Antoninus Pius had succeeded in governing the Empire by means of prudent and vigilant diplomacy. But during the reign of Marcus Aurelius (who had

348 ROME: SARCOPHAGUS OF ONE OF MARCUS AURELIUS'S GENERALS (DETAIL). DYING BARBARIAN. ROME, MUSEO NAZIONALE

349 EQUESTRIAN STATUE OF MARCUS AURELIUS (DETAIL). ROME: THE CAPITOL

immediately taken Lucius Verus as co-Emperor) the pressure on the frontiers, first in the East, then in the North, became so great that recourse to military action was virtually inevitable. Anything less would have risked breaking the hinge that held the Empire's Eastern and Western halves together. This crucial central point lay in the general area of the Danube, covering the provinces of Noricum, Pannonia and Moesia, against which the Sarmatian tribes were exerting strong pressure. In the East the Parthian Empire – the only power that had always been capable of holding its own against the Romans – was now challenging Rome's supremacy in Armenia, and imperilling the safety of the commercial caravan-routes into Central Asia.

Chinese annals for the year AD 166 record the arrival from Amman of an embassy sent by Ngan-toun (or Ant-toun) – that is, Marcus Aurelius Antoninus. This embassy, passed over in silence by our Roman sources, shows how important a role commercial relations were coming to assume. In all likelihood the mission consisted of merchants rather than official envoys; and the gifts with which they arrived in China – ivory, rhinoceros-horns and tortoise-shells – had undoubtedly been acquired during the course of their journey. This penetration of the Far East was encouraged by the recent discovery of the regular monsoon winds.

Marcus Aurelius detested war; but when the affairs of State seemed to demand it, he went out on campaign, enduring all the hardships involved with that lofty sense of duty which inspired all his actions (see p. 326). For him, philosophy was more than an intellectual game; and in this respect he showed more insight than did his tutor Fronto, whose correspondence with Marcus Aurelius and Lucius Verus still survives. For Marcus Aurelius, Stoic philosophy had become a religion. In his wholly humanist creed, reason, which proceeded from God, was the common measure of all good men, whatever their race or condition; reason drew them all naturally together, as members of the same human family. Moral law, here conceived as divine law, was in itself a religious act; when practised, it brought its own reward, and no one could look to it for any further recompense, in this world or the next. All that one got from it was that satisfaction which a man experiences when he obeys his sense of duty, in accordance with his nature as a reasonable being, and with the general laws both of the world and of God. Such sentiments are often voiced in Marcus Aurelius's *Meditations* (e.g. 12.29). Composed in Greek, the language of philosophy,

350 EQUESTRIAN STATUE OF MARCUS AURELIUS. ROME: THE CAPITOL

this man's spiritual journal, written to achieve self-mastery and self-guidance – as the original title, 'To Himself', makes clear – still remains one of the noblest documents of true humanism, one of the most agonizing accounts of a life sacrificed to duty, ever written. 'A little while yet, and I shall be dead, and everything ended for me. What purpose, then, in seeking further, if now I conduct myself as an intelligent, sociable being, obedient to the same laws as those of God?' (8.2.1-2). The religious anguish which one senses on every page of the *Meditations* is a typical feature of the age in which they were composed. Without the sustaining curb of rational discipline, such a state of mind soon lapsed into superstition, and was wide open to irrational excesses of every sort, magic in particular. No one better exemplified this process than Marcus Aurelius's son Commodus.

For the Eastern campaign, Lucius Verus held the supreme command, but the actual conduct of operations was in the hands of a number of distinguished generals. Two armies entered Mesopotamia in 165, crossed the Euphrates in the direction of Doura-Europos, reached the Tigris, and occupied both Seleucia and Ctesiphon, where the royal palace was destroyed. Lucius took the title of *Parthicus Maximus*; before the war was over, we find him writing to Fronto, asking him to hold himself in readiness for the task of composing an account of the campaign. Fronto is to emphasize how badly things had gone before Lucius's arrival, making it 'crystal clear' that until then the Parthians had had things very much their own way (Fronto, *Ad Verum Imp*. 2.3, ed. Haines, Vol. 2, pp. 194f.). This attitude of Lucius's is symptomatic of the general psychological climate which was, at the same moment, driving Lucian to compose his stinging essay on 'How to Write History'. This piece is directed against the gross flatterers who compare 'our captain to Achilles and the Persian monarch to Thersites, not realizing that their Achilles would cut a better figure if instead of Thersites he had Hector as his opponent', and who, 'quite shamelessly', wrote that 'at the Europos there perished 370,236 of the enemy, while the Romans had only two dead and nine wounded' (Lucian, *Quomodo Hist. est Conscrib*. 14.2, 20.3). Here we see the first reflection of that contemptuous attitude towards the enemy which so sharply distinguishes the sculptured scenes on the two great Columns, those of Trajan and Marcus Aurelius, being wholly absent from the first and predominating in the second. For centuries to come this new mood was to obliterate the spirit of tolerance and justice which had remained a living force throughout Marcus Aurelius's reign, the legacy of Greek *paideia*.

In 166, the towns of Carrhae and Doura became Roman *coloniae*, and Rome's authority over Armenia was secure. That same year, after a campaign that had lasted five years and cost a fortune, the two emperors celebrated their triumph. At Lucius's suggestion, the two sons of Marcus Aurelius – the five-year-old Commodus, and Annius Verus, now three – each received the title of Caesar. It was half a century since the citizens of Rome had witnessed a triumph; and the last one, Trajan's, had been celebrated posthumously.

However, in the winter of 166/7 there took place the first invasion by tribesmen from the North, an event which marked the beginning of their great migrations. Six thousand Lombards and Obii swarmed into Upper Pannonia, and in due course were hurled back. There followed an attack on the Dacian gold-mines. Behind these invaders came the

Marcomanni and the Quadi. who in fact represented a vast coalition of Germanic tribes under the leadership of Ballomar, the king of the Marcomanni. The returning Eastern army brought an epidemic with it, which spread from one staging-post to the next, finally reaching Rome, where it caused many deaths. It may have been either smallpox, exanthematous typhus or true plague. The famous physician Galen came to Rome in person, but soon afterwards returned to Pergamum. The fact that people at once ascribed some kind of magical or religious origin to this epidemic is typical of the increase in superstitious beliefs during the period. Nor was there any lack of impostors, from Rome to the furthest Eastern provinces, who made it their business to profit by such credulity. As a sop to public opinion, the city of Rome was purified by priests of every religion. Marcus Aurelius wrote (9.2.4): 'The name of plague I bestow – and with better reason – on the corruption of human intelligence, rather than on that comparable infection and metamorphosis of the atmosphere we breathe. The latter plague does but attack animals in their animal natures, whereas the former infects men as human beings.' Throughout this period Lucius was throwing extravagant parties in his villa on the Via Claudia, and surrounding himself with a crowd of actors he had brought back from Syria and Alexandria. As the historian Julius Capitolinus later remarked (*Vita Veri* 8.6-11), 'One might have thought he had just won a war against the theatre.'

A story which typifies this whole period is that of Glycon, a supposed reincarnation of Asclepius, whose cult, from the reign of Antoninus Pius onwards, flourished in Paphlagonia, Dacia and Moesia, perhaps even in Rome. Mysteries, complete with full sacred ritual, were instituted in his honour. At Parium, his cenotaph and cult-statue were displayed in the market-place (Athenagoras, 26). Both cult and oracle were in fact the work of a hoaxer called Alexander, who started the whole thing in the town of Abono-teichos. A handsome man, and by nature a cheerful opportunist, he claimed to be the disciple of Apollonius of Tyana, and actually succeeded in marrying off his daughter to a former proconsul of Asia. This dignitary, Rutilianus, protected him on a number of occasions, even when his activities came very close to sedition. To help in creating the 'oracle of Glycon', Alexander made use of a large tame snake which he had brought back from Pella in Macedonia. This creature he fitted out with a quasi-human movable head, made of painted cloth and horsehair. In this guise his improvised deity bore some resemblance to the widely known hypostasis of Khnum, the creator god of late Egyptian mythology, who features on numerous Gnostic gems as a lion-headed serpent. Although that sceptical freethinker Lucian of Samosata had, on several occasions, unmasked the false prophet as a common charlatan (Lucian, *Alexander Pseudomantis* 13-19), the cult of Glycon lasted for about a century, and is represented on some coin-issues of the period. His image has been found at Tomis (*pl. 352*).

In the spring 168 the two Emperors set out on an expedition against the Marcomanni and the Quadi, and established their camp at Aquileia. Despite Marcus Aurelius's insistence that they must take a personal part in the conduct of the campaign, Lucius Verus was determined to return to Rome. On his way back, near Altinum, he died in an accident. After his death the military command was given to Tiberius Claudius Pompeianus, a Syrian from Antioch who belonged to the Equestrian Order and for the past two years had been Governor of Lower Pannonia. Pompeianus subsequently married

Lucius Verus's widow, Lucilla, the daughter of Marcus Aurelius. As son-in-law of the sole surviving Emperor, and commander-in-chief during a war which required several campaigns before it was wound up, he is portrayed in close attendance upon the Imperial person in all the sculptured monuments which we are shortly going to examine.

Meanwhile fresh attacks broke out in other frontier areas, and at one point the barbarians invaded Italy itself, penetrating as far south as Verona. The financial situation deteriorated so far that Marcus Aurelius was driven to auction off items from the Imperial collection – rich robes, tableware, statues and paintings – in order to avoid having to impose yet more taxes. These factors, together with the constant pressure being brought to bear in the Danube region, led the Emperor to decide on a large-scale expedition, the object of which would be to establish a new province beyond Dacia. From 171 to 173 Marcus Aurelius remained in camp with the legions based on Carnuntum (near Vienna). In 174 the Marcomanni and Quadi were defeated, and it become possible to deal more summarily with the Sarmatians, probably from an advance base at Aquincum (near Budapest). A revolt in the Near East forced Marcus Aurelius to hurry off to Syria, taking Faustina with him. The leading rebel was Avidius Cassius, a general with a distinguished record in the Parthian Wars, who had been granted wide powers after his successful expedition to put down an uprising in Egypt. Although Cassius's revolt had been quelled by the intervention of the Governor of Cappadocia before Marcus Aurelius appeared, the Emperor remained in the East until 176. On their way home Faustina died. In Rome, on 27 November, accompanied by Commodus, whom he had associated with himself as co-Emperor, Marcus Aurelius celebrated his second triumph – and also his return to the capital, after an eight years' absence. However, fresh trouble on the Danube front soon took him back again. On 17 March 180, in camp at Vindobona (modern Vienna), he fell victim to the epidemic which was still taking toll of his troops.

I have spent longer than usual on the events of Marcus Aurelius's reign because the chronological and interpretative problems raised by contemporary sculptures with a historical theme are closely related to them. In Rome, such sculptures not only provide evidence for the art of the Antonine period, but represent a fundamental turning-point in the formal language of Roman art as a whole.

Outside Rome, in the provinces, the most important single work of sculpture from this period is the great frieze at Ephesus, celebrating the achievements of the Antonines from the adoption of Antoninus Pius to Lucius Verus's victories over the Parthians. This frieze, with its lifesize figures carved in high relief, has not survived in its original form. Like the great frieze of Trajan (to which it constitutes a unique parallel) it was re-used at a later period, to enclose the basin of a nymphaeum built into the façade of that architectural jewel, the library-*heroön* of Celsus Aquila Polemeanus at Ephesus (datable to the first decade of Hadrian's reign). This great frieze, now in the Kunsthistorisches Museum in Vienna, must have required the collaboration of several master-artists; and the one responsible for the battle scenes was a genuine innovator.. Here, too, we may note a formal link with the Hellenistic sculptures at Pergamum; but in view of the greater emphasis on spatial freedom, the liveliness of the figures, and the novelty of the iconographic patterns employed, one could equally well posit the direct influence of the

Maestro della gesta di Traiano. We may note, above all, a predilection for placing figures obliquely, so that they seem to be moving either out of the background towards the spectator or vice-versa; the constant search for tonal effect; and the restrained use of the ground-auger (see p. 316) – here virtually limited to the hair, though it had been constantly utilized by Ephesian artists ever since the earliest monuments of Hadrian's reign.

We now come to one of the most hotly debated problems of Roman sculpture from this period: that of the three reliefs preserved on the staircase of the Palazzo dei Conservatori on the Capitol, and those other eight reliefs, of the same size, now inserted in the Attic storey of the Arch of Constantine. Although in the latter the head of the Emperor has been replaced (first by that of Constantine, then by other restored heads), the presence in each one of a recurrent character, identifiable as Tiberius Claudius Pompeianus, and always in the Emperor's immediate entourage, proves that these eleven reliefs all came from one or more monuments erected in honour of Marcus Aurelius. Discussion has centred on the original purpose of these reliefs, together with the type and location of the architectural monuments they were used to decorate. These arguments, which properly fall within the competence of the archaeologist, have obscured the importance of subjecting the works in question to a careful stylistic analysis. The three reliefs in the Palazzo dei Conservatori come from a church which stood in the Forum Romanum, on the site of an arch put up in honour of Marcus Aurelius to celebrate his triumph in 176. It follows that they probably came from this arch in the first place. But the eight reliefs from the Arch of Constantine are, beyond doubt, the products of a workshop which operated on very different lines. Hence the problem: did they form part of the same triumphal arch, or must we posit the existence of another monument? Both these hypotheses are possible; neither, at present, admits of conclusive proof. All that matters, as regards the history of artistic form, is that the thematic material of the eleven reliefs is taken from events which probably

351 EPHESUS: MONUMENT OF MARCUS AURELIUS AND L. VERUS. VIENNA

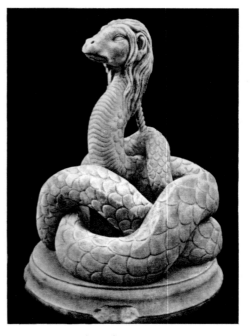

352 CONSTANTZA (TOMIS): THE SERPENT GLYCON

353 ROME: MARCUS AURELIUS SACRIFICING. ROME, P. DEI CONSERVATORI

occurred during a period after the death of Lucius Verus (that is, the wars against the Northern barbarians) but which perhaps antedated the triumph of 176. We may also ask ourselves whether Commodus was not originally portrayed on the reliefs, and, if so, whether his image may not have been effaced as a result of the *damnatio memoriae* which the Senate proclaimed immediately after his death in 192. Such a possibility exists, though the evidence is not clinching.

Another problem which now poses itself is working out just what relation there may have been between this series of reliefs and the sculptures on the Antonine Column, which was certainly complete by 193. In fact we possess a document attesting the fact that, in this same year, a portion of the timber which had served as scaffolding was made over to the custodian of the monument, so that he could build himself a little house with it. Yet as far as the history of art is concerned, what really emerges is the fact that between the three reliefs in the Palazzo dei Conservatori and the eight from the Arch of Constantine we can discern a radical change of artistic direction. This is not just a matter of taste or personal inclination. It represents the beginning of a wholly new concept, something destined to culminate in a genuine break with tradition. What we can trace here are the origins of the so-called *Spätantike*, the art of Late Antiquity in its pre-medieval phase.

That sculptors with quite different concepts of art should have collaborated on the same monument is perfectly possible. The important fact is that the three reliefs belong, without any doubt, to a traditional artistic phase of development, whereas the eight other ones exemplify a wholly new trend. The former, those in the Palazzo dei Conservatori, portray Marcus Aurelius in three scenes: on horseback, receiving the defeated barbarians; in his triumphal chariot (with a blank space beside him, where Commodus might have been shown); and offering sacrifice outside the Capitoline temple. These scenes, which one might label respectively as *Clementia*, *Victoria* and *Pietas Augusti* (there must have been a fourth to complete the series) reveal thematic links

314

and a close affinity of style. The composition of these sculptures still strikes a 'neoclassical' note, and their relief carving achieves a restrained tonal effect which makes it hard to distinguish from the sculpture of Antoninus Pius's reign, as exemplified in those specifically Roman monuments which we have already studied.

In order to appreciate the difference between these three reliefs and those on the Arch of Constantine, let us examine the way that each approaches and resolves an identical theme, that of sacrifice. The relief in the first series which portrays this scene divides it sharply into two parts: a crowded foreground, with most of the figures shown in profile, and a background which portrays an architectural motif, still with firm, precise lines, though the actual relief-work is less prominent. The iconographic pattern is a traditional one, contrived in such a way that the scene unfolds before the spectator's eyes. In the relief from the second series, this pattern undergoes considerable modification. The procession, which is shown advancing towards the spectator, moves from left to right past the Emperor (who is performing a sacrificial libation) and then curves away again, towards the background. In contrast to the official solemnity which marks the other relief, what we see here (realistically rendered, and conveyed with a limited number of figures) is the confused impression of a crowd moving forward across an open space. The habit of composing these figures as though they were coming out towards the spectator, or moving away from him into their own background, is typical of Ephesian reliefs executed during the Antonine period. The latter, as we have already seen, were inspired by Pergamene art; here at Rome, however, the influence of the Pergamum reliefs is less immediately obvious, and what we tend to find is a compromise with the narrative style of the Roman historical relief – itself plebeian in origin.

In other reliefs from the same series a more classically balanced pattern of composition can be found – e.g. in the one (No. 7) which represents an Imperial *liberalitas*, and is composed on two separate levels, one above the other. Two figures – that of the

354 ROME: SCENE OF SACRIFICE. ROME, ARCH OF CONSTANTINE

355 ROME: A 'LIBERALITAS' OF MARCUS AURELIUS. ARCH OF CONSTANTINE ▶

Emperor himself, set almost full-face in the upper row, and in particular the one at ground level seen from behind – are pointers towards a new concept of figurative space. One comparison will suffice: the parallel scene from Trajan's Arch at Beneventum (*pl. 261*). In the relief of Marcus Aurelius we can still make out, beside the figure of the Emperor himself, the foot of another person who must have occupied the space to his left. It has been suggested that this was originally a portrait of Commodus, erased after his death; but the space available is perhaps insufficient for the representation of an adult – that is, to judge by the height of the restored background, easily ascertainable from a study of the original, which shows the point at which the background had been visible from the start.

In almost all the other reliefs of this series, even if the Emperor is shown seated or in profile, according to the traditional patterns of composition, the sculptor has introduced some motif suggestive of lively movement, either towards the background, or from the background towards the viewer. By this means the viewer is no longer outside the composition, but is made to take part in it. This trend goes with a technique for handling detail which has been labelled 'illusionist', in that the effect it produces is based on an optical illusion. Rather than execute a fold of drapery with the swelling that real cloth would have, the artist obtains an identical effect by means of a far flatter relief, while at the same time emphasizing the outlines of the fold with deep shadow-work. The latter is produced either by a series of juxtaposed round holes, made with a stone-drill, or else by a deep continuous furrow, for which the running ground-auger was used. This tool is portrayed on a sarcophagus now in the Archbishop's Palace Museum at Urbino. We see the occupant of the tomb, a sculptor named Eutropos – his name is inscribed in Greek – carving a lion's head on another sarcophagus, while an assistant works the ground-auger for him. This consists of a straight metal drill with a helicoidal bit, worked by a twist of cord held in either hand and run vigorously to and fro. With this technique it becomes possible to produce the illusion of far deeper and sharper relief-work than in fact exists. The process had long been employed for the less important parts of traditional sculpture, because it was quicker, and therefore more economical. In Hadrian's day, if not before, it was being used by the production centres of Asia Minor as an instrument for expressing one particular style. In the great Ephesus frieze its application still shows sober restraint, being restricted to the hair of the sculptured figures, and even then not employed on every plaque. But in those reliefs from the Arch of Constantine which can be ascribed to the Antonine period it is deliberately used – on the heads in particular – to create a striking effect. This process gave a tremendous boost (even though by somewhat rough and ready methods) to that straining after pictorial effect which also appeared in Rome during Hadrian's reign, and grew more pronounced under Antoninus Pius. The technique tended to eliminate both objective naturalism and formal organic cohesion, just as in painting the 'blocking-out' technique had destroyed that naturalism which was the result of using a quasi-impressionist technique.

Thus, both in their concept of figurative space and in their illusionist relief technique, these Antonine reliefs from the Arch of Constantine mark a decisive turning-point in Roman art, datable to the reign of Commodus. The turning-point was a decisive one, since this new formal language and mode of expression did not remain an isolated

356 ROME: A BARBARIAN CHIEFTAIN SURRENDERS. ROME, ARCH OF CONSTANTINE

phenomenon. It was, indeed, to develop in a way which laid increasing emphasis on its penchant for illusion, its departure from the tradition of Hellenistic naturalism and classical organic cohesion of form. The trend which had its beginnings here led directly to a final break with the classical tradition: by the end of the third century this break was unmistakable.

The genesis of this turning-point needs, if possible, to be analysed from two quite separate angles. It will not suffice simply to outline the new features which these reliefs display, and then insert them in one's historical survey of the period, as (for instance) Alois Riegl did at the beginning of this century. Nor is it enough to describe the sculptures, and manufacture a tag such as 'Marcus Aurelius's master-artist' to serve, eventually, for classifications that will be employed in schools and museums. Ideally, we ought to do two things: first, establish the relationship between the studio-workshops and the actual process of production; and, second, attempt to grasp the inner significance of this formal change, which must be seen as the expression (or, more precisely, the structure) of a predetermined historical, social and ethical situation.

As regards the first of these problems, the fact that our sequence of material evidence

317

357 ROME: MONUMENT OF MARCUS AURELIUS. RELIEF (DETAIL). ROME, ARCH OF CONSTANTINE

358 ROME: MONUMENT OF MARCUS AURELIUS. A BARBARIAN CHIEFTAIN SURRENDERS (DETAIL). ROME, ARCH OF CONSTANTINE

359 ROME: A BARBARIAN CHIEFTAIN SURRENDERS (DETAIL). ROME, ARCH OF CONSTANTINE ▶

360 ROME: MARCUS AURELIUS'S COLUMN. THE 'MIRACLE OF THE THUNDERBOLT' (DETAIL)

contains numerous lacunae precludes the possibility of our reaching any firm conclusions. Here we can do no more than frame a hypothesis. My own conviction is that we must recognize as a verifiable fact the existence of a link with the master-artists responsible for the great Ephesus frieze – executed ten years previously. It is possible that some sculptors trained at Ephesus formed their own school in Rome – a school that forged a style in which the art of Pergamum, with Ephesus as its intermediary, acquired a completely new form. It would also have derived much benefit from the knowledge bequeathed to all Roman workshops by the great school that flourished under Trajan.

361 ROME: MARCUS AURELIUS'S COLUMN. THE 'MIRACLE OF THE RAIN' (DETAIL)

The latter's influence can still be traced in the fluidity of design, and a certain emphasis on pathos which marks the facial expressions. In this connection we should make a particularly close study of relief No. 8, which represents the submission of an old barbarian chieftain, supported by a young man with an intensely sorrowful expression on his face.

Then we have the other question – that is, how far this artistic turning-point reflects changing conditions in the period generally. Unless we are prepared to embark on a long digression, it must suffice to recall the close connection which can repeatedly be detected

in the history of art between naturalism, organic form, and a basically rational concept of the world; and conversely between formal abstraction, decomposition of organic form, and an irrational reliance on metaphysical solutions for the world's problems. These relationships have been known and formulated since time began: in prehistory, in the Middle Ages, today. Their applicability to the period with which we are directly concerned, that of Commodus, can be made clear simply by recalling what was said earlier on the subject of religious anxiety, and how it degenerated into superstition from the beginning of the Antonine period. This trend assumed really threatening proportions under Commodus, with the prevalence of philosophical sects attached to the Eastern mystery-cults, and the consequent daily expectation of miracles. Appropriately enough, it is now that the miracle appears for the first time in the history of ancient art. There are at least two such episodes on the Antonine Column: the miracle of the thunderbolt (scene XIa) and the miracle of the rain (scene XVII).

The Antonine Column was set up to commemorate Marcus Aurelius's campaigns on the Danube frontier, against the Marcomanni, the Quadi and the Sarmatians. It is quite plainly an imitation of Trajan's

363 ROME: MARCUS AURELIUS'S COLUMN. THE BASE (ENGRAVING BY G. B. PIRANESI)

◀ 362 ROME: MARCUS AURELIUS'S COLUMN

364 ROME, MARCUS AURELIUS'S COLUMN (DETAIL)

Column, but the eighty years which separate them have brought about a profound change in artistic language, and when we turn to the reliefs we find only an occasional detail which still echoes the style of Trajan's period. Nevertheless, the most important turning-point had taken place only during the preceding few years, between 176 and 190, as I have tried to show. At the same time I do not feel inclined to accept that theory according to which the relationship between the eight reliefs by 'Marcus Aurelius's master-artist' and the studios that worked on the column is identical with that which existed between Trajan's great frieze and Trajan's Column. In the latter case it can be shown that we have to do with one and the same artistic personality, who was in control of *both* workshops.

Undoubtedly the reliefs on the Antonine Column should be related to the new concept of art which we have already seen in the Antonine reliefs from the Arch of Constantine; but there is far less trace of Hellenistic influence, far less boldness in the composition or vigour in the general structure. Trajan's Column shows us a great master at work; in all likelihood the entire concept and design of the frieze was his alone. But what we see on the Antonine Column is the collective labour of a workshop. The master-craftsmen who worked on Marcus Aurelius's column were less cultivated, had less individual character; they remain more closely linked to the 'plebeian' Roman tradition of historical narrative. There is another great difference between Marcus Aurelius's column and that of Trajan: the former lacks unity of conception no less than unity of form; it never achieves that unflaggingly original narrative flow. Not only do we find several different sculptors charged with the work's execution, but several different master-artists providing the designs, as a detailed analysis makes clear. Here the sequence of events does not follow a chronological order, and there is reason to believe that certain scenes, on which it was desired to lay emphasis (e.g. the 'miracle of the rain'), were shifted back in time – which meant placing them lower, where they could more easily be seen.

The original base of the column is still recognizable in certain ancient engravings. In its present reduced form (complete with the inscriptions of Pope Sixtus V) it dates from 1589, when the slabs bearing figured reliefs were chiselled down. Today the general ground-level is nearly thirteen feet higher than it was in antiquity. Originally, the column-base stood some ten feet *above* the road; this must have enhanced its monumental quality, since it meant that the actual shaft was over thirty feet clear of the passer-by. The column itself (base and capital included) consisted of nineteen separate blocks, together with a cylindrical plinth which supported the statue of the Emperor, placed on top. The column's overall height, then, was over one hundred feet. The relief unfolds in twenty-one spiral turns, two less than on Trajan's Column; as a result the figures are larger, while the actual stone-cutting is more pronounced. This plays havoc with the column's architectonic proportions – besides depriving it of that faint swelling (*entasis*) over two-thirds of its length, a legacy from Greek structural sensibility, which Trajan's Column had still preserved.

It is noteworthy that Commodus does not appear in any scene (the identifications suggested by J. Morris in 1952 are not wholly convincing). He was probably represented on the relief which decorated the base, together with the dedication; but his absence (*not* as a result of *damnatio memoriae*) provides yet another reason for re-examining the question raised by the eleven reliefs of Marcus Aurelius. What seems clear is that until 175 Marcus Aurelius conducted the campaign single-handed.

On Trajan's Column, the Emperor is represented in whatever attitude may best suit the action depicted; and when on the march or giving audience he is always shown in profile. On Marcus Aurelius's column, however, the figure of the Emperor is generally shown full face – a sign of the change that had come about in the artist's technical and conceptual outlook. This is invariably the case with 'official' scenes, such as a review of troops or a presentation of prisoners, and nearly always when an *allocutio* (address) is involved. To portray the Emperor in this manner may be associated either with the new conception of figurative space (as exemplified on p. 315 by the reliefs on the Arch of Constantine dating from Marcus Aurelius's reign), or else with an iconographic device to convey the notion of Imperial majesty. The latter acquired fixed characteristics after the great crisis at the end of the third century, and was to provide a direct link with the concept of the Emperor's 'divine majesty' (*divina maiestas*); this idea, Iranian in origin, was already coming in.

Despite Marcus Aurelius's clear-headed rationalism, he was already being credited with supernatural gifts. The 'miracle of the thunderbolt', datable to 172, was interpreted by a later biographer, Julius Capitolinus, as having been brought about by the Emperor's

365 ROME, MARCUS AURELIUS'S COLUMN. DECAPITATION OF PRISONERS (DETAIL)

prayers (*Vit. Marc.* 24). On the Column, the scene showing the effects of the thunderbolt is followed, shortly afterwards, by the 'miracle of the rain' (*pl. 360, 361*). The date of the latter has been much debated, and oscillates between 171 and 174. Nor is it certain whether it should be located in the territory of the Cottians or in that of the Quadi. About the nature of the 'miracle' itself, however, there is no doubt: it saved the desperately thirsty Romans, and spelt ruin for their enemies, who were washed away by the resultant flood. The miracle was sometimes attributed to Hermes Aerios, sometimes to the intervention of the Egyptian priest Harnouphis, and, somewhat later, to the prayers of the Christian troops of the XIIth Legion, which bore the title *Fulminata*. In any case, the representation of this scene produced a quite new iconographic pattern. We see a huge winged figure, whose features – more akin to those of a river-deity than to Jupiter – are glimpsed through a thick curtain of rain. (This rain does not emanate from the figure itself, and indeed continues well beyond it.) In the foreground, bodies and pack-animals are borne away by the flood while the Roman legionaries advance refreshed.

366 ROME, MARCUS AURELIUS'S COLUMN. THE EMPEROR ON THE BATTLEFIELD (DETAIL)

On the Antonine Column there are numerous general scenes put in simply to fill up space; but those of real importance show a dramatic character and an effectiveness which had hitherto never been attained by such simple means. We have come a long way from the powerful and dramatic descriptive techniques of the scenes on Trajan's Column. Here, the effect is obtained by a few comparatively simple devices: the repetition of a gesture or movement or conventional pattern. Such procedures, as well as the trick of showing figures moving towards or away from the viewer (already noted in the eight reliefs, and similarly employed on the actual Column), are fundamentally those rediscovered by modern poster art. The object, in both cases, is to simplify the composition, to make it immediately comprehensible.

These compositions present totally new iconographic features: a scene showing prisoners being beheaded by auxiliary troops who are themselves barbarians; a scene showing village huts being set on fire, with women screaming and trying to protect their children (Renaissance artists drew on this source when they came to portray the

367 ROME: MARCUS AURELIUS'S COLUMN. BARBARIAN WOMEN BEING CARRIED OFF (DETAIL) ▶

368 ROME: NERO'S 'DOMUS AUREA'. MURAL DECORATIONS WITH ARCHITECTURAL MOTIFS AND PAINTED LANDSCAPES

Massacre of the Innocents); a wholly new portrayal of the Emperor appearing in front of a fortress, while a messenger, down below, is entering it. On the basis of such compositions, the 'masters of the Antonine Column' must surely be ranked among the most original contributors to Roman art.

In the age of the Antonines, decorative mural painting, like other media, moved away from that naturalism which had always – even among the most fantastic fancies of *trompe-l'oeil* architectural invention – remained the basis of schemes of decoration. If we compare a wall of Nero's *Domus Aurea*, first with a wall in Ostia contemporary with Antoninus Pius, and then with another from Commodus's day, we see that by the time

328

369 OSTIA: MURAL DECORATION FROM THE ERA OF ANTONINUS PIUS

370 OSTIA: 'HOUSE OF THE PAINTINGS'. YELLOW ROOM: MURAL DECORATIONS FROM COMMODUS'S REIGN

372 MARINO: MITHRAEUM. SOLAR DIVINITY

we get to this last example, nothing is left but a pale reflection of the traditional type of architectural decor, in the shapes assumed by a purely linear pattern. Here we have a direct predecessor of the still more abstract and linear fashion in design which held the field from about 230 onwards (the house under the basilica of S. Sebastiano, on the Via Appia), and acquired a new lease of life as decoration for the Christian catacombs.

As regards the painting of large-scale compositions with figures, on the other hand, we have certain frescoes which display a broader vision and are executed with remarkably fresh and fluid brushwork. Some of these are found in certain underground shrines sacred to the cult of Mithras (such as the grotto at Marino, near Rome). Mithraism, originally an Iranian creed, became increasingly popular during this period, especially

373 ROME: HOUSE OF SS. JOHN AND PAUL. MYTHICAL SCENE

374 MARINO: MITHRAEUM. MITHRAS AS BULL-SLAYER (TAUROCTONUS)

375 ROME: HOUSE OF SS. JOHN AND PAUL. MYTHICAL SCENE (DETAIL) ▶

376 OSTIA: VOTIVE RELIEF WITH SYMBOLIC MOTIFS. ROME, MUSEO TORLONIA

in the army. We also have some individual variations on a mythological scene; the meaning of this scene remains unknown, although several interpretations have been attempted. It shows an island, on which are portrayed a number of heroic figures (including a cup-bearing goddess); the sea around them is also peopled with various figures. The best example is located above a fountain in a house on the Mons Caelius, owned by one Pammachius, and afterwards dedicated to the almost legendary martyrs John and Paul, officials under Julian the Apostate.

One votive relief from Ostia offers, in a sense, a concentration of all the artistic trends from the late Antonine period. In this work, the pictorial style affected by the sculpture of the day blends with an obvious indifference to true proportions or naturalistic representation. The latter is typical of plebeian-type reliefs, and exactly matches those magical and religious tendencies prevalent at the time. The symbolic element has been greatly increased, as is shown, in the clearest possible way, by the large apotropaic eye which stands out in the middle of the relief, without any formal connection between it

334

377 OSTIA: VOTIVE RELIEF WITH SYMBOLIC MOTIFS (DETAIL). THE APOTROPAIC EYE. ROME, MUSEO TOROLONIA

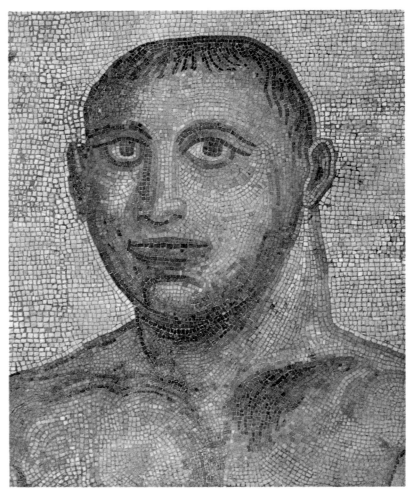

378 ROME: BATHS OF CARACALLA. GLADIATOR. ROME, MUSEO NAZIONALE

and the rest. Objects portrayed include the Ostia lighthouse; a ship with painted sails, on which tiny figures can be seen at work; the statue of Neptune, together with a second ship; and various other statues, presumably meant to denote well-known sites in the town of Ostia. Last but not least, in the upper part of the background, we can see an Attic storey surmounted by an elephant-drawn *quadriga*. This was a characteristic feature of the *aditus Urbis*, the triumphal gate close to the Forum Boarium by which one entered Rome when coming from Ostia. Yet it was certainly not *visible* from Ostia, which lay some sixteen miles away.

We have spoken of a social crisis in the ancient world. This crisis became open and explicit under Commodus, who was himself both its product and its protagonist. After the attempt on his life in 188, he placed himself under the protection of the goddess Cybele, the Phrygian Great Mother, while a Phrygian freedman became his Praetorian Prefect (chief minister). Commodus next took up the workship of Neptune-Serapis, Dolichenus and Mithras, all Eastern deities belonging to mystery-cult religions that promised both salvation and a life in the hereafter. Finally he sought refuge and protection from the Egyptian goddess Isis, and picked a new Praetorian Prefect who was an

336

379 ROME: PORTRAIT OF THE EMPEROR CARACALLA. ROME, PALAZZO DEI CONSERVATORI

Egyptian too. His political actions were always getting mixed up with his vein of irrational mysticism. There was also his well-known passion for dressing up as Heracles and taking part in gladiatorial combats. A few years later gladiators were to reach dizzy social heights as the new idols of the populace – a phenomenon clearly reflected in certain mosaic portraits from the Baths of Caracalla, which bring out all their ugliness and brutality. We have come a long way from the classical ideal of harmonious beauty, as

337

380 ROME: PORTRAIT OF POPE CALLISTUS. PARIS. BIBLIOTHÈQUE NATIONALE, CABINET DES MÉDAILLES

represented by the gymnasium-trained Greek athlete. Irrationality and a weakness for the primitive, brutal, direct element in man always tend to go together. As though in reaction against the examples of his predecessors, so constantly displayed before him, and magnified by official propaganda – the suavity and discretion of Augustus, the clemency of Titus and Trajan, the austere self-discipline of Marcus Aurelius – Caracalla chose to be portrayed with a fierce, brutal expression, his head turned to one side, as though seized by some suspicion, or the abrupt decision to give an order.

The reign of Commodus had similarly ushered in a new concept of sovereignty. The Roman prince was now becoming an Oriental-style god-king. It has rightly been said that Commodus was 'the first European sovereign to style himself both king of the world and servant of God' (W. Weber, *Röm. Herrschertum u. Reich*). Here, too, we glimpse not only the end of Antiquity, but also the dawn of the Middle Ages.

Like the many other Eastern religions in circulation at this time, all of them promising individual salvation and a life after death, Christianity was making steady progress. In 177/8 a number of Christians were brought to trial at Lugdunum, the modern Lyons, and forty-eight of them were executed – mostly immigrants from the East. These are the first martyrs to be mentioned by any pagan historical source. If the Christians alone suffered persecution, this was because their religion was the only one which called in question the eternal and absolute character of the Roman Empire – simply by looking forward to a different eternity, another kind of universalism. The Christians were also the only people

338

who rejected the cult of the Emperor's person. In the *Acts* of Justin Martyr, 'a Christian philosopher', we undoubtedly have some echo of Justin's actual trial, which would seem to have taken place in 167. The Prefect Q. Junius Rusticus, who had instructed the Emperor Marcus Aurelius in Stoic doctrine (Eusebius, *Hist. Eccles.* 4.16), was chosen to judge this Christian, whose writings enumerated the resemblances between Stoicism and Christianity in the field of ethics. It looks as though Rusticus really wanted to find out the nature of Christian doctrine; but over the cult of the Emperor he ran into an insurmountable obstacle. Quite apart from its wide-reaching organization, the great strength of Christianity (something the ruling classes could never appreciate except in a negative fashion) lay in the fact that, ever since its struggle against Gnosticism, it had steadfastly rejected any kind of intellectual deviation, however seductive. As a result, it had won a solid popular backing. All the other mystery religions were complex, intellectual creeds. That with the least intellectual content, Mithraism, likewise proved Christianity's most dangerous rival. This was the period when the school of rhetoric founded by Herodes Atticus was flourishing in Athens, and when Marcus Aurelius – in conscious opposition to the principles behind this type of teaching – established the first Chair of Philosophy in Rome. Yet at the same time another Chair existed in the capital, which took its name from the Apostle Peter. It was the most rudimentary of the three, the least well endowed, yet already it had begun to attract certain upper-class adherents, especially women (see S. Mazzarino, 'Prima cattedra', in *Mélanges offerts à André Piganiol*, 1966, p. 1653f).

In this connection it is worth glancing at the remarkable story of Pope Callistus, who organized the property-holdings of the Roman Church and arranged for the acquisition of the catacombs (the largest still bears his name). Callistus was a slave who ran a bank on behalf of his master. Accused by the Jews, he found himself condemned, at some point between 186 and 189, to hard labour in the mines of Sardinia, where he would undoubtedly have perished. However, he was a Christian, and so was Commodus's favourite concubine, Marcia; in 190 or 192 she asked for, and obtained, Callistus's release and return to Rome. In 218, after an acrimonious quarrel with one Hippolytus, he was elected head of the Roman community. His likeness is preserved for us on a gilded glass of the fourth century. Stylistically, it is without doubt based on a third-century model, and may well derive from an authentic portrait.

C·SEPTIMO·OPT·LEG·I·
...LDESIDERATVS·EST

381 HUNGARY: FUNERARY STELE OF THE LEGIONARY C. SEPTIMUS. BUDAPEST, NATIONAL MUSEUM

Conclusion

THIS book is an attempt to survey, in broad outline, the origins and evolution of a form of art proper to the Roman period, in a world which for over five hundred years had been dominated by Greek art. We have studied its birth and subsequent development at the political heart of the new world which slowly crystallized around Rome. Rome to begin with was a secondary Mid-Italic centre, favourably situated to handle trade, but in an area where neither the arable land nor the pasturage was of more than mediocre quality. First Rome became the political and economic hub controlling the Mediterranean, with all its vast wealth. Then she extended this authority to include much of the territory that was afterwards to make up Europe. Her historical position was so exceptional that it has seemed justifiable, in the present work, to study only the art produced by this centre, where the political power resided. As a centre it was, moreover, open to any external influence: on it there converged all the active forces, good and bad alike, from every corner of the Mediterranean basin. Yet in the sphere of the figurative arts, Rome contrived (after an initial period of eclecticism) to stamp this aggregate of borrowed artistic trends with a recognizable and appropriate physiognomy all its own. This was a remarkable achievement. Quite apart from being called on to imitate classical Greek works, primarily for decorative purposes, Rome's slowly evolving creative tradition was always closely tied down by specific requirements, of a social and political nature.

I have tried to bring out the part which Classical and Hellenistic Greece (as represented by the still-flourishing cities of Asia Minor and Syria) played in the formation of a specifically Roman art. At the same time I have also attempted to indicate the influence exerted by that provincial variety of Hellenistic art which I call Mid-Italic, and which got a new lease of life in the 'plebeian' trend of Roman art. To make a full study of Mid-Italic art production (and, generally speaking, of such production in all regions of Italy before the Roman conquest) requires a book to itself, and the subject will, in fact, eventually be treated as a separate volume in this series.

Having, in the present work, reached the principate of Commodus – that is, the final years of the second century – I realize that in studying later periods it would be wrong to restrict my survey to Rome alone. The provinces of the Empire now assumed a leading historical role, both politically and as regards the organization of Rome's civil service and finances. As a result, they also became involved in Roman art and culture. From now on, Rome entered a phase of cultural passivity: she remained, as it were, a parasitic centre, ready to assimilate whatever came her way. Later still, we see the provinces regain their autonomy, the price of independence being a general drop in standards – economic no less than cultural and artistic. In these often difficult and troubled circumstances, the peripheral areas slowly worked out formal traditions of their own, the effect of which was felt only later. Though the concept of Europe had already been adumbrated by certain classical Greek authors, and found an ardent latterday champion in Pliny (*NH* 3.4), it was not destined to be realized for many centuries. Yet the reality it achieved would have been quite different in its modes of artistic expression had there not existed, throughout the provinces, a common substructure of Roman art. This, too, will form the subject of a separate volume in this series.

I would like to conclude by drawing the reader's attention to the funeral stele of a soldier, Caius Septimus, stationed with the Ist Legion on garrison duty by the Danube (*pl. 381*). This stele symbolizes, in striking fashion, the parts played, after Marcus Aurelius's day, by the provinces of the Empire, both as victims and as arbiters of Roman history. We see a barbarian (most probably a Sarmatian) beaten to his knees among his dead or fleeing comrades, and still clutching the broken butt-end of a spear in one hand. Behind him stands a Roman soldier, sword drawn, on the point of cutting off his head. From a strictly classical viewpoint one could justifiably describe this sculpture as crude; but considered as plebeian provincial expressionism, and judged in terms of the new movement in Roman art, it is a masterpiece. As far as content and formal expression go, the Roman soldier is not the protagonist. Though this little monument is dedicated to him, he stands there frozen in a conventional pose, stiff, mechanical, and about as threatening as a marionette. The true central figure is the barbarian, so close to death, who kneels there with mouth open and one hand upraised. This is no desperate plea for mercy, but the intensely human gesture of a man in whom all feeling and sensation are stilled for one brief instant as he awaits the ineluctable stroke which means his death. In itself this is a modest enough provincial relief, vaguely influenced by the school which executed the Marcus Aurelius column. Yet at the same time it sums up the profound transformation which ancient culture had undergone. Apart from a frame with two little pillars, there is no longer anything to recall the glorious past of classical art; on the contrary, this relief strongly suggests the future language of Christian art in medieval Europe. The irrational element which first crept into ancient art during Commodus's reign had come to stay; it was never to disappear again throughout the entire history of the Western tradition in art.

PART TWO

General Documentation

TECHNICAL EDITOR: MADELEINE DANY

Supplementary Illustrations

COINS AND MEDALLIONS

Portraits

Architecture

Coins and medallions are presented in chronological order.

382 TITUS TATIUS

383 THE ELDER BRUTUS

384 SCIPIO AFRICANUS

385 PERSEUS OF MACEDONIA

386 MITHRIDATES IV

387 MITHRIDATES VI

388 A. POSTUMIUS ALBINUS

389 L. CORNELIUS SULLA

390 C. ANTIUS RESTIO

391 DOMITIUS AHENOBARBUS

392 POMPEY

393 SEXTUS POMPEIUS

394 JULIUS CAESAR

395 THE YOUNGER BRUTUS

396 MARK ANTONY

397 AUGUSTUS

398 OCTAVIA

399 AGRIPPA

400 TIBERIUS

401 GERMANICUS

402 THE ELDER AGRIPPINA

403 ANTONIA

404 THE YOUNGER DRUSUS

405 CALIGULA

406 CLAUDIUS

407 THE YOUNGER AGRIPPINA

408 NERO

349

409 GALBA

410 OTHO

411 VITELLIUS

412 VESPASIAN

413 TITUS

414 JULIA

415 DOMITIAN

416 NERVA

417 TRAJAN

418 PLOTINA   419 HADRIAN   420 SABINA

421 ANTONINUS PIUS   422 THE ELDER FAUSTINA   423 THE YOUNGER FAUSTINA

424 MARCUS AURELIUS   425 LUCIUS VERUS   426 COMMODUS

427 ROME: THE PALATINE. TEMPLE OF VESTA

428 ROME: TEMPLE OF CONCORD

429 ROME: TEMPLE OF VENUS GENETRIX

430 ROME: ARCH OF TRAJAN'S FORUM

431 ROME: TEMPLE DEDICATED TO MATIDIA

432 ROME: TEMPLE OF BACCHUS

433 ROME: TEMPLE DEDICATED TO CYBELE

434 ROME: DOMITIAN'S STADIUM

435 ROME: THE RESTORED TEMPLE OF VESTA

Plans

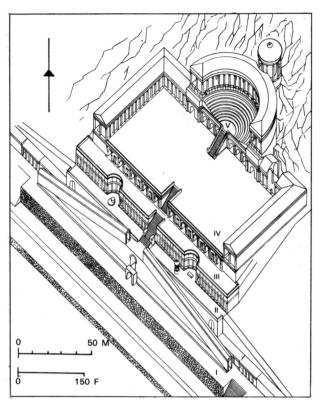

436 PALESTRINA: TEMPLE OF FORTUNE. RECONSTRUCTION (LEVELS I-V)

437 TIVOLI: SANCTUARY OF HERCULES RECONSTRUCTION

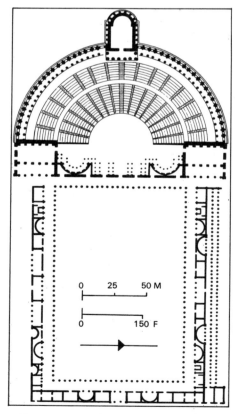

438 ROME: POMPEY'S THEATRE

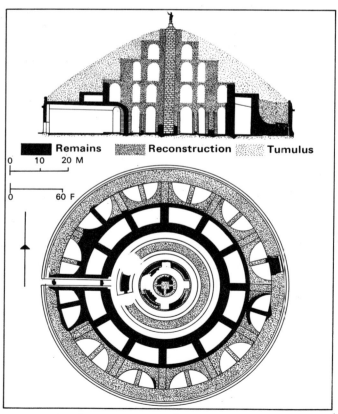

Remains   Reconstruction   Tumulus

439 ROME: THE MAUSOLEUM OF AUGUSTUS. SECTION AND GROUND-PLAN

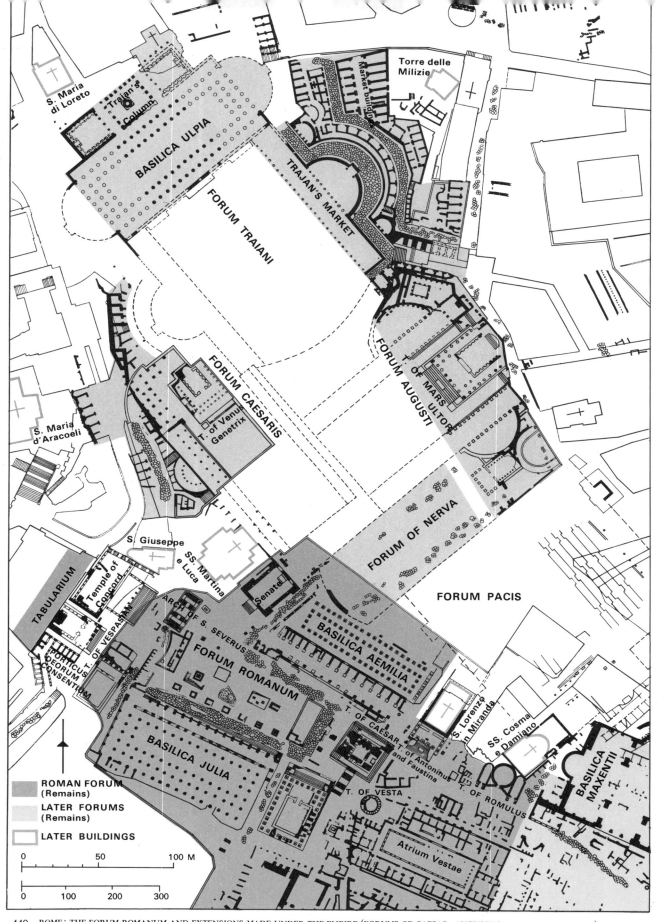

S. Maria
di Loreto

Trajan's
Column

BASILICA ULPIA

FORUM TRAIANI

Market building

Torre delle
Milizie

TRAJAN'S MARKET

FORUM CAESARIS

T. of Venus
Genetrix

FORUM OF MARS ULTOR

FORUM AUGUSTI

S. Maria
d'Aracoeli

FORUM OF NERVA

FORUM PACIS

TABULARIUM

Temple of
Concord

S Giuseppe

SS. Martina
e Luca

Senate

BASILICA AEMILIA

T. OF VESPASIAN

PORTICUS
DEORUM
CONSENTIUM

ARCH OF S. SEVERUS

FORUM ROMANUM

T. OF CAESAR

S. Lorenzo
in Miranda

SS. Cosma
e Damiano

T of Antoninus
and Faustina

BASILICA JULIA

T. OF VESTA

T. OF ROMULUS

BASILICA
MAXENTII

Atrium Vestae

ROMAN FORUM
(Remains)

LATER FORUMS
(Remains)

LATER BUILDINGS

0   50   100 M

0   100   200   300

440   ROME: THE FORUM ROMANUM AND EXTENSIONS MADE UNDER THE EMPIRE (FORUMS OF CAESAR, AUGUSTUS, NERVA AND TRAJAN)

355

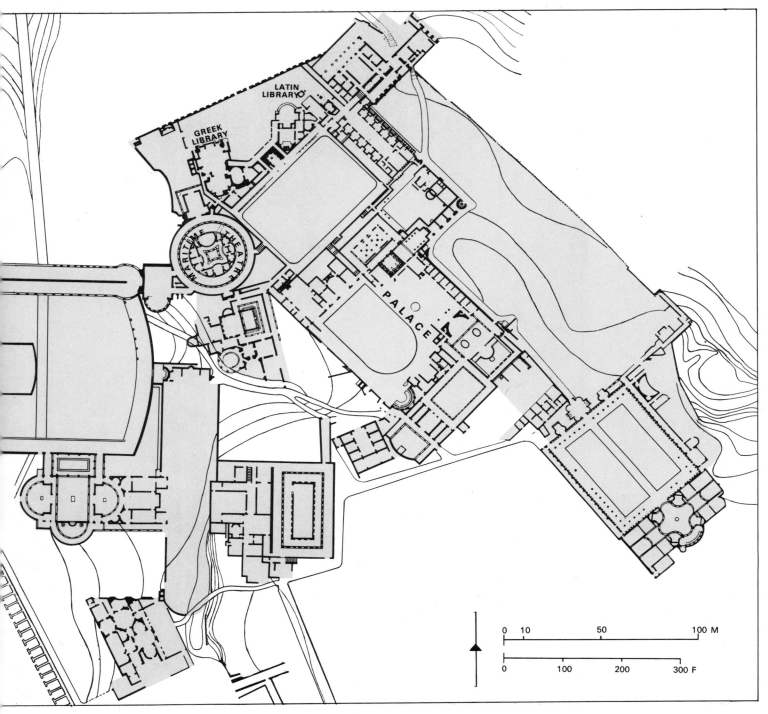

GREEK
LIBRARY

LATIN
LIBRARY

MARITIME THEATRE

PALACE

0 10   50   100 M

0   100   200   300 F

441 TIVOLI (TIBUR): HADRIAN'S VILLA. PARTIAL GROUND-PLAN

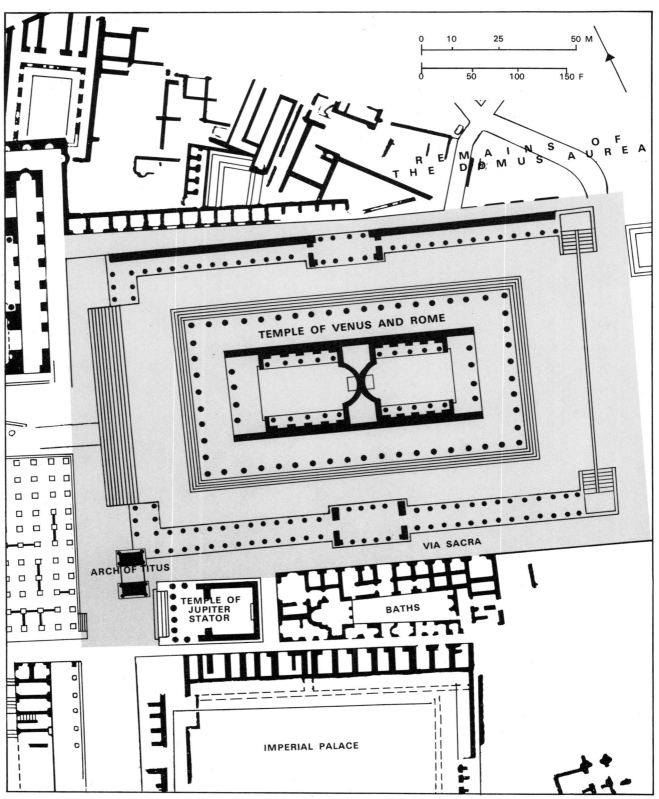

TEMPLE OF VENUS AND ROME

VIA SACRA

ARCH OF TITUS

TEMPLE OF
JUPITER
STATOR

BATHS

IMPERIAL PALACE

THE REMAINS OF DOMUS AUREA

0 10   25   50 M

0   50   100   150 F

442 ROME: TEMPLE OF VENUS AND ROME

443   OSTIA: HOUSES BUILT TO A STANDARDIZED PLAN. INSULAE XII AND XIII IN REGIO III (TRAJAN'S REIGN)

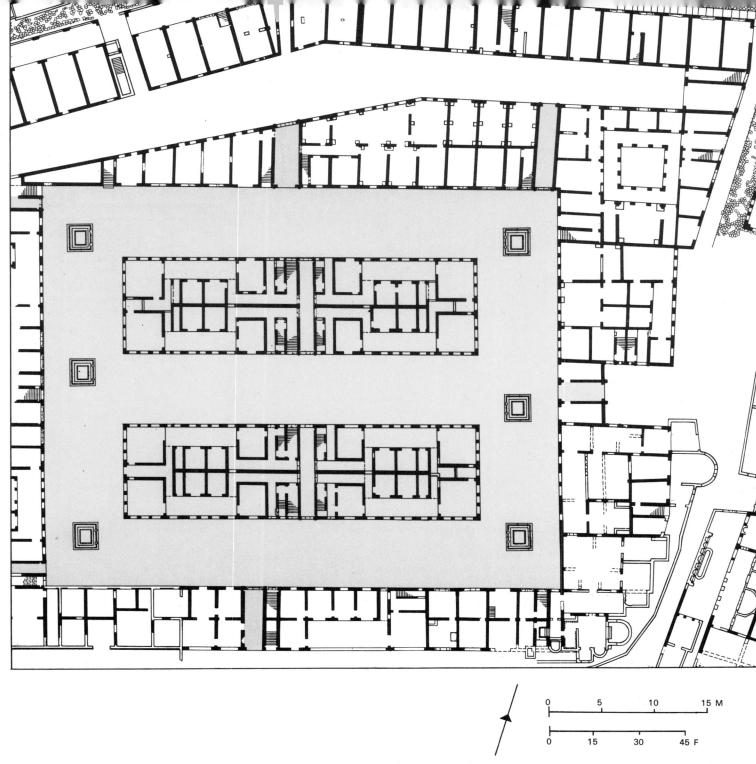

444 OSTIA: TWO BLOCKS OF HOUSES BUILT TO A STANDARDIZED PLAN, SET IN A GARDEN DECORATED
WITH SIX FOUNTAINS AND SURROUNDED BY HOUSES AND SHOPS (HADRIAN'S REIGN)

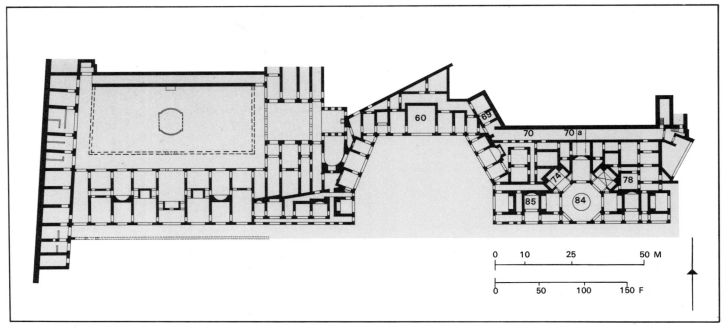

445 ROME: NERO'S 'DOMUS AUREA'

Numbers are given only for those rooms which are illustrated in this book.
The numbering follows the traditional scheme:

No. 60   'Room with the gilded vaulting', pl. 174
No. 69   Small passage beside the 'Room with masks', pl. 142
No. 70   Corridor, pl. 173
No. 70a Transverse passage, pl. 139
No. 74   Cruciform room, pl. 141
No. 78   Room with architectural motifs and painted landscapes, pl. 368
No. 84   Octagonal room, pl. 175
No. 85   'Room of Achilles on Scyros': walls, pl. 143, 144; ceiling, pl. 145

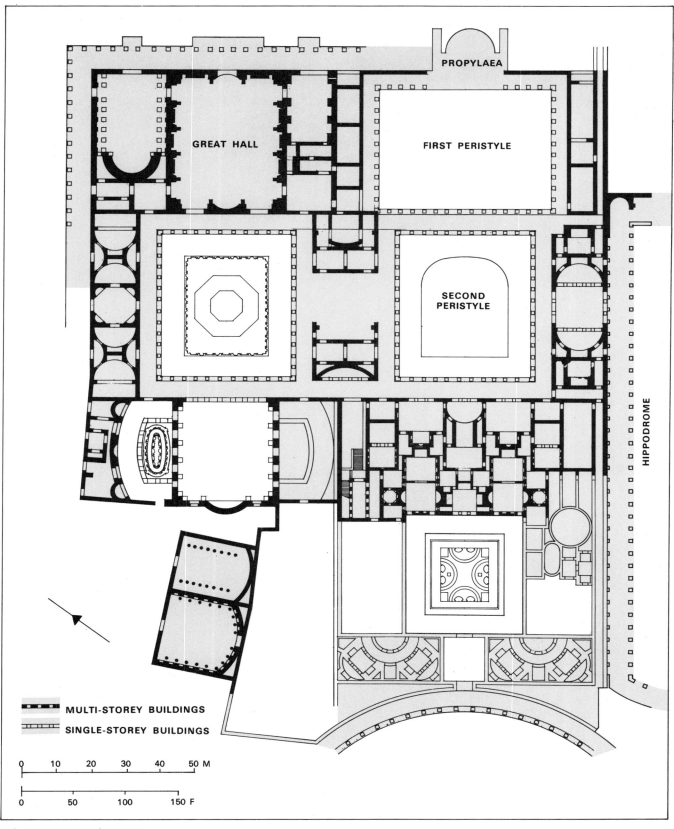

PROPYLAEA

GREAT HALL

FIRST PERISTYLE

SECOND
PERISTYLE

HIPPODROME

MULTI-STOREY BUILDINGS
SINGLE-STOREY BUILDINGS

0 10 20 30 40 50 M

0 50 100 150 F

446   ROME: DOMITIAN'S PALACE

447 ROME: TRAJAN'S MARKET

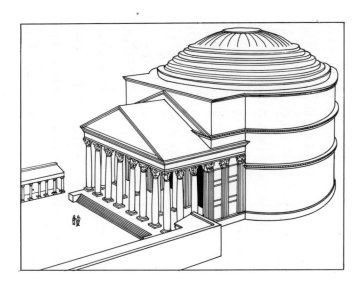

448 ROME: THE PANTHEON

362

Chronological Table

	MEN	EVENTS
850		
	753. Romulus, according to legend, founds Rome. Between 753 and 509, tradition posits a sequence of seven kings at Rome: Titus Tatius, Numa Pompilius, Tullus Hostilius, Ancus Martius, the Elder Tarquin, Servius Tullius, Tarquinius Superbus.	753 (21st April). Traditional date of the foundation of Rome.
750		750. First Greek settlements at Ischia, Cumae, and Naxos in Sicily.
		About 575. Earliest level of the Forum Romanum and the Forum Boarium.
		540. Victory of the Carthaginians and Etruscans over the Phocaeans off Alalia (Corsica).
	509. Lucius Junius Brutus and Lucius Tarquinius Collatinus consuls.	509. The Etruscans driven from Rome. Traditional date for the foundation of the Republic. (The tyrant Hippias was expelled from Athens in 510.)
500		494. Creation of the *tribuni plebis*. Institution of the *Comitia tributa*.
	493. Second consulship of Spurius Cassius Vecellinus.	493. *Foedus Cassianum*: Rome joins the Latin League.
	480. Gelon tyrant of Gela and Syracuse (491-478 BC).	480. Victory of the Syracusans over the Carthaginians at Himera (and of the Athenians over the Persians at Salamis).
	474. Hieron I tyrant of Syracuse (478-467/6 BC).	474. Victory of the Syracusans over the Etruscans at Cumae.
		473. Victory of the Iapygians and the Messapians over the inhabitants of Tarentum and Rhegium.
450	451. The decemvirs.	451. Organization of the army by centuries.
		443. Institution of the Censorship (two Censors).
		431. Victory of the Romans over the Aequi on the high plateau of Carsioli. (Athens: outbreak of the Peloponnesian War).
		426. Rome conquers Fidenae (Veii's bridgehead on the Tiber).
		406. Institution of the twenty-first tribe. Beginning of the war against Veii.
400		400. The Celts cross the Alps and penetrate as far as the Po Valley.
		399. Plebeians admitted to the College of *tribuni consulares*.
	396. Marcus Furius Camillus dictator.	396 (traditonal date). Capture and sack of Veii.
		389/7. Establishment of four new tribes in the territory of southern Etruria.
	387. Brennus chieftain of the Gauls.	387. The Gauls march on Rome. The Romans defeated at the Allia. Praeneste sacked.

THE ARTS	THOUGHT	
850. Villanovan huts (Phase II) on the Palatine.		850
		750
About 500. Altars at Lavinium. The Manios fibula. Sculptures from the temple on the Capitol (Vulca?).		500
493. Traditional date for the dedication of the Temple of Ceres near the Circus Maximus (which can certainly be assigned to the fifth century), with its terracotta ornaments and paintings by Damo-philos and Gorgasos, from Magna Graecia. When Augustus restored the temple, these paintings and terracottas were removed and framed (Pliny, *NH* 35.154).		
484?. First bronze statue made in Rome: dedicated to Ceres by Sp. Cassius (Pliny, *NH* 34.15). The She-Wolf of the Capitol (struck by lightning in 65 BC, Cicero, *Catilin.* 3.19).		
	456. Aeschylus, the first great Greek tragedian, dies at Gela in Sicily.	
	451. Laws of the XII Tables.	450
439. L. Minucius Esquilinus Augurinus, *prefectus annonae*, has a statue on a column erected in his honour (Pliny, *NH* 34.21; cf. 18.15, and Livy, 4.17.6).		
438. Statues erected on the Rostra in memory of four ambassadors sent to Fidenae and murdered by the King of the Veians (Pliny, 34.23; Livy, 4.7.6).	438. Athens: work concluded on the statue of Athena for the interior of the Parthenon (Pheidias).	
	406/5. Athens: death of Sophocles (born 497/6) and Euripides (born about 480).	
		400
	399. Athens: death of Socrates.	
About 390. Reconstruction of the Servian Wall.		

MEN	EVENTS
366. Caius Licinius Stolon and Lucius Sextius tribunes of the people (*tribuni plebis*), and pass the *Lex Licinia-Sexta*.	366. Plebeians admitted to the consulship.
	357/4. The Falisci and the Etruscans in alliance against Rome.
	354. Praeneste and Tibur (Tivoli) join Rome.
	353. Peace with Caere (annexed as a *civitas sine suffragio*).
	351. Forty-year truce with Tarquinia and Falerii.
	348. First treaty with Carthage.
	346/5. Third Gallic invasion.
	343/1. First Samnite War.
340/338. Titus Manlius Imperiosus Torquatus and Publius Decius Mus consuls.	340/338. Conflict with the Latin-Campanian League.
	338. Dissolution of the Latin League. (In Greece, the Battle of Chaeronea, which established the supremacy of Macedonia.)
	335/4. Capua and other towns in Campania ally themselves with Rome.
334. Alexander the Molossian King of Epirus (*c*.362-331 BC).	334. The King of Epirus lends aid to Tarentum against the tribes of Bruttium.
	326. Beginning of the Second Samnite War.
323. Death of Alexander the Great.	321. Roman defeat near Caudium (the Caudine Forks).
312. Appius Claudius Caecus Censor.	
307. Appius Claudius Caecus consul.	
	304. End of the Second Samnite War.
	300. Plebeians admitted to the Sacred College of Pontiffs and Augurs (*lex Ogulnia*).
	298. The Samnites form an alliance with the Sabines, Etruscans and Umbrians. Outbreak of the Third Samnite War.
	295. Roman victory at Sentinum (Umbria).
	290. End of the Third Samnite War.
281. Pyrrhus King of Epirus (*c*.319-272 BC).	281. Pyrrhus in Italy, as a result of an appeal by Tarentum; he defeats the Romans at Heraclea (280 BC) and at Asculum (279 BC).
	275. The Romans defeat Pyrrhus at Beneventum.
272. Manius Curius Dentatus Censor.	272. Capture of Tarentum.
	270. Capture of Rhegium.
	264/241. First Punic War.
260. Caius Duilius consul.	
256. Marcus Attilius Regulus consul.	

Left margin dates: 350, 300

THE ARTS	THOUGHT	

380. Statue of Jupiter Imperator brought from Praeneste and placed in the temple on the Capitol (Livy, 6.29.8-9).

About 350. Temple C at Largo Argentina.

340/312. Bronze statues, some of them equestrian, placed in the Forum to honour victorious consuls and Pythagoras.

340/310. The François Tomb (Vulci) decorated with Etruscan paintings on historical and mythological themes.

312. The Appian Way and the aqueduct known as the *Aqua Appia*.

305. Large bronze statue of Hercules erected on the Capitol (Livy, 9.44.16).

303. The Temple of Health decorated by Fabius Pictor (Pliny, 35.19; Val.Max., 8.14.6).

300. The 'Ficoroni Cist' (bronze receptacle signed by Novios Plautios).

304. Acting on the commission of Appius Claudius, Cn. Flavius collects the rules of procedure into a single book (*ius Flavianum*).

296. Cn. and Q. Ogulnius aediles. Bronze doors and small silver tables added to the Capitoline temple, and a bronze quadriga placed on its rooftop. Statue of the She-wolf suckling the Twins in the Forum.

293. Colossal bronze statue of Jupiter, with the donor's statue facing it, dedicated by Sp. Carvilius Maximus after his victory over the Samnites (Pliny, 34.43).

About 280. The citizens of Thurii dedicate statues to the consul C. Fabricius and the *tribunus plebis* C. Albius in gratitude for the assistance they received against the Lucanians and the Bruttians. (In Alexandria, Sostratos builds the Pharos.)

280. Appius Claudius's speech against the ambassadors of Pyrrhus.

272. The *Anio Vetus* aqueduct completed (M. Curius Dentatus).

About 270. Coinage: the *as libralis*.

268. Coinage: the silver *denarius*.

264. Sack of Volsinii (Bolsena): numerous bronze statues removed thence to Rome (Pliny, 34.34). Picture of the battle in which he defeated the Carthaginians and Hiero hung on a side-wall of the Curia Hostilia by M. Valerius Maximus Messala (Pliny, *NH* 35.22).

260. The *columna rostrata* of C. Duilius set up after his naval victory over the Carthaginians at Mylae (Pliny, 34.20).

272. Livius Andronicus, brought to Rome as a slave after the capture of Tarentum, translates Homer's *Odyssey* into Latin Saturnians.

254/251. Plautus, the greatest comic Latin poet, born at Sarsina in Umbria, a Latin *colonia* since 266. His creative activity spanned the period between 207 and 184 BC.

350

300

	MEN	EVENTS
250		241. Institution of the thirty-fifth, and last, Roman tribe.
		231. Sardinia and Corsica (occupied since 238) formed into a Roman province.
	229. Teuta, Queen of the Illyrian pirates.	229/8. First Illyrian War.
225		225. Battle against the Gauls at Cape Telamon (Etruria).
	222. Marcus Claudius Marcellus consul.	222. Defeat of the Insubrian Gauls at Clastidium.
	220. Hannibal, Carthaginian general (247/6-183 BC).	220. Hannibal, in Spain, attacks Rome's ally Saguntum.
		218. Outbreak of the Second Punic War. Placentia and Cremona become Latin *coloniae*
		217. Debasement of the coinage (*as sextans*) [*lex Flaminia*].
		216. The Romans defeated at Cannae by the Carthaginians.
	214. Marcus Claudius Marcellus, elected consul after the resumption of hostilities in Sicily, remains C.-in-C. of the armed forces for the next two years.	
		212. Capture of Syracuse and death of Archimedes.
	211. Publius Cornelius Scipio, known as 'Africanus' (died 183 BC).	211. Scipio, in the capacity of *privatus cum imperio* (an ordinary citizen appointed commander-in-chief of the army) opposes Hannibal.
	204. Marcus Porcius Cato, known as 'the Censor' (234-149 BC), quaestor in Sicily. On his way back to Rome, he spends time in Sardinia.	
		202. Roman victory at Zama. End of the Second Punic War.
	201. Massinissa King of Numidia (*c.*240-148 BC).	201. Alliance with Massinissa.

THE ARTS	THOUGHT	
250. Plate with elephant decoration.		250
	240. Traditional date of the first dramatic performance in Rome, of a work by Livius Andronicus (Cicero, *Brutus* 18.72). Afterwards he was to compose numerous tragedies and comedies.	
	239. Ennius born at Rudiae, a Messapian city between Brindisi and Taranto. As a poet he wrote tragedies, comedies, minor philosophical works, and an epic poem in hexameters, the *Annals*.	
	235. Performance of the first tragedy by Cn. Naevius, an enfranchised plebeian from Campania, who wrote tragedies, comedies, and an epic poem on the First Punic War, the *Bellum Poenicum*.	
	234. Birth at Tusculum of M. Porcius Cato, the author of various encyclopedic and didactic works on agriculture, and the first major Latin work in prose, the *Origines*.	
	About 230. Statius Caecilius born, perhaps at Mediolanum (Milan): an Insubrian Gaul, he composed a number of comedies.	
		225
	222. Statius Caecilius brought to Rome after being taken prisoner and enslaved.	
220. The Flaminian Circus built.	About 220. Birth, at Brindisi, of M. Pacuvius, tragedian, musician and painter.	
218. Bronze statue of Jupiter dedicated by Rome's matrons on the Aventine (Livy, 22.1.12).		
217. Debasement of the *as libralis*.		
216. Golden statue of Victory offered to the Senate by the ambassadors of Syracuse (Livy, 22.37.2-5).		
214. Banquet for the soldiers and citizens of Beneventum portrayed in a picture which the consul Tiberius Sempronius Gracchus has painted in the Temple of Liberty on the Aventine (Livy, 24.16.16-19).		
212. Capture of Syracuse: numerous works of art removed to Rome (Livy, 25.40.1-3; Plut., *Marc.*21). Statues of *Honos*, Honour, and *Virtus*, Valour. (Val. Max., 1.1.8; Livy, 34.4.4, puts these words into Cato's mouth: 'Believe me, the statues they have brought to this city from Syracuse will do more harm than good. Already I have heard far too many people whose praise and admiration goes only to ornaments from Corinth or Athens, and who sneer at the terracotta decorations which our Roman deities receive.')		
212/11. *Imago clipeata* of Hasdrubal, in silver, brought from Spain to Rome (Livy, 25.39.11-17; Pliny, *NH* 35.14).		
212/200. An Asiatic painter, who subsequently takes the name of Marcus Plautius, executes pictures in the temple of Ardea (Pliny, *NH* 25.115).		
210. Bronze statue carried off from Capua (Livy, 26.34.11). Cf. the 'Brutus' on the Capitol.		
209. Capture of Tarentum: quantities of statues and gold and silver vessels carried off to Rome (Livy, 27.16.7).		
208. Three statues dedicated to Ceres by the aediles (Livy, 27.36.9), among them a colossal bronze statue of Heracles by Lysippus (Strabo, 6.3.1, C.278; Pliny, *NH* 34.40; Plut., *Fab.Max.*22.8).		
207. Two statues of *Juno Regina* (Queen Juno), carved in cypress-wood, borne in solemn procession and dedicated in her temple (Livy, 27.37.11-15).	207. Hymn in honour of Juno Queen of Heaven composed by Livius Andronicus and sung in procession. Performance of Plautus's comedy the *Asinaria*.	
	About 205. Performance of Plautus's *Miles Gloriosus* ('The Braggart Soldier'), with allusion to the captivity of Naevius.	
	204. Ennius, serving as a soldier in Sardinia, is brought to Rome by Cato.	

	MEN	EVENTS
200		200/196. Battles against the Gauls in the Po Valley.
		199. The Romans invade Macedonia. Alliance with the Aetolian League.
	198. Sextus Aelius Paetus Catus consul.	
	197. Titus Quinctius Flamininus proconsul. Philip V King of Macedon (221-179 BC).	197. Spain divided into two provinces. Defeat of Philip V at Cynoscephalae.
		196. Freedom for all the Greeks proclaimed by the Romans at Corinth.
	195. Antiochus III King of Syria (223-187 BC). Marcus Porcius Cato consul.	195. Antiochus III invades Greece. Rebellion in Spain put down by Cato.
	190. Lucius Cornelius Scipio, surnamed 'Asiaticus' and brother of Scipio Africanus, consul.	190. Antiochus III beaten by the Romans at Magnesia-by-Sipylus.
		189. Bononia (Bologna) becomes a Latin *colonia*.
		188. Treaty of Apamea concluded with Antiochus III.
	184. Marcus Porcius Cato and Publius Valerius Flaccus Censors.	
		181. Aquileia becomes a Latin *colonia*.
		180. Pisa becomes a Roman *colonia*.
	179. Marcus Aemilius Lepidus and M. Fulvius Nobilior, Censors.	
		177-176. Tiberius Sempronius Gracchus's campaign in Sardinia.
175		
	174. Antiochus IV Epiphanes (175-164 BC).	
	171. Perseus King of Macedon (179-168 BC).	171. Outbreak of the Third Macedonian War.
	169. Tiberius Sempronius Gracchus Censor.	

THE ARTS	THOUGHT	

THE ARTS

About 200. Sarcophagus of C. Scipio Barbatus. Bronze equestrian statue of Fabius Maximus.

About 198. Statues and paintings carried off by T. Quinctius Flamininus from Eretria (Livy, 32.16.7).

196. After his victory in Spain L. Stertinius has two arches erected in the Forum Boarium and another in the Circus, with gilded statues on top of them (Livy, 33.27.3-4). Note: statues set on an architrave joining two columns are attested from Greece from the middle of the third century BC onwards.

194. Triumph of T. Quinctius Flamininus: statues in bronze and marble (first mention of the latter), silver and gold vessels, finely wrought armour (Livy, 34.52.4-5). Statue of Jupiter on the Capitol (Cicero, *Verrines* 2.4.129-30). Bronze statue of Flamininus with Greek inscription (Plut., *Titus* 1.1). Greek-style statue of L. Scipio on the Capitol (Val. Max., 3.6.2).

193. Construction of the Porticus Aemilia, where merchandise coming up-river from Ostia was unloaded.

192. The sanctuary of Jupiter Vejovis built on the Capitol.

190. Before his departure for Asia, P. Cornelius Scipio Africanus, in association with his brother Lucius, the consul, has an arch set up in the street approaching the Capitol, together with seven gilded statues and two fountain-basins in front of them.

189. Capture of Ambracia: numerous works of art (statues and paintings) looted from Pyrrhus's palace (Livy, 38.9.13; 38.35.5-6; Pliny, 35.66: statues of the Muses).

188. Triumph of Lucius Scipio Asiaticus: cf. Livy, 37.59.3-5. Luxury had come to stay in Rome, and we see no more wooden or terracotta statues (Pliny, 34.34: *in delubris dicata usque ad devictam Asiam, unde luxuria*; 33.148; 16.216). Numerous artists are now brought from Asia Minor to Rome (Livy, 39.22.9-10). Paintings on historical themes deposited in the temple on the Capitol by Lucius Scipio.

186. Triumph of C. Manlius: furniture and fine fabrics brought to Rome from Asia (Livy, 39.6.7-9; Pliny, 34.14).

184. The Basilica Porcia built in the Forum.

179. Construction of the Pons Aemilius and the Basilica Fulvia (renamed the Aemilia after 78 BC). M. Aemilius Lepidus restored the temple on the Capitol and removed the statues with which it was cluttered up; he also dedicated the temples of Diana and Juno Queen of Heaven.

174. A picture of Sardinia, showing the battles of T. Sempronius Gracchus, together with an explanatory inscription, is placed in the temple of *Mater Matuta* (Livy, 41.28.8-10). Antiochus IV Epiphanes summons the Roman architect Cossutius to Rome for the construction of the temple of Olympian Zeus.

170. Construction of the Basilica Sempronia (destroyed by Caesar in 54).

THOUGHT

198. Sextus Aelius Paetus Catus, jurisconsult, writes a commentary on the Laws of the XII Tables (*Tripertita*).

195/194. Birth in Carthage of Terence, a manumitted slave of the senator C. Terentius Lucanus, one of the greatest Latin comedy-writers.

191. Plautus's comedy *Pseudolus* performed.

190/173. Ennius composing the *Annals*.

189. Ennius accompanies M. Fulvius Nobilior during the annexation of Ambracia, which he celebrates in a poem.

188. Plautus's *Amphitryon* performed.

184. Performance of the *Casina*, Plautus's last comedy. Ennius takes part in the foundation of the colony of Pisaurum (Pesaro) and becomes a Roman citizen.

180. C. Lucilius, a satirical poet who described the *mores* of his age, born at Suessa Aurunca.

174. Cato starts work on the *Origines*.

About 173. The Epicurean philosophers Alcaeus and Philiscus expelled from Rome.

170. Birth – possibly at Pisaurum – of Accius, author of tragedies, didactic writings, and treaties on agriculture (in verse).

169/8. Death of Ennius in Rome.

200

175

	MEN	EVENTS
	168. Aemilius Paulus, surnamed 'Macedonicus', consul.	168. The Romans defeat Perseus at Pydna.
		166. Delos made a free port.
150	155. Ptolemy VIII Euergetes King of Cyrene and Egypt (died 116 BC).	155. In his will Ptolemy VIII Euergetes makes the Roman people residuary legatees of Cyrenaica (will executed 96 BC).
		154/138. Revolt in Lusitania.
	149. Andriscus, a Macedonian adventurer, passes himself off as the son of Perseus.	149. Revolt in Macedonia under Andriscus.
		149/146. Third Punic War.
	147. Scipio Aemilianus, son of Aemilius Paulus—adopted by Scipio Africanus—consul (died 129 BC).	
	146. Lucius Mummius Achaicus consul.	146. Carthage conquered and destroyed by Scipio Aemilianus. Corinth captured by L. Mummius. Africa, Achaea and Macedonia become Roman provinces.
		143/133. Revolt of the Celtians.
		134/132. First Sicilian Slave War.
	133. Attalus III King of Pergamum (138-133 BC). P. Mucius Scaevola and Tiberius Sempronius Gracchus (162-133 BC) consuls.	133. Scipio Aemilianus conquers Numantia. End of the Celtiberian revolt. Attalus III bequeaths his kingdom to the Romans. Tiberius Gracchus's agrarian laws and assassination.
		130. Asia constituted as a province.
125		125/121. Conquest of Cisalpine Gaul.
	123. Caius Sempronius Gracchus (154-121 BC).	123. Caius Gracchus, tribune of the people, ratifies the agrarian laws proposed by his brother.
		121. Assassination of Caius Gracchus. End of the Gracchan reforms.
		121/111. First reaction against the Gracchan reforms.
	118. Death of Micipsa, son of Massinissa, King of Numidia. Jugurtha, Micipsa's nephew and adopted son (died 104 BC).	118. Narbo Martius (Narbonne) established as a Roman *colonia*.
	107. Caius Marius's first consulship.	118/105. War against Jugurtha successfully wound up by Marius.
	104/100. Caius Marius consul.	105. Marius's army reforms.
	102. Quintus Lutatius Catulus consul.	102. Marius defeats the Teutons near Aquae Sextiae (Aix-en-Provence), and the Cimbri at Campi Raudii, near Vercellae (101).

THE ARTS	THOUGHT	
168. Triumph of Aemilius Paulus, with statues of gold, marble and ivory, paintings on wood, fine silks, wrought silver and gold (Livy, 45.39.5-6); also works attributed to Pheidias (an Athena in bronze: Plut., *Aem.* 32-33; Pliny, *NH* 34.54). Aemilius Paulus asked the Athenians for a philosopher to instruct his children and a painter to celebrate his triumph. They sent him Metrodorus (Pliny, *NH* 35.135) who was capable of fulfilling both roles. Construction of the Porticus Octavia, with bronze capitals. (In Pergamum, the construction of the Great Altar.)	168. Crates of Mallus, Stoic grammarian, opens a school in Rome. C. Sulpicius Gallus, author of works on astronomy, predicts the lunar eclipse of 21 June 168.	
	168/167. Death of Statius Caecilius, probably in Rome.	
164. The 'topographic' painter Demetrius entertains his king-in-exile, Ptolemy Philometor, in Rome (Diod., *Exc.* 31.18.1-3).	167/166. The future Greek historian Polybius, of Megalopolis, is brought to Rome as a hostage. Terence's first comedy, the *Andria* ('Woman of Andros') is performed.	
	160. Last performances of the *Adelphi* and the *Hecyra*, both comedies by Terence, on the occasion of the funeral games in honour of Aemilius Paulus.	
158. All statues placed in the Forum other than by decree of the people or the Senate are removed.	159. Death of Terence during a voyage to Greece.	
	154. Three philosophers, Diogenes the Stoic, the Peripatetic Critolaus, and Carneades, Head of the Academy, expelled from Rome.	150
	149. Death of Cato in Rome.	
146. Triumph of Q. Caecilius Metellus, conqueror of Macedonia. In the portico which he caused to be erected, in Rome, he placed a great bronze group by Lysippus, with numerous figures in it, commemorating Alexander's victory at the Granicus (Pliny, *NH* 34.64; Vell. Paterc., 1.11.3).		
146. Sack of Corinth and other Greek cities by the consul Lucius Mummius (Strabo, 8.6.23, C.381; Pliny, *NH* 34.36).		
146/45. Hostilius Mancinus, as part of his electoral campaign, puts up in the Forum a picture showing him at the capture of Carthage, together with a written commentary. For other pictures in the Forum, see Pliny, *NH* 35.24-5.		
144/140. The aqueduct *Aqua Marcia* constructed by the praetor Q. Marcius Rex.		
136. Consecration of the temple of Mars by Decius Junius Brutus.	136. Performance of the *Brutus* by Accius during festivities organized by Decius Junius Brutus to celebrate the consecration of the temple of Mars.	
	133. P. Mucius Scaevola, jurisconsult, opposes the Gracchi.	
	133/132. The eloquence of the Gracchi reaches its apogee.	
	About 130. Death of Pacuvius at Tarentum.	
125. Construction of the *Aqua Tepula* aqueduct.		125
121. Q. Fabius Maximus has a triumphal arch erected in the Forum to celebrate his victory over the Allobroges (reconstructed in 56 BC and afterwards destroyed).		
109. Construction of the Milvian Bridge.	116. Birth at Reate of M. Terentius Varro: historian, archaeologist, man of letters, linguist, poet, and author of various didactic works.	
	106. M. Tullius Cicero, the greatest Roman orator – also an author of philosophic and didactic works – born near Arpinum.	
	102. Q. Lutatius Catulus writes his *Memoirs*, and gathers round him a circle of poets who draw their inspiration from Hellenistic erotic poetry.	
	101/100. Birth of C. Julius Caesar.	

MEN	EVENTS
100. Lucius Appuleius Saturninus tribune of the people (*tribunus plebis*).	100. Rome in a state of siege.
	96. Ptolemy Apion, King of Cyrenaica, bequeaths his kingdom to Rome.
95. Mithridates VI Eupator King of Pontus (111-63 BC). Quintus Mucius Scaevola consul.	95/91. Mithridates VI occupies Armenia, Paphlagonia and southern Cappadocia.
92. Lucius Cornelius Sulla (138-78 BC).	92. Sulla propraetor in Cilicia. First contact with the Parthians.
	91/88. The Social War (the Italian Allies against Rome).
	90/89. The right of Roman citizenship is extended to all loyal Italians and to those who lay down their arms.
88. Lucius Cornelius Sulla consul.	88. Siege of Nola: Sulla's victory over the last remaining Italian rebels.
87. Lucius Cornelius Cinna (Marius's adherent) consul.	87. Sulla's campaign in Greece against Mithridates.
	86. Proscriptions held in Rome by Cinna and Marius. 17 January: death of Marius.
	86/5. Sulla's victorious campaign against Mithridates.
	84. Death of Cinna.
	83/2. Sulla in Italy. Victory over the Sabines at the Colline Gate, Rome (1 November 82). Ruthless massacres and proscriptions.
	82/79. Sulla, established as Dictator from December 82, reforms the Constitution by re-establishing the absolute authority of the Senate.
	81. Sulla's Triumph: Pliny, *NH* 33.1.16; Lucian, *Zeuxis* 3.
	80/72. Revolt of the Lusitanians under Quintus Sertorius.
	78. Death of Sulla.
75. Nicomedes IV Philopator King of Bithynia (94-75 BC).	75. Nicomedes IV bequeaths his kingdom to the Romans.
74. Lucius Licinius Lucullus consul.	74. After prolonged resistance Cyrenaica becomes a Roman province. Third campaign against Mithridates VI conducted between 74 and 69 by Lucullus.
73. Spartacus, a Thracian slave, leads a revolt. Caius Verres *legatus* in Asia (80-79), praetor (74), propraetor in Sicily (73).	73/71. Third Slave War, with the insurgents under the leadership of Spartacus, bloodily repressed by Crassus. Verres propraetor in Sicily.
72. Marcus Licinius Crassus consul (*c.*115-53 BC).	
70. Crassus and Pompey consuls. Cn. Pompeius Magnus (106-48 BC).	
69. Caius Julius Caesar (100-44 BC).	69. Lucullus besieges Tigranocerta, the capital of Armenia. Julius Caesar holds the quaestorship.
	67. Pompey, appointed commander of the fleet, with extraordinary powers, puts down the Cilician pirates.
	66/64. Pompey's campaign in Asia: he defeats Mithridates VI and conquers both Pontus and Palestine. Pontus absorbed into a single province with Bithynia (already a province since 74).
63. Marcus Tullius Cicero consul (106-43 BC). Lucius Sergius Catilina (108-62 BC).	63. Cicero circumvents the Catilinarian Conspiracy.
	62. Catiline dies on the field of battle at Pistoria (Pistoia). Syria and Cilicia become Roman provinces.
	61. Pompey's Asiatic triumph. Caesar propraetor in Spain.

100

75

THE ARTS	THOUGHT	
100. The Roman architect C. Mucius builds the temple of *Honos et Virtus*.		100
100/80. Paintings in the 'House of the Griffins'.	98/96. T. Lucretius Carus, poet and Epicurean, born: perhaps in Pompeii. The *De Rerum Natura* was published after his death by Cicero.	
100/70. The so-called 'Altar of Domitius Ahenobarbus'.	95. Q. Mucius Scaevola writes the first systematic treatise on civil law (Pomponius, *Dig.st.*I.ii.2.41).	
	90/80. During Sulla's ascendancy those popular farces known as Atellane Comedy (by authors like Novius and Pomponius) were much in vogue. Sulla himself composed his *Memoirs* in Greek (Plut., *Sulla* 6).	
	87. During the Marian proscriptions C. Caesar Strabo, an author of tragedies, lost his life, and Q. Lutatius Catulus committed suicide.	
	87/84. Catullus, the most subtle of the Latin elegiac poets, born at Verona.	
	86. C. Sallustius Crispus (Sallust, the historian) born at Amiternum.	
	82. Q. Mucius Scaevola killed by Sulla's hired assassins.	
	81/80. Cicero's first speech, the *Pro Quinctio*.	
80/78. The Tabularium. Temple of *Fortuna Primigenia* at Praeneste (82-79?).	80/79. Cicero defends S. Roscius Amerinus.	
	79/78. Cicero in Greece.	
	76/75. Birth (at Teate Marrucinorum or in Rome) of Asinius Pollio, poet, orator and historian.	75
74. Colossal bronze statue of Apollo (30 cubits, or about 44 ft. carried off by Lucullus from Apollonia on the Euxine and consecrated on the Capitol (Strabo, 7.6.1, C.319; Pliny, *NH* 34.39).		
	73. Parthenius of Nicaea, Greek elegiac poet and mythographer, is brought to Rome as a slave.	
	70. The prosecution of Verres: two speeches (the Verrine Orations) by Cicero. P. Vergilius Maro (Virgil) born at Andes (Pietole), near Mantua.	
	69. C. Cornelius Gallus, elegiac poet, born at Forum Julii (Fréjus) in Gallia Narbonensis.	
	68. Beginning of the correspondence between Cicero and Atticus.	
	65. Q. Horatius Flaccus (Horace) born at Venusia, on the borders of Lucania and Apulia.	
63. Triumph of Lucullus, who amasses quantities of statues and paintings in his private house (Plut., *Lucullus* 39).	63. The trial of Catiline: four speeches *Against Catiline* delivered by Cicero.	
	62. Beginning of Cicero's correspondence *ad familiares* (to his friends).	
61. Triumph of Pompey: silver statues taken from the King of Pontus, a silver and gold chariot. Importation of jewellery, furniture and fabrics (Pliny, *NH* 33.151; 37.12-14).		

MEN	EVENTS
	60. First triumvirate of Pompey, Caesar and Crassus.
59. Julius Caesar consul.	
58. Publius Clodius Pulcher *tribunus plebis*. Marcus Aemilius Scaurus aedile.	58. Caesar proconsul of Hither and Further Gaul and Illyria.
	58/51. Caesar's conquest of Gaul.
57. Annius Milo organizing armed gangs.	57. Reaction by Pompey's supporters. Cicero recalled from exile.
	56. The Congress of Lucca, at which the triumvirs decided that Caesar should have Gaul, Pompey Spain, and Crassus Syria.
55. Pompey and Crassus consuls.	
	53. Crassus defeated and killed by the Parthians at Carrhae, in Mesopotamia.
	52. Pompey sole consul and *Princeps Senatus*.
49. Mark Antony and Quintus Cassius Longinus, Caesar's supporters, *tribuni plebis*.	49. The Senate orders Caesar to disband his legions. A state of siege proclaimed. On 12 January Caesar crosses the Rubicon and marches on Rome. Pompey flees to Macedonia.
48. Ptolemy XIV King of Egypt (61-47 BC). Pharnaces II King of the Cimmerian Bosporus (63-47 BC): this was the son of Mithridates VI, King of Pontus.	48. Pompey, defeated by Caesar at Pharsalus, flees to Egypt, where he is killed by order of Ptolemy XIV.
	47. Caesar's victory over Pharnaces at Zela, followed by his campaign in North Africa against Pompey's supporters.
46. Titus Labienus Caesar's legate.	46. Caesar elected Dictator for ten years, and celebrates a triumph. Titus Labienus's campaign against Pompey's supporters in Spain.
	45. Caesar's decisive victory over Pompey's partisans at Munda.
44. Marcus Junius Brutus (85-42 BC). Caius Cassius Longinus (died 42 BC).	44. February: Caesar made Dictator for life. 15 March: Caesar assassinated by a group of conspirators under Brutus and Cassius.
43. Hirtius and Vibius Pansa consuls. Caius Julius Caesar Octavianus (63 BC-AD 14): Caesar's adopted son, and from 27 BC known as 'Augustus'. Mark Antony (c.82-30 BC). Marcus Aemilius Lepidus (died 13 BC).	43. The 'War of Modena': Mark Antony defeated by Octavian. 27 November: formation of the Second Triumvirate, with Octavian, Antony and Lepidus. Antony's proscriptions: the assassination of Cicero.
	42. Defeat of the conspirators at Philippi: Brutus and Cassius commit suicide.
40. Asinius Pollio (76 BC-AD 5).	40. The Treaty of Brindisi: Antony gets the East, while Gaul goes to Octavian. The Parthians invade Syria.
37. Cleopatra Queen of Egypt (51-30 BC). Caius Cilnius Maecenas (c.69-8 BC).	39. The Treaty of Misenum ratified with Sextus Pompeius, now in command of a powerful fleet. Asinius Pollio's success in Dalmatia.
39. Sextus Pompeius (died 35 BC), son of Pompey the Great.	37/35. Failure of Antony's Parthian expedition. He marries Cleopatra, and repudiates Octavian's sister Octavia.

50

THE ARTS	THOUGHT		
60. Pasiteles (sculptor).	59. Birth in Padua of Livy the historian. Cicero undertakes the defence of Valerius Flaccus, charged with maladministration in Asia (*Pro Flacco*).		
59. Certain paintings from Sparta, originally executed on brick walls, are removed, set in wooden frames, and brought to the *Comitium* (Pliny, *NH* 37.173).	58. Cicero goes into voluntary exile at Thessalonice and Dyrrhachium, for a period of eighteen months.		
58. Numerous paintings of the 'Sicyon School' are purchased in Sicyon and brought to Rome (Pliny, *NH* 35.127). along with three thousand statues (Pliny, *NH* 34.36). M. Aemilius Scaurus is the first person to own a collection of precious stones, which is subsequently eclipsed by that of Pompey, captured from King Mithrates and dedicated in the temple of the Capitol. Caesar, following this precedent, offered up six collections of rings, *dactyliothecae*, in the temple of *Venus Genetrix*, while Marcellus consecrated another in the temple of Apollo on the Palatine.)	58/54. Death of Catullus in Rome.		
55. Construction of Pompey's Theatre in the Campus Martius (the first stone-built theatre in Rome).	55. Cicero withdraws from politics, and between 54 and 51 writes the *De Oratore* and the *De Republica*.		
54/46. The *Forum Caesaris*.	55/53. Lucretius commits suicide, perhaps in Rome.		
	54. Caesar writes a grammatical and philological treatise entitled *De Analogia*.		
50/40. Paintings of the *Odyssey*.	51. Cicero proconsul in Cilicia.		
50/10. The Theatre of Marcellus.	50. Caesar writes the *De Bello Gallico* ('On the Gallic Wars'), 57-51 BC.	50	
About 50. Portrait of Pompey (like that in the Ny Carlsberg Glyptotek).	About 50. Albius Tibullus, the elegiac poet, born (perhaps at Gabii).		
	About 47. Sextus Propertius, the elegiac poet, born in Umbria.		
	47(?). Caesar writes his *De Bello Civili* ('On the Civil War'), 49-48 BC.		
	47/46. Cicero's second retirement.		
	46. Cicero writes the *Brutus*, the *Orator*, and the *Paradoxa Stoicorum*.		
	45. Lavish games held to celebrate Caesar's fifth triumph. Publius Syrus, young actor and author of mimes, arrives in Rome. Cicero writes his *Academica* and the *De finibus bonorum et malorum*. P. Nigidius Figulus, moving force in Rome behind the Neo-Pythagorean and astrological movement, dies an exile.		
	44. Cicero writes the *Tusculanae Disputationes*, the *De Natura Deorum*, the *Cato Maior*, the *De Officiis*, and the first four *Philippics* against Antony.		
	44/35. Sallust, having retired from political life, writes the *De Coniuratione Catilinae*, the *Bellum Jugurthinum*, and his *Historiae*, covering the period between 78 and 67 BC.		
	43. Cicero composes the ten remaining *Philippics* against Antony. On 7 December he is murdered by the Triumvir's agents at Formiae. Ovid, the elegiac poet, born at Sulmona. His works include the *Amores*, the *Heroides*, the *Ars Amatoria* ('Art of Love'), the *Metamorphoses*, the *Fasti*, the *Tristia*, and the *Epistulae ex Ponto*.		
	42/39. Virgil writes the *Eclogues*.		
40/30. Bronze portrait in the Hermitage Museum (Leningrad).	39. Asinius Pollio founds the first public library in Rome.		
	37. Maecenas, with Virgil and Horace accompanying him, travels to Brindisi to heal the breach between Octavian and Antony.		
	37/29. Virgil composes his *Georgics*.		

377

MEN	EVENTS
36. Marcus Vipsanius Agrippa (63-12 BC), Octavian's friend and general.	36. Agrippa's final victory over Sextus Pompeius off Naulochus. Lepidus receives no appointment save that of Pontifex Maximus. Octavian has tribunician *sacrosanctitas* conferred on him.
	35/34. Octavian's Illyrian and Dalmatian expedition.
31/23. Octavian consul.	31 (2 September). Octavian defeats Antony and Cleopatra in the naval battle off Actium. The Parthians occupy Armenia.
	30. Antony and Cleopatra commit suicide. Egypt becomes a Roman Prefecture. The tribunician *ius auxilii* is conferred on Octavian.
	27 (13 January). Proconsular power conferred on Octavian for ten years. 16 January: Octavian receives the title of 'Augustus'. Formation of the province of Achaea, including Thessaly and Epirus.
	27/19. War against the Cantabri, successfully concluded by Agrippa.
25. Death of Amyntas, the last King of Galatia. Juba II King of Mauretania. M. Claudius Marcellus, son of Octavia (died 23 BC).	25. Galatia becomes a Roman province. Mauretania handed over to Juba II as a client-kingdom. Marcellus marries Augustus's daughter Julia.
	23. The *imperium maius*, proconsular authority over all the provinces, together with the tribunician right of veto, conferred on Octavian Augustus. Death of Marcellus, Augustus's nephew and successor-designate.
	22. Cyprus becomes an autonomous province.
	21. Agrippa marries Augustus's daughter Julia.
20. Phraates IV King of the Parthians (37-2 BC).	20. Phraates IV gives back the legionary standards taken from Crassus after the defeat at Carrhae. Augustus granted the right to legislate.
	17. Celebration of the *Ludi Saeculares* (Secular Games).
	16. Noricum becomes a Roman province.
15. Nero Claudius Drusus (38-9 BC), son of Livia, adopted by Augustus. Tiberius (42 BC-AD 37), son of Livia, adopted by Augustus, Emperor from AD 14.	15. Raetia and Vindelicia conquered by Drusus and Tiberius, and made into Roman provinces.
	14. Settlement of the Alpine region: the *Alpes Cottiae* become a vassal-kingdom, and the *Alpes Maritimae* a province.
	12. Augustus, *aet.* 50, becomes Pontifex Maximus.
10. Tiberius Claudius Nero Germanicus, son of Drusus, the future Emperor, born at Lyons (Lugdunum).	9. Drusus dies in action on the Elbe, fighting the Germans.
8. Marbod King of the Marcomanni (8 BC-AD 17).	8. Marbod and the Marcomanni invade Bohemia and found a kingdom there.
5. Birth of the future Emperor, Galba.	
4. Herod, King of Palestine (37-4 BC).	4. Death of Herod, the last King of Palestine.
2. Lucius, son of Julia and Agrippa.	2. Death of Augustus's adopted son Lucius.
4. Caius, son of Julia and Agrippa.	4. Death of Augustus's adopted son Caius. Adoption of Tiberius, who is now named as successor-designate.
	6/9. Insurrections in Pannonia put down by Tiberius. Judaea becomes a Roman province.

25

0

THE ARTS	THOUGHT	
	36/35. Sallust dies in Rome.	
	35. The first book of Horace's *Satires* published.	
About 31. Portrait of Octavian in the Capitol Museum.	About 31. Vitruvius publishes his *De Architectura*, in ten books.	
30/25. House near the Farnesina (paintings and stuccos).	30. Horace publishes the *Epodes* and the second book of the *Satires*.	
30/10. Monument of Eurysaces.	29. Victory games to celebrate Actium, with performances of tragedies.	
29. First stone amphitheatre, built by Caius Statilius Taurus (burnt during Nero's great fire). Consecration of the temple of Divus Julius in the Forum Romanum.	29/19. Virgil composing the *Aeneid*.	
27/20. Cameo of Livia (The Hague). Dioscorides of Aegae (modern Nemrut Calesi), a town in Cilicia; famous engraver of precious stones. His sons and disciples included Eutychides, Herophilos and Hylos (Pliny, *NH* 37.1.[4]: Suetonius *Aug.* 50). Another gem-engraver we may note is Pamphilos.	About 28. Publication of the first book of Propertius's *Elegies*.	
	27. Varro dies in Rome.	
	27/25. Livy embarks on his *History (Ab Urbe Condita)*.	
	26. The poet C. Cornelius Gallus commits suicide in Rome.	
	25. Propertius publishes the second book of his *Elegies*.	25
	23. Horace publishes the first three books of his *Odes*.	
	About 22. Publication of the third book of Propertius's *Elegies*.	
21. The Arch of Augustus in the Forum Romanum.	20. Horace publishes the first book of his *Epistles*.	
20 *et seq*. Frieze of the temple of Apollo Sosianus.	19. 21 September: Virgil dies at Brindisi, on his return from Greece.	
19. The Baths of Agrippa.	19/18 Death of Tibullus.	
	17. Horace composes the *Carmen Saeculare*, to be sung by a double choir of young boys and girls on the occasion of the Secular Games.	
	14(?). Publication of the fourth book of Propertius's *Elegies*.	
13. Work begun on the *Ara Pacis Augustae*. Balbus's Theatre built.	13. Horace publishes the second book of the *Epistles* and the fourth book of the *Odes*.	
12. Tomb of C. Cestius Epulo, in the shape of a pyramid.		
11. Completion of Marcellus's Theatre, begun by Caesar.		
9. Dedication of the *Ara Pacis Augustae*.		
	8. 27 November: Death of Horace in Rome.	
	About 4. Seneca, the tragedian and Stoic philosopher, born at Cordova.	
About 1. Historical frieze painted in the 'House of Livia' on the Palatine. 'Arezzo-type' vases by Perennius on the Esquiline.		0
2. Altars of the *vicomagistri*, 'street-commissioners' or municipal magistrates.		
	4/5. Death of Asinius Pollio at Tusculum.	
7/10. The temple of Concord in the Forum.		
	8. Ovid exiled to Tomis (Constantza) on the Black Sea, at the mouth of the Danube.	

MEN	EVENTS
9. Arminius, chieftain of the Cherusci (19 BC-AD 19). P. Quintilius Varus (consul in 13 BC; died AD 9). Birth at Reate of Vespasian, the future Emperor.	9. Pannonia becomes a Roman province. Arminius (Hermann) destroys Varus's legions in the Teutoberger Forest.
14. Tiberius Emperor (AD 14-37). Drusus Julius Caesar Minor, son of the Emperor Tiberius (died AD 23). Lucius Aelius Sejanus (AD 14-31). Germanicus, son of Drusus, grandson and adopted son of Tiberius (died AD 19).	14. Death of Augustus, *aet.* 76. Tiberius succeeds him. Drusus puts down a revolt of the legions in Pannonia. Sejanus becomes Prefect of the Praetorian Guard.
	14/17. Punitive expeditions into Germany under the command of Germanicus.
15. Birth of the future Emperor Vitellius.	15. Moesia absorbed into a single province with Macedonia and Achaea.
17. Tacfarinas, tribal chieftain of the Mauretanians.	17/18. Germanicus in the East: Cappadocia and Commagene become Roman provinces. A vassal-king on-the throne of Armenia.
	17/24. Revolt in Africa under Tacfarinas.
	23. Death of Drusus, Tiberius's son, perhaps poisoned at Sejanus's orders.
	26. Tiberius retires to Capri.
30. Vipsania Agrippina (the Elder), daughter of Agrippa and Julia, wife of Germanicus (died AD 33).	30. Agrippina, Germanicus's widow, and her children (except C. Caligula) banished to the island of Pandateria. Sejanus granted proconsular powers by Tiberius.
32. Birth of the future Emperor Otho.	31. Sejanus made joint-consul with Tiberius. His subsequent condemnation and death.
	33. Agrippina dies in exile with her children.
37. C. Caligula, Emperor (AD 37-41).	37. Tiberius dies on Capri, *aet.* 78.
39. Birth of the future Emperor Titus.	38. Numidia becomes an autonomous province.
40. Ptolemy King of Mauretania (died AD 40).	40. Caligula has Juba II's son Ptolemy assassinated.
41. Claudius Emperor (AD 41-54).	41 (January). Caligula assassinated by Cassius Chaerea, a tribune of the Praetorian Guard.
	42. Mauretania divided into two provinces.
	43. Claudius conquers Britain as far north as the line formed by the Trent and the Severn. Lycia and Pamphylia become a single Roman province.
	44. Britain becomes a Roman province.
	46. Thrace becomes a Roman province.
48. Death of the Empress Messalina.	48. Claudius has his wife Messalina executed for immoral behaviour.
49. Julia Agrippina the Younger (15 BC-AD 59), daughter of Germanicus.	49. Claudius marries his niece Agrippina, and adopts her son Nero.
53. The future Emperor Trajan born at Italica, in Spain.	
54. Nero Emperor (AD 54-68).	54. Death of Claudius at the age of 64 (perhaps poisoned by Agrippina).

THE ARTS	THOUGHT	

9. Arch of Augustus at Susa (Piedmont).

About 12. Trogus Pompeius, born in Gallia Narbonensis, writes the *Historiae Philippicae* (on the history of the Macedonian kingdom and the Parthians).

14/29. Statue of Augustus at Prima Porta.

17. Livy dies in Padua. Ovid dies at Tomis.

23/24. Birth at Comum of C. Plinius Secundus (the Elder Pliny): historian, grammarian, encyclopedist.

25. Silius Italicus, the epic poet, born – perhaps at Corfinium (Corfinio). His main work was the *Punica*, on the Second Punic War (88-*c*.101).

29. Velleius Paterculus, a Campanian by origin, publishes a historical study (covering the period from 'the origins' to the year 30), which he dedicates to M. Vinicius, consul-designate.

About 30. Phaedrus writing fables in the manner of Aesop. Birth of Sextus Julius Frontinus, author of treatises on architecture, surveying, and military topics.

31/32. Valerius Maximus publishes his *Memorable Facts and Sayings* – *Factorum ac dictorum memorabilium libri IX*, dedicated to Tiberius.

34. A. Persius Flaccus, member of the Equestrian Order and author of the *Satires*, born at Volaterrae (Volterra).

35/40. M. Fabius Quintilianus (Quintilian), rhetorician and orator, born at Calagurris Nassica (Calahorra) in Hispania Tarraconensis.

39. M. Annaeus Lucanus (Lucan), nephew of Seneca the Philosopher, and an epic poet (*Belli Civilis Libri*, better known as the *Pharsalia*), born at Cordova.

About 40. M. Valerius Martialis (Martial), author of the *Epigrams*, born at Bilbilis (modern Bambola) in Hispania Tarraconensis.

40/50. Birth at Naples of P. Papinius Statius, poet, author of the *Silvae*, the *Thebaid* and the *Achilleid*.

41/49. Seneca in exile on Corsica, where he writes the *De Ira*, the *Consolatio ad Polybium*, the *Consolatio ad Helviam matrem*, and the *De Providentia*.

42/54. Claudian aqueduct completed.

About 49. Monument of Lusius Storax (Chieti).

49. Seneca recalled to Rome by the Empress Agrippina as Nero's tutor.

50/60. The *Ara Pietatis*. Underground basilica by the Porta Maggiore.

50/60. Birth at Aquinum of D. Iunius Iuvenalis (Juvenal), the satirical poet.

52. Rome: Porta Maggiore (Claudian Aqueduct).

54. Seneca composes the satire *Ludus de morte Claudii*, otherwise known as the *Apocolocyntosis,* or 'Pumpkinification'.

25

50

MEN	EVENTS
55. Death of Britannicus, the son of Claudius and Massalina.	55. Nero has Britannicus poisoned.
58. Otho marries Poppaea Sabina.	
60. Boadicea Queen of the Iceni.	60. Boadicea's rebellion in Britain. Nero has his mother Agrippina assassinated.
	61. Suetonius Paulinus and Petilius Cerialis put down the rising in Britain.
62. Death of Octavia, the daughter of Claudius and Messalina. Poppaea Sabina Empress (AD 62-65). Tigellinus Prefect of the Praetorian Guard.	62. Nero has his wife Octavia done to death and marries Poppaea.
	63. War against Parthia: Corbulo as commander-in-chief. Greater Armenia established as a client-kingdom under a Parthian prince.
	64. The Great Fire of Rome (ten out of fourteen districts gutted). First persecution of the Christians.
65. Piso and Seneca commit suicide.	65. Discovery of a conspiracy against Nero, led by Calpurnius Piso.
66/67. Corbulo commits suicide.	66. Outbreak of rebellion among the Jews, subsequently put down by Vespasian. Conspiracy against Nero, with Corbulo among those involved. The Parthian prince Tiridates crowned King of Armenia in Rome.
	67. Nero in Greece, which is now declared, not a province, as hitherto, but a federal ally of Rome.
68. Julius Vindex Governor of Gallia Lugdunensis. Sulpicius Galba Governor of Hispania Tarraconensis, and subsequently Emperor (June 68-January 69).	68. Julius Vindex, Galba, and Otho, Governor of Lusitania, all revolt. June: Nero commits suicide. End of the Julio-Claudian dynasty.
69. Otho Emperor (January-April 69). Vitellius Emperor (April-December 69). Vespasian Emperor (December AD 69-79). Beginning of the Flavian dynasty.	69 (15 January). Galba killed by the Praetorians. 16 April: Otho commits suicide after being defeated by Vitellius at Bedriacum, near Cremona. The Eastern legions, with those of Moesia and Pannonia, acclaim Vespasian Emperor. The Batavi, led by Julis Civilis, revolt. October: Vitellius is defeated near Cremona by Vespasian's troops under Antonius Primus. December: Antonius Primus occupies Rome, and Vitellius is assassinated.
70. Titus, Vespasian's son.	70. The revolt of Julius Civilis is put down. Titus conquers Jerusalem and destroys the city. Judaea becomes a Roman province.
76. Birth of the future Emperor Hadrian.	
77. Agricola, Tacitus's father-in-law, Governor of Britain.	77. The conquest of Scotland begun (completed in 84).
79. Titus Emperor (AD 79-81).	79. 24 June: Vespasian dies, *aet.* seventy. October: Eruption of Vesuvius, destroying Pompeii, Herculaneum, and other towns.
81. Domitian Emperor (AD 81-96).	81. 13 September: Titus dies at the age of forty-one.
	83. War against the Chatti. Reinforcement of the *limes*.
	84. All Britain, including Scotland, subdued by Agricola.
85. Decebalus, chieftain of the Dacians.	85. War against Decebalus on the Lower Danube (continues until 89).
86. Birth of the future Emperor Antoninus Pius.	89. War against the Suevi and Sarmatians on the Middle Danube (continues until 97).
93. Death of Agricola.	93/94. Persecution of the Jews.
96. Nerva Emperor (AD 96-98).	96. Domitian dies, the victim of a conspiracy, aged forty-four.
97. Tacitus, the historian, *consul suffectus*.	97. Trajan named as co-partner in the Principate.
98. Trajan Emperor (AD 98-117).	98. Nerva dies, aged about seventy.

75

THE ARTS	THOUGHT
	About 55. L. Junius Moderatus Columella, of Cadiz(?), composes treatise on agriculture, the *De Re Rustica*. Birth of Tacitus, orator and Roman historian, who wrote a biography of Agricola (*De vita Iulii Agricolae*), a treatise on Germany (*De origine et situ Germanorum*), and two longer works, the *Histories* and the *Annals*.
	61/62. The Younger Pliny, orator and author of the *Letters*, born at Comum.
	62. Seneca withdraws from public life, to write the *Naturales Quaestiones*, nine tragedies, and the *Letters to Lucilius*. Persius dies in Rome.
64/68. Construction of the *Domus Aurea*.	
	65. The 'Conspiracy of Piso' uncovered. Seneca, Lucan, and Petronius, author of the *Satiricon*, all commit suicide.
70. Work begun on the construction of the Coliseum.	70/75. Birth of C. Suetonius Tranquillus, historian and biographer, best known for his *De viris illustribus* and the *De vita Caesarum* ('Lives of the Twelve Caesars').
	75/79. Flavius Josephus composes his *Jewish War*.
	77. Publication of the Elder Pliny's *Naturalis Historia*.
79. Destruction of Pompeii, Herculaneum, Stabiae, etc.	79. 24 August: Death of the Elder Pliny, during the eruption of Vesuvius, while commanding the fleet at Misenum.
80. Inauguration of the Flavian Amphitheatre, or Coliseum.	80. Martial publishes his first thirty epigrams (*Liber spectaculorum*) for the inauguration of the Flavian amphitheatre.
80/90. Palace of the Flavian Emperors built on the Palatine.	
81. Arch of Titus.	81. The *Dialogus de Oratoribus*, attributed to Tacitus (the imaginary discussion is supposed to take place in 74/75).
	85. The first book of Martial's *Epigrams* published.
	88. Tacitus the historian becomes praetor and *quindecemvir sacris faciundis*.
	About 90/96. The *Revelations* of St John the Divine.
	93/94. Flavius Josephus publishes his *Jewish Antiquities*.
	95. Expulsion of the philosophers from Rome.
96. Consecration of Nerva's Forum.	95/96. Death of Quintilian. Publication of his *Institutio Oratoria*, a treatise on education and training in oratory.
	About 96/100(?). Death of Statius.
	97. Frontinus, as *curator aquarum*, or Inspector-General of Aqueducts, writes his *De Aquaeductu Urbis Romae* ('The Aqueducts of the City of Rome').
	98. Publication of Tacitus's treatise on Germany (see above).

75

	MEN	EVENTS
100	100. The Younger Pliny *consul suffectus*.	100. Foundation of Timgad (Thamugadi) in Numidia (Algeria).
		101/2. First Dacian War.
		105/7. Second Dacian War.
		106. Arabia becomes a Roman province.
		113. Trajan leaves Rome on a campaign against the Parthians (spring 114).
		114. Armenia, together with Cappadocia and Lesser Armenia, formed into a new Roman province.
		116. Mesopotamia and Assyria become Roman provinces.
	117. Hadrian Emperor (AD 117-138).	117. August: Trajan dies in Cilicia. Greater Armenia once more becomes an independent kingdom.
		122. Hadrian's journey to the North (Britain).
125		
		128-132. Hadrian and Sabina travelling in Greece, Asia Minor and Egypt.
	130. Antinoüs, Hadrian's favourite, dies in Egypt, in mysterious circumstances.	130. Foundation of Antinoöpolis.
		132/135. The revolt of the Jews in Palestine is harshly repressed.
	138. Antoninus Pius Emperor (AD 138-161).	138. 10 July: Death of Hadrian. Beginning of the Antonine dynasty.
	140. Marcus Aurelius holds his first consulship.	
150		
	161. Marcus Aurelius Emperor (AD 161-180) with Lucius Aurelius Verus as his associate in power (AD 161-169).	161. Death of Antoninus Pius.
		162/165. War against the Parthians: destruction of Seleucia.
		165. Western Mesopotamia once more becomes a Roman province.
		166. Roman merchants reach Western China. Marcus Aurelius and Lucius Verus celebrate their triumph. Plague and famine.
	169. (January or February): Death of Lucius Verus at Altinum.	167. Campaigns against the Pannonians, Germans and Sarmatians.
175		175. The Sarmatian and German campaigns concluded. Revolt of Avidius Cassius in the East.
	176. Commodus consul: takes title of Augustus in 177.	176. 27 November: Marcus Aurelius celebrates his triumph. 23 December: Commodus does likewise.
		178. Fresh attack by the Marcomanni and Iapygians.
	180. Commodus Emperor (AD 180-192).	180. 17 March: Death of Marcus Aurelius.
		192. 31 December: Commodus assassinated.
	193. Pertinax Emperor (1st January-28th March AD 193). Septimius Severus becomes the new Emperor.	

THE ARTS	THOUGHT	
	100. The Younger Pliny publishes his *Panegyric* on Trajan.	100
	101. Death of Silius Italicus.	
	102. The twelfth book of Martial's *Epigrams* published.	
	103/104. Death of Frontinus.	
108. Portrait of Trajan, commissioned on the tenth anniversary of his accession.		
109. Consecration of the Adamklissi trophy.	111/113. The Younger Pliny Governor of Bithynia: during this period he has his correspondence with Trajan, which provides the material for the tenth book of the *Letters*.	
112/113. January: Consecration of Trajan's Column and Forum.		
113. Reconstruction of the temple of *Venus Genetrix* in the *Forum Caesaris*.	About 113. Death of the Younger Pliny.	
115/127. Reconstruction of Agrippa's Pantheon.	116/120(?). Death of Tacitus.	
	119/121. Suetonius writes his *Lives of the Twelve Caesars*.	
121. Work begun on the construction of the temple of Venus and Rome.	About 120. Lucian, the author of many satirical works, born at Samosata. M. Cornelius Fronto, orator and rhetorician, born at Cirta in North Africa (*Principia historiae, De Orationibus*). Second version of the *Gospel according to St Matthew*, and probable compilation (? in Syria) of the *Didaké* [Instruction] *of the Twelve Apostles* (Christian literature).	
122. Hadrian's Wall in Britain.		
125/135. Hadrian's Villa at Tibur (Tivoli).		125
	About 126. Death of Plutarch.	
	129. Birth at Pergamum of Claudius Galenus (Galen), anatomist, physiologist and doctor (*Medical Method, On the Art of Medicine*, etc.).	
132. Work begun on the construction of Hadrian's mausoleum.		
135. The temple of Venus and Rome inaugurated.	135/140. Deaths of Juvenal and of Epictetus, the Stoic philosopher.	
139. Hadrian's mausoleum now completed. Secular paintings in what was later to be the 'House of the Martyrs John and Paul' on the Caelian Hill. At Ostia, the Pharos baths.	135/145. *The Shepherd* of Hermas and the *Acts of the Apostles* (first version 80/90).	
	140/150. Death of Suetonius. Marcion, the Gnostic philosopher, in Rome.	
145. Temple of the Divine Hadrian (reliefs from the provinces).	150. Justin Martyr's *Apology for the Christian Religion*.	150
150/160. Tomb of the Pancratii on the Via Latina.		
	155/160. Birth in Carthage of Quintus Septimius Florens Tertullianus (Tertullian), Christian apologist and writer. Death of Marcion the Gnostic. Work begun on deciding the genuine canonical writings of the New Testament.	
161/162. The Column of Antoninus Pius and Faustina (base with procession and apotheosis in the Vatican).		
	165. The *Letter* of Polycarp (*Epistula ad Philippenses*). Montanism.	
	About 169. Aulus Gellius, scholar and grammarian, writes his *Noctes Atticae* ('Attic Nights'). Pausanias compiles the *Hellados Periegesis*, or *Description of Greece*.	
	170/174. Marcus Aurelius embarks on his *Meditations*.	275
176. Arch of Marcus Aurelius (reliefs from the Capitol).	About 177. Athenagoras, *Legatio pro Christianis* ('Apology for the Christians').	
About 178. Tomb of Annia Regilla built.	About 178. Irenaeus, Bishop of Lyons, writes the treatise *Adversus Haereses* ('Against Heresies').	
180. Monument in honour of Marcus Aurelius (?) [reliefs inserted in the Arch of Constantine]. Work begun on the Antonine Column. Ostia: paintings in the 'House of Ganymede' (the traditional style's first real crisis).		
193. Work completed on the Antonine Column.		

385

GENEALOGICAL TREE OF THE ANTONINES

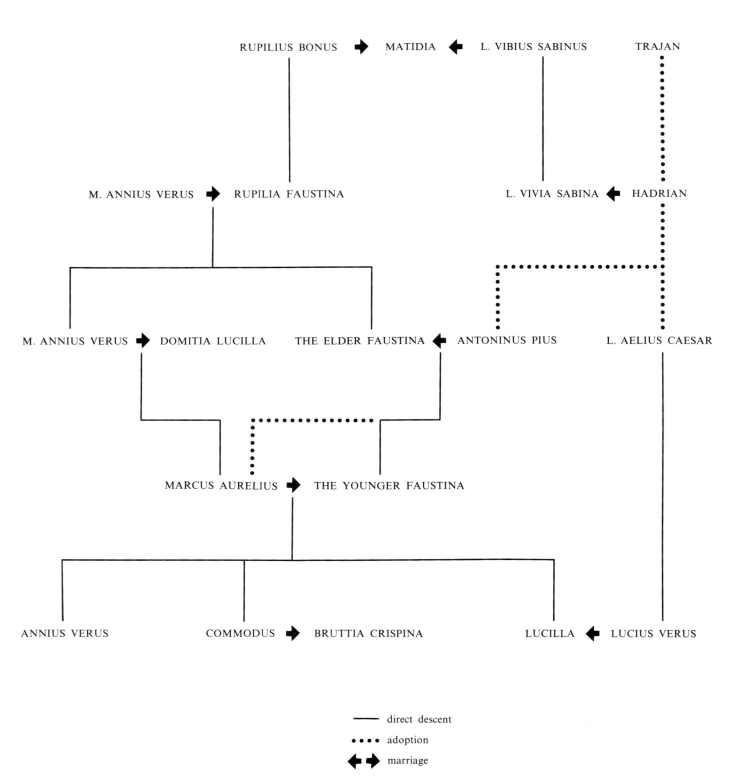

RUPILIUS BONUS ➡ MATIDIA ⬅ L. VIBIUS SABINUS   TRAJAN

M. ANNIUS VERUS ➡ RUPILIA FAUSTINA   L. VIVIA SABINA ⬅ HADRIAN

M. ANNIUS VERUS ➡ DOMITIA LUCILLA   THE ELDER FAUSTINA ⬅ ANTONINUS PIUS   L. AELIUS CAESAR

MARCUS AURELIUS ➡ THE YOUNGER FAUSTINA

ANNIUS VERUS   COMMODUS ➡ BRUTTIA CRISPINA   LUCILLA ⬅ LUCIUS VERUS

——— direct descent

•••• adoption

⬅ ➡ marriage

ANCIENT SOURCES

AMMIANUS MARCELLINUS *Rerum gestarum Libri XXXI (The Histories)*

ATHENAGORAS *Apology*

AUGUSTUS *Res Gestae (Record of Enterprises,* or *Testament)*

CICERO *Ad Atticum (Letters to Atticus)*
   Actiones in Verrem (Speeches against Verres)
   Ad Familiares (Letters to his Friends)
   Tusculanae Disputationes (Tusculan Disputations)
   Cato Maior or *De Senectute (Cato the Elder,* or *On Old Age)*
   De Haruspicum Responsis (On the Responses of Diviners)

DIO CASSIUS *Roman History*

EPICTETUS *Discourses*

EUSEBIUS *Ecclesiastical History*

FLAVIUS JOSEPHUS *The Jewish War*

FRONTO *Ad Verum Imperatorem (Letters to the Emperor Lucius Verus)*

GAIUS *Institutiones (Institutes)*

HORACE *Epoden Liber (Epodes)*
  Sermones (Satires)
  Carmina (Odes) Carmen Saeculare (Secular Hymn)

JULIUS CAPITOLINUS *Historia Augusta (History of the Emperors)* for Lucius Verus and Marcus Aurelius

LIVY (T. LIVIUS) *Ab Urbe Condita (Roman History)*
    Epitome (Summaries)

LUKE, ST *The Acts of the Apostles*

LUCIAN *Alexander Pseudomantis (Alexander the False Prophet)*
  Quomodo Historia est Conscribenda (How to Write History)

MACROBIUS *Saturnalia Libri septem (Saturnalia)*

MARCUS AURELIUS *Meditations*

MARTIAL *Epigrammaton Liber (Epigrams)*

PETRONIUS *Satiricon (Satiricon)*

PLATO *Timaeus*
  Critias

PLAUTUS *Casina (Casina)*

PLINY THE ELDER *Naturalis Historia (Natural History)*

PLUTARCH *Parallel Lives* for Numa and Marcellus

POLYBIUS *History*

SALLUST *De Bello Jugurthino (The Jugurthine War)*

SENECA *Epistolae and Lucilium (Letters to Lucilius)*

SUETONIUS in *De Vita Caesarum (Lives of the Twelve Caesars)* for Nero and Augustus

TACITUS *Annales ab excessu divi Augusti (Annals).*

VARRO *De Lingua Latina (On the Latin Tongue)*

VIRGIL *Bucolicae (Eclogues)*

VITRUVIUS *De Architectura libri decem (On Architecture)*

Bibliography

GENERAL WORKS

REFERENCE BOOKS

1 BIANCHI BANDINELLI (Ranuccio) and BECATTI (Giovanni), eds., *Enciclopedia dell'arte antica classica e orientale*, Rome, Istituto della Enciclopedia italiana, 1958-1966, 7 vol.

2 BRUNN (Heinrich) and ARNDT (Paul), *Griechische und römische Porträte*, Munich, Verlagsanstalt für Kunst und Wissenschaft, 1891 sq. (Published in fascicles, text by various authors.)

3 CAGNAT (René) and CHAPOT (Victor), *Manuel d'archéologie romaine*, Paris, A. Picard, 1916-1920, 2 vol.

4 DAREMBERG (Charles), SAGLIO (Edmond) and POTTIER (Edmond), eds., *Dictionnaire des antiquités grecques et romaines d'après les textes et les monuments*, Paris, Hachette, 1877-1919, 9 vol in 5.

5 HERRMANN (Paul) and BRUCKMANN (Friedrich), *Denkmäler der Malerei des Altertums*, Munich, F. Bruckmann, 1906 sq. (Published in fascicles, text by various authors.)

6 *Monumenti della pittura antica scoperti in Italia*, Rome, Libreria dello Stato, 1938 sq. (Documentary fascicles, texts by various authors.)

GENERAL SURVEYS

7 BECATTI (Giovanni), *Arte e gusto negli scrittori latini*, Florence, Sansoni, 1951.

8 BECATTI (Giovanni), *L'età classica*, in *Le grandi epoche dell'arte*, Florence, Sansoni, 1955, pp. 285-352.

9 BIANCHI BANDINELLI (Ranuccio), with contributions by Hans Jürgen Eggers and Filippo Coarelli, *Romana Arte*, in *Enciclopedia dell'arte antica classica e orientale*, VI, Rome, Istituto della Enciclopedia italiana, 1965, pp. 939-1024.

10 BORDA (Maurizio), *La pittura romana*, Milan, Società editoriale italiana, 1958.

11 BREGLIA (Laura), *Numismatica antica. Storia e metodologia*, Milan, Feltrinelli, 1964.

12 BRILLIANT (Richard), *Gesture and Rank in Roman Art*, 'Memoirs of the Connecticut Academy', XIV, New Haven, Conn., 1963.

13 BYVANCK (Alexander Willem), *De Kunst der Oudheid*, IV and V, Leiden, E. J. Brill, 1960-1965.

14 FROVA (Antonio), *L'arte di Roma e del mondo romano*, 'Storia universale dell'arte', II, Turin, Unione tipografica editrice torinese, 1961.

15 GARCIA Y BELLIDO (Antonio), *Arte romano*, Madrid, Blass, 1955.

16 GRABAR (André), *The Beginnings of Christian Art*, 'Arts of Mankind', London, Thames and Hudson, 1967, and, under the title *Early Christian Art*, New York, Odyssey, 1968.

17 HANFMANN (George M. A.), *Roman Art*, London, Cory, Adams and Mackay, and Greenwich, Conn., New York Graphic Society, 1964.

18 KÄHLER (Heinz), *Rome and Her Empire*, 'Art of the World Library', London, Methuen, and New York, Crown, 1963.

19 KASCHNITZ-WEINBERG (Guido von), *Römische Kunst*, I-III, Reinbeck, Rowohlt Verlag, 1961-1962. (Published by Helga von Heintze in *Rowohlts Deutsche Enzyklopädie*, nos. 133, 134, 137, 150.)

20 KRAUS (Theodor), *Das römische Weltreich*, 'Propyläen-Kunstgeschichte', II, Berlin, A. Springer, 1967.

21 LEE THOMPSON (Mary), *Monumental and Literary Evidence for Programmatic Painting in Antiquity*, in *Marsyas*, IX, 1960, pp. 36 sq.

22 PICARD (Gilbert-Charles), *L'Art romain*, Paris, Presses universitaires de France, 1962.

23 SCOTT RYBERG (Inez), *Rites of the State Religion in Roman Art*, in *Memoirs of the American Academy in Rome*, XXII, Rome, 1955.

24 STRONG (Eugenie), *Roman Sculpture*, London, Duckworth & Co., 1911.

25 STRONG (Eugenie), *La scultura romana da Augusto a Costantino* (Italian edn. of no. 24, translated by Giulio Gianelli), Florence, Alinari, 1923-1926, 2 vol. (Trans. rev. and enlarged by the author.)

26 TECHNAU (Werner), *Die Kunst der Römer*, 'Geschichte der Kunst des Altertums', II, Berlin, 1940.

27 WIRTH (Fritz W.), *Römische Wandmalerei vom Untergang Pompejis bis ans Ende des III. Jahrhunderts*, XII, Berlin, Verlag für Kunstwissenschaft, 1934.

CATALOGUES

28 CAGIANO DE AZEVEDO (Michelangelo), *Le antichità di Villa Medici*, Rome, Libreria dello Stato, fourth edition, 1951.

29 CALZA (Raissa), *Scavi di Ostia, I Ritratti*, I, 'Scavi di Ostia', V, Rome, Istituto poligrafico dello Stato, 1964.

30 DELLA SETA (Alessandro), *Catalogo del Museo de Villa Giulia*, Rome, Danesi, 1918.

31 ELIA (Olga), *Pitture murali e mosaici nel Museo nazionale di Napoli*, 'Le guide dei musei italiani', Rome, Libreria dello Stato, 1932.

32 FELLETTI MAJ (Bianca Maria), *Catalogo dei ritratti nel Museo nazionale romano*, 'Cataloghi dei musei e gallerie d'Italia', Rome, Libreria dello Stato, 1953.

33 HELBIG (Wolfgang), *Führer durch die*

öffentlichen Sammlungen klassischer Altertümer in Rom, Tubingen, Ernst Wasmuth, 1963-1966-1968, 3 vol. (4th edn., edited by H. Speier).

34 JONES (Henry Stuart), A Catalogue of the Ancient Sculptures in the Municipal Collections of Rome. The Sculptures of the Museo capitolino, Oxford, The Clarendon Press, 1912.

35 MORETTI (Mario), Il Museo nazionale di Villa Giulia, Rome, Tipografia artistica, 1963.

36 MUSTILLI (Domenico), Il Museo Mus-

solini (Museo nuovo dei Conservatori), Rome, Istituto poligrafico dello Stato, 1939.

37 PARIBENI (Roberto), Le Terme di Diocleziano e il Museo nazionale romano, 'Le guide dei musei italiani', Rome, Libreria dello Stato, 1928, definitive edn.

38 PIETRANGELI (Carlo), Il Museo Barracco, Rome, Istituto grafico tiberino, 1963.

39 SCHEFOLD (Karl), Die Wände Pompeijs. Topographisches Verzeichnis der Bild-

motive, Berlin, Walter de Gruyter & Co., 1957.

40 Vaticano (Città del), in Enciclopedia dell'arte antica classica e orientale, VII, Rome, Istituto della Enciclopedia italiana, 1966, pp. 1094-1103. (Article written by several contributors, the principal one being H. Speier, with short descriptions of the ancient collections and a bibliography of their catalogues.)

41 VISCONTI (Pietro Ercole), Catalogo del Museo Torlonia di sculture antiche, Rome, Tipografia tiberina, 1883-1884.

SPECIAL STUDIES

ROMAN HISTORY

42 ALFÖLDI (Andréas), Early Rome and the Latins, 'Jerome Lectures', 7th Series, Ann Arbor, University of Michigan Press, n.d. [1963].

43 AYMARD (André), Rome et son empire, 'Histoire générale des civilisations', II, Paris, Presses universitaires de France, 1954.

44 BLOCH (Raymond), Traditions celtiques dans l'histoire des premiers siècles de Rome, in Mélanges...Carcopino, Paris, Hachette, 1966, pp. 125 sq.

45 The Cambridge Ancient History, VIII-XII, Cambridge, The University Press, 1928-1939. (Various contributors.)

46 CESANO (Secondina Lorenzina), I fasti della Repubblica romana sulla moneta di Roma, in Studi di numismatica, I, 2, 1942.

47 FRANK (Tenney), ed., An Economic Survey of Ancient Rome, Paterson, New Jersey, 1933-1940; reprinted 1959, 5 vol.

48 GAGÉ (Jean), Les Classes sociales dans l'Empire romain, Paris, Payot, 1964.

49 GRANT (Michael), The World of Rome, London, Weidenfeld and Nicolson, and Cleveland, Ohio, World, 1960.

50 KOVALIOV (S. I.), Istoria Rima, Leningrad, University of Leningrad, 1948.

51 MAZZARINO (Santo) and GIANNELLI (Giulio), Trattato di storia romana, Rome, Tumminelli, 1953-1956, 2 vol.

52 MÜLLER-KARPE (Hermann), Vom Anfang Roms, in Mitteilungen des Deutschen Archäologischen Instituts. Römische Abteilung, Heidelberg, 1959.
    Collection of archaeological evidence for protohistory, with conclusions on such topics as social history, religion and urban topography.

53 MÜLLER-KARPE (Hermann), Zur Stadtwerdung Roms, in Mitteilungen des Deutschen Archäologischen Instituts. Römische Abteilung, Heidelberg, 1962.
    Collection of archaeological evidence for protohistory, with conclusions on such topics as social history, religion and urban topography.

54 PIGANIOL (André), La Conquête romaine, Paris, Presses universitaires

de France, 1967, 5th edn., revised. From the origins until the fall of the Republic.

55 ROSTOVTZEFF (Mikhail), Social and Economic History of the Roman Empire, ed. P. M. Frazer, Oxford, The Clarendon Press, 1926; 2nd edn., 1957, 2 vol.

56 SESTON (William), Marius Maximus et la date de la 'Constitutio Antoniniana', in Mélanges . . . Carcopino, Paris, Hachette, 1966, pp. 877 sq.

57 SYME (Ronald), The Roman Revolution, Oxford, The Clarendon Press, 1939; 2nd edn., 1952.

58 VULPE (Radu), Dion Cassius et la campagne de Trajan en Mésie inférieure, in Studii clasice, VI, Bucharest, 1964, pp. 205-232.

59 WEBER (Wilhelm), Römisches Herrschertum und Reich im II. Jahrhundert nach Christus, Stuttgart-Berlin, W. Kohlhammer, 1937.

60 WEBER (Wilhelm), The Cambridge Ancient History, XI, IX, 8, Cambridge. The University Press, 1954.

THE HISTORY OF ART

THE PROBLEM OF ROMAN ART

61 BIANCHI BANDINELLI (Ranuccio), *Römische Kunst zwei Generationen nach Wickhoff*, in *Klio*, XXXVIII, 1960, pp. 267 sq. (Reprinted in *Archeologia e cultura*, Milan-Naples, 1961, pp. 234 sq., trans. into Italian.)

62 BRENDEL (Otto), *Prolegomena to a Book on Roman Art*, in *Memoirs of the American Academy in Rome*, XXI, Rome, 1953, pp. 9 sq.

63 BYVANCK (Alexander Willem), *Le Problème de l'art romain*, in *Bulletin Vereeniging v. antieke Beschaving*, XXXIII, 1958, pp. 1 sq.

64 CURTIUS (Ludwig), *Geist der römischen Kunst*, in *Die Antike*, V, 1929, pp. 187-213.

65 HINKS (Roger Packmann), *Carolingian Art*, London, Sidgwick & Jackson, 1935; 2nd edn., Ann Arbor, 1962.

66 KÄHLER (Heinz), *Wesenzüge der römischen Kunst*, Saarbrücken, Universität des Saarlandes, 1958.

67 LEVI (Doro), *L'arte romana, schizzo della sua evoluzione e sua posizione nella storia dell'arte antica*, in *Annuario della Scuola archeologica italiana di Atene*, XXIV-XXVI, 1946-1948, pp. 229 sq. (Published in 1950.)

68 RIEGL (Alois), *Die spätrömische Kunstindustrie nach den Funden in Österreich-Ungarn*, Wien, Druck und Verlag der kaiserlich-königlichen Hof und Staatsdruckerei, 1901, part 1, 2 vol. (Subsequently published under the title *Spätrömische Kunstindustrie*, Österreichische Staatsdruckerei, Vienna, 1927.)

69 RODENWALDT (Gerhart), *Römisches in der antiken Kunst*, in *Archäologischer Anzeiger*, XXXVIII-XXXIX, 1923-1924, pp. 364 sq.

70 SCHEFOLD (Karl), *Vom Ursprung und Sinn 'römischer' Reliefkunst*, in *Charites. Studien zur Altertumswissenschaft herausgegeben von Konrad Schauenburg*, Bonn, Athenäum-Verlag, Junker & Dünnhaupt, 1957, pp. 187 sq.

71 SCHWEITZER (Bernhard), *Die europäische Bedeutung der römischen Kunst*, in *Zur Kunst der Antike. Ausgewählte Schriften*, II, Tübingen, Ernst Wasmuth, 1963, pp. 198 sq.

72 SNIJDER (Geerto Aelko Seebo), *Het Probleem der Romeinse Kunst*, in *Tijdschrift voor Geschiedenis*, XLIX, 1934, pp. 1 sq.

73 STRZYGOWSKI (Josef), *Orient oder Rom?*, Leipzig, W. Brugulin, 1901.

74 WICKHOFF (Franz), *Die Wiener Genesis*, Prague-Vienna-Leipzig, Télpsky, Freytag, 1895. (Introduction published separately under the title *Roman Art*, London, Heinemann, and New York, Macmillan, 1900.)

REPUBLICAN PERIOD

75 BIANCHI BANDINELLI (Ranuccio), *Sulla formazione del ritratto romano*, in *Archeologia e cultura*, Milan-Naples, R. Ricciardi, 1961, pp. 172-188.

76 BIANCHI BANDINELLI (Ranuccio), COARELLI (Filippo), FRANCHI (Luisa), GIULIANO (Antonio), LA REGINA (Adriano) and TORELLI (Mario), *Sculture municipali dell'area sabellica tra l'età di Cesare e quella di Nerone*, in *Studi miscellanei*, X, Rome, 1966.

77 BONNAFFÉ (Edmond), *Les Collectionneurs de l'ancienne Rome. Notes d'un amateur*, Paris, Aubry, 1867.

78 CASTAGNOLI (Ferdinando), *Dedica arcaica lavinate a Castore e Polluce* in *Studi e materiali di storia delle religioni*, XXX, 1, Rome, Cesare Mazioli, 1959, pp. 109-117.

79 CASTAGNOLI (Ferdinando), *Sulla tipologia degli altari di Lavinio*, in *Bollettino comunale*, LXXVII, Rome, 1959-1960.

80 COLONNA (Giovanni), *Il santuario di Pyrgi alla luce delle recenti scoperte*, in *Studi etruschi*, XXXIII, 1965, pp. 191-219.
Concerning the discovery of Etruscan and Phoenician inscriptions at Pyrgi.

81 COLONNA (Giovanni), GARBINI (Giovanni) and PALLOTTINO (Massimo), *Scavi nel santuario etrusco di Pyrgi: relazione preliminare della VIIª campagna*, in *Archeologia classica*, XVI, Rome, 1964, pp. 49-117.
Concerning the discovery of Etruscan and Phoenician inscriptions at Pyrgi.

82 FRANK (Tenney), *Roman Buildings of the Republic*, in *Memoirs of the American Academy in Rome*, Rome, 1924.

83 JUCKER (Hans), *Vom Verhältnis der Römer zur bildenden Kunst der Griechen*, Frankfurt/Main, V. Klostermann, 1950.

84 KASCHNITZ-WEINBERG (Guido von), *Studien zur etruskischen und frührömischen Porträtkunst*, in *Mitteilungen des Deutschen Archäologischen Instituts. Römische Abteilung*, XLI, Rome, 1926, pp. 133-211.

85 KASCHNITZ-WEINBERG (Guido von), *Über die Grundformen der italisch-römischen Struktur*, *Mitteilungen des Deutschen Archäologischen Instituts*, III, Munich, 1950, pp. 148 sq.

86 KASCHNITZ-WEINBERG (Guido von), *Vergleichende Studien zur italisch-römischen Struktur*, I, *Baukunst*, in *Kleine Schriften zur Struktur*, I, Berlin, Gebr. Mann, 1965, pp. 109-145.

87 MICHEL (Dorotea), *Alexander als Vorbild für Pompeius, Caesar und Marcus Antonius*, 'Collection Latomus', XCIV, Bruxelles, Latomus, 1967.

88 PARIBENI (Roberto), *Ariccia: Stipe votiva in località Castelletto*, in *Notizie degli scavi*, Rome, 1930, pp. 370 sq.

89 POULSEN (Frederik), *Die Römer der republikanischen Zeit und ihre Stellung zur Kunst*, in *Die Antike*, XIII, 2, 1937, pp. 125-150.

90 PUGLIESE CARRATELLI (Giovanni), *Intorno alle lamine di Pyrgi*, in *Studi etruschi*, XXXIII, 1965, pp. 221-235.
Concerning the discovery of Etruscan and Phoenician inscriptions at Pyrgi.

91 SCHWEITZER (Bernhard), *Die Bildnis-*

kunst der römischen Republik, Leipzig-Weimar, Koehler & Amelang, 1948.

92 SCOTT RYBERG (Inez), *An Archaeological Record of Rome from the VIIth to the IInd Century B.C.*, in *Studies and Documents*, XIII, I, 2, London, Christophers, 1940.

93 STRONG (Eugenie), *The Art of the Roman Republic*, in *The Cambridge Ancient History*, IX, Cambridge, The University Press, 1932.

94 STUCCHI (Sandro), *Statua di Apollo saettante dalle rovine del tempio Sosiano*, in *Bollettino comunale*, LXXV, Rome, 1953-1955 (1956), pp. I sq.

95 VAN ESSEN (Carel Claudius), *Literary Evidence for the Beginnings of Roman Art*, in *Journal of Roman Studies*, XXIV, 1934, pp. 154-162.

96 VESSBERG (Olaf), *Studien zur Kunstgeschichte der römischen Republik*, 'Acta Instituti Romani Regni Sueciae', VIII, Lund-Leipzig, C.W.K. Gleerup-O. Harrassowitz, 1941.

97 ZINSERLING (Georg), *Studien zu den Historiendarstellungen der römischen Republik*, in *Wissenschaftliche Zeitschrift der Friedrich-Schiller-Universität Jena*, IX, Jena, 1959-1960, pp. 403-448.

THE JULIO-CLAUDIAN PERIOD

98 BIANCHI BANDINELLI (Ranuccio), Review of *Antike Plastik*, IV, Berlin, 1965, in *Dialoghi di archeologia*, I, I, Milan, Saggiatore, pp. 125-129.
On the third Grimani relief.

99 BRENDEL (Otto), *Novus Mercurius*, in *Mitteilungen des Deutschen Archäologischen Instituts. Römische Abteilung*, L, 1935, pp. 231-259.

100 CARETTONI (Gianfilippo), *I problemi della zona Augustea del Palatino*, in *Rendic. Pontificia Accad.*, XXXIX, 1966-1967, pp. 55-75.

101 CHARBONNEAUX (Jean), *L'Art au siècle d'Auguste*, Lausanne, Clairefontaine, 1948.

102 FUCHS (Werner), *Die Vorbilder der neuattischen Reliefs*, in *Jahrbuch des Instituts*, Berlin, De Gruyter, 1965.

103 GABRIEL (Mabel M.), *Livia's Garden Room at Prima Porta*, New York, University Press, 1955.

104 GRIMAL (Pierre), *Les Jardins romains à la fin de la République et aux deux premiers siècles de l'Empire*, «Bibliothèque des Écoles françaises d'Athènes et de Rome», 155, Paris, E. de Boccard, 1943.

105 KRAUS (Theodor), *Die Ranken der Ara Pacis*, Berlin, Gebr. Mann, 1953.

106 KÜTHMANN (Harald), *Untersuchungen zur Toreutik des zweiten und ersten Jahrhunderts vor Chr.*, Inaugural lecture. Basel, Typogr. Lassleben, Kallmünz (Oberpfalz), 1959.

107 MÖBIUS (Hans), *Alexandria und Rom*, 'Bayerische Akademie der Wissenschaften', n.s. 59, Munich, 1964.

108 MORETTI (Giuseppe), *Ara Pacis Augustae*, Rome, Istituto poligrafico dello Stato, 1948, 2 vol.

109 RODENWALDT (Gerhard), *Kunst um Augustus*, Berlin, Walter de Gruyter & Co., 1942.

110 SIMON (Erika), *Toreutica*, in *Enciclopedia dell'arte antica, classica e orientale*, VII, Rome, Istituto della Enciclopedia italiana, 1966, pp. 919-948. (Contains an important bibliography.)

111 SIMON (Erika), *Ara Pacis Augustae*, 'Monumenta Artis antiquae', I, Tübingen, Ernst Wasmuth, 1967.

112 STROCKA (Volker Michael), *Die Grimanischen Reliefs*, in *Antike Plastik*, IV, Berlin, 1965, pp. 87-102.

113 STRONG (Eugenie), *The Art of the Augustean Age*, in *The Cambridge Ancient History*, X, Cambridge, The University Press, 1934, pp. 545 sq.

114 ZANKER (Paul), *Forum Augustum*, 'Monumenta Artis antiquae', II, Tübingen, Ernst Wasmuth, 1968.

THE FLAVIAN PERIOD

115 BLANCKENHAGEN (Peter Heinrich von), *Flavische Architektur und ihre Dekoration untersucht am Nervaforum*, Berlin, Gebr. Mann, 1940.

116 BLANCKENHAGEN (Peter Heinrich von), *Elemente der römischen Kunst am Beispiel des flavischen Stils*, in *Das neue Bild der Antike*, II, Leipzig, Koehler & Amelang, 1942, pp. 310-341.

117 CASTAGNOLI (Ferdinando), *Gli edifici rappresentati in un rilievo del sepolcro degli Haterii*, in *Bollettino comunale*, LXIX, Rome, 1941, pp. 59-69.

118 CHAMOUX (François), *Observations sur la survivance des thèmes helléniques dans la sculpture provençale*, 'Publications de l'Université de Dijon', XVI, Dijon, Imprim. Bernigaud et Privat, 1958.

119 MAGI (Filippo), *I rilievi Flavi del palazzo della Cancelleria*, Rome, Bardi, 1946.

120 PICARD (Gilbert-Charles), *Glanum et les origines de l'art romano-provençal*, in *Gallia*, XXI, Paris, Centre national de la recherche scientifique, 1963, pp. III sq.

121 PICARD (Gilbert-Charles), *La Peinture romaine jusqu'à la destruction de Pompéi*, in *Revue des Etudes Latines*, XLII, Paris, Les Belles-Lettres, 1964, pp. 378 sq.

122 SCHEFOLD (Karl), *Probleme der pompejanischen Malerei*, in *Mitteilungen des Deutschen Archäologischen Instituts. Römische Abteilung*, LXXII, Heidelberg, 1965, pp. 116-126.

TRAJAN AND HADRIAN'S REIGNS

123 ANDREAE (Bernhard), *Studien zur römischen Grabkunst*, in *Mitteilungen des Deutschen Archäologischen Instituts. Römische Abteilung*, Heidelberg, 1963.

124 BIANCHI BANDINELLI (Ranuccio), *Gusto e valore dell'arte provinciale*, in *Storicità dell'arte classica*, Florence, Electa editrice, 2nd edn., 1950, pp. 229 sq.

125 BIANCHI BANDINELLI (Ranuccio), *Il 'Maestro delle imprese di Traiano'*, in *Storicità dell'arte classica*, Florence, Electa editrice, 2nd edn., 1950, pp. 209 sq.

126 CARANDINI (Andrea), *Vibia Sabina*, Florence, Olschki, 1968.

127 GRAINDOR (Paul), *Athènes sous Hadrien*, Cairo, Impr. Misr., 1932.

128 GROSS (Walter Hatto), *Bildnisse Trajans*, in *Das römische Herrscherbild*, II, 2, Berlin, Gebr. Mann, 1940.

129 HAMBERG (Peer Gustaf), *Studies in Roman Imperial Art. The State Relief of the Second Century*, Copenhagen, Almqvist-Munksgaard, 1945.

130 HASSEL (Franz Josef), *Der Trajansbogen in Benevent. Ein Bauwerk des römischen Senates*, Mainz, Zabern, 1966.

131 KÄHLER (Heinz), *Hadrian und seine Villa bei Tivoli*, Berlin, Gebr. Mann, 1950.

132 LEHMANN-HARTLEBEN (Karl), *Die Trajanssäule*, Berlin, Walter de Gruyter & Co., 1926.

133 PARIBENTI (Roberto), *Optimus Princeps*, Messina, Principato, 1926-1927.

134 PASSARELLI (Vincenzo), *Rilievo e studio di restituzione dello Hadrianeum*, in *Atti III° Convegno di storia dell'architettura 1938*, Rome, 1940, pp. 123 sq.

135 TOYNBEE (Jocelyn Mary Catherine), *The Hadrianic School. A Chapter in the History of Greek Art*, Cambridge, The University Press, 1934.

136 WEITZMANN (Kurt), *The Joshua Roll*, Princeton, The University Press, 1947.

THE ANTONINE PERIOD

137 BECATTI (Giovanni), *La colonna coclide istoriata*, Rome, L'Erma di Bretschneider, 1960.

138 BIANCHI BANDINELLI (Ranuccio), *Osservazioni sulla forma artistica in Oriente e in Occidente*, in *Problemi attuali di scienza e cultura: Convegno su tardo antico e alto medioevo*, Accademia dei Lincei, April 1967, Rome, 1968, section no. 105, pp. 289-308.

139 BIRLEY (Anthony), *Marcus Aurelius*, London, Eyre and Spottiswoode, 1966.

140 COARELLI (Filippo), *La porta trionfale*, in *Dialoghi di archeologia*, II, I, Milan, Saggiatore, 1968.

141 COLINI (Antonio Maria), GATTI (Guido) et coll., *La colonna di Marco Aurelio. Studi e materiali, Museo dell'Impero*, Rome, l'Erma di Bretschneider, 1955.

142 MAZZARINO (Santo), *Prima cattedra*, in *Mélanges d'archéologie et d'histoire offerts à André Piganiol*, Paris, S.E.V.-P.E.N., 1966, pp. 1635 sq.

143 MORRIS (John), *The Dating of the Column of Marcus Aurelius*, in *Journal of the Warburg and Courtauld Institute*, XV, London, 1952, pp. 33 sq.

144 RODENWALDT (Gerhard), *Über den Stilwandel in der antoninischen Kunst*, in *Abhandlungen der Preussischen Akademie der Wissenschaften*, III, Berlin, 1935.

145 RODENWALDT (Gerhard), *Art from Nero to the Antonines*, in *The Cambridge Ancient History*, XI, Cambridge, The University Press, 1936, pp. 775-805.

146 SCOTT RYBERG (Inez), *Panel Reliefs of Marcus Aurelius*, New York, The Archaeological Institute of America, 1967.

147 WEGNER (Max), *Die kunstgeschichtliche Stellung der Marcussäule*, in *Jahrbuch des Deutschen Archäologischen Instituts*, XLVI, Berlin, 1931, pp. 61 sq.

148 WEGNER (Max), *Die Herrscherbildnisse in antoninischer Zeit*, in *Das römische Herrscherbild*, I, Berlin, Gebr. Mann, 1939.

ARCHITECTURE AND TOWN PLANNING

ASHBY (Thomas). *See no. 167.*

149 BLAKE (Marion Elizabeth), *Ancient Roman Construction in Italy from the Prehistoric Period to Augustus*, Washington, D.C., Carnegie Institution, 1947.

150 BLAKE (Marion Elizabeth), *Roman Construction in Italy from Tiberius through the Flavians*, Washington D.C., Carnegie Institution, 1959.

151 BLOCH (Herbert), *I bolli laterizi e la storia dell'edilizia romana*, Rome, Comune di Roma, 1947.

152 BROWN (Donald Frederick), *Temples of Rome as Coin Types*, 'Numismatic Notes and Monographs', XC, New York, American Numismatic Society, 1940.

153 CALZA (Guido), *La necropoli del porto di Roma nell'Isola sacra*, Rome, Istituto poligrafico dello Stato, 1940.

154 CARETTONI (Gianfilippo), COLINI (Antonio Maria), COZZA (Luigi) and GATTI (Guido), *La pianta marmorea di Roma antica*, Rome, Comune di Roma, 1955-1960, 2 vol.

155 CREMA (Luigi), *L'architettura romana*, Turin, Società editrice internazionale, 1959.

156 DELBRÜCK (Richard), *Hellenistische Bauten in Latium*, Strassburg, K. J. Trübner, 1907-1912, 2 vol.

157 VAN DEMAN (Esther Boise), *The Building of Roman Aqueducts*, Washington D.C., Carnegie Institution, 1934.

158 FASOLO (Furio) and GULLINI (Giorgio), *Il santuario della Fortuna Primigenia a Palestrina*, Rome, Istituto di archeologia, University of Rome, 1953, 2 vol.

159 GERKAN (Armin von), *Griechische und römische Architektur*, in *Bonner Jahrbücher*, 1952, Bonn, 152, pp. 21 sq.

160 GIOVANNONI (Gustavo), *La tecnica della costruzione presso i Romani*, Rome, Società editrice d'arte illustrata, n.d. [1926].

161 LUGLI (Giuseppe), *I monumenti antichi di Roma e suburbio*, Rome, Bardi, 1931-1940, 4 vol.

162 LUGLI (Giuseppe), *Roma antica. Il centro monumentale*, Rome, Bardi, 1946.

163 MACDONALD (William Lloyd), *The Architecture of the Roman Empire*, New Haven-London, Yale University Press, 1965.

164 MEIGGS (Russell), *Roman Ostia*, Oxford, The Clarendon Press, 1960.

165 NASH (Ernst), *The Pictorial Dictionary of Ancient Rome*, London, Thames and Hudson, rev. edn. 1968, 2 vol.

166 PALCHETTI (Anna-Maria) and QUILICI (Lorenzo), *Il tempio di Giunone Regina nel Portico di Ottavia*, in *Studi di topografia romana (Quaderni dell'Istituto di topografia antica)*, V, Rome, 1968, pp. 77-78.

167 ASHBY (Thomas) and PLATNER (Samuel Ball), *A Topographical Dictionary of Ancient Rome*, Oxford, The Clarendon Press, 1929.

168 QUILICI (Lorenzo), *Sull'acquedotto Vergine dal Monte Pincio alle sorgenti*, in *Studi di topografia romana (Quaderni dell'Istituto di topografia antica)*, V, Rome, 1968, pp. 125-160.
   Account of the first modern attempt to explore the interior of the Roman water-conduit (the Aqua Virgo, completed in 19 BC), with documentary photographs.

169 *Roma*, in *Enciclopedia dell'arte antica classica e orientale*, VI, Rome, Istituto della Enciclopedia italiana, 1965, pp. 764-939. (Written by several contributors, the foremost being Ferdinando Castagnoli.)

395

BIBLIOGRAPHY

ROMAN ANTIQUITIES IN RENAISSANCE DRAWINGS

170 BARTOLI (Alfonso), *I monumenti antichi di Roma nei disegni degli Uffizi di Firenze*, 3 vol.: I, II, Rome, C. A. Bontempelli, 1914-1915; III, Florence, Alinari, 1922.

171 HÜLSEN (Christian), *Il libro di Giuliano da Sangallo*, Lipsia, Harrassowitz, 1910, 2 vol. (Cod. Vat. Barb. Lat. 4424).

172 HÜLSEN (Christian) and EGGER (Hermann), *Die römischen Skizzenbücher von Marten van Heemskerk*, Berlin, Julius Bard, 1913-1916, 4 vol.

INDEX TO THE BIBLIOGRAPHY

ALFÖLDI, 42.
ANDREAE, 123.
ARNDT, 2.
ASHBY, 167.
AYMARD, 43.

BARTOLI, 170.
BECATTI, 1, 7, 8, 137.
BIANCHI BANDINELLI, 1, 9, 61, 75, 76, 98, 124, 125, 138.
BIRLEY, 139.
BLAKE, 149, 150.
BLANCKENHAGEN, 115, 116.
BLOCH (H.), 151.
BLOCH (R.), 44.
BONNAFFÉ, 77.
BORDA, 10.
BREGLIA, 11.
BRENDEL, 62, 99.
BRILLIANT, 12.
BROWN, 152.
BRUCKMANN, 5.
BRUNN, 2.
BYVANCK, 13, 63.

CAGIANO DE AZEVEDO, 28.
CAGNAT, 3.
CALZA (G.), 153.
CALZA (R.), 29.
CARANDINI, 126.
CARETTONI, 100, 154.
CASTAGNOLI, 78, 79, 117.
CESANO, 46.
CHAMOUX, 118.
CHAPOT, 3.
CHARBONNEAUX, 101.
COARELLI, 76, 140.
COLINI, 141, 154.
COLONNA, 80, 81.
COZZA, 154.
CREMA, 155.
CURTIUS, 64.

DAREMBERG, 4.
DELBRÜCK, 156.
DELLA SETA, 30.

EGGER, 172.
ELIA, 31.

FASOLO, 158.
FELLETTI MAJ, 32.

FRANK, 47, 82.
FROVA, 14.
FUCHS, 102.

GABRIEL, 103.
GAGÉ, 48.
GARBINI, 81.
GARCIA Y BELLIDO, 15.
GATTI, 141, 154.
GERKAN, 159.
GIANNELLI, 51.
GIOVANNONI, 160.
GIULIANO, 76.
GRABAR, 16.
GRAINDOR, 127.
GRANT, 49.
GRIMAL, 104.
GROSS, 128.
GULLINI, 158.

HAMBERG, 129.
HANFMANN, 17.
HASSEL, 130.
HELBIG, 33.
HERRMANN, 5.
HINKS, 65.
HÜLSEN, 171, 172.

JONES, 34.
JUCKER, 83.

KÄHLER, 18, 66, 131.
KASCHNITZ-WEINBERG, 19, 84, 85, 86.
KOVALIOV, 50.
KRAUS, 20, 105.
KÜTHMANN, 106.

LA REGINA, 76.
LEE THOMPSON, 21.
LEHMANN-HARTLEBEN, 132.
LEVI, 67.
LUGLI, 161, 162.

MacDONALD, 163.
MAGI, 119.
MAZZARINO, 51, 142.
MEIGGS, 164.
MICHEL, 87.
MÖBIUS, 107.
MORETTI (G.), 108.
MORETTI (M.), 35.
MORRIS, 143.
MÜLLER-KARPE, 52, 53.

MUSTILLI, 36.

NASH, 165.

PALCHETTI, 166.
PALLOTTINO, 81.
PARIBENI, 37, 88, 133.
PASSARELLI, 134.
PICARD, 22, 120, 121.
PIETRANGELI, 38.
PIGANIOL, 54.
PLATNER, 167.
POTTIER, 4.
POULSEN, 89.
PUGLIESE CARRATELLI, 90.

QUILICI, 166, 168.

RIEGL, 68.
RODENWALDT, 69, 109, 144, 145.
ROSTOVTZEFF, 55.

SAGLIO, 4.
SCHEFOLD, 39, 70, 122.
SCHWEITZER, 71, 91.
SCOTT RYBERG, 23, 92, 146.
SESTON, 56.
SIMON, 110, 111.
SNIJDER, 72.
STROCKA, 112.
STRONG, 24, 25, 93, 113.
STRZYGOWSKI, 73.
STUCCHI, 94.
SYME, 57.

TECHNAU, 26.
TORELLI, 76.
TOYNBEE, 135.

VAN DEMAN, 157.
VAN ESSEN, 95.
VESSBERG, 96.
VISCONTI, 41.
VULPE, 58.

WEBER, 59, 60.
WEGNER, 147, 148.
WEITZMANN, 136.
WICKHOFF, 74.
WIRTH, 27.

ZANKER, 114.
ZINSERLING, 97.

Notes on the Illustrations

Abbreviations: H = Height, B = Breadth, D = Diameter, Ph. = Photo.
Dates without suffix are AD dates.

Frontispiece. Mid-Italic art. ROME. Portrait: fragment of a statue traditionally identified as the Elder Brutus. Third cent. BC. Rome: Capitol, Palazzo dei Conservatori. Bronze. H 0.69 m. Ph. U.D.F. – La Photothèque.

This head has been known since the sixteenth cent.; it was bequeathed to the city of Rome by Cardinal di Carpi, and attached to a modern bust. The eyes, of ivory and glass paste, are ancient. The identification with Brutus, the first consul, has no basis in fact.

1 Roman art. ROME. Cameo: Eagle with Symbols of Victory. Augustan period (27-14 BC). Vienna: Kunsthistorisches Museum, Antikensammlung. Onyx. D 0.22 m. Ph. Erwin Meyer, Vienna.

The setting dates only from the Renaissance (cf. 208).

2 Mid-Italic art. ROME. The She-Wolf of Rome, detail (cf. 9). Fifth cent. BC. Rome: Capitol, Palazzo dei Conservatori. Ph. U.D.F. – La Photothèque.

3 The Seven Hills of Rome. Map. From A. Malet and J. Isaac, *Histoire romaine.* Paris (Hachette), 1924, p. 30.

4 ROME, Palatine Hill. Foundations of protohistorical huts. Ninth cent. BC. *In situ.* Rock. Ph. U.D.F. – La Photothèque.

5 ROME, Capitol. The Tarpeian Rock. *In situ.* Ph. Anderson, Rome.

6 ROME, Insula Tiberina. *In situ.* Ph. U.D.F. – La Photothèque.

7 Italian art. Anonymous artist. Rome: Forum Romanum looking towards the Capitol (seventeenth century). Rome, Antiquarium del Foro. Oil painting on canvas. H 0.92 m. B 1.30 m. Ph. U.D.F. – La Photothèque.

8 Roman art. ROME. Horatius Cocles holding the Tiber bridge: medallion of Antoninus Pius, 138-61. Paris: Bibliothèque Nationale, Cabinet des Médailles. Bronze. D 0.039 m. Ph. U.D.F. – La Photothèque.

9 Mid-Italic art. ROME. The She-Wolf of Rome. Fifth cent. BC. Rome: Capitol,

Palazzo dei Conservatori. Bronze. H 0.75 m. B overall: 1.14 m. Ph. U.D.F. – La Photothèque.

References to this portrayal of the Roman She-Wolf are known as early as the tenth century AD. The figures of the Twins – suppressed in this illustration – were added during the Renaissance.

10 Roman art. LARINO (ancient LARINUM). Mosaic pavement: Shepherds discovering the She-Wolf and the Twins. Third cent. Larino: Town Hall. Coloured marble. Ph. U.D.F. – La Photothèque.

11 Roman art. PRATICA DI MARE (ancient LAVINIUM). The Thirteen Archaic Altars. Sixth and fifth cents. BC. *In situ.* Limestone. Ph. U.D.F. – La Photothèque.

12 Roman art. PRATICA DI MARE (ancient LAVINIUM). Plaque bearing a dedication, in Latin, to the Dioscuri. About 500 BC. Rome: Museo Nazionale. Bronze. Ph. Soprintendenza alle Antichità di Roma.

The inscription reads: 'Castorei Podlouqueique/qurois'.

13 Etruscan art. VULCI, the 'François Tomb'. Mcstrna and other characters in the local legend. 300-280 BC. Rome: Villa Albani. Fresco. H 1.28 m. Ph. U.D.F. – La Photothèque.

14 Etruscan art. VULCI, the 'François Tomb'. Episode from Theban legend: Eteocles and Polyneices. 300-280 BC. Rome: Villa Albani. Fresco. H 1.28 m. Ph. U.D.F. – La Photothèque.

15 Etruscan art. ROME. Etruscan bowl, with inscription. Sixth cent. BC. Rome: Museo Capitolino. Terracotta. D 0.173 m. Ph. U.D.F. – La Photothèque.

The inscription reads: 'mi araziia laraniia' (name of the owner). Found in Rome, near the Civus Capitolinus.

16 Etruscan art. ROME. Fragment of an Etruscan architectural relief. Late sixth cent. BC. Rome: Museo Capitolino. Terracotta. H 0·22 m. Ph. U.D.F. – La Photothèque.

This piece comes from an area near the Ara Coeli on which, somewhat later (344 BC) the temple of Juno Moneta was

built; it must be connected with an earlier building, itself probably a temple.

17 Art from Latium. Found in 1738, at PALESTRINA (ancient PRAENESTE). Novios Plautios. The Ficoroni Cist, executed in Rome. About 300 BC. Rome: Museo Nazionale (Villa Giulia). Bronze. H 0.74 m. Ph. U.D.F. – La Photothèque.

The scene engraved on the body of the receptacle represents the punishment of Amycus (cf. 18) and the Argonauts. The lid is engraved with a hunting-scene (boar and stag), and topped with statuettes of Dionysus accompanied by two satyrs. The three claw-type feet are decorated in relief with representations of Hercules between Iolaus and Eros.

18 Art from Latium. PALESTRINA (ancient PRAENESTE). Novios Plautios. The Ficoroni Cist (detail): The punishment of Amycus (cf. 17). About 300 BC. Rome: Museo Nazionale (Villa Giulia). Ph. U.D.F. – La Photothèque.

19 Art from Latium. PALESTRINA (ancient PRAENESTE). Novios Plautios. The Ficoroni Cist (detail, lid): Dionysus between two satyrs (cf. 17). About 300 BC. Rome: Museo Nazionale (Villa Giulia). Ph. U.D.F. – La Photothèque.

20 Art from Latium. PALESTRINA (ancient PRAENESTE). Novios Plautios. The Ficoroni Cist (detail, lid): the inscription (cf. 17). About 300 BC. Rome: Museo Nazionale (Villa Giulia). Ph. U.D.F. – La Photothèque.

The portion of the inscription visible in this illustration reads as follows: 'Dindia. Macolnia. fileai dedit'. (C.I.L., I³, 561).

21 Roman art. ROME. The serpent of Asclepius landing on the Insula Tiberina: medallion of Antoninus Pius, 138-61. Paris: Bibliothèque Nationale, Cabinet des Médailles. Bronze. D 0.039 m. Ph. U.D.F. – La Photothèque.

The cult of Asclepius (Aesculapius) was introduced to Rome in 293 BC.

22 Etruscan art. PALESTRINA (ancient PRAENESTE). Etruscan-type brooch known as the 'Manios Fibula', with inscription in Latin. Sixth cent. BC.

Rome: Museo Preistorico-Etnografico L. Pigorini. Gold. B 0.115 m. Ph. U.D.F. – La Photothèque.

The inscription reads: 'Manios: med: fhe: fhaked: Numasioi' (C.I.L., I³, 3) – i.e. 'Manios made me for Numasios (or Numerius)'.

23-4 Roman art. ROME. The oldest known Roman coin. Obverse: head of Janus. Reverse: prow of a ship. Fourth cent. BC. Rome: Museo Nazionale. Bronze. D 0.06 m. Ph. U.D.F. – La Photothèque.

This is the 'as libralis', weighing a Roman pound, i.e. 272.87 gr.

25 VEII. A sanctuary, with a Roman road running past it. *In situ.* Ph. U.D.F. – La Photothèque.

26 Roman art. ROME. Defensive fortifications: the so-called 'Servian Wall'. Fourth cent. BC. *In situ.* Tufa. Ph. U.D.F. – La Photothèque.

27 Roman art. SANTA MARIA DI FALLERI (ancient FALERII NOVI). Gate in the city-wall. About 210 BC. *In situ.* Limestone. Ph. U.D.F. – La Photothèque.

28 Art from Latium. Dish with war-elephant decoration. About 250 BC. Rome: Museo Nazionale (Villa Giulia). Terracotta. D 0.295 m. Ph. U.D.F. – La Photothèque.

29 Roman art. ROME. Tomb of the Scipios on the Via Appia. Sarcophagus of Lucius Cornelius Scipio Barbatus. About 250 BC. (The inscription can be dated to about 200.) Musei Vaticani. Volcanic rock (peperino). H 1.42 m. B 2.77 m. Ph. Anderson, Rome.

This member of the Scipio family was consul in 298 BC. For the inscription see C.I.L., I², 29.30 (= VI 1284/5).

30 Italic art. LUCERA. Local relief showing a shepherd. 3rd-1st cent. BC. Lucera: Museo Provinciale. Limestone. L of fragment: about 0.40 m. Ph. A. Giuliano, Rome.

31 Roman art. ROME. Orpheus and the animals. Late second cent. BC. Rome: Capitol, Palazzo dei Conservatori. Volcanic stone (peperino). H 0.90 m. Ph. U.D.F. – La Photothèque.

Found in Rome near the Porta Tiburtina. The generally presumed connection with the college of flute-players is erroneous. At the singer's feet we see a hare and a lion, while an owl is perched on his left leg.

32 Roman art. ISERNIA. Relief of a battle-scene. Isernia Museum. Limestone. Ph. U.D.F. – La Photothèque.

33-4 Roman art. Coin. Obverse, woman's head and the inscription 'Italia'. Reverse: military oath-taking ceremony. 91-88 BC. Paris: Bibliothèque Nationale, Cabinet des Médailles. Silver. D 0.019 m. Ph. U.D.F. – La Photothèque.

Coin struck by the Allies during the Social War.

35 Art from Latium. CERVETERI (ancient CAERE). Votive head. 2nd-1st cent. BC. Vatican: Museo Etrusco Gregoriano. Terracotta. H 0.27 m. Ph. Archivio Fotografico Gallerie e Musei Vaticani.

36 Roman art. ARICCIA (ancient ARICIA). Statue of Demeter. 2nd-1st cent. BC. Vatican: Museo Etrusco Gregoriano. Terracotta. H 1.05 m. Ph. U.D.F. – La Photothèque.

This belongs to the same group as nos. 37 and 38.

37 Roman art. ARICCIA (ancient ARICIA). Statue of Koré-Persephone (cf. 36 and 38: all these statues are from the same group). 2nd-1st cent. BC. Rome: Museo Nazionale. Terracotta. H 1.14 m. Ph. U.D.F. – La Photothèque.

38 Roman art. ARICCIA (ancient ARICIA). Bust of Demeter. 2nd-1st cent. BC. Rome: Museo Nazionale. Terracotta. H 0.73 m. Ph. U.D.F. – La Photothèque.

The ear-rings belong to a type of jewellery known from Tarentum (3rd-2nd cents. BC). Cf. nos. 36 and 37.

39 Roman art. CERVETERI (ancient CAERE). Portrait of a man. First cent. BC. Rome: Museo Nazionale (Villa Giulia). Terracotta. H of face: 0.25 m. Ph. De Antonis, Rome.

40 Roman art. ROME, Via Statilia. Funerary relief, detail (for the *vue d'ensemble*, see no. 102), 50-30 BC. Rome: Capitol, Palazzo dei Conservatori, Museo Nuovo. Limestone. Ph. U.D.F. – La Photothèque.

41 Roman art. ROME. Portrait of Pompey the Great. About 50 BC. Copenhagen: Ny Carlsberg Glyptotek. Marble. H of the head: 0.28 m. (modern bust). Ph. Glyptotek.

42 Roman art. ROME. Denarius bearing the portrait of M. Claudius Marcellus. 42 BC. Paris: Bibliothèque Nationale, Cabinet des Médailles. Silver. D 0.018 m. Ph. U.D.F. – La Photothèque.

Struck in 42 BC, this coin very prob-ably reproduces a contemporary portrait of the general who reduced Syracuse in 212 BC.

43 Graeco-Roman art. GREECE. Attic stater bearing the portrait of the consul T. Quinctius Flamininus, 194 BC. East Berlin: Staatliche Museen, Münzkabinett. Gold. D 0.019 m. Ph. U.D.F. – La Photothèque.

Flamininus concluded the conquest of Macedonia in 198 and celebrated his triumph in 194 BC.

44 Roman art. HERCULANEUM. House with wooden framework. First cent. BC – first cent. AD. *In situ.* Masonry and timber. Ph. U.D.F. – La Photothèque.

45 Roman art. POMPEII. Tomb of C. Vestorius Priscus. Silver dinner-service on a table. First cent. *In situ.* Fresco. Ph. U.D.F. – La Photothèque.

46 Graeco-Roman art. POMPEII, Via dell' Abbondanza. Lampstand in the form of an ephebe. First cent. Naples: Museo Archeologico Nazionale. Bronze. H 1.50 m. Ph. U.D.F. – La Photothèque.

47 Graeco-Roman art. ROME. Kleomenes, son of Kleomenes. A member of Augustus's family, as Hermes the Orator (*Logios*). 50-40 BC. Paris: Louvre. Marble. H 1.80 m. Ph. U.D.F. – La Photothèque.

The portrait has been identified as that of Germanicus, but without certainty.

48 Graeco-Roman art. ROME, Ludovisi Collection. M. Kossoutius Menelaos. Orestes and Electra. First half of first cent. Rome: Museo Nazionale. Marble. H 1.92 m. Ph. U.D.F. – La Photothèque.

49 Graeco-Roman art. ROME, Ludovisi Collection. M. Kossoutius Menelaos. Orestes, detail (cf. 48). First half of first cent. Rome: Museo Nazionale. Ph. Anderson, Rome.

50 Roman art. POMPEII. A baker and his customers. First cent. Naples: Museo Archeologico Nazionale. Fresco. H 0.50 m. B 0.56 m. Ph. U.D.F. – La Photothèque.

51 Roman art. ROME. The so-called 'Altar of Domitius Ahenobarbus' (detail). Procession of Poseidon and Amphitrite. About 100 BC. Munich: Staatliche Antikensammlungen. Marble. H 0.78 m. B 5.59 m. Ph. Felbermeyer (Museum).

Formerly in the Palazzo Santacroce, in Rome (cf. 52).

52 Roman art. ROME. 'Altar of Domitius Ahenobarbus'. Procession of Poseidon and Amphitrite, detail (cf. 51). About 100 BC. Munich: Staatliche Antikensammlungen. Ph. Felbermeyer (Mus.).

53 Roman art. ROME. 'Altar of Domitius Ahenobarbus' (detail). Administrative and religious ceremony. About 100 BC. Paris: Louvre. Marble. H 0.82 m. B 5.59 m. Ph. U.D.F. – La Photothèque. Formerly in Rome (Palazzo Santacroce: cf. 54).

54 Roman art. ROME. 'Altar of Domitius Ahenobarbus' (detail). Administrative and religious ceremony (cf. 53). About 100 BC. Paris: Louvre. Ph. U.D.F. – La Photothèque.

55 Roman art. ROME. 'Altar of Domitius Ahenobarbus' (detail). Administrative and religious ceremony (cf. 53). About 100 BC. Paris: Louvre. Ph. U.D.F. – La Photothèque.

56 Roman art. SUSA. Arch of Augustus (detail from the frieze). About 9-8 BC. In situ. Marble. H 0.52 m. Overall B 10.75 m. Ph. Soprintendenza Antichità, Turin.

57 Roman art. ROME. 'Altar of the Four Street-Commissioners (vicomagistri)', responsible for the streets of the vicus Aesculetus. 4 BC-2 AD. Rome: Capitol, Palazzo dei Conservatori. Marble. H 1.05 m. Ph. U.D.F. – La Photothèque.
The altar bears this inscription: 'Magistri vici Aescleti anni VIIII' (C.I.L., VI, 30957), indicating the ninth year after the reorganization of the cult of the Lares carried out by Augustus.

58 Roman art. ANGERA. Altar dedicated by two seviri: libation and bull-sacrifice. First cent. Milan: Museo Archeologico. Marble. H 1.06 m. B 0.73 m. Ph. Archivio Fotografico dei Civici Musei, Milan.

59 Roman art. SAN GUGLIELMO AL GOLETO. Relief from a funerary monument. First cent. BC. San Guglielmo al Goleto: medieval tower. Marble. Ph. F. Coarelli, Rome.

60 Roman art. SAN VITTORINO (ancient AMITERNUM). Relief showing a funeral cortège. Second half of the first cent. BC. L'Aquila: Museo Nazionale d' Abruzzo. Limestone. H 0.65 m. B 1.64 m. Ph. U.D.F. – La Photothèque.

61 Roman art. SAN VITTORINO (ancient AMITERNUM). Relief showing a funeral cortège, detail (cf. 60). Second half of the first cent. BC. L'Aquila: Museo Nazionale d'Abruzzo. Ph. U.D.F. – La Photothèque.

62 Roman art. CHIETI (ancient TEATE MARRUCINORUM). Fragments of the funerary monument of Lusius Storax, sevir of Teate Marrucinorum. About 50. Chieti: Museo Nazionale. Limestone. Upper relief: H 0.61 m., B 2.79 m. Lower relief: H 0.61 m. B 0.60 m. Ph. U.D.F.-La Photothèque.

63 Roman art. CHIETI (ancient TEATE MARRUCINORUM). Funerary monument of Lusius Storax (detail): Assembly of Magistrates (cf. 62). About 50. Chieti: Museo Nazionale. Limestone. H 0.61 m., B 1.14 m. Ph. U.D.F. – La Photothèque.

64 Roman art. CHIETI (ancient TEATE MARRUCINORUM). Funerary monument of Lusius Storax, detail of frieze showing gladiators (cf. 62). About 50. Chieti: Museo Nazionale. Limestone. B 1.08 m. Ph. U.D.F. – La Photothèque.

65 Roman art. ESTE (ancient ATESTE). Votive relief dedicated by a tinsmith. First cent. Este: Museo Nazionale. Limestone. Ph. Tuzza, Este.

66 Roman art. OSTIA (Rome), necropolis on the Isola Sacra, tomb 78. Brick relief showing a mill. Second cent. Ostia Museum. Brick. H 0.395 m. B 0.40 m. Ph. Soprintendenza, Ostia.
A similar composition is to be found on a marble sarcophagus in the Vatican (Museo Chiaramonti, Inv. no. 1370).

67 Roman art. SAN VITTORINO (ancient AMITERNUM) [?]. Pediment of a funerary monument, with tools carved in relief. First cent. L'Aquila: Museo Nazionale d'Abruzzo. Limestone. H 0.56 m. Ph. U.D.F. – La Photothèque.

68 Roman art. SAN VITTORINO (ancient AMITERNUM) [?] Pediment from a funerary monument, with armour. First cent. L'Aquila: Museo Nazionale d'Abruzzo. H 0.90 m. Ph. U.D.F. – La Photothèque.

69 Roman art. OSTIA. Greengrocer-poulterer's shop-sign. Second half of the second cent. Ostia Museum. Marble. B 0.55 m. Ph. Gabinetto Fotografico Nazionale, Rome.

70 Roman art. POMPEII. The brawl in the amphitheatre. Naples: Museo Archeologico Nazionale. Fresco. H 1.70 m. B 1.85 m. Ph. U.D.F. – La Photothèque.

This painting was found in a private house (Reg. 1, 3. 25). The brawl itself, between spectators from Pompeii and Nucera, took place in 59.

71 Roman art. OSTIA, Via di Diana. Sign of a public snack-bar (thermopolium). First cent. In situ. Fresco. H 0.50 m. (approx.). B 1.05 m. Ph. U.D.F. – La Photothèque.

72 Roman art. ROME, Via Portuense. Painting at the entrance to a tomb: basket of flowers. Second cent. Rome: Museo Nazionale. Fresco. B 1.07 m. Ph. U.D.F. – La Photothèque.
The paintings shown in pl. 99 and 149-51 are taken from the same tomb.

73 Roman art. ROME, Via Praenestina, by the Porta Maggiore. Tomb of the master-baker M. Vergilius Eurysaces (detail from frieze). Various stages of bread-making (cf. 164). End of the first cent. BC. In situ. Limestone (travertine). Ph. U.D.F. – La Photothèque.
For the entire monument cf. 164

74 Roman art. ROME, Via Latina. Mosaic inscription at the entrance to a columbarium. First cent. In situ. Mosaic. Ph. U.D.F. – La Photothèque.
The inscription gives the name of the founder of the burial-club, Cn. Pomponius Hylas, and of his wife, Pomponia Vitalinis (C.I.L., VI, 2, 5552).

75 Roman art. SAN VITTORINO (ancient AMITERNUM). Relief from a funerary monument: banqueting scene. First cent. Pizzoli: Church of S. Stefano, embedded in the wall of the presbytery. Limestone. B 1.12 m. Ph. U.D.F. – La Photothèque.

76 Roman art. ESTE (ancient ATESTE). Relief from a funerary monument: banqueting scene. First cent. Este. Limestone. Ph. Tuzza, Este.

77 Roman art. SEPINO (ancient SAEPINUM). Relief: banqueting scene. First cent. Ancona: Museo Nazionale. Limestone. Ph. Tran., Ancona.

78 Roman art. ROME, Temple of Apollo Sosianus near the Theatre of Marcellus. Detail from frieze: Triumphal procession. About 20 BC. Rome: Capitol, Palazzo dei Conservatori. Marble H 0.85 m. Ph. U.D.F. – La Photothèque.
This frieze was inside the temple.

79 Roman art. ROME, Palazzo della Cancelleria. Altar-base showing sacrificial procession. Middle of the first cent.

Vatican: Museo Pio Clementino. Marble. H 1.05 m. B 5 m. Ph. Archivio Fotografico Gallerie e Musei Vaticani.

80 Roman art. ROME. Portrait of a Roman patrician (cf. 84). First half of the first cent. BC. Rome: Museo Torlonia. Marble. H 0.35 m. (minus the bust). Ph. U.D.F. – La Photothèque.

81 Mid-Italic art. SAN GIOVANNI SCIPIONI. Portrait: fragment of a statue. 3rd-2nd cent. BC. Paris: Bibliothèque Nationale, Cabinet des Médailles. Bronze. H 0.27 m. Ph. U.D.F. – La Photothèque.
    Provenance: this is generally agreed to have been Bovianum. See Giovanni Colonna, in 'Studi Etruschi', 25 (1957), pp. 567ff.

82 Roman art. TARENTUM, Roman necropolis. Funerary cippus. First cent. Taranto: Museo Nazionale. Limestone. Ph. Carrano Gennaro, Soprintendenza alle Antichità, Taranto.

83 Roman art. ROME. Supposed portrait of Sulla. 80-75 BC. Venice: Museo Archeologico. Marble. H 0.26 m. Ph. Osvaldo Böhm, Venice.
    This identification depends on comparison with later coin-portraits.

84 Roman art. ROME. Portrait of a patrician (cf. 80). First half of the first cent. BC. Rome: Museo Torlonia. Marble. H 0.35 m. (minus the bust). Ph. U.D.F. – La Photothèque.

85 Roman art. ROME, Barberini Collection. Patrician carrying two portrait-busts: the so-called 'Barberini Statue'. End of the first cent. BC. Rome: Capitol, Palazzo dei Conservatori. Marble. H 1.65 m. Ph. U.D.F. – La Photothèque.
    The chronology followed in the text for the original of this portrait – that proposed by Schweitzer – has recently been revived by H. von Heintze from 50 to 40-30 BC. (Helbig⁴ II, no. 1615), who also suggests that the pattern of kinship with the sitter (grandfather and father) should be reversed.

86 Roman art. ROME, Barberini Collection. 'Barberini Statue' (detail): the portrait-bust held in the right hand (cf. 85). End of the first cent. BC. Rome: Capitol, Palazzo dei Conservatori. Ph. U.D.F. – La Photothèque.

87 Roman art. ROME, Barberini Collection. 'Barberini Statue' (detail): the portrait-bust held in the left hand (cf. 85). End of the first cent. BC. Rome: Capitol, Palazzo dei Conservatori. Ph. U.D.F. – La Photothèque.

88 Roman art. LATIUM. Portrait of a girl. Late first cent. BC. Berlin: Staatliche Museen, Antikensammlungen. Terracotta. H 0.19 m. Ph. U.D.F. – La Photothèque.

89 Roman art. PALESTRINA (ancient PRAENESTE). Funerary bust. Second cent. BC. Palestrina: Museo Prenestino-Barberiniano. Limestone. H 0.43 m. Ph. U.D.F. – La Photothèque.

90 Roman art. CERVETERI (ancient CAERE). Bust of a woman. First half of the first cent. BC. Vatican: Museo Etrusco Gregoriano. Terracotta. H 0.347 m. Ph. Archivio Fotografico Gallerie e Musei Vaticani.

91 Roman art. ROME (?). Portrait of a man (bust). About 43-32 BC (Second Triumvirate). Leningrad: Hermitage Museum. Bronze. H 0.39 m. Ph. Museum.
    This piece was acquired in 1928.

92 Mid-Italic art from Etruria. TARQUINIA. Portrait of a man. 2nd-1st cent. BC. Tarquinia: Museo Nazionale. Terracotta. H 0.23 m. Ph. De Antonis, Rome.

93 Roman art. TIVOLI (ancient TIBUR). Statue of a general from the period of the Mithridatic Wars. First half of the first cent. BC. Rome: Museo Nazionale. Marble. H 1.88 m. H (with the base): 1.94 m. Ph. U.D.F. – La Photothèque.

94 Roman art. ROME. Portrait of a young girl. Middle of the first cent. BC. Rome: Villa Albani. Marble. H 0.34 m. Ph. U.D.F. – La Photothèque.
    The eyes were originally inset with glass paste.

95 Roman art. CAMPANIA. Funerary statue. First cent. BC. Naples: Museo Archeologico Nazionale. Limestone. H 2.10 m. Ph. U.D.F. – La Photothèque

96 Roman art. RAVENNA. Funerary stele of the family of P. Longidienus, shipbuilder. First cent. Ravenna: Museo Nazionale. Marble. H 2.66 m. Ph. Museum.

97 Roman art. CAMPANIA. Funerary statue (detail). First cent. BC. Naples: Museo Archeologico Nazionale. Limestone. H 1.78 m. Ph. U.D.F. – La Photothèque.

98 Roman art. OSTIA. Portrait on a shield (imago clipeata). First cent. Ostia Museum. Marble. H 0.80 m. Ph. U.D.F. – La Photothèque.

99 Roman art. ROME, Via Portuense. Portrait painted in a tomb. Second cent. Rome: Museo Nazionale. Fresco. Ph. U.D.F. – La Photothèque.
    The paintings reproduced in pl. 72 and 149-51 come from the same tomb.

100 Roman art. POMPEII. Portraits on shields (clipeatae) hung in a building. First cent. Pompeii: House of the Impluvium. Fresco. Ph. U.D.F. – La Photothèque.

101 Roman art. ROME or LATIUM. Portrait based on a funeral mask. First cent. BC. Paris: Louvre. Terracotta. H 0.195 m. Ph. U.D.F. – La Photothèque.
    Formerly at Rome, Campana Coll.

102 Roman art. ROME, Via Statilia. Funerary stele of man and wife, both of the middle classes. Mid-first cent. BC. Rome: Capitol, Palazzo dei Conservatori, Museo Nuovo. Rough marble. H 1.80 m. Ph. U.D.F. – La Photothèque.

103 Roman art. ROME, Via Praenestina. Funerary stele of the master-baker M. Vergilius Eurysaces and his wife (?). End of the first cent. BC. Giardini Pantanella, Via Labicana. Marble. H 1.90 m. Ph. Fototeca Unione pr. Accademia Americana, Rome.
    This piece is shortly to be rehoused in the Antiquarium on the Capitol. The head of the woman is now lost.

104 Roman art. ROME (?). Fragment of alto-relievo: portrait of a woman. First cent. Provenance unknown (purchased on the antiquities market). Marble. Ph. Deutsches Archäologisches Institut, Rome.

105 Roman art. PALOMBARA SABINA. Portrait of an elderly lady. Augustan period. Rome: Museo Nazionale. Marble. H 0.32 m. Ph. U.D.F. – La Photothèque.

106 Roman art. ROME (found in the Tiber). Portrait of a priest in the service of Isis. First cent. Rome: Museo Nazionale. Marble. H 0.33 m. Ph. U.D.F. – La Photothèque.

107 Roman art. OSTIA, Porta Laurentina necropolis. Fragment of alto-relievo from a funerary monument: portrait of a man. About 55-65. Ostia Museum. Marble. H 0.22 m. Ph. U.D.F. – La Photothèque.

108 Roman art. POMPEII. Portrait of a municipal magistrate and his wife. First cent. Naples: Museo Archeologico

Nazionale. Fresco. H 0.58 m. Ph. U.D.F. – La Photothèque.

The frequently repeated identification of this couple as the baker Pacuvius Proculus and his wife is dubious.

109 Art of the Roman period in Egypt. FAYUM. Portrait of a middle-aged woman. Second cent. Berlin: Staatliche Museen, Antikensammlungen. Encaustic on wood. H 0.35 m.; B 0.18 m. Ph. U.D.F. – La Photothèque.

110 Roman art. ROME. Portrait of a lady from the period between Titus and Trajan, i.e. 90-100. Rome: Museo Capitolino. Marble. H 0.63 m. Ph. U.D.F. – La Photothèque.

U. Hausmann ('Arch. Jahrbuch', 74, 1960, pp. 200ff.) suggests an identification with Vibia Matidia the Younger, the elder sizter of Hadrian's wife Sabina.

111 Roman art. ROME. Portrait of an elderly lady from the Flavian era. Late first cent. Vatican (Museo Laterano). Marble. H 0.24 m. (minus the bust). Ph. Alinari, Florence. Formerly Mus. Lat. Inv. no. 10203.

112 Roman art. ROME, between the Via Appia and the Via Latina: Vigna Codini (Cencelli estate). Columbarium of the Freedmen in the Julio-Claudian Imperial household. First half of the first cent. *In situ.* Ph. U.D.F. – La Photothèque.

113 Roman art. ROME. Funerary altar of Vitellius Successus (Flavian period). Late first cent. Vatican: Museo Pio Clementino (Galleria delle statue). Marble. H 0.93 m. B 0.66 m. Ph. Alinari, Florence.

The altar was dedicated by the dead man's wife, whose bust can be seen in the niche beside her husband's. She is also present, lower down, at his funeral feast: this type of representation was very widespread in Greece. For the inscription, see C.I.L. VI 29088 a. (Formerly at Rome, in the Palazzo Mattei.)

114 Roman art. ROME, tomb of the Esquiline. Painting of historical scene, detail (cf. 117). Third cent. BC. Rome: Capitol, Palazzo dei Conservatori. Ph. U.D.F. – La Photothèque.

115 Graeco-Roman art. HERCULANEUM, basilica. Theseus liberating the children of Athens. Between 60 and 79. Naples: Museo Archeologico Nazionale. Fresco. H 1.90 m. B 1.53 m. Ph. U.D.F. – La Photothèque.

This fresco comes from the basilica of Herculaneum: inv. no. 9049.

116 Roman art. POMPEII, house of Gavius Rufus (Reg. VII. 2.16). Theseus liberating the children of Athens. Between 60 and 79. Naples: Museo Archeologico Nazionale. Fresco. H 0.90 m. B 0.80 m. Ph. U.D.F. – La Photothèque.

117 Roman art. ROME, tomb on the Esquiline. Painting on a historical theme. Third cent. BC. Rome: Capitol, Palazzo dei Conservatori. Fresco. H 0.875 m. B 0.45 m. Ph. U.D.F. – La Photothèque.

118 Art from Latium. TARQUINIA. Small ceramic bowl manufactured in Latium (Rome?). First half of third cent. BC. Tarquinia: Museo Nazionale. Terracotta. D 0.157 m. Ph. U.D.F. – La Photothèque.

119 Graeco-Roman art. ROME, house on the Esquiline. Landscape connected with the *Odyssey* (detail from a frieze). Arriving in the land of the Laestrygonians. 50-40 BC. Vatican: Biblioteca Apostolica. Fresco. B 1.55 m. Ph. Bibl. Apost.

This frieze with landscapes, divided by a series of 'trompe-l'œil' painted pilasters, ran round the upper level of the wall in a room. The episodes are all connected with Bks IX-XII of the 'Odyssey'.

120 Graeco-Roman art. ROME, house on the Palatine known as the 'House of the Griffins'. Mural decoration with *trompe-l'œil* perspective. 90-80 BC. Rome: Palatine Antiquarium. Fresco. Dimensions of the room: 4 × 3 m. Height from skirting to epistyle: 3.08 m. Ph. U.D.F. – La Photothèque.

121 Roman art. ROME, tomb on the Esquiline known as the 'Tomb of the Statilii'. Painting on a historical theme (detail). Late first cent. BC or beginning of first cent. AD. Rome: Museo Nazionale. Fresco. H 0.37 m. Ph. U.D.F. – La Photothèque.

122 Roman art. ROME, tomb on the Esquiline known as the 'Tomb of the Statilii'. Frieze: the legend of Aeneas. End of the first cent. BC. Rome: Museo Nazionale. Fresco. B 1.96 m. Ph. U.D.F. – La Photothèque.

123 Roman art. ROME, house near the Farnesina. Wall decorated with *trompe-l'œil* architectural motifs. 30-25 BC. Rome: Museo Nazionale. Fresco. B 2.32 m. Ph. U.D.F. – La Photothèque.

124 Roman art. ROME, house near the Farnesina. Picture on a white ground

(cf. 123). 30-25 BC. Rome: Museo Nazionale. Fresco. H 0.30 m. Ph. U.D.F. – La Photothèque.

125 Graeco-Roman art. ROME, house near the Farnesina. A garland (detail). 30-25 BC. Rome: Museo Nazionale. Fresco. B between the columns 0.91 m. Ph. U.D.F. – La Photothèque.

126 Graeco-Roman art. ROME, house near the Farnesina. Maritime scene with boats. 25-19 BC. Rome: Museo Nazionale. Fresco. B 0.73 m. Ph. U.D.F. – La Photothèque.

127 Graeco-Roman art. ROME, house near the Farnesina. Masks (detail). 25-19 BC. Rome: Museo Nazionale. Fresco. H 0.23 m. Ph. U.D.F. – La Photothèque.

128 Roman art. ROME, hall on the Palatine, the so-called *Aula Isiaca*, or 'Hall of Isis'. Decorations on walls and ceiling (detail). 30-20 BC. Rome: Palatine Antiquarium. Fresco. Ph. U.D.F. – La Photothèque.

This hall, some 4.50 m. high, was found 7.90 m. below the basilica of Domitian's palace on the Palatine. The paintings were detached in 1956 and provisionally relocated in a chamber of Domitian's Palace.

129 Roman art. ROME, hall on the Palatine (*Aula Isiaca*). Detail of frieze, showing emblems associated with the cult of Isis (cf. 128). 30-20 BC. Rome: Palatine Antiquarium. Ph. U.D.F. – La Photothèque.

130 Roman art. PRIMA PORTA, Livia's villa. Main salon with mural fresco of garden and birds (cf. 131 and 133 for other details). First half of the first cent. Rome: Museo Nazionale. Fresco. B 5.95 m. Ph. U.D.F. – La Photothèque.

131 Roman art. PRIMA PORTA, Livia's villa. Main salon with mural fresco (detail). First half of the first cent. Rome: Museo Nazionale. Ph. U.D.F. – La Photothèque.

132 Roman art. ROME, Via Merulana. Nymphaeum, known as 'Maecenas's recital-room'. First half of first cent. *In situ.* Ph. U.D.F. – La Photothèque.

133 Roman art. PRIMA PORTA, Livia's villa. Detail of mural decoration. First half of first century. Rome: Museo Nazionale. Ph. U.D.F. – La Photothèque.

134 Roman art. ROME, house on the Palatine known as the 'House of Livia'.

Mural decoration. The central panel represents Io being watched over by Argus. Early first cent. *In situ*. Fresco. H 2.30 m. B 1.60 m. Ph. U.D.F. – La Photothèque.

135 Roman art. ROME, house on the Palatine known as the 'House of Livia'. Mural decoration (detail). Early first cent. *In situ*. B of detail view: 1.90 m. Ph. U.D.F. – La Photothèque.

136 Graeco-Roman art. ROME, house on the Palatine known as the 'House of Livia'. Frieze with landscape. Early first cent. *In situ*. Fresco. H 0.29 m. Ph. U.D.F. – La Photothèque.
The frieze is placed above the garlands (cf. 135).

137 Roman art. ROME, house on the Palatine known as the 'House of the Masks'. Mural decoration (detail). First cent. *In situ*. Fresco. Ph. U.D.F. – La Photothèque.

138 Roman art. ROME, the Palatine: Nero's *Domus Transitoria*. Decoration on the vaulting in a Nymphaeum. 54-64. Rome: Palatine Antiquarium. Fresco. Ph. U.D.F. – La Photothèque.
The room containing the remains of frescoes on the vaulting was a nymphaeum 6.375 × 5.50 m., its walls faced with pieces of coloured marble.

139 Roman art. ROME, the Palatine: Nero's *Domus Aurea*. Corridor no. 70, vaulting in the cross-passage (no. 70a). Cf. 445. Date: 64-68. *In situ*. Fresco. Ph. U.D.F. – La Photothèque.

140 Roman art. ROME, the Palatine: Nero's *Domus Transitoria*. Decoration on the vaulting in a nymphaeum. (Another detail-shot: cf. 138). Date: 54-64. Rome: Palatine Antiquarium. Fresco. Ph. U.D.F. – La Photothèque.

141 Roman art. ROME, Nero's *Domus Aurea*. Cruciform room (no. 74). Cf. 445. Date: 64-68. *In situ*. Fresco. Ph. Gabinetto Fotografico Nazionale, Rome.

142 Roman art. ROME, Nero's *Domus Aurea*. Small passage beside the 'Room with Masks' (no. 69). Niche with *trompe-l'œil* window-decoration (cf. 445). Date: 64-68. *In situ*. Fresco. Ph. U.D.F. – La Photothèque.

143 Roman art. ROME, Nero's *Domus Aurea*. Chamber of Achilles on Scyros (no. 85), mural decoration, detail (cf. 445). Date: 64-68. *In situ*. Fresco. Ph. U.D.F. – La Photothèque.

144 Roman art. ROME, Nero's *Domus Aurea*. Chamber of Achilles on Scyros (no. 85), mural decoration, detail (cf. 445). Date: 64-68. *In situ*. Fresco. Ph. U.D.F. – La Photothèque.

145 Roman art. ROME, Nero's *Domus Aurea*. Fabullus (?). Ceiling in the chamber of Achilles on Scyros (no. 85). Cf. 445. Date: 64-68. *In situ*. Fresco. Ph. U.D.F. – La Photothèque.

146 Roman art. OSTIA, 'House of the Painted Ceilings'. Mural decoration (detail). Date: 54-68. *In situ*. Fresco. Ph. U.D.F. – La Photothèque.

147 Graeco-Roman art. POMPEII, 'House of the Quadrigae' (Reg. VII. 2.25). The forge of Hephaestus (detail). Date: 68-79. *In situ*. Fresco. Ph. U.D.F. – La Photothèque.

148 Graeco-Roman art. BOSCOTRECASE, house known as that of Agrippa Postumus. Landscape. First quarter of the first cent. Naples: Museo Archeologico Nazionale (Inv. no. 147502). Fresco. H 1 m. B 1.30 m. Ph. U.D.F. – La Photothèque.

149 Roman art. ROME, tomb on the Via Portuense. Mural decoration showing children at play (cf. 72, 99, 150, 151 for other detail shots). Second cent. Rome: Museo Nazionale. Fresco. H 0.90 m. Ph. U.D.F. – La Photothèque.

150 Roman art. ROME, tomb on the Via Portuense. Mural decoration, detail (cf. 149). Second cent. Rome: Museo Naz. Ph. U.D.F. – La Photothèque.

151 Roman art. ROME, tomb on the Via Portuense. Children at play (cf. 149). Second cent. Rome: Museo Nazionale. Ph. U.D.F. – La Photothèque.

152 Roman art. TIVOLI (ancient TIBUR): Hadrian's Villa. Brick-work (detail). Date: 130-138. *In situ*. Ph. Gabinetto Fotografico Nazionale, Rome.

153 Roman art. ROME, the Capitol. An arcade of the Tabularium (Record Office). Date: 80-78 BC. *In situ*. Limestone. Ph. U.D.F. – La Photothèque.

154 Roman art. ROME, Via Praenestina. The bridge of Nona (detail). Date: about 80 BC. *In situ*. Limestone. Ph. U.D.F. – La Photothèque.

155 Roman art. ROME, Forum Romanum. The temple of Saturn. Date: 42 BC-AD 320. *In situ*. Marble and limestone. Ph. U.D.F. – La Photothèque.

156 Roman art. PALESTRINA (ancient PRAENESTE). Temple of Fortune. One of the two ramps (cf. 436). Date: 112-70 BC. *In situ*. Ph. Deutsches Archäologisches Institut, Rome.

157 Roman art. PALESTRINA (ancient PRAENESTE). Temple of Fortune. The fourth level (cf. 436). Date: 112-70 BC. *In situ*. Ph. U.D.F. – La Photothèque.

158 Roman art. ROME, Pompey's Theatre, on the ancient plan of the city of Rome. Rome: Museo Capitolino. Marble. Ph. Fototeca Unione pr. Accademia Americana, Rome.
A plan of the whole city was drawn up between 203 and 209, under the Severi, engraved on marble plaques (of which fragments still survive) and set up on a wall of the Forum Pacis. The scale was approximately 1 : 240.

159 Roman art. ROME. Coin showing the interior of the Basilica Aemilia. Date: about 65 BC. Rome: Museo Nazionaie. Silver. D 0.019 m. Ph. U.D.F. – La Photothèque.
The coin is a denarius struck by M. Aemilius Lepidus about 65 BC.

160 Roman art. ROME. Marcellus's Theatre. Between 50 and 10 BC. *In situ*. Limestone (travertine). Ph. U.D.F. – La Photothèque.

161 Roman art. ROME, Forum Caesaris. Large shops. Date: 51-46 BC. *In situ*. Limestone and brick. Ph. U.D.F. – La Photothèque.

162 Roman art. ROME, Forum Caesaris. Entablature of the temple (Trajan). Date: 113-120. *In situ*. Marble. Ph. U.D.F. – La Photothèque.

163 Roman art. ROME, the Palatine. Domitian's Palace. Entablature (detail). Date: 81-96. *In situ*. Marble. Ph. U.D.F. – La Photothèque.

164 Roman art. ROME, Via Praenestina, near the Porta Maggiore. Tomb of the master-baker M. Vergilius Eurysaces (cf. 73, 103, 169). End of the first cent. BC. *In situ*. Limestone (travertine). Ph. U.D.F. – La Photothèque.

165 Roman art. ROME. Coin of Octavian showing the Temple of Neptune. End of the first cent. BC. London: British Museum. Gold. D 0.017 m. Ph. Museum.

166 Roman art. ROME. Coin of Octavian showing the Altar of Julius Caesar. End of the first cent. BC. London:

NOTES ON THE ILLUSTRATIONS

British Museum. Gold. D 0.017 m. Ph. Museum.

167 Roman art. ROME. Coin showing the Arch of Augustus in the Forum. Date: between 17 and 15 BC. Rome: Museo Nazionale. Silver. D 0.017 m. Ph. U.D.F. – La Photothèque.

This arch was set up by the Senate after peace was concluded with the Parthians in 19 BC. The coin itself is a denarius struck by L. Vinicius between 17 and 15 BC.

168 Roman art. ROME. Coin showing the palace of Tiberius. Date: 95-96. Rome: Museo Nazionale. Bronze. D 0.03 m. Ph. Fototeca Unione pr. Accademia Americana, Rome.

Coin struck under Domitian, in 95/6; the ante-chamber and audience-hall visible in the foreground were Domitian's additions to the original palace of Tiberius.

169 Roman art. ROME, Porta Maggiore. The Aqua Claudia and the tomb of M. Vergilius Eurysaces (cf. 164). *In situ.* Limestone. Ph. U.D.F. – La Photothèque.

The gateway was constructed in 52.

170 Roman art. ROME, near the Via Appia. The ruins of the Aqua Claudia. Date: 42-54. *In situ.* Limestone. Ph. Anderson, Rome.

171 Roman art. ROME. Precinct-wall of the Forum Augusti (detail). First cent. *In situ.* Ph. U.D.F. – La Photothèque.

172 Roman art. Near TIVOLI (ancient TIBUR). Tomb of the Plautii and bridge across the Anio. First cent. *In situ.* Ph. Alinari, Rome.

173 Roman art. ROME, Nero's *Domus Aurea.* A corridor (no. 70). Cf. 445. Date: 64-68. Ph. U.D.F. – La Photothèque.

174 Flemish art. Francisco de Hollandia. Water-colour reproducing the decoration on a vault of Nero's Golden House. The 'Chamber with gilded vaulting' (no. 60). Cf. 445. Date: about 1538. El Escorial: Biblioteca. Watercolour on parchment. H 0.35 m. B 0.50 m. Ph. Enciclopedia dell'Arte Antica, Rome.

175 Roman art. ROME, Nero's *Domus Aurea.* Octagonal room (no. 84). Cf. 445. Date: 64-68. *In situ.* Brick. Ph. Fototeca Unione pr. Accademia Americana, Rome.

176 Roman art. ROME, the Coliseum. Exter-ior view. Date: 70-90. *In situ.* Limestone (travertine). H 48.50 m. Ph. U.D.F. – La Photothèque.

177 Roman art. ROME. Coin showing the Central Market constructed by Nero. Date: 59. Rome: Museo Nazionale. Bronze. D 0.03 m. Ph. U.D.F. – La Photothèque.

Coin struck under Nero.

178 Roman art. ROME. Coin of Titus portraying the Coliseum. Date: 79-81. Rome: Museo Nazionale. Bronze. D 0.03 m. Ph. U.D.F. – La Photothèque.

179 Roman art. ROME, the Coliseum. First-floor corridor. Date: 70-90. *In situ.* Limestone (travertine). Ph. U.D.F. – La Photothèque.

180 Roman art. ROME, monument of the Haterii. Buildings erected in Rome under the Flavian Emperors. Vatican (Lateran Museum). Marble. H 0.42 m. B 1.58 m. Ph. Anderson, Rome.

This relief formed part of the funerary monument belonging to the Haterii family (cf. 242-5).

181 Roman art. ROME, the Coliseum. Vaulting decorated with stucco. Date: 70-90 (cf. 182). *In situ.* Stucco on masonry. Ph. U.D.F. – La Photothèque.

182 Roman art. ROME, the Coliseum. Reconstruction of stucco-work according to a sketch made during the Renaissance. Ph. Bibliothèque Nationale, Paris. After Pierre Crozat, *Recueil d'estampes d'après les plus beaux dessins qui sont en France, dans le Cabinet du Roy, dans celui de Monseigneur le duc d'Orléans et dans d'autres cabinets,* Paris 1729, fol. 77.

Crozat's engraving followed a sketch made by Giovanni da Udine (1487-1564).

183 Roman art. ROME, the Coliseum. View of the interior. Date: 70-90. *In situ.* D maximum: 188 m. Ph. U.D.F. – La Photothèque.

In the centre we can see various substructures which once formed part of the off-stage complex servicing the arena, but which were then roofed in beneath it.

184 Roman art. ROME, the Palatine. Palace of the Flavians. Aerial view. Second cent. *In situ.* Ph. Fotocielo, Rome.

185 Roman art. ROME, the Palatine. Approach to the Flavian Palace. Second cent. *In situ.* Brick-built. Ph. U.D.F. – La Photothèque.

186 Roman art. ROME, the Palatine. Domitian's Palace: detail of the vaulting. Date: 80-90. *In situ.* Ph. U.D.F. – La Photothèque.

187 Roman art. ROME, the Palatine. Palace of the Flavians: façade overlooking the gardens. Date: 80-90. *In situ.* Ph. U.D.F. – La Photothèque.

188 Roman art. ROME, Piazza Sallustio. Ruins of a palace in the Gardens of Sallust. Second cent. *In situ.* Ph. U.D.F. – La Photothèque.

189 Roman art. ROME. Entablature of the temple of Vespasian (detail). Date: 79-80. Rome: Capitol (Tabularium or Record Office). Marble. Ph. U.D.F. – La Photothèque.

190 Roman art. ROME (?). Relief showing a view of a town, in perspective (detail). Second cent. Avezzano, Palazzo Torlonia. Marble. Ph. Alinari, Florence.

191 Roman art. ROME, Forum Nervae. Frieze (detail). Date: 96-98. *In situ.* Marble. Ph. Anderson, Rome.

192 Roman art. ROME, the Portland Vase (cf. 221-2). First cent. London: British Museum. Glass cameo. H 0.247 m. Ph. Museum.

193 Roman art. LATIUM. Votive head. End of the first cent. BC. Vatican: Museo Etrusco Gregoriano. Terracotta. H 0.26 m. Ph. De Antonis, Rome.

194 Graeco-Roman art. RHODES (?). Coin of Octavian, struck in the East. Date: 30-29 BC. Forli: Piancastelli Collection. Silver. D 0.023 m. Ph. Comune di Roma.

195 Roman art. ROME: House near the Farnesina. Octavian as Hermes-Thoth. Date: 30-25 BC. Rome: Museo Nazionale. Stucco. Ph. U.D.F. – La Photothèque.

Cf. 232, which shows a detail shot of the same building.

196 Greek art of the Roman period. POMPEII. Copy of the 'Doryphoros' (spear-bearer) by Polycletus. The original was of the fifth cent. BC., the copy of the first cent. BC. Naples: Museo Archeologico Nazionale. Marble. H 2.01 m. Ph. U.D.F. – La Photothèque.

197 Roman art. PRIMA PORTA. Portrait-statue of the Emperor Augustus. Date: 14-29. Vatican: Museo Chiaramonti. Marble. H 2.04 m. Ph. Anderson, Rome.

Found in 1863, in Livia's villa at Prima Porta, near Rome.

198 Roman art. OSTIA. A couple portrayed as Mars and Venus. Date: 150-60. Rome: Museo Nazionale. Marble. H 2.16 m.; H with the plinth, 2.28 m. Ph. U.D.F. – La Photothèque.

199 Roman art. ROME. Young woman portrayed as Omphale. Beginning of the third cent. Vatican (Museo Pio Clementino). Marble. H 1.82 m. Ph. Archivio Fotografico Gallerie e Musei Vaticani.

200 Roman art. ROME, *Ara Pacis Augustae*, the altar commemorating the peace established by the Emperor Augustus. Exterior view. Date: 13-9 BC. Rome: Ara Pacis. Marble. B 11 × 10 m. Ph. U.D.F. – La Photothèque.
The altar originally stood on the Via Flaminia (today the Corso), as far up as the Via in Lucina. The first fragments were discovered in the sixteenth century. During the years 1937-8 all the remaining fragments came to light, and were reconstructed (in a way which one cannot unreservedly approve) near the mausoleum of Augustus.

201 Roman art. ROME, the *Ara Pacis Augustae*. View from inside the precinct (detail). Date: 13-9 BC. Rome: Ara Pacis. Marble. Ph. U.D.F. – La Photothèque.

202 Roman art. ROME, the *Ara Pacis Augustae*. Precinct: Aeneas and the sanctuary of the Penates (cf. 200). Date: 13-9 BC. Rome: Ara Pacis. Marble. H 1.55 m. B 2.37 m. (approx.). Ph. U.D.F. – La Photothèque.

203 Roman art. ROME, the *Ara Pacis Augustae*. Precinct (detail): Aeneas. Cf. 202. Date: 13-9 BC. Rome: Ara Pacis. Ph. U.D.F. – La Photothèque.

204 Roman art. ROME, the *Ara Pacis Augustae*. Precinct: the procession (detail, restored). Date: 13-9 BC. Rome: Ara Pacis. Ph. U.D.F. – La Photothèque.
In this detail shot, taken from the north side, all the heads in alto-relievo are restorations, probably done during the eighteenth century.

205 Etruscan art. TARQUINIA, the necropolis. 'Tomb of the Bulls'. Mural decoration (detail). Date: 530-20 BC. *In situ.* Fresco. H 1.65 m. B 1.30 m. Ph. U.D.F. – La Photothèque.

206 Graeco-Roman art. ROME, formerly in the Grimani Collection. Relief from a fountain: lioness with cubs. Date: 14-37 (reign of Tiberius). Vienna: Kunsthistorisches Museum. Marble. H 0.94 m. B 0.81 m. Ph. Museum.

207 Graeco-Roman art. PALESTRINA (ancient PRAENESTE). Relief from a fountain: wild sow and young boars. Date: 14-37 (reign of Tiberius). Palestrina: Museo Prenestino Barberiniano. Marble. H 0.94 m. B 0.815 m. Ph.A. Giuliano, Rome.
This relief served as decoration for one of the four niches of an oval fountain, discovered near Palestrina: the excavation is still unpublished.

·208 Roman art. ROME (?). Cameo: eagle with symbols of victory (cf. 1). Date: 27 BC-AD 14 (reign of Augustus). Vienna: Kunsthistorisches Museum, Antikensammlung. Onyx. D 0.22 m. Ph. Erwin Meyer, Vienna.
The setting, of gold and silver, dates from the second half of the sixteenth century, and was executed at Milan, in the Piccinino studio.

209 Roman art. ROME (?). Cameo. The 'Gemma Augustea' with Rome and Tiberius. Date: 15-37. Vienna: Kunsthistorisches Museum, Antikensammlung. Onyx. H 0.19 m. B 0.23 m. Ph. Erwin Meyer, Vienna.
This piece was preserved at Saint-Sernin (Toulouse) until 1533, and is mentioned there as early as 1246.

210 Roman art. ROME (?). The great 'Cameo of France'. First cent. Paris: Bibliothèque Nationale, Cabinet des Médailles. Sard. H 0.31 m. B 0.255 m. Ph. Bibl. Nat.
This piece has been interpreted in various ways. For a résumé of the hypotheses, see the 'Enciclopedia dell'arte antica classica e orientale', II, pp. 295-8. This cameo was preserved in the Sainte-Chapelle, Paris, from the Middle Ages until 1791.

211 Roman art. ROME (?). The 'Gemma Augustea' (detail): Rome and Tiberius (cf. 209). Date: 15-37. Vienna: Kunsthistorisches Museum, Antikensammlung. Ph. Erwin Meyer, Vienna.

212 Graeco-Roman art. ROME (?). Amethyst signed by Pamphilos. Achilles playing the lyre. Date: 27 BC-AD 14 (reign of Augustus). Paris: Bibliothèque Nationale, Cabinet des Médailles. Amethyst. D 0.017 m. Ph. U.D.F. – La Photothèque.

213 Roman art. ROME (?). Octavia, Augustus's sister. Date: 60-30 BC. Paris: Bibliothèque Nationale, Cabinet des Médailles. Cameo. D 0.087 m. Ph. U.D.F. – La Photothèque.

214 Roman art. Livia, Augustus's wife. Date: 27-10 BC. The Hague: Koninklijk Penningkabinet. Cameo. H 0.063 m. B 0.056 m. Ph. Koninklijk Penningkabinet.

215 Roman art. ROME, formerly in the Albani Collection. Bust of Octavian about the time of the Battle of Actium. Date: between 35 and 29 BC. Marble. H of the head: 0.37 m. Ph. U.D.F. – La Photothèque.

216 Roman art. ROME, Via Labicana. Augustus as Pontifex Maximus (detail). Beginning of the first cent. Rome: Museo Nazionale. Marble. H 2.07 m. H with the plinth: 2.17 m. H of the head: 0.39 m. Ph. U.D.F. – La Photothèque.

217 Graeco-Roman art (Neo-Attic). ROME. Base of altar (detail). Nymph and Satyr. First cent. BC. Venice: Museo Archeologico. Marble. H 0.93 m. B 0.95 m. D 0.67 m. Ph. Osvaldo Böhm, Venice.

218 Graeco-Roman art. CASTELLAMMARE DI STABIA (ancient STABIAE). Bowl with Egyptian motifs. First cent. Naples: Museo Archeologico Nazionale. Obsidian, enamel and gold. H 0.12 m. Ph. U.D.F. – La Photothèque.

219 Roman art. AREZZO. Workshop of Marcus Perennius. Fragment of a bowl. End of the first cent. BC or beginning of the first cent. AD (reign of Augustus). Arezzo: Museo Archeologico. Red ceramic. H 0.15 m. Ph. Scala, Florence.

220 Graeco-Roman art. BOSCOREALE. Carafe. First cent. Paris: Louvre. Silver. Ph. U.D.F. – La Photothèque.

221 Roman art. ROME. The Portland Vase (cf. 192). First cent. London: British Museum. Ph. Museum.

222 The Portland Vase: a reconstruction (cf. 192). From E. Simon, *Die Portlandvase*, Mainz, 1953, pl. V, i.

223 Roman art. BOSCOREALE. Cup (detail): homage to Augustus. First cent. Now destroyed, formerly in the Rothschild Collection. Silver. Ph. Deutsches Archäologisches Institut, Rome.

224 Graeco-Roman art. BOSCOREALE. Carafe, detail (cf. 220). First cent. Paris: Louvre. Ph. U.D.F. – La Photothèque.

225 Graeco-Roman art. POMPEII, house near the Porta Marina. Glass plaque cut to resemble a cameo (detail). Cf. 226. Beginning of the first cent. Naples: Museo Archeologico Nazionale. Ph. U.D.F. – La Photothèque.

226 Graeco-Roman art. POMPEII, house near the Porta Marina. Glass plaque cut to resemble a cameo: Dionysiac scene. Beginning of the first cent. Naples: Museo Archeologico Nazionale. Glass. B 0.39 m. Ph. U.D.F. – La Photothèque.
This plaque, with others like it, was set in the wall as part of its decoration.

227 Graeco-Roman art. BOSCOREALE. Vase and salt-cellars. First cent. Paris: Louvre. Silver. H of vase: 0.155 m. H of salt-cellars: 0.055 m. Ph. U.D.F. – La Photothéque.

228 Roman art. ROME. Fragment of Claudius's *Ara Pietatis*. Date: 50-60. Rome: Villa Medici (Académie de France). Marble. Ph. Oscar Savio, Rome.

229 Roman art. ROME. Fragment of Claudius's *Ara Pietatis*. Date: 50-60. Rome: Villa Medici (Académie de France). Marble. H 1.14 m. B 1.12 m. Ph. Oscar Savio, Rome.

230 Roman art. ROME, Via Praenestina: underground basilica. View of an aisle. Middle of the first cent. *In situ.* Stucco decoration. Ph. U.D.F. – La Photothèque.

231 Roman art. ROME, Via Praenestina: underground basilica. Sappho's Leap. Middle of the first cent. *In situ.* Stucco. Ph. U.D.F. – La Photothèque.

232 Graeco-Roman art. ROME, house near the Farnesina. Stucco decoration on vaulting (landscape). Date: 30-25 BC. Rome: Museo Nazionale. White stucco. B 0.65 m. Ph. U.D.F. – La Photothèque.
The following illustrations also show decorations from the same house: 123, 124, 125, 126, 127, 195.

233 Roman art. ROME, Ponte Mammolo. Tomb-decoration: Dionysus inebriated. First cent. Rome: Museo Nazionale. Stucco. H 0.95 m. Ph. U.D.F. – La Photothèque.

234 Roman art. ROME. Vespasian (private portrait). Date: 69-79. Copenhagen: Ny Carlsberg Glyptotek. Marble. H 0.29 m. Ph. Glyptotek.

235 Roman art. ROME. Vespasian (official portrait). Date: 69-79. Rome: Museo Nazionale. Marble. H 0.40 m. Ph. U.D.F. – La Photothèque.

236 Roman art. ROME, Cancelleria. Detail from a relief: the Senate and Roman people in procession. Date: 80-90. Musei Vaticani. Marble. H 2.06 m. B 5.08 m. Ph. Archivio Fotografico Gallerie e Musei Vaticani.
This detail shot comes from the frieze normally designated by the letter A.

237 Roman art. ROME. Arch of Titus. The Triumph of Titus: the Emperor. Date: 80-85. *In situ.* Marble. B 3.80 m. H 2.04 m. Ph. Alinari, Florence.

238 Roman art. ROME. Arch of Titus. The Triumph of Titus: spoils from the Temple of Jerusalem, destroyed in the year 70. Date: 80-85. *In situ.* Marble. H 2.04 m. Ph. Alinari, Florence.

239 Roman art. ROME. Arch of Titus. The Triumph of Titus, detail (cf. 237). Date: 80-85. *In situ.* Ph. Deutsches Archäologisches Institut, Rome.

240 Roman art. ROME. Arch of Titus. The Triumph of Titus: spoils from the Temple of Jerusalem, detail (cf. 238). Date: 80-85. *In situ.* Ph. U.D.F. – La Photothèque.

241 Roman art. ROME. Arch of Titus. Summit of the vault in the triumphal arch: apotheosis of Titus. Date: 80-85. *In situ.* Marble. Ph. U.D.F. – La Photothèque.

242 Roman art. ROME, tomb of the Haterii (detail). Hoist, buildings, and various funerary emblems. Date: 100-110. Vatican (Lateran Museum). Marble. H 1.04 m. Ph. Anderson, Rome.
Pl. 180, 243-5 are taken from the same funerary monument.

243 Roman art. ROME, tomb of the Haterii (detail). Pillar wreathed with climbing roses. Date: 100-110. Vatican (Lateran Museum). Marble. H 1.45 m. Ph. Anderson, Rome.

244 Roman art. ROME, tomb of the Haterii (detail). Portrait of a woman member of the Haterii family. Date: 100-110. Vatican (Lateran Museum). Marble. H of bust: 0.54 m. H of shrine: 0.74 m. Ph. Anderson, Rome.

245 Roman art. ROME, tomb of the Haterii (detail). Portrait of an infant (cf. 242). Date: 100-110. Vatican (Lateran Museum). Ph. Deutsches Archäologisches Institut, Rome.

246 Roman art. ROME. Sarcophagus of Bellicus Tebanius, consul in 87. Date: 90-100. Pisa: Camposanto. Marble. H 0.78 m. B 1.06 m. Depth 0.92 m. Ph. Deutsches Archäologisches Institut, Rome.

247 Roman art. ROME, the Capitol steps. Domitian's trophy. Date: between 84 and 90. *In situ.* Marble. H 4.23 m. Ph. U.D.F. – La Photothèque.
This trophy, and another one close by, are commonly known as the 'trophies of Marius'; but their connection with Domitian's victories over various Germanic tribes is assured. The figure in the foreground represents a captive.

248 Roman art. ROME. Mural relief: Priapus among vines. Date: about 100-120 (Flavian era). Vatican (Lateran Museum). Marble. H 0.85 m. Ph. Anderson, Rome.

249 Roman art. POMPEII, tavern by the 'House of Laocoön' (Reg. VI. 14.28A). Sketch for a painting: Bacchus and Mercury. Date: 68-79. *In situ.* Lime coating. Ph. Deutsches Archäologisches Institut, Rome.

250 Roman art. ANKARA. Bust of Trajan in old age. Date: about 117. Ankara: Archaeological Museum. Bronze. H of bust: 0.322 m. H of head: 0.25 m. B 0.638 m. Ph. Antonello Perissinotto, Padua.

251 Roman art. ROME, Via Latina. Vault of a tomb. Second cent. *In situ.* Stucco and frescoes. Ph. U.D.F. – La Photothèque.

252 Roman art. ROME. Bust of Trajan commissioned to celebrate the tenth anniversary of his reign. Date: 108. London: British Museum. Marble. H 0.75 m. Ph. Museum.

253 Roman art. ROME. Trajan's Column. Maestro della Gesta di Traiano. Trajan and Sura (detail). Date: 110-13. *In situ.* Marble. Overall H of figures: 0.70 m. (approx.). Ph. Deutsches Archäologisches Institut, Rome.

254 Roman art. ROME. Trajan's Column (detail). Date: 110-13. *In situ.* Marble. D 3.83 m. Ph. U.D.F. – La Photothèque.

255 Roman art. ROME. Maestro della Gesta di Traiano. The Great Frieze of Trajan (restoration-work on the mouldings). Date: 100-17. Rome: Museo della Civiltà Romana (moulding). Plaster. H 3 m. Overall B 18 m. Ph. U.D.F. – La Photothèque.

The moulding links up the reliefs, which are inserted as decoration on different levels of the Arch of Constantine, but formed a continuous frieze when in Trajan's Forum.

256 Roman art. ROME. Maestro della Gesta di Traiano. The Great Frieze (detail). The Emperor on horseback, attacking the enemy (cf. 255). Date: 100-17. Arch of Constantine (central thoroughfare). Marble. H 3 m. B 4.60 m. Ph. Gabinetto Fotografico Nazionale, Rome.

257 Greek art of the Hellenistic era. PERGAMUM. The Great Altar. Frieze of Telephus (detail). Date: 160-155 BC. East Berlin: Staatliche Museen. Marble. B 0.223 m. Ph. U.D.F. – La Photothèque.

258 Roman art. ROME. Maestro della Gesta di Traiano. The Great Frieze, detail (cf. 255). Date: 100-17. Rome: Museo della Civiltà Romana (moulding). Plaster. Ph. UDF – La Photothèque.

259 Roman art. ROME. Maestro della Gesta di Traiano. The Great Frieze, detail (cf. 255). Date: 100-17. Rome: Museo della Civiltà Romana (moulding). Plaster. Ph. U.D.F. – La Photothèque.

260 Roman art. BENEVENTUM. Trajan's Arch. Date: 114-20. *In situ.* Marble. H 8.60 m. B 15.60 m. Ph. U.D.F. – La Photothèque.

261 Roman art. BENEVENTUM. Trajan's Arch. Trajan's *Institutio alimentaria* (detail). Date: 114. *In situ.* Marble. H 2.40 m. Ph. U.D.F. – La Photothèque.

262 Roman art. ROME. Trajan's Market (detail). Date: 108-17. *In situ.* Ph. U.D.F. – La Photothèque.

263 Roman art. ROME. Trajan's Market (detail): the great market-hall. Date: 108-17. *In situ.* Ph. U.D.F. – La Photothèque.

264 Renaissance art. ROME. Enea Vico. Trajan's Column. Date: 1523-67. Rome: Gabinetto delle Stampe. Engraving on paper. Ph. Gabinetto Fotografico Nazionale. Rome.

265 Roman art. ROME. Trajan's Column. The base. Date: 110-13. *In situ.* Marble. H of base: 5.37 m. H of plinth: 1.68 m. Ph. Anderson, Rome.

266 Roman art. ROME. Trajan's Column. Internal staircase. Date: 110-13. *In situ.* Marble. Ph. Gabinetto Fotografico Nazionale, Rome.

267 Roman art. ROME, Trajan's Column. Entrance to the burial-chamber. Date: 110-13. *In situ.* Marble. Ph. Gabinetto Fotografico Nazionale, Rome.

268 Roman art. ROME. Trajan's Column. Cavalry from Mauretania (detail). Date: 110-13. *In situ.* Marble. Ph. Deutsches Archäologisches Institut, Rome.
   C. Cichorius, 'Die Relief der Trajanssäule', Berlin 1896-1900, scene lxiv.

269 Roman art. ROME. Trajan's Column. Mass suicide of the Dacians. Date: 110-13. *In situ.* Marble. Ph. Deutsches Archäologisches Institut, Rome.
   Cichorius, scene cxx.

270 Roman art. ROME. Trajan's Column. Mass deportation of tribes (detail). Date: 110-13. *In situ.* Marble. Ph. Deutsches Archäologisches Ins., Rome.
   Cichorius, scenes cxxvi-cxxvii.

271 Roman art. ROME. Trajan's Column. Hecatomb of Barbarians. Date: 110-13. *In situ.* Marble. Ph. Deutsches Archäologisches Institut, Rome.
   Cichorius, scene xli (Battle of Adamklissi?).

272 Roman art. ROME. Trajan's Column. The pursuit through the woods. Date: 110-13. *In situ.* Marble. Ph. Istituto Luce, Rome.
   Cichorius, scene lxxxii, 112.

273 Roman art. ROME. Trajan's Column. Battle of the Danube. Date: 110-13. *In situ.* Marble. Ph. Istituto Luce, Rome.
   Cichorius, scene xxxi.

274 Roman art. ROME. Trajan's Column. Assault on a Dacian fortress. *In situ.* Marble. Ph. Deutsches Archäologisches Institut, Rome.
   Cichorius, scene lxx.

275 Roman art. ROME. Trajan's Column. The Dacians in battle. Date: 110-13. *In situ.* Marble. Ph. Deutsches Archäologisches Institut, Rome.
   Cichorius, scene cxxii.

276 Roman art. ROME. Trajan's Column. The flight of the Dacian chieftain Decebalus. Date: 110-13. *In situ.* Marble. Ph. Deutsches Archäologisches Institut, Rome.
   Cichorius, scenes cxliii-cxliv.

277 Romano-Gallic art. SAINT-RÉMY-DE-PROVENCE (GLANUM). Funerary monument of the Julii (detail). Third quarter of the first cent. BC. *In situ.* Limestone. H 2.19 m. B 3.37 m. Ph. U.D.F. – La Photothèque.

278 Roman art. OSTIA. Bust of Hadrian from the beginning of his reign. Date: 117-18. Ostia Museum. Marble. H 0.43 m. Ph. U.D.F. – La Photothèque.

279 Roman art. ANKARA. Bust of Trajan in old age, detail (cf. 250). Date: about 117. Ankara: Archaeological Museum. Ph. Antonello Perissinotto, Padua.

280 Roman art. ROME. Bust of Trajan's wife Plotina. Date: 100-20. Rome: Museo Capitolino. Marble. H 0.55 m. Ph. U.D.F. – La Photothèque.

281 Roman art. OSTIA. Posthumous portrait of Trajan. Date: 120-30. Ostia Museum. Marble. H 0.38 m. Ph. U.D.F. – La Photothèque.

282 Roman art. ROME, Forum Romanum. Parapet showing an episode from Trajan's reign (cf. 283). Date: 117-20. *In situ.* Ph. U.D.F. – La Photothèque.

283 Roman art. ROME, Forum Romanum. Parapet showing an episode from Trajan's reign. Date: 117-20. *In situ.* Marble. H 1.68 m. B 5.21 m. Ph. U.D.F. – La Photothèque.
   This relief is matched by another one of the same dimensions. The two of them have, on their obverse, the figures of a pig, a sheep and a bull ready for sacrifice (the 'suovetaurilia').

284 Roman art. ROME, house near the Porto Flumentano. Decoration of a room. Date: 131. Fresco. Ph. Gabinetto Fotografico Nazionale, Rome.
   This fresco is at present in Rome, in the Museo Nazionale.

285 Roman art. ROME, house near the Porto Flumentano. Mural decoration (detail). Date: 131. Rome: Museo Nazionale. Fresco. H of part shown: 1 m. Ph. U.D.F. – La Photothèque.

286 Roman art. ROME. Temple of Venus and Rome built by Hadrian. View of the apse. Date: 121-40. *In situ.* Ph. U.D.F. – La Photothèque.

287 Greek art of the Roman period. ROME. Antinoüs, Hadrian's favourite (detail). Date: 130-38. Naples: Museo Archeologico Nazionale. Marble. H of statue overall: 2.03 m. H of face: 0.15 m. Ph. U.D.F. – La Photothèque.

288 Roman art. OSTIA. Portrait from the Hadrianic period (detail). Date: 135-40. Ostia Museum. Marble. H of bust overall: 0.66 m. H of the head: 0.27 m. Ph. U.D.F. – La Photothèque.

289 Graeco-Roman art. OSTIA. Necropolis on the Isola Sacra. Attic sarcophagus. Date: 120-40. Ostia Museum. Marble. B 1.24 m. Ph. U.D.F. – La Photothèque.

290 Roman art. ROME, Forum Caesaris. Frieze of the temple of Venus Genetrix, restored under Trajan. Date: 113-20. Rome: Capitol, Palazzo dei Conservatori. Marble. H of the frieze: 0.49 m. B 1.92 m. Ph. U.D.F. – La Photothèque.
The Amorini are shown preparing a bath for Venus and playing with the arms of Mars.

291 Roman art. ROME. Arch of Constantine (detail). *In situ.* Marble. Ph. Alinari, Florence.
The Arch of Constantine, built in 312-15, is decorated with eight medallion-type reliefs dating from the reign of Hadrian.

292 Roman art. ROME. Arch of Constantine. Hadrian as lion-hunter (cf. 191). Date: 130-38. *In situ.* Marble. D 2.40 m. Ph. Anderson, Rome.

293 Roman art. ROME. Arch of Constantine. Hadrian's hunt: sacrifice to Diana (detail). Date: 130-38. *In situ.* Marble. Ph. Deutsches Archäologisches Institut, Rome.

294 Roman art. OSTIA (?). Funerary relief of a magistrate (*aedile*) responsible for circus entertainment. Date: 120-40. Vatican (Lateran Museum). Marble. H 0.50 m. B 0.97 m. Ph. Alinari, Rome.

295 Roman art. ROME, Via Portuense. The reclining Hercules, an image revered by circus charioteers. Second cent. Rome: Museo Nazionale. Tufa. B 0.30 m. Ph. U.D.F. – La Photothèque.
The sanctuary of Hercules Cubans was situated on what is now the Via Portuense.

296 Roman art. ROME. The Pantheon (as reconstructed during Hadrian's reign). Date: 117-38. *In situ.* Ph. Anderson, Rome.

297 Roman art. ROME. Antonio Sarti. The Pantheon: view of the interior. Date: 1829. Rome: Calcografia Nazionale. Engraving. Ph. U.D.F. – Photothèque.

298 Roman art. BAIA (ancient BAIAE). Bathhouse. End of the first cent. BC or beginning of the first cent. AD. *In situ.* Ph. Alinari, Florence.
This building is popularly known as the 'Temple of Diana'.

299 Roman art. ROME. Hadrian's Mausoleum (detail). Date: 130-40. *In situ.* Ph. U.D.F. – La Photothèque.
This mausoleum forms the basis of the Castello Sant'Angelo, the former Papal fortress.

300 Roman art. TIVOLI (ancient TIBUR). Ruins of Hadrian's Villa (detail). Date: 120-38. *In situ.* Ph. U.D.F. – La Photothèque.

301 Italian art. Giambattista Piranesi (1720-78). Ruins of Hadrian's Villa at Tivoli. Rome: Calcografia Nazionale. Engraving. Ph. U.D.F. – La Photothèque.

302 Roman art. TIVOLI (ancient TIBUR). Hadrian's Villa. The *Teatro marittimo,* detail (cf. 441). Date: 130-38. *In situ.* Ph. U.D.F. – La Photothèque.

303 Roman art. TIVOLI (ancient TIBUR). Hadrian's Villa. The *Teatro Marittimo,* detail (cf. 441). Date: 130-38. *In situ.* Ph. U.D.F. – La Photothèque.

304 Roman art. TIVOLI (ancient TIBUR). Hadrian's Villa. Centaur and wild beasts. Mosaic picture. Date: 130-38. Berlin: Staatliche Museen. Pavement mosaic. B 0.62 m. Ph. U.D.F. – La Photothèque.

305 Roman art. TIVOLI (ancient TIBUR). Hadrian's Villa, guest chambers. Mosaic flooring. Date: 130-38. *In situ.* Pavement mosaic. Ph. U.D.F. – La Photothèque.

306 Roman art. TIVOLI (ancient TIBUR). Hadrian's Villa. Pavement mosaic, detail (cf. 304). Date: 130-38. Berlin: Staatliche Museen. Ph. U.D.F. – La Photothèque.

307 Roman art. TIVOLI (ancient TIBUR). Hadrian's Villa. Pavement mosaic, detail. Date: 130-38. Vatican: Museo Pio Clementino. B of entire picture: 0.62 m. Ph. De Antonis, Rome.

308 Roman art. TIVOLI (ancient TIBUR). Hadrian's Villa. Interior view of the 'canopus' (detail). Date: 120-38. *In situ.* Ph. U.D.F. – La Photothèque.

309 Graeco-Roman art. TIVOLI (ancient TIBUR). Hadrian's Villa. Copy of the 'Amazon' of Pheidias. Original: fifth cent. BC (bronze). Copy: 117-38 (marble). Tivoli: Hadrian's Villa (Museum). Marble. H 2 m. (approx.). Ph. U.D.F. – La Photothèque.

310 Roman art. Sarcophagus with garlands and scenes from the myth of Diana (detail). Date: 130-40. Paris: Louvre. Marble. Ph. U.D.F. – La Photothèque.

311 Roman art. ROME. Tomb near the Porta Viminalis. Sarcophagus portraying the Orestes myth. Date: 130-34. Vatican (Lateran Museum). Greek marble. H 1.12 m. B 2.15 m. H of the consoles: 0.23 m. Ph. Anderson, Rome.
The sarcophagi in pl. 311 and 312 were found in the same chamber, built with bricks dated 132 and 134.

312 Roman art. ROME: Tomb near the Porta Viminalis. Sarcophagus portraying the myth of Niobe and her children. Date: 130-34. Vatican (Lateran Museum). Italian marble. H 0.92 m. B 2.09 m. H of the consoles: 0.24 m. Ph. Anderson, Rome.

313 Roman art. ROME: Tomb near the Porta Viminalis. Sarcophagus portraying the Orestes myth (detail): the death of Aegisthus (cf. 311). Date: 130-34. Vatican (Lateran Museum). Ph. Anderson, Rome.

314 Roman art. ROME: Tomb near the Porta Viminalis. Sarcophagus portraying the myth of Niobe and her children (detail): Niobe (cf. 312). Date: 130-34. Vatican (Lateran Museum). Ph. Anderson, Rome.

315 Roman art. ROME, Palazzo Giustiniani. Sarcophagus portraying the Orestes myth. Date: 130-40. Rome: courtyard of the Palazzo Giustiniani. Marble. B 2.10 m. Ph. Deutsches Archäologisches Institut, Rome.

316 Roman art. ROME: House of SS. John and Paul on the Caelian Hill. Mythical scene, detail (cf. 373). End of second or beginning of third cent. *In situ.* Fresco. Ph. U.D.F. – La Photothèque.

317 Roman art. ROME, Hadrian's Temple. Fragment of relief portraying two Roman provinces. Date: 139-45. Rome: Capitol, Palazzo dei Conservatori. Marble. H of base: 2.08 m. H of the figures: 1.51 m. Ph. U.D.F. – La Photothèque.

318 Roman art. ROME. Fragment of alto-relievo: portrait of Lucius Verus. Date: 161-69. Rome: Museo Nazionale. Marble. H. 0.27 m. Ph. U.D.F. – La Photothèque.
Formerly in the Von Kopf Collection.

319 Roman art. ROME: Forum Romanum. Portrait of Marcus Aurelius as a youth. About 147. Rome: Antiquarium del Foro. Marble. H 0.27 m. Ph. U.D.F. – La Photothèque.

NOTES ON THE ILLUSTRATIONS

This portrait matches the coin-portraits of 147, the year in which Marcus Aurelius was made joint-Emperor by Antoninus Pius. At the time he was twenty-six. Compare the portraits in pl. 349 and 366.

320 Roman art. ROME. The apotheosis of Sabina. Date: 136-38. Rome: Capitol, Palazzo dei Conservatori. Marble. H 2.68 m. B 2.10 m. Ph. U.D.F. – La Photothèque.
This relief, with another similar matching one, was used to decorate a monument in memory of Sabina, and afterwards transferred to a Late Empire arch on the Corso. The arch was demolished in 1662. The head and hand of the figure representing Hadrian (seated) are restored.

321 Roman art. ROME: Piazza di Montecitorio. Base of Antoninus Pius's Column: the apotheosis of Antoninus and Faustina. Date: 160-61. Vatican: Cortile della Pigna. Marble. H 2.72 m. B 3.38 m. Ph. De Antonis, Rome.
Discovered in 1703 in the Piazza di Montecitorio. The monolithic column of red granite (with a statue of the Emperor on top) which was erected over this base was used in the restoration of the obelisk that was put in its place.

322 Roman art. ROME. Base of Antoninus Pius's Column: cavalcade. Date: 160-61. Vatican: Cortile della Pigna. Marble. H 2.72 m. B 3.38 m. Ph. De Antonis, Rome.

323 Roman art. ROME. Base of Antoninus Pius's Column: detail of the cavalcade (cf. 322). Date: 160-61. Vatican: Cortile della Pigna. Ph. De Antonis, Rome.

324 Roman art. Relief: races in the circus. Date: 180-90. Foligno: Museo Archeologico. Plaster moulding: Rome, Museo della Civiltà Romana. Ph. Alinari, Florence.

325 Roman art. Relief: races in the circus (detail of the moulding). Cf. 324. Date: 180-90. Foligno: Museo Archeologico. Moulding. Ph. Alinari, Florence.

326 Roman art. ROME, Forum Romanum. Temple of Antoninus and Faustina. About 150. *In situ.* Marble. Ph. U.D.F. – La Photothèque.

327 Roman art. ROME. Coin of Antoninus Pius portraying the Temple of Faustina. Date: 142. Rome: Museo Nazionale. Bronze. D 0.03 m. Ph. U.D.F. – La Photothèque.

328 Roman art. OSTIA, necropolis on the Isola Sacra. Portrait of C. Volcacius Myropnous. About 160. Ostia Museum. Marble. H of bust overall: 0.55 m. Ph. U.D.F. – La Photothèque.

329 Roman art. LATIUM. Villa near Lanuvium. Bust of the young Commodus. About 176. Rome: Museo Capitolino. Marble. H with the base: 0.72 m. Ph. U.D.F. – La Photothèque.
Official bust of the young prince, at the age of about fifteen. It was now (in 176) that he took part in the triumph over the Germans and Sarmatians, and was elevated to the rank of Imperator.

330 Roman art. ROME. Portrait of Commodus. About 180. Vatican: Museo Pio Clementino. Sala dei busti (portrait-bust gallery). Marble. H 0.44 m. Ph. De Antonis, Rome.
In 180, when, barely twenty years of age, Commodus succeeded his father on the throne.

331 Roman art. ROME, the Esquiline. Bust of Commodus as Hercules. About 190. Rome: Capitol, Palazzo dei Conservatori. Marble. H 1.18 m. Ph. U.D.F. – La Photothèque.

332 Roman art. ROME, the Vatican. Necropolis in the Grotte Vaticane: Tomb of the Valerii. Stucco head. About 160. *In situ.* White stucco. H of the head: 0.12 m. Ph. De Antonis, Rome.
This fragment comes from the Tomb of the Valerii, situated underneath St Peter's Basilica in Rome.

333 Roman art. ROME, the Vatican. Necropolis in the Grotte Vaticane: Tomb of the Valerii. Decorated niche (cf. 332). About 160. *In situ.* Stucco. Ph. De Antonis, Rome.

334 Roman art. ROME. House under the Basilica S. Sebastiano on the Appian Way. Mural decoration (detail): villas by the seaside. About 180. *In situ.* Fresco. B 1.04 m. Ph. U.D.F. – La Photothèque.
This landscape forms part of the decoration on the remains of a villa now 2.50 m. below ground level, with the Basilica S. Sebastiano built over it.

335 Roman art. OSTIA. 'House of the Painted Ceilings'. Ceiling of a room. About 150. *In situ.* Fresco. Ph. U.D.F. – La Photothèque.

336 Roman art. OSTIA. Necropolis on the Isola Sacra. Ceiling of a tomb (detail): Mercury. About 150. Ostia Museum. Fresco. Ph. U.D.F. – La Photothèque.

337 Roman art. ROME. Pavement mosaic: a Maenad. Late second or early third cent. Rome: Museo Nazionale. Marble. H 1.40 m. B 1.40 m. Ph. U.D.F. – La Photothèque.

338 Roman art. OSTIA. Porta Laurentina: the necropolis. First-century tombs. About 50. *In situ.* Brick. Ph. U.D.F. – La Photothèque.

339 Roman art. ROME, Via Appia. Tomb of Annia Regilla. Date: 160-61. *In situ.* Brick. 8 × 8 m. (approx.). Ph. Alinari, Florence.
This edifice has been known, ever since the Renaissance, as the 'Temple of the God Rediculus'.

340 Italian Renaissance art. FLORENCE. Antonio Sangallo the Younger (1483-1546). Sketch of the tomb of Annia Regilla. Florence: Uffizi. Department of Drawings. Ink on paper. H 0.278 m. B 0.210 m. Ph. Soprintendenza alle Gallerie – Gabinetto Fotografico, Florence.

341 Roman art. ROME, Via Appia. Sarcophagus portraying a battle against the Galatians. About 160-70. Rome: Museo Capitolino. Carrara marble. H 1.25 m. B 2.11 m. Ph. U.D.F. – La Photothèque.
The sarcophagus comes from a tomb in the Vigna Ammendola, Via Appia, discovered in 1830. The composition of the relief is inspired by some lost Hellenistic painting.

342 Roman art. OSTIA. Sarcophagus portraying the myth of Alcestis. Date: 161-70. Vatican: Museo Chiaramonti. Marble. H 0.795 m. B 2.10 m. Ph. Anderson, Rome.
The inscription gives the names of the occupants: C. Junius Eunodus, who was, at the time of the twenty-first 'lustrum', an officer in the Ostia Guild of Carpenters (which gives us a date between 161 and 170), and Metilia Acte, his wife, a priestess of Cybele.

343 Roman art. ROME, the Via Appia. Sarcophagus showing battle against the Galatians (detail). Cf. 341. About 160-70. Rome: Museo Capitolino. Ph. U.D.F. – La Photothèque.

344 Roman art. ROME, Via Casilina. Sarcophagus of one of Marcus Aurelius's generals (detail). Cf. 345. Date: 180-90. Rome: Museo Nazionale. Ph. U.D.F. – La Photothèque.

345 Roman art. ROME, Via Casilina. Sarcophagus of one of Marcus Aurelius's

generals. Battle against the barbarians. Date: 180-90. Rome: Museo Nazionale. Marble. H 1.50 m. B 2.39 m. Ph. U.D.F. – La Photothèque.

346 Roman art. ROME, Via Casilina. Sarcophagus of one of Marcus Aurelius's generals (detail): captive barbarians (cf. 345). Date 180-90. Rome: Museo Nazionale. Ph. U.D.F. – La Photothèque.

347 Roman art. ROME, Via Casilina. Sarcophagus of one of Marcus Aurelius's generals (detail): captive barbarians (cf. 345). Date: 180-90. Rome: Museo Nazionale. Ph. U.D.F. – La Photothèque.

348 Roman art. ROME, Via Casilina. Sarcophagus of one of Marcus Aurelius's generals (detail). Dying barbarian (cf. 345). Date: 180-90. Rome: Museo Nazionale. Ph. U.D.F. – La Photothèque.

349 Roman art. ROME. Equestrian statue of Marcus Aurelius (detail). Cf. 350. Date: 166-80. Rome: Piazza del Campidoglio. Gilded bronze. H of head: 0.585 m. Ph. U.D.F. – La Photothèque.

350 Roman art. ROME. Monument of Marcus Aurelius. Date: 166-80. Rome: Piazza del Campidoglio. Gilded bronze. Overall H 4.24 m. H of horse (head): 3.52 m. Overall B: 3.87 m. Ph. U.D.F. – La Photothèque.

In the tenth century this group stood in the Piazza del Laterano (once the site of the house where he was born). Through an erroneous impression that it was in fact a representation of Constantine, it survived. In 1538, at Michelangelo's instigation, it was transferred to the Capitol. The crouching figure of a conquered barbarian originally, it would seem, was located beneath the horse's raised hoof.

351 Roman art. EPHESUS. Monument of Marcus Aurelius and L. Verus (detail). Date: 166-70. Vienna: Kunsthistorisches Museum. Marble. H 2 m. Overall B 18 m. (approx.). Ph. Museum.

352 Art of the Roman period. CONSTANTZA (ancient TOMIS). The serpent Glycon. Second cent. Constantza: Muzeul de Arheologie. Marble. H 0.60 m. (approx.). Ph. Mircea Boca.
This is the only surviving representation in the round. It was found in the ruins of a sanctuary at Constantza (Rumania), ancient Tomis, the town to which Ovid was exiled.

353 Roman art. ROME. Church of Santa Martina. Marcus Aurelius sacrificing before the temple of Jupiter on the Capitol. Date: 176-80. Rome: Capitol, Palazzo dei Conservatori. Marble. H 3.14 m. B 2.10 m. Ph. U.D.F. – La Photothèque.
The temple of Jupiter Capitolinus, as reconstructed during Domitian's reign, can be identified by the adornment of the pediment, even though the artist has reduced it (four columns instead of six).

354 Roman art. ROME. Monument of Marcus Aurelius. Scene of sacrifice. Date: 180-90. Rome, Arch of Constantine: attic storey. Marble. H 3.14 m. B 2.10 m. Ph. Soprintendenza ai Monumenti del Lazio.
This and the two following reliefs (355, 356) originally belonged to a monument of Marcus Aurelius, but were afterwards re-used for the Arch of Constantine (built between 312 and 315). The emperor's head is modern (eighteenth century).

355 Roman art. ROME. Monument of Marcus Aurelius. A *liberalitas* of Marcus Aurelius. Date: 180-90. Rome, Arch of Constantine, attic storey. Marble. H 3.14 m. B 2.10 m. Ph. Soprintendenza ai Monumenti del Lazio.

356 Roman art. ROME. Monument of Marcus Aurelius. A barbarian chieftain surrenders. Date: 180-90. Rome, Arch of Constantine, attic storey. Marble. H 3.14 m. B 2.10 m. Ph. Soprintendenza ai Monumenti del Lazio.

357 Roman art. ROME. Monument of Marcus Aurelius. Detail from one of the reliefs. Date: 180-90. Rome: Arch of Constantine. Marble. Ph. Deutsches Archäologisches Institut, Rome.

358 Roman art. ROME. Monument of Marcus Aurelius. A barbarian chieftain surrenders (detail of 356). Date: 180-90. Rome, Arch of Constantine. Ph. Deutsches Archäologisches Institut, Rome.

359 Roman art. ROME. Monument of Marcus Aurelius. A barbarian chieftain surrenders (detail of 356). Date: 180-90. Rome, Arch of Constantine. Ph. Deutsches Archäologisches Institut, Rome.

360 Roman art. ROME. Piazza Colonna: Marcus Aurelius's Column. The 'miracle of the thunderbolt' (detail).

Date: 180-92. *In situ.* Marble. Ph. Deutsches Archäologisches Institut, Rome.

361 Roman art. ROME. Piazza Colonna: Marcus Aurelius's Column. The 'miracle of the rain' (detail). Date: 180-92. *In situ.* Marble. H 1.30 m. (approx.). Ph. Anderson, Rome.

362 Roman art. ROME. Piazza Colonna: Marcus Aurelius's Column (cf. 360, 361, 363-7). Date: 180-92. *In situ.* Marble. Overall height (minus statue): 41.951 m. D 3.80 m. Ph. Alinari, Florence.

363 Roman art. ROME. Giambattista Piranesi. Base of Marcus Aurelius's Column before 1589. Rome: Calcografia Nazionale. Engraving on paper. Ph. U.D.F. – La Photothèque.
This engraving by Piranesi (1720-78) follows a sketch of Cavalieri's, made prior to the changes carried out by D. Fontana under Pope Sixtus V (1589).

364 Roman art. ROME. Marcus Aurelius's Column. Detail from a relief. Date: 180-92. *In situ.* Marble. Ph. Deutsches Archäologisches Institut, Rome.

365 Roman art. ROME. Marcus Aurelius's Column. Decapitation of prisoners (detail). Date: 180-92. *In situ.* Marble. Ph. Anderson, Rome.

366 Roman art. ROME. Marcus Aurelius's Column. The Emperor on the battlefield (detail). Date: 180-92. *In situ.* Marble. Ph. Deutsches Archäologisches Institut, Rome.

367 Roman art. ROME. Marcus Aurelius's Column. Barbarian women being carried off (detail). Cf. 445. Date: 180-92. *In situ.* Marble. Ph. Deutsches Archäologisches Institut, Rome.

368 Roman art. ROME. Nero's *Domus Aurea.* Room with architectural motifs and painted landscapes (no. 78). Date: 64-68. *In situ.* Fresco. Ph. U.D.F. – La Photothèque.

369 Roman art. OSTIA. Mural decoration from the era of Antoninus Pius. Date: 140-60. *In situ.* Fresco. Ph. Soprintendenza, Ostia.

370 Roman art. OSTIA. 'House of the Paintings': Yellow Room. Mural decorations dating from Commodus's reign. Date: 180-90. *In situ.* Fresco. Ph. U.D.F. – La Photothèque.

371 Roman art. ROME. House of SS. John

and Paul on the Caelian Hill. Mythical scene (detail): goddess with a cup (cf. 373). Late second or early third cent. *In situ.* Ph. U.D.F. – La Photothèque.

372 Roman art. MARINO. Mithraeum. Solar divinity, detail (cf. 374). Date: 160-70. *In situ.* Fresco. From the *Enciclopedia dell'Arte Antica Classica e Orientale,* V, 1963, p. 492.

373 Roman art. ROME. House of SS. John and Paul on the Caelian Hill. Mythical scene above a fountain (for details, cf. 371, 375). Late second or early third cent. *In situ.* Fresco. Ph. U.D.F. – La Photothèque.

374 Roman art. MARINO. Mithraeum. Mithras as bull-slayer (*tauroctonus*). Date: 160-70. *In situ.* Fresco. B 3.40 m. From the *Enciclopedia dell'Arte Antica Classica e Orientale,* V, 1963, p. 116.

375 Roman art. ROME. House of SS. John and Paul on the Caelian Hill. Mythical scene, detail (cf. 373). Late second or early third cent. *In situ.* Ph. U.D.F. – La Photothèque.

376 Roman art. OSTIA. Necropolis. Votive relief with ships and symbolic motifs. Date: 180-90. Rome: Museo Torlonia. Marble. B 1.22 m. Ph. U.D.F. – La Photothèque.

377 Roman art. OSTIA. Necropolis. Votive relief (detail): the apotropaic eye (cf. 376). Date: 180-90. Rome: Museo Torlonia. Ph. U.D.F. – La Photothèque.

378 Roman art. ROME. Baths of Caracalla. Pavement mosaic: portrait of a gladiator (detail). About 212. Rome: Museo Nazionale. Pebbles. H 0.96 m. Ph. U.D.F. – La Photothèque.
Other fragments of the same mosaic are preserved in the Vatican (Lateran Museum).

379 Roman art. ROME, Via dei Fori Imperiali. Portrait of the Emperor Caracalla. Date: 211-17. Rome: Capitol, Palazzo dei Conservatori. Marble. H 0.28 m. Ph. U.D.F. – La Photothèque.

380 Roman art. ROME. Portrait of Pope Callistus. Third cent. Paris: Bibliothèque Nationale, Cabinet des Médailles. Glass and gold leaf. D 0.046 m. Ph. U.D.F. – La Photothèque.

381 Roman art. HUNGARY (ancient PANNONIA). Funerary stele of the legionary C. Septimus, deceased in Pannonia (plaster cast). Date: 180-200. Magyar Nemzeti Múzeum. Plaster moulding: Rome, Museo della Civiltà Romana. Limestone. Ph. Alinari, Florence.

382 Roman art. ROME. Titus Tatius, legendary king of the Sabines and of Rome. Denarius of L. Titurius Sabinus. Date: 87 BC. Rome: Museo Nazionale Romano. Silver. D 0.018 m. Ph. Pozzi Bellini.
On the reverse: Tarpeia between two warriors. Inscription: 'L. Tituri'.

383 Roman art. ROME. The Elder Brutus (L. Iunius Brutus), first consul of the Roman Republic. Denarius of M. Iunius Brutus. Date: 59-58 BC. Rome: Museo Nazionale Romano. Silver. D 0.018 m. Ph. Pozzi Bellini.
On the reverse: a portrait of Servilius Ahala. Inscription: 'Ahala'.

384 Roman art. ROME. P. Cornelius Scipio Africanus, who defeated Hannibal in 202, and died about 183 BC. Denarius of Cn. Cornelius Cn. f. Blasio. Date: 99-91 BC. Rome: Museo Nazionale Romano. Silver. D 0.018 m. Ph. De Antonis, Rome.
On the reverse: the three Capitoline deities. Inscription: 'Roma'.

385 Hellenistic art. ATHENS. Perseus of Macedonia, the last Macedonian king. Tetradrachm. Date: 178-168 BC. East Berlin: Münzkabinett. Silver. D 0.033 m. From Kurt Lange, *Herrscherköpfe des Altertums,* Berlin 1938.
On the reverse: an eagle perched on a thunderbolt. Inscription: 'Basileos Perseos'.

386 Hellenistic art. AMASIA or SINOPE (?). Mithridates IV, who ruled over the kingdom of Pontus from 170 to 150 BC. Tetradrachm. 170-50 BC. East Berlin: Münzkabinett. Silver. D 0.032 m. Ph. U.D.F. – La Photothèque.
On the reverse: the inscription gives the name of the King with the additional titles of Philopator (in honour of his father) and Philadelphos (with reference to his sister Laodice, who was also his wife).

387 Hellenistic art. SINOPE. Mithridates VI. The last king of Pontus (132-63 BC), who took the title of Eupator Dionysus; the Romans found him a formidable and determined adversary. Tetradrachm. Date: 90-89 BC. East Berlin: Münzkabinett. Silver. D 0.034 m. From Kurt Lange, *Herrscherköpfe des Altertums,* Berlin 1938.
On the reverse: Pegasus. Inscription reads: 'Basileos Mithradatou Eupatoros'.

388 Roman art. ROME. A. Postumius Albinus, consul in 99 BC. Denarius of D. Postumius Albinus, son of the Brutus who was one of Caesar's murderers. Coin struck in 44-43 BC. Paris: Bibliothèque Nationale, Cabinet des Médailles. Silver. D 0.018 m. Ph. U.D.F. – La Photothèque.
On the reverse: a wreath of corn-ears round the inscription with the name of the mint-official.

389 Roman art. ROME. Sulla. L. Cornelius Sulla, consul in 88, and Dictator from 82 to 79 BC. Reverse of a denarius struck by Q. Pompeius Rufus, son of the consul of that name, who had been in office with Sulla for 88, and married his daughter. Date: 58-57 BC. Paris: Bibliothèque Nationale, Cabinet des Médailles. Silver. D 0.018 m. Ph. U.D.F. – La Photothèque.

390 Roman art. ROME. C. Antius Restio, *tribunus plebis* about 74 or 71 BC. Denarius struck by his son. Inscription: 'Restio'. Date: 46 BC. Rome: Museo Nazionale Romano. Silver. D 0.018 m. Ph. Pozzi Bellini.
Reverse: the figure of Hercules, with trophy and club, and the inscription: 'C. Antius. C.F.'.

391 Roman art. ROME. Domitius Ahenobarbus. We have here a portrait either of Cn. Domitius, victor of the naval engagement off Brindisi (42 BC), or else of his father, L. Domitius, consul in 54 BC. Denarius of Cn. Domitius, struck between 42 and 36 BC. Rome: Museo Nazionale Romano. Gold. D 0.018 m. Ph. Pozzi Bellini.
On the reverse: inscription and temple of Neptune.

392 Roman art. ROME. Pompey. Cn. Pompeius Magnus (71-48 BC). Denarius struck by Q. Nasidius at the order of Sextus Pompeius, the Triumvir's son, with the inscription 'Neptuni' (son of Neptune). Coin minted in 38-36 BC. East Berlin: Münzkabinett. Silver. D 0.017 m. Ph. U.D.F. – La Photothèque.

393 Roman art. SPAIN. Sextus Pompeius, son of Pompey the Great. Inscription: 'Magnus. Imp[erator]. Iter[um]'. Coin struck in Spain, 39 BC. East Berlin: Münzkabinett. Gold. D 0.017 m. From L. von Matt, *Römische Münzbilder,* Hirmer, Munich, 1966.
On the reverse: heads of Pompey the Great and Cnaeus Pompeius.

394 Roman art. ROME. Julius Caesar. Inscription: 'Caesar Dict[ator]. Perpetuo'. Denarius of L. Aemilius Buca.

Date: 44 BC. Rome: Museo Nazionale Romano. Silver. D 0.019 m. Ph. U.D.F. – La Photothèque.
On the reverse: winged caduceus and fasces, a globe, an axe, and two clasped hands.

395 Roman art. ROME. Brutus the Younger (M. Iunius Brutus), the anti-Caesarian conspirator. Inscription: 'Brutus Imp [erator]'. Coin struck between 44 and 42 BC. East Berlin: Münzkabinett. Gold. D 0.019 m. Ph. U.D.F. – La Photothèque.
On the reverse: inscription 'Casca Longus', with the representation of a trophy set on the prows of two ships.

396 Roman art. ROME. Marcus Antonius, the triumvir of 43 BC (with Octavian and Lepidus), who committed suicide in 30 BC after his defeat at Actium. Denarius of P. Sepullius Macer. Antony is shown wearing a beard, in token of mourning for the assassination of Caesar. Date: 44 BC. Rome: Museo Nazionale Romano. Silver. D 0.018 m. Ph. Pozzi Bellini.

397 Roman art. ROME. Augustus (born in 63 BC, received the title of 'Augustus' in 27 BC, died AD 14). Coin struck by his successor Tiberius. Inscription: 'Divus Augustus pater'. East Berlin: Münzkabinett. Bronze. D 0.030 m. Ph. U.D.F. – La Photothèque.

398 Roman art. ROME. Octavia, Augustus's sister and the wife of M. Antonius. Inscription on the obverse: 'M. Antonius M.F.N. Augur Imp[erator]ter' and portrait of M. Antonius. Coin struck 38-37 BC. London: British Museum. Gold. D 0.018 m. Ph. Comune di Roma.

399 Roman art. ROME. M. Agrippa (63-12 BC). Commemorative coin struck under Tiberius. Inscription: '[Marcus] Agrippa. L[uci]. F[ilius]. Co[nsul]. III'. Agrippa had married Augustus's daughter. He served as admiral of the fleet, and on coins is shown wearing the *corona navalis*. His third consulship was in 27 BC. Rome: Museo Nazionale Romano. Bronze. D 0.028 m. Ph. Pozzi Bellini.

400 Roman art. ROME. Tiberius, Emperor from 14 to 37. Inscription: 'Ti[berius]. Caesar. Divi. Aug[usti]. F[ilius]. Augustus'. Coin struck in AD 15. Rome: Museo Nazionale Romano. Gold. D 0.019 m. Ph. Pozzi Bellini.
On the reverse: 'Pontif[ex]. Maxim [us]', with a portrait of Livia, shown seated.

401 Roman art. CAESAREA in CAPPADOCIA. Germanicus, son of Tiberius's brother the Elder Drusus, and the adopted son of Tiberius himself. While proconsul in Asia, he struck a coin (silver drachma) at Caesarea in Cappadocia, bearing his portrait, in AD 18, the year of his death. Inscription: 'Germanicus Caes [ar] Ti[berio] Aug[usto] Cos. II P[ontifex] M[aximus]'. Date: AD 18. London: British Museum. Silver. D 0.019 m. Ph. Museum.

402 Roman art. ROME. Agrippina the Elder, the daughter of Augustus's daughter Julia by Agrippa, and the wife of Germanicus. Mother of Caligula. Died in exile, 33. Inscription: 'Agrippina M[arci]. F[ilia]. Mat[er]. C[aii]. Caesaris. Augusti'. Date: AD 33-34. Rome: Museo Nazionale Romano. Bronze. D 0.033 m. Ph. Pozzi Bellini.
On the reverse: 'S.P.Q.R. Memoriae. Agrippinae', and the representation of a waggon drawn by two mules.

403 Roman art. ROME. Antonia, daughter of Octavia by Mark Antony, and the mother of Germanicus and Claudius. Died AD 33. Coin struck under Claudius. Date: about 41-42. Rome: Museo Nazionale Romano. Bronze. D 0.028 m. Ph. Pozzi Bellini.

404 Roman art. ROME. Drusus the Younger, son of Tiberius, died in 23. Coin struck by Tiberius. Inscription on the obverse: 'Drusus. Caesar. Ti[berii]. Aug[usti]. Fi[lius]. Divi. Aug[usti]. N[epos]'. Date: AD 23. Rome: Museo Nazionale Romano. Bronze. D 0.028 m. Ph. Pozzi Bellini.

405 Roman art. ROME. Caligula. The title by which we know Caius Caesar Germanicus, Agrippina's son by Germanicus, who was Emperor from AD 37 to 41. Inscription on the obverse: 'C. Caesar. Aug[ustus]. Germanicus. Pon [tifex]. Max[imus]. Tr[ibunicia]. Pot [estate]'. Coin struck in AD 37. Rome: Museo Nazionale Romano. Bronze. D 0.033 m. Ph. Pozzi Bellini.
On the reverse: Caligula's three sisters represented as Securitas, Concordia, and Fortuna. Inscription: 'Agrippina, Drusilla, Julia'.

406 Roman art. ROME. Claudius, Antonia's son and Caligula's uncle, emperor from 41 to 54. The coin is a sestertius, and and bears the inscription: 'Ti[berius]. Claudius Caesar Aug[ustus] P[ontifex] M[aximus] Tr[ibunicia] P[otestate] Imp [erator]'. Date: AD 41. East Berlin: Münzkabinett. Bronze. D 0.033 m. Ph. U.D.F. – La Photothèque.

407 Roman art. ROME. Agrippina the Younger, sister of Caligula and Nero's mother (his father being Cn. Domitius Ahenobarbus), and from 48 married to her uncle, the Emperor Claudius. Born at Cologne in 16, died in 59. Coin struck by Nero in 51 when he received the title *Princeps Iuventutis*, during Claudius's reign. Date: AD 51. Rome: Museo Nazionale Romano. Silver. D 0.019 m. Ph. Pozzi Bellini.

408 Roman art. ROME. Nero, emperor from 54 to 68, son of the Younger Agrippina; committed suicide *aet.* 31. This coin bears the inscription: 'Nero Claudius Caesar Aug[ustus] Ger[manicus] P[ontifex] M[aximus] Tr[ibunicia] P [otestate] Imp[erator] P[ater] P[atriae]'. Date: between 54 and 68. Rome: Museo Nazionale Romano. Bronze. D 0.033 m. Ph. Pozzi Bellini.

409 Roman art. ROME. Galba, emperor in 68-69. The coin, a sestertius, bears this inscription: 'Imp[erator] Ser[vius] Sulpic[ius] Galba Caes[ar] Aug[ustus] Tr [ibunicia] P[otestate]'. Date: AD 68-69. East Berlin: Münzkabinett. Bronze. D 0.033 m. Ph. U.D.F. – La Photothèque.

410 Roman art. ROME. Otho, emperor in 69. This coin bears the inscription: 'Imp [erator] M[arcus] Otho Caesar Aug [ustus] Tr[ibunicia] P[otestate]'. Date: AD 69. Rome: Museo Nazionale Romano. Gold. D 0.019 m. Ph. De Antonis, Rome.

411 Roman art. ROME. Vitellius, emperor in AD 69. This coin, a dupondius, bears the inscription: 'A[ulus] Vitellius Germa[nicus] Imp[erator] Aug[ustus] P[ontifex] M[aximus] Tr[ibunicia] P [otestate]'. Date: AD 69. East Berlin: Münzkabinett. Bronze. D 0.028 m. From Kurt Lange, *Herrscherköpfe des Altertums*, Berlin 1938.

412 Roman art. ROME. Vespasian, emperor from 69 to 79. Inscription: 'Caes[ar] Vespasianus P[ater] P[atriae] Pon[tifex] Tr[ibunicia] Pot[estate] Co[n]s[ul] III'. Date: AD 71. Rome: Museo Nazionale Romano. Bronze. D 0.028 m. Ph. Museum.

413 Roman art. ROME. Titus, Vespasian's son, emperor from 79 to 81, died *aet.* 40. Inscription: T[itus] Caes[ar] Imp [erator] Vesp[asianus] Cens[or]'. Date: AD 76. Rome: Museo Nazionale Romano. Gold. D 0.018 m. Ph. Pozzi Bellini.
On the reverse: 'Co[n]s[ul] V'. The reference to Titus's fifth consulship provides the date.

414 Roman art. ROME. Julia, daughter of the Emperor Titus: died in 91. Coin struck in her honour by Domitian. Inscription: 'Julia Imp[eratoris] T[iti] Aug[usti] F[ilia] Augusta'. Date: AD 91. Rome: private collection. Bronze. D 0.028 m. Ph. Comune di Roma, from a cast.
On the reverse, the figure of Vesta, seated.

415 Roman art. ROME. Domitian, second son of the emperor Vespasian, reigned from 81 to 96. Inscription: 'Imp[erator] Caes[ar] Domit[ianus] Aug[ustus] Germ[anicus] P[ontifex] M[aximus] Tr[ibunicia] P[otestate] XI'. Coin minted in AD 91. Rome: Museo Nazionale Romano. Silver. D 0.019 m. Ph. Pozzi Bellini.

416 Roman art. ROME. Nerva, emperor from 96 to 98. The coin, a sestertius, bears this inscription: 'Imp[erator] Nerva Caes[ar] Aug[ustus] P[ontifex] M[aximus] Tr[ibunicia] P[otestate] Co[n]s[ul] III P[ater] P[atriae]'. Coin minted in AD 97. East Berlin: Münzkabinett. Bronze. D 0.035 m. Ph. U.D.F. – La Photothèque.

417 Roman art. ROME. Trajan, adopted son of Nerva, emperor from 98 until 117. The coin, struck after his sixth consulship (to which it refers), can be dated between 112 and 114, when Trajan was 59-61 years old. Inscription: 'Imp[erator] Traianus Aug[ustus] Ger[manicus] Dac[icus] P[ontifex] M[aximus] Tr[ibunicia] P[otestate] Co[n]s[ul] VI P[ater] P[atriae]'. Paris: Bibliothèque Nationale, Cabinet des Médailles. Gold. D 0.033 m. Ph. U.D.F. – La Photothèque.

418 Roman art. ROME. Plotina, wife of the emperor Trajan, born about 70, died in 129. This coin was struck by order of Hadrian that same year and bears the inscription: 'Plotina Aug[usta] Imp[eratoris] Traiani[uxor]'. Date: AD 129. East Berlin: Münzkabinett. Bronze. D 0.034 m. Ph. U.D.F. – La Photothèque.

419 Roman art. ROME. Hadrian, adopted by Trajan, was the son of one of his cousins, and emperor from 117 to 138. The medallion bears the inscription: 'Hadrianus Aug[ustus] Co[n]s[ul] III P[ater] P[atriae]'. Medallion struck in AD 119. Rome: Museo Nazionale Romano. Bronze. D 0.035 m. Ph. Pozzi Bellini.

420 Roman art. ROME. Sabina, Trajan's great-niece and the daughter of Mati-

dia: married to Hadrian. Inscription: 'Sabina Augusta Imp[eratoris] Hadriani Aug[usti] P[atris] P[atriae] [uxor]'. Date: AD 128-34. Paris: Bibliothèque Nationale, Cabinet des Médailles. Gold. D 0.020 m. Ph. U.D.F. – La Photothèque.

421 Roman art. ROME. Antoninus Pius, Hadrian's adopted son, and emperor from 138 to 161. Inscription: 'Antoninus Aug[ustus] Pius P[ater] P[atriae] Tr[ibunicia] P[otestate] XXIII'. This last detail gives the date as AD 160. Rome: Museo Nazionale Romano. Bronze. D 0.033 m. Ph. Pozzi Bellini.

422 Roman art. ROME. Faustina the Elder, wife of Antoninus Pius, mother of Faustina the Younger: died in 141. This coin was struck in the same year, and bears the inscription: 'Faustina Aug[usta] Antonini Aug[usti] P[atris] P[atriae] [uxor]'. Rome: Museo Nazionale Romano. Gold. D 0.018 m. Ph. Pozzi Bellini.
On the reverse, the seated figure of Concord, with the inscription: 'Concordia Aug[usta]'.

423 Roman art. ROME. Faustina the Younger, the Elder Faustina's daughter by Antoninus Pius, and married to Marcus Aurelius: died 175-76. Inscription: 'Diva Faustina Pia'. Date: AD 175-76. Rome: Museo Nazionale Romano. Gold. D 0.033 m. Ph. Pozzi Bellini.
On the reverse: 'Aeternitas', with the figure of Eternity, seated, holding a sceptre and a globe surmounted by a phoenix.

424 Roman art. ROME. Marcus Aurelius, emperor from 161 to 180. The medallion bears this inscription: 'M[arcus] Antoninus Aug[ustus] Germ[anicus] Sarm[aticus] Tr[ibunicia] P[otestate] XXXI'. Date: AD 177. Milan: Brera. Bronze. D 0.036 m. Ph. Museum.
The reverse of this medallion commemorates Marcus Aurelius's eighth Imperial 'acclamatio' and third consulship. It shows the emperor, with Commodus, in a processional quadriga: this composition much resembles one of the reliefs from the Palazzo dei Conservatori in Rome, on which the image of Commodus would appear to have been effaced.

425 Roman art. ROME. Lucius Verus, adopted brother of Marcus Aurelius, associated in power with him from 161: died in 169. The coin, dating from 163, bears the inscription: 'L[ucius] Verus Aug[ustus] Armeniacus'. It was struck

to commemorate the conquest of Armenia. Rome: Museo Nazionale Romano. Gold. D 0.018 m. Ph. U.D.F. – La Photothèque.

426 Roman art. ROME. Commodus, son of Marcus Aurelius and Faustina the Younger: emperor from 180 to 192. The inscription on the medallion reads: 'M[arcus] Commodus Antoninus Pius Felix Aug[ustus] Brit[annicus]'. Medallion struck in AD 191. Rome: Museo Nazionale Romano. Bronze. D 0.035 m. Ph. Pozzi Bellini.

427 Roman art. ROME. Temple of Vesta on the Palatine, dedicated by Augustus on 28 April 12 BC. Coin struck under Tiberius, between AD 14 and 37. Rome: Museo Nazionale Romano. Bronze. D 0.033 m. Ph. U.D.F. – La Photothèque.

428 Roman art. ROME. Temple of Concord. Coin struck under Tiberius between AD 34 and 37. Rome: Museo Nazionale Romano. Bronze. D 0.033 m. Ph. U.D.F. – La Photothèque.

429 Roman art. ROME. Temple of Venus Genetrix and its porticos in the Forum Caesaris, restored by Trajan. Inscription: 'S[enatus] P[opulus] q[ue] R[omanus] Optimo Principi'. Below: 'S[enatu] C[onsulto]'. Coin struck under Trajan, between AD 104 and 111. Rome: Museo Nazionale Romano. Bronze. D 0.033 m. Ph. U.D.F. – La Photothèque.

430 Roman art. ROME. Arch of Trajan's Forum on a medallion struck about AD 114. Inscription: 'Forum Traian[um]'. Rome: Museo Nazionale Romano. Gold. D 0.020 m. Ph. U.D.F. – La Photothèque.
This honorific arch reveals six frontal and six lateral columns, with a passage-way through the middle. The six columns are separated by four niches, in each of which there stands a statue, with a medallion above every niche and another over the archway itself. On the podium we see a six-horse chariot, with Trajan mounted in it, holding a branch (laurel? palm?) and crowned by Victory. Other coins of Trajan show a great central thoroughfare, flanked by four relief-sequences set one above the other. These end, at the upper level, in a frieze, over which are set yet further reliefs, as decoration for the attic storey. Highest of all comes the six-horse chariot. The date assigned to these issues is between 104 and 111.

431 Roman art. ROME. Temple dedicated to Matidia. A medallion of Hadrian's, with the inscription: 'Divae Matidiae

socrui', and a picture of the temple which he dedicated to his mother-in-law. Date AD 120-21. Vienna: Kunsthistorisches Museum. Bronze. D 0.033 m. Ph. Museum.

The temple was on two levels, and between two wings. Remains of it have been found between the Piazza Capranica and the Via dei Pastini in Rome. E. Nash, 'Pictorial Dictionary of Ancient Rome', II, pp. 36-37.

432 Roman art. ROME. Forum Romanum. Temple of Antoninus Pius and Faustina, restored by Antoninus Pius and adorned with a hemicyclic portico. Coin refers (obverse) to the fourth consulship of Antoninus. thus giving a *terminus post quem* of 145. Date: AD 145-61. Paris, Bibliothèque Nationale, Cabinet des Médailles. Bronze. D 0.033 m. Ph. U.D.F. – La Photothèque.

The remains of this little temple are still visible in front of Constantine's Basilica. See Nash, I, p. 165.

433 Roman art. ROME. Temple dedicated to Cybele. The image of the goddess can be seen inside, sitting on a throne flanked by lions, and holding a tambourine in her left hand. Inscription: 'Matri De[or]um salutari'. Coin struck about AD 141 under Antoninus Pius. Paris: Bibliothèque Nationale, Cabinet des Médailles. Bronze. D 0.033 m. Ph. U.D.F. – La Photothèque.

434 Roman art. ROME. Domitian's Stadium, on a coin of Septimius Severus, struck on the occasion of Severus's and Caracalla's return to Rome – and in honour of the latter's marriage to Plautilla, which was celebrated by games in the stadium. Date: AD 202-3. London: British Museum. Gold. D 0.019 m. Ph. Museum.

The interior of this stadium, built by Domitian between 92 and 96, was located on the present site of the Piazza Navona, in Rome.

435 Roman art. ROME. Restored Temple of Vesta. This temple stood close to the Forum Romanum, a little distance from the Via Sacra. Destroyed by fire during the reign of Commodus, it was restored by Septimius Severus's wife

Julia Domna. Coin struck between AD 196 and 211. East Berlin: Münzkabinett. Silver. D 0.018 m. Ph. Fototeca Unione pr. Accademia Americana, Rome.

The composition of this design repeats a typological formula first worked out for certain coins of Faustina the Elder and Commodus's sister Lucilla.

436 PALESTRINA (ancient PRAENESTE). Temple of Fortune. Reconstruction (levels I-V). After Heinz Kähler, *Das Fortuna-Heiligtum von Palestrina Praeneste*, in *Annales Universitatis Saraviensis, Philosophie-Lettres*, VII, 1958, p. 198.

437 TIVOLI (ancient TIBUR). Sanctuary of Hercules. Reconstruction. After Kähler, p. 216.

438 ROME. Pompey's Theatre. Plan. After Kähler, p. 222.

439 ROME. Augustus's Mausoleum. Section and ground-plan. After G. Q. Giglioli, 'Il mausoleo di Augusto', in *Capitolium*, no. 11, November 1930, p. 563.

440 ROME. The Forum Romanum and extensions made under the Empire (the Forums of Caesar, Augustus, Nerva and Trajan). Plan. After Gianfilippo Carettoni, Antonio Colini, Lucos Cozza, Guglielmo Gatti, *La pianta marmorea di Roma antica*, Comune di Roma, 1960, p. 72, pl. xx.

441 TIVOLI (ancient TIBUR). Hadrian's Villa. Partial ground-plan. From the *Enciclopedia dell'Arte Antica Classica e Orientale* I, Rome (Istituto poligrafico dello Stato), 1958, pl. 122.

442 ROME. Temple of Venus and Rome. Ground-plan. After Giuseppe Lugli, *Roma antica. Il centro monumentale*, Rome (G. Bardi), 1946, pl. iv.

443 OSTIA. Houses built to a standardized plan. Insulae XII and XIII in Regio III (contemporary with Trajan). After *Scavi di Ostia*, I, Rome (Libreria dello Stato), 1953, plans 1 and 6.

444 OSTIA. Two blocks of houses built to a standardized plan, set in a garden

decorated with six fountains and surrounded by houses and shops (contemporary with Hadrian). After *Scavi di Ostia*, I, Rome (Libreria dello Stato), 1953, plans 6 and 11.

445 ROME. Nero's *Domus Aurea*. Ground-plan. After W. L. Macdonald, *The Architecture of the Roman Empire*, Yale University Press, 1965, pl. 24.

The numbering of the rooms, according to Weege's traditional plan, is limited to those rooms illustrated in the present work: 60, 'Room with the gilded vaulting' (cf. 174); 69, small passage beside the 'Room with masks' (cf. 142); 70, corridor (cf. 173); 70a, transverse passage (cf. 139); 74, cruciform room (cf. 141); 78, room with architectural motifs and painted landscapes (cf. 368); 84, octagonal room (cf. 175); 85, 'Room of Achilles on Scyros', (a) walls (cf. 143, 144), (b) ceiling (cf. 145).

446 ROME, the Palatine. Domitian's Palace. Ground-plan. After W. L. Macdonald, *The Architecture of the Roman Empire*, Yale University Press, 1965, pl. 40.

447 ROME. Trajan's Market. Perspective drawing. After Macdonald, pl. 75.

448 ROME. The Pantheon: reconstruction carried out in Hadrian's day. After Macdonald, pl. 8.

449 Map of Central Italy, about 300 BC. After A. Piganiol, *La Conquête romaine*, Paris (Presses Universitaires de France), 1967; and the *Grosser historischer Weltatlas*, Munich (Bayerischer Schulbuch-Verlag), 1954, p. 28.

450 Map of the Roman Empire, from the Second Punic War till the death of Hadrian (201 BC-AD 138). Based on André Aymard, *Rome et son Empire*, 'Histoire générale des civilisations' II, Paris (Presses Universitaires de France), 1954, pp. 82, 252; and André Grabar, *The Beginnings of Christian Art*, 'Arts of Mankind', London (Thames and Hudson), 1967, pl. 312.

451 Plan of Republican Rome, about 50 BC, and of Imperial Rome during the Age of the Antonines, about AD 138-92.

The plans were executed by Claude Abeille, and the maps by Jacques Person.

Glossary - Index

ABONOTEICHOS. Ancient town on the coast of Paphlagonia (Asia Minor), today known as Inebolu (Turkey): 311.

ABRUZZI. Region of southern Italy: 74.

ACHAEAN LEAGUE. Federation of twelve Greek cities, defeated by the Romans at Pydna in 168, and broken up after the fall of Corinth in 146 BC: 75.

ACHILLES. The most valiant of the heroes whom Homer describes in the *Iliad*: 52, 132, 139, 310; *pl. 143-145, 212.*

ACTAEON. In Greek myth, a huntsman of royal birth, who was metamorphosed into a stag and torn to pieces by his own hounds for having surprised Artemis bathing in a river: 274.

ACTIUM. Promontory on the Gulf of Arta, off which there took place the decisive naval engagement between Octavian and Mark Antony, on 2 September 31 BC. From this battle dates Rome's supremacy throughout the Mediterranean, and the end of the Hellenistic Age: 180, 198; *map 450.*

ADRIATIC SEA: 4.

AEGISTHUS. In Greek legend, a son of Thyestes and cousin of Agamemnon: *pl. 313.*

AELIUS CAESAR (Lucius). Father of L. Aelius Aurelius Verus, who married the daughter of Marcus Aurelius: 282.

AELIUS CATO. Consul in 172 BC: 40.

AEMILIUS (Marcus). Roman consul (78 BC) who adorned the Basilica Aemilia – named after one of his ancestors – with family portraits fixed on shields (*imagines clipeatae*), and was the first person in Rome to put up such things in a private house (his own): 89, 152.

AEMILIUS PAULUS MACEDONICUS (Lucius). Roman consul, who defeated Perseus, King of Macedonia, at Pydna, in 168 BC: 40, 49.

AENEAS. Trojan hero, son of Anchises and Aphrodite. According to legend he disembarked in Latium, married Lavinia, daughter of King Latinus, and thus became the founder of the Roman *gens Iulia*: 8, 119, 155, 189, 192; *pl. 122, 202, 203.*

AEQUI. Ancient Italian people subjugated by Rome during the Samnite Wars (304 BC): 19.

AETERNITAS. Symbol of the eternity of Imperial power. Deified in Rome from the Augustan Age: 286.

AETOLIA. Region of Greece situated between Epirus, Thessaly, the Gulf of Corinth and Acarnania; subjugated by the Romans in 189 BC: 40.

AFRICA. Province of the Roman Empire, entitled *Africa Proconsularis,* and situated between Numidia and Cyrenaica. A senatorial province after 146 BC: 177, 281.

AGORA. In Greek towns, a public place in which markets and political meetings were held: 152, 311.

AGRIPPA. General and admiral of Augustus, whose daughter Julia he married: 44, 105, 123, 148, 179, 208, 264; *pl. 399.*

AGRIPPA POSTUMUS. Owner of a house in Pompeii: *pl. 148.*

AGRIPPINA THE ELDER (Vipsania Agrippina Maior). Daughter of Agrippa and Julia, and Augustus's granddaughter, she married Germanicus, by whom she had Caligula and Agrippina the Younger: *pl. 402.*

AGRIPPINA THE YOUNGER (Julia Agrippina Minor). Daughter of Germanicus and Agrippina the Elder. Married Domitius Ahenobarbus (by whom she had Nero) and, *en troisièmes noces,* her uncle Claudius: *pl. 407.*

AHENOBARBUS. *See* DOMITIUS.

AIÔN. Greek divinity, the son of Chronos. He represents the idea of time as eternal duration: 286, 287.

ALBA LONGA (Albe-la-Longue). Ancient capital of the Latins, situated near the modern town of Albano. Traditionally supposed to have been destroyed by the Romans under their king Tullus Hostilius: 155.

ALBANO. A town of Latium, situated in the hills, by the lake of the same name, and not far from Alba Longa, the ancient capital of the Latins: 18.

ALBERTI (Leon Battista), 1404-1472. Italian architect, sculptor, mathematician and writer: one of the most eminent humanists of the Italian Renaissance in Florence: 153, 161.

ALCESTIS. Wife of Admetus, king of Thessaly. She volunteered to take her dying husband's place, but was brought back to the world of the living by Heracles. The myth was taken up by Euripides as the theme for one of his tragedies; during the Roman period it came to symbolize the notion of a new life after death: 302, 305; *pl. 342.*

ALEXANDER III of Macedon (ALEXANDER THE GREAT), 356-323 BC. Son of Philip II of Macedon and Olympias: conqueror of Greece, Egypt and Persia (336-323). His reign marked the end of the classical period in Greece, and the advent of the Hellenistic Age: x, 11, 26, 30, 184, 235, 262, 281.

ALEXANDER OF ABONOTEICHOS. A hoaxer and charlatan who announced himself as a disciple of Apollonius of Tyana. During the reign of Antoninus Pius, he launched the cult of Glycon, creating an oracle to go with it: 311.

ALEXANDRIA. Founded by Alexander in 332 BC, Alexandria became the principal city of Hellenistic Egypt, a role it maintained in Graeco-Roman and Byzantine times. It stood on the Mediterranean, at the western extremity of the

Nile Delta: 11, 49, 108, 121, 125, 177, 198, 203, 204, 265, 274, 311: *map 450.*

ALGERIA. 281.

ALTINUM (Altino). Roman *colonia* in the territory of the Veneti, near the ancient mouth of the Piave: 311.

AMAZONS. A legendary race of female warriors, traditionally located in the north-east part of Asia Minor, and against whom both Heracles and Theseus fought. Together with their queen, Penthesilea, they played a part in the Trojan War: 71: *pl. 309.*

AMITERNUM. A Roman municipality in Sabine territory, on the Via Caecilia; its modern name is San Vittorino: 59, 66, 67; *pl. 60, 61, 67, 68, 75; map 449.*

AMMIANUS MARCELLINUS. Roman historian, born at Antioch; flourished during the second half of the fourth cent. AD: 238.

AMPHITRITE. A Nereid, the wife of Poseidon: *pl. 51, 52.*

AMYCUS. A Giant, the son of Poseidon: *pl. 18.*

ANATOLIA. The area usually referred to as ASIA MINOR.

ANCONA. A town of Central Italy, the capital of the Marches, on the Adriatic coast. Near the port there stands an arch set up in honour of Trajan, who set out from Ancona on his campaign against the Dacians: 67.

ANDRONIKOS KYRRHESTES. Greek architect, born at Cyrrhus (Syria), who designed the 'Tower of the Winds' in Athens. *Fl.* early first cent. BC: 163.

ANFOUCHI. A necropolis of Alexandria, in Egypt (Hellenistic period): 125.

ANGERA. A commune in Lombardy, on Lake Maggiore: provenance of a Roman altar: 58; *pl. 58.*

ANIO VETUS. An aqueduct which brought water into Rome from the Tibur (Tivoli) area: *pl. 172.*

ANKARA. Formerly Ancyra; in Asia Minor. Today the capital of Turkey: 252; *pl. 250.*

ANNIA REGILLA. The wife of Herodes Atticus. Her tomb still stands on the Via Appia, near Rome: 301; *pl. 339, 340.*

ANNIUS VERUS (Marcus). Consul in 97, 121, 126; grandfather of Marcus Aurelius: 282.

ANNIUS VERUS (M.). Father of the emperor Marcus Aurelius: 282.

ANNIUS VERUS (Marcus). Marcus Aurelius's son: 310.

ANTINOÜS. A Bithynian youth, of extraordinary beauty, beloved by the emperor Hadrian, who established a cult in his honour after his mysterious death in the Nile (AD 130): 258; *pl. 287.*

ANTIOCHUS. A city on the Orontes: capital of Syria (both as a kingdom and latterly as a Roman province). Founded by King Seleucus I in 300 BC: 11, 311: *map 450.*

ANTIOCHUS I. King of Syria (281-261 BC), son of Seleucus I Sotor, who founded the Seleucid dynasty: 72.

ANTIOCHUS III, known as 'The Great'. King of Syria (223-187 BC). Defeated by the Romans in 190 near Magnesia-by-Sipylus: 37, 51.

ANTIOCHUS IV EPIPHANES. Seleucid King of Syria (175-164 BC): 281.

ANTIUS RESTIO (C.). *Pl. 390.*

ANTONIA THE YOUNGER. Wife of Drusus; mother of Germanicus, Claudius, and Livia (or Livilla): *pl. 403.*

ANTONINUS PIUS (Titus Aelius Hadrianus Antoninus Pius). Roman emperor (138-161). Born in 86 at Lanuvium: his family originally came from Gallia Narbonensis. Adopted by Hadrian, he gave his name to the Antonine dynasty: 223, 224, 258, 282, 292, 306, 311, 312, 315, 316, 328; *pl. 321, 421.*

ANTONINES, THE. Dynasty of Roman emperors, from Nerva to Commodus (96-192): x, 63, 109, 183, 223, 258, 281-339.

ANTONIUS, MARCUS (known as MARK ANTONY), 82-30 BC. In 43, together with Octavian and Lepidus, he formed the Second Triumvirate. Defeated – together with Cleopatra – at Actium (31 BC), he committed suicide in Alexandria: 49, 79, 179, 180, 182; *pl. 396.*

ANXUR. Ancient Volscian town near the Tyrrhenian Sea, so called after the god Anxur, whose sanctuary stood above it. The Romans called it Terracina, a name it still preserves: 4, 5, 146; *map 449.*

APAMEA. An ancient Syrian town on the Orontes, occupied by Pompey: 11; *map 450.*

APENNINES. 29, 281.

APHRODISIAS. Ancient city of Caria, in Asia Minor, famous for its school of sculpture: 259; *map 450.*

APOLLO. One of the most important Greek divinities: son of Zeus and Leto, brother of Artemis. God of light, oracles, music and poetry: 5, 38, 69, 180, 182, 262, 275.

APOLLODORUS OF DAMASCUS. Greek civil and military architect, employed by the emperor Trajan from about 100 until 117: 237-239, 250, 255.

APOLLONIUS OF TYANA. Philosopher and prophet, born at Tyana in Cappadocia (Asia Minor). Flourished during the second half of the first cent. AD. Attempted to integrate Neo-Pythagorean theories with elements from Indian religions: 311.

APOTHEOSIS. Greek term equivalent to 'deification'. From Julius Caesar on, all Roman emperors were deified after their death (symbolized by the title *divus*): 87, 214, 284, 286; *pl. 241, 320, 321.*

APOTROPAIC. Greek term signifying anything with the power of fending off harmful spirits or the Evil Eye: 334; *pl. 377.*

APULIA. Ancient region of Italy, roughly equivalent to modern Puglia, but also including part of what are now Campania and Basilicata (Lucania). Principal city, Tarentum (Taranto): 11, 29, 114.

AQUILA, L'. Italian town in the Abruzzi, 37 miles east of Terni: 62.

AQUILEIA. Town of Friuli (Forum Iulii, Venetia) which became a Roman *colonia* in 181 BC. It stood at the head of the Via Aemilia and the Via Postumia: from here the latter went on to the Roman province of Noricum (modern Austria): 51, 311; *map 450.*

AQUINCUM. Roman town in Pannonia, and an important military headquarters. Today it is known as Buda (Hungary): 312; *map 450.*

ARA PACIS AUGUSTAE. Monumental altar, in marble, commissioned by decree of the Senate in 13 BC, and inaugurated on 30 March 9 BC, in honour of Augustus, to celebrate the peace that had been established throughout the Empire: 69, 182, 186, 188, 189, 191, 193, 198, 209; *pl. 200-204.*

ARA PIETATIS AUGUSTAE. Monumental altar commissioned by decree of the Senate in AD 22, during the reign of Tiberius, and finally consecrated by the emperor Claudius in AD 43: 209; *pl. 228, 229.*

ARABIA. 261.

ARCESILAUS. Sculptor from southern Italy, who executed the statue of Venus Genetrix for the temple which Julius Caesar built in the Forum: 48, 49, 155.

ARCHAIC STYLE. Term used to define Greek art from the mid-seventh century BC up to 480 BC: 121, 177.

ARCHAIZING STYLE. Imitation of the archaic style, most popular towards the end of the first century BC.

ARCHIMEDES (287-212 BC). Famous mathematician from Syracuse, who was killed during the capture of the city by the Romans: 36.

ARDEA. Ancient city of Latium, and the capital of Turnus, legendary king of the Rutulians: later a Roman *colonia:* 116.

AREZZO. Italian town in Tuscany: an Etruscan centre, and later a Roman *colonia* (Aretium), well-known for its production of red terracotta pottery with relief decorations: 203; *pl. 219; map 450.*

ARGONAUTS. Heroes of Greek mythology, the crew of the *Argo,* the vessel in which they and Jason set forth to bring back the Golden Fleece from Colchis, on the Black Sea: 17.

ARGUS. Giant with a hundred eyes, to whom Hera gave the task of watching over Io: *pl. 134.*

ARICCIA. A town in Latium, on the Via Appia (formerly Aricia): 32; *pl. 36-38; map 449.*

ARIKAMEDU. Site located south of Pondicherry, on the east coast of the Deccan: 203.

ARISTIDES. Greek painter from Thebes: *fl.* in the first half of the fourth cent. BC. Regarded as the founder of the Attic School of painting: 37, 38.

ARMENIA. A region of Western Asia situated between the Euxine and the Caspian: conquered by Lucullus in 67 BC, and organized as a Roman province under Trajan: 223, 241, 261, 309, 310.

ARNO. Italian river (Tuscany) which rises on M. Falterona and flows into the Tyrrhenian Sea: 3, 40.

ARPINUM (Arpino). Small town in Latium, in the Liris Valley, the birthplace of Cicero. In early times it belonged to the Volscians, and subsequently to the Samnites. It was conquered by the Romans in 305 BC: 43; *map 449.*

ARTA. Small Greek town of Epirus (ancient Ambracia), which lent its name to the nearby gulf; the southern end of this gulf is marked by the promontory of Actium, off which, on 2 September 31 BC, was fought the naval battle that guaranteed Octavian's supremacy: 180.

ARTEMIS. Greek divinity, daughter of Zeus and Leto, sister to Apollo. Patron goddess of hunting and chastity: 275.

ARVERNI. A Gallic tribe from the Auvergne, occupying an area between the headwaters of the Allier and the Dordogne: 130.

ASCLEPIUS, or AESCULAPIUS. Greek divinity, son of Apollo and a nymph, Coronis: doctor and healer: 19, 311; *pl. 21.*

ASIA MINOR. 51, 79, 116, 121, 130, 145, 177, 224, 259, 265, 274, 275, 284, 316, 341.

ASSYRIANS. 262.

ATHENA. Greek divinity, born from the head of Zeus, invoked both as warrior and as patron of the arts and sciences. Under the title of Athena Polias, she was the protectress of Athens: 240.

ATHENAGORAS. Athenian philosopher, and one of the earliest Christian apologists, who addressed an *Apologia for the Christians* to Marcus Aurelius: 311.

ATHENS. Capital of Greece; in antiquity the most famous of classical Greek cities, and a great cultural centre: 5, 11, 38, 43, 49, 75, 108, 177, 179, 182, 198, 202, 203, 261, 274, 281, 339; *map 450.*

ATISTIA. Wife of Eurysaces, an important Roman master-baker: 93; *pl. 103.*

ATRIUM. The principal room in an ancient Italian house, consisting (during the Roman period) of a large central hall which often had an opening *(impluvium)* in the centre of its roof: 77, 175.

ATTALUS II. King of Pergamum (159-138 BC): 36, 37.

ATTALUS III. King of Pergamum who bequeathed his kingdom to the Roman people on his death (133 BC).

ATTICUS (T. Pomponius). Wealthy Roman, publisher and intimate friend of Cicero: 43.

AUGURS. These were priests who interpreted omens from the flight of birds. Originally three in number, their numbers had risen to sixteen by Caesar's day: they constituted a sacerdotal College in Rome, which was established, traditionally, during the reign of Numa (legendary king): 25.

AUGUSTUS. Title voted to Octavian by the Senate in January 27 BC, and thenceforth bestowed *ex officio* on every Roman emperor: 38, 40, 41, 57, 58, 67, 80, 86, 93, 105, 121, 123, 128, 146, 148, 153, 155, 157, 180, 182, 183, 186, 190, 194, 198, 202, 204, 208, 212, 213, 249, 286, 338; *pl. 167, 197, 397, 439.*

AUGUSTINE (Saint), 354-430. One of the greatest Fathers and Doctors of the Latin Church. Born at Thagaste in Numidia: 44.

AVELLINO. Italian town (Campania), originally the main city of the Irpini, later a Roman *colonia:* 59.

AVEZZANO. An Italian town (Abruzzi): 175; *pl. 190.*

AVIANUS EVANDER (Caius). Athenian sculptor and goldsmith of the first century BC, who worked in Alexandria and Rome: 49.

AVIDIUS CASSIUS. One of Marcus Aurelius's generals, who in 166 defeated the Parthians. Nine years later (175) he had himself proclaimed Emperor in the East, but his usurpation lasted only three months: 312.

BACCHUS. Roman god of wine, identified with the Greek god Dionysus: 283; *pl. 249, 432.*

BAIAE (Baia). Natural harbour, situated on the Campanian coast (southern Italy) between Naples and Cumae. Its hot springs made it a popular resort: 146, 265; *pl. 298.*

BALLOMAR. King of the Marcomanni, a Germanic tribe settled in Bohemia, which – together with the Quadi and the Obii – in 166-167 crossed the Danube and invaded northern Italy. This was the first barbarian invasion under the Empire: 311.

BAROQUE. One of the major trends in European art; according to some, it first appeared in the seventeenth century, with Rome as its diffusion-point: 273, 291.

BASILICA. A type of building with an elongated ground-plan, and generally divided into three aisles or naves, of which the central one is higher, and often ends in an apse. Among the Romans the basilica was used both as a market-hall and for the dispensation of justice. Under Christianity it was adapted as a cult-centre: 152, 153; *pl. 159.*

BELLICUS NATALIS TEBANIUS (G.). Roman consul (AD 87) whose sarcophagus is preserved at Pisa: 274; *pl. 246.*

BELLONA. Italian divinity absorbed by the Romans, who worshipped her as the Goddess of War; the sister (or wife) of Mars: 89.

BENEVENTUM (Benevento). Italian town (Campania) which got its name from the Romans after they had defeated Pyrrhus there in 275 BC: 69, 235, 237, 250, 316; *pl. 260, 261; maps 449, 450.*

BEYEN (H.G.). Dutch archaeologist (1905-65): 123.

BITHYNIA. Ancient region of Asia Minor, between the Propontis and the Black Sea. An independent kingdom until the death of King Nicomedes IV in 74 BC; afterwards a Roman province: 258.

BLACK SEA. Large inland sea located between Anatolia, southern Russia and the Balkan peninsula: the ancient *Pontus Euxinus*, or Euxine: 241, 261.

BOCCHORIS. An Egyptian Pharaoh, *c.* 720-712 BC (XXIVth Dynasty), popularly regarded, by Greek historians, as the embodiment of all a just and wise judge should be: 121.

BOHEMIA. 261.

BOII: A Celtic tribe settled in what is now Bohemia: 51.

BOLOGNA (Bononia). Italian town (Emilia); its old Etruscan name of Felsina was changed after its occupa-

tion by the Gauls. From 189 BC it was a Roman *colonia:* 51; *map 450.*

BORGHESE. 184.

BOSCOREALE. Small town in the province of Naples; buried at the time of the eruption of Vesuvius in AD 79. A Roman villa with important wall-paintings has been unearthed here (paintings now in Naples, New York and Mariemont); the site has also yielded a treasure of silver vessels now in the Louvre: 204; *pl. 220, 223, 224, 227.*

BOSCOTRECASE. Near Pompeii: *pl. 148.*

BOSPHORUS. Straits linking the Propontis (Sea of Marmara) and the Euxine (Black Sea): X.

BOSPORUS, Kingdom of. Graeco-Scythian kingdom on the northern shores of the Black Sea, with its capital at Panticapaeum (Kertsch): *map 450.*

BOVIANUM UNDECIMANORUM. Capital of the Samnites before the Roman conquest; now Boiano in the Abruzzi: 74; *map 449.*

BRINDISI. Italian town (Puglia), known in antiquity as Brundisium. Occupied by the Romans in 226 BC. Used as a port for commerce with Greece and the East: 235; *map 450.*

BRUTUS (Lucius Junius). According to legend, he and Tarquinius Collatinus were the first consuls of the Roman Republic, after the expulsion of the last king, Tarquinius Superbus, in 509 BC: 28, 74; frontispiece, *pl. 383.*

BRUTUS (Marcus Junius), 85-42 BC. One of the leaders of the conspiracy to murder Caesar. Committed suicide in 42, after the defeat at Philippi: 80; *pl. 395.*

BUDAPEST. 312, 342.

BYZANTIUM. City on the Bosphorus, founded by Dorian colonists (600 BC); subsequently (AD 330) became the new capital of the Roman Empire, under the name of Constantinople: X; *map 450.*

CAECILIA METELLA. Daughter of Q. Caecilius Metellus Creticus, consul in 69 BC. Her tomb beside the Appian Way still survives: 154.

CAECILIUS METELLUS MACEDONICUS (Quintus). Roman general and politician. As consul, he conquered Macedonia (146 BC.): 146.

CAERE (Cerveteri). One of the main cities in the Etruscan federation, it lay northwest of Rome: 11, 23, 35; *pl. 35, 39, 90; map 449.*

CAESAR (Caius Julius), 100-44 BC. Roman politician and general: conqueror of the Gauls (58-51), Dictator, assassinated by a group of conspirators whose leaders were Brutus and Cassius: 40, 49, 79, 80, 152, 154, 155, 157, 177, 179, 181, 182; *pl. 166, 394.*

CALIGULA. The nick-name (from *caliga,* a boot) by which we know the Roman emperor Caius Caesar Augustus Germanicus (37-41), the son of Germanicus and Agrippina: 94, 123, 196, 208; *pl. 405.*

CALLISTUS I, Pope (217-222). 339; *pl. 380.*

CALLOT (Jacques), 1592-1635. French painter and engraver: 123.

CAMEO. Engraved stone: the intaglio technique employed takes full advantage of the different coloured layers which compose it: 194; *pl. 1, 208-214.*

CAMPANA COLLECTION. Large collection of antiquities assembled about the middle of the nineteenth century, in Rome, by the Marchese Giampetro Campana and subsequently dispersed (Louvre, British Museum, Hermitage, etc.): 93.

CAMPANIA. Region of southern Italy, situated between Latium and Lucania. The coastal district was colonized by the Greeks. Occupied by the Romans during the course of the fourth and third centuries BC: 4-6, 9, 11, 12, 17, 19, 25, 29, 30, 40, 41, 86, 110, 114, 115, 146, 159, 265; *pl. 95, 97.*

CANEPHORAE. This was the title given at Athens, in classical times, to the young girls who carried baskets on their heads, in religious processions, with sacred objects inside them: 43.

CAPPADOCIA. Region of Asia Minor between the Euxine, Armenia, Anti-Taurus and the Halys River: 312.

CAPUA (Santa Maria Capua Vetere). One of the oldest towns in Campania. Originally belonging to the Oscans, it was occupied first by the Etruscans and afterwards by the Romans, and in 59 BC became a *colonia:* 40; *maps 449, 450.*

CARACALLA (Marcus Aurelius Severus Antoninus, known as). Roman emperor

(AD 211-217), known by this nick-name because of the Gallic dress he habitually wore: 148, 282, 337; *pl.* 378, 379.

CARCOPINO (Jérôme). French historian (b. 1881): 209.

CARNUNTUM. Ancient Celtic town on the Danube, in Upper Pannonia (now Petronell, near Vienna, in Austria): 312.

CARPATHIANS. 241.

CARRHAE (Harran). Town in Mesopotamia (Turkey) near which Crassus suffered the first defeat which the Parthians ever inflicted on a Roman army: 310; *map 450.*

CARTHAGE. City founded by Phoenicians from Tyre on the North African littoral, near modern Tunis. Destroyed by the Romans in 146 BC, after a century-long struggle between the two powers: 9, 23, 26, 38, 40, 51, 75, 114, 180; *map 450.*

CASTELLAMMARE DI STABIA *See* STABIAE.

CASTELLETTO. *See* ARICCIA.

CASTOR. *See* DIOSCURI.

CATHERINE DE MEDICI. 196.

CATILINA (Lucius Sergius), 108-62 BC. A Roman patrician, and moving force behind a conspiracy to take over power in Rome. The conspiracy was anticipated by Cicero: 180.

CATO (Marcus Porcius, known as CATO THE ELDER), 234-149 BC. Roman politician and writer, famous for his austerity. Censor in 184, and an implacable enemy of Carthage: 43, 192.

CAUCASIANS. 5.

CAVEA. Elliptical or semi-circular pit formed by the tiers of an amphitheatre or theatre: 152.

CELER. Roman architect: in association with Severus he built the *Domus Aurea* for Nero: 130, 163.

CELSUS AQUILA POLEMEANUS (T. Julius). Roman senator and magistrate during Trajan's reign. His son built a library at Ephesus in his memory; the library also housed his mausoleum: 312.

CELTS. Generic name for tribes settled in western and northern Europe (Gaul, Belgium, Britain), some of whom also emigrated to Spain (the Celtiberi) or

Asia Minor (the Galatians). A wave of Celtic invaders penetrated Italy, advancing as far as Rome itself: 8, 51, 80, 305.

CENSORS. Roman magistrates, first appointed in 443 BC, whose task it was to supervise State revenues and public morals: 24, 75.

CENTOCELLE. A Roman suburb, through which the Via Casilina runs: 215.

CERVETERI. *See* CAERE.

CHARLES IX. 196.

CHIETI. *See* TEATE.

CHIGI (Agostino), 1465-1520. Wealthy Italian banker and patron of the arts: 119.

CHINA. 18, 309.

CHRONOS. Greek divinity, the youngest of the Titans: son of Ouranos (Sky) and Ge (Earth), father of Zeus and other leading gods, symbol of eternal time: 287.

CICERO (Marcus Tullius), 106-43 BC. Great Roman orator, writer and politician. Born at Arpinum, banished by Mark Antony, and finally executed near Formia: 43, 44, 49, 59, 60, 177, 181.

CILICIA. Region on the southern coast of Asia Minor, between Syria and Pamphylia: a Roman province from the first century BC (now part of Turkey): *map 450.*

CIPPUS. A small pillar, very often rectangular, put up as a gravestone: 74; *pl. 82.*

CISTI PRAENESTINI. Bronze receptacles, nearly always cylindrical in shape, with a lid, feet decorated with small figures in relief, and engraved surfaces; they date from the fourth and third centuries BC, and the greater part of them has been found at Praeneste (Palestrina): 17.

CISTOPHOROS. Silver Asiatic coin (originally worth four drachmas) on one side of which was represented the cylindrical cist associated with the cult of Dionysus: 38.

CIVITAVECCHIA (Centumcellae). Italian town (Latium): 239.

CLAUDIUS (Tiberius Claudius Nero Germanicus), 10 BC-AD 54. Roman emperor (41-54): 32, 148, 157, 204, 208, 209, 210; *pl. 169, 170, 406.*

CLAUDIUS PULCHER (Appius). Roman consul in 79 BC: 89.

CLEOPATRA (69-30 BC). Queen of Egypt, restored to her throne by Julius Caesar (in 46), married Mark Antony, and committed suicide after her defeat at Actium: 49, 180.

CNIDOS or CNIDIA. Ancient Greek city of Caria, opposite the island of Cos, especially famous for its school of medicine: 33.

COLONIES (COLONIAE). These were of two kinds, Roman and Latin. (1) They were Roman when Roman citizens were settled on a portion of the *ager publicus* to administer it in conjunction with the authorities in the Capital. (2) They were Latin when the colonized town kept its own laws, currency and magistrates, while acquiring rights of trade and intermarriage with Rome. In return for these privileges it undertook to furnish Rome military support at need.

COLUMBARIUM. In cemeteries, a special building containing numbers of little niches, each of which accommodated the ashes of a deceased person who belonged to the same burial club: 67, 103; *pl. 74, 112.*

COMES. Official accompanying the *Princeps* and acting as his adviser: 229.

COMMODUS (Lucius Aurelius). Roman emperor (180-192), son and successor of Marcus Aurelius: x, 100, 130, 173, 249, 282, 292, 310, 312, 314, 316, 322, 324, 328, 336, 338, 339, 341, 342; *pl. 329-331, 426.*

CONSTANTINE THE GREAT (Flavius Valerius Constantinus). Roman emperor (306-337), who transferred the capital of the Empire to Constantinople (Byzantium) and became a Christian convert: 42, 107, 185, 204, 223, 313.

CONSTANTINOPLE (Istanbul). Ancient Byzantium, elevated to be the capital of the Roman Empire on 11 May 330, by Constantine: x, 282.

CONSTANTIUS II (Flavius Julius Constantinus), 318-361. Roman emperor, son of Constantine: 238.

CONSTANTZA. *See* TOMIS.

CONSTITUTIO ANTONINIANA. Edict of the emperor Caracalla, issued in AD 212, by which every freeborn male throughout the Empire received Roman citizenship: x, 282.

CONSUL. One of the two magistrates who, from 449 BC onwards, held supreme civil and military power at Rome; elected annually by the *Comitia centuriata*: 37, 40, 75, 77.

CORINTH (Korinthos). One of the oldest and most flourishing cities of Greece: sacked by the Roman consul L. Mummius in 146 BC, reconstructed by Julius Caesar and raised to the rank of *colonia*, 44 BC: 5, 26, 36, 38, 51; *map 450*.

CORNELIUS SCIPIO AEMILIANUS (Publius). Adopted son of Scipio Africanus, who utterly destroyed Carthage in 146 BC: 38, 75.

CORNELIUS SCIPIO AFRICANUS MAIOR (Publius). Defeated Hannibal at Zama in 202 BC: 180; *pl. 384*.

CORNELIUS SCIPIO ASIATICUS (Lucius). Brother of Scipio Africanus, he was consul in 190 BC: 37.

CORNELIUS SCIPIO BARBATUS (Lucius). Consul in 298 BC, during the Third Samnite War: 26; *pl. 29*.

CORNELIUS SCIPIO NASICA SERAPIO. Consul in 138 BC, and leader of the aristocratic party: 180.

CORSICA. Island in the central Mediterranean, occupied by the Romans in 238 BC From 227 BC it and Sardinia together formed a Roman province: 26.

COSA (Ansedonia). Latin *colonia* on the coast of central Etruria, founded in 273 BC. Its ramparts survive, near the modern town of Orbetello: 24.

COTINI (Cottians). Germanic tribe settled on the River Tibiscus (Tisza), between the frontiers of Hungary and the Ukraine: 325.

COTTIUS (M. Julius). King of the Segusians, a Ligurian tribe settled in the maritime Alps and on Mt Cenis. In 9 BC he signed a treaty with Augustus, placing all his tribes under the authority of Rome. The Emperor became Prefect of the Roman province thus founded: 57.

CRASSUS (Marcus Licinius), 115-53 BC. Roman banker and politician, who with Pompey and Julius Caesar formed the First Triumvirate (60 BC). In 71 he suppressed the slave-revolt led by Spartacus, showing ruthless and bloody severity to the conquered rebels. He died at Carrhae, fighting against the Parthians: 40, 154, 180.

CROTON. Italian city on the east coast of ancient Bruttium (Calabria), a Greek colony occupied by the Romans from 277 BC: 39; *map 450*.

CTESIPHON. Ancient city on the left bank of the Tigris, opposite Seleucia: capital first of the Parthian, and afterwards of the Sassanid, Empire. Its ruins are located 20 miles south of Baghdad (Iraq): 310.

CUMAE. One of the oldest Greek colonies in Italy, and the furthest north (11 miles south-west of Naples). It was off the coast here that the Etruscans, who were settled in Campania, suffered a decisive naval defeat in 474 BC: 9, 19; *maps 449, 450*.

CURULE CHAIR. A backless seat made of ivory, to which only the highest Roman magistrates were entitled: 76.

CYBELE. Phrygian divinity identified by the Greeks with Rhea, the wife of Chronos (Time), and with the Anatolian Great Goddess, whose rites were of an orgiastic nature. Her cult was introduced to Rome in 204 BC: 283, 336; *pl. 433*.

CYNICISM. Greek school of philosophy, founded by Antisthenes (fourth cent. BC). Its name derives from the gymnasium of Cynosarges, at Athens: 224.

CYPRUS. The largest island in the Eastern Mediterranean, originally taken over by the Romans as part of Cilicia, but from 22 BC an autonomous Roman province: 5.

CYRENE. Capital of ancient Cyrenaica, a region on the North African coast west of Syrtis Maior, colonized by Dorian Greeks: 177; *map 450*.

DACIA. Region situated north of the Danube, towards its lower reaches: conquered by Trajan in two wars (AD 101-102 and 105-107) and thereafter a Roman province (107): 223, 229, 241, 242, 261, 310, 312; *pl. 269, 276*.

DALMATIA. Region on the Balkan coast of the Adriatic: a Roman province from 27 BC onwards: 26.

DAMASCUS. Ancient capital of Coele-Syria, conquered by the Romans in 66 BC: 237, 238; *map 450*.

DAMNATIO MEMORIAE. A condemnation inflicted by the Senate on some public figure after his death, which was tantamount to the official obliteration

of his memory; it included the erasure of his name from public inscriptions, and the destruction of his portraits: 130, 314, 324.

DANUBE. River of Central and Eastern Europe which runs from the Black Forest to the Black Sea: 223, 239, 241, 281, 308, 312, 322, 342; *pl. 273*.

DECEBALUS. Last king of the Dacians, who committed suicide in AD 106, after his defeat by Trajan: 249; *pl. 276*.

DECURSIO. Procession of armed troops round the mortal remains of a person whom it was wished to honour: 288.

DELLA VALLE (Andrea), 1463-1534. Italian cardinal: 209.

DEMETER. Greek divinity: daughter of Chronos and goddess of Earth, revered with her daughter Kore in the Eleusinian Mysteries: 32; *pl. 36, 38*.

DIANA. Italian divinity identified with the Greek goddess Artemis, goddess of hunting and the moon: 38, 262; *pl. 293, 310*.

DINDIA MACOLNIA. Name engraved on Ficoroni Cist as that of donatrix: 17.

DIO CASSIUS (Dio Cassius Cocceianus), *c.* 155-235. Greek historian from Nicaea who wrote a *Roman History* from the origins up to the year AD 229, of which only fragments survive: 179, 249.

DIO CHRYSOSTOM (*c.* 50-117). Greek orator and writer, born at Prusa in Bithynia: resident at Rome under Domitian and Trajan: 224, 226.

DIONYSUS. Greek divinity, of Thracian origin, son of Zeus and Semele, god of Nature and Wine, identified at Rome with Bacchus: 17, 36, 182; *pl. 17, 19, 20, 233*.

DIOSCURI. Twin brothers, Castor and Pollux, the sons of Zeus and Leda, protectors of horsemen, and generally invoked by those in danger: 8, 19; *pl. 12*.

DOLICHENUS. Oriental divinity (Baal) from the village of Doliché, in Commagene: assimilated to Jupiter under the Antonines: 336.

DOMITIAN (Titus Flavius Domitianus). Roman emperor (81-96), son of Vespasian, brother and successor to Titus: 123, 158, 167, 168, 209, 212, 215, 224, 238, 239, 241, 265; *pl. 163, 186, 247, 415*.

DOMITIUS AHENOBARBUS (Cneius). Roman politician, the friend of Brutus and Cassius; in 42 BC he won a resounding naval victory, and afterwards dedicated, in the temple of Neptune, a sculptured group of marine deities by Scopas. He has also been credited with the erection of an altar, identified in a sculptured frieze (Louvre and Munich Museums); but the latter has, by some, been attributed to another Domitius Ahenobarbus, and though the name remains linked with this monument, it probably did, in fact, have a different origin: 52, 69, 192; *pl. 51-55, 391.*

DONATELLO (1386-1466). One of the most eminent Florentine sculptors: 242.

DORYPHOROS (i.e. 'The Spear-bearer'). A famous bronze statue by Polycletus: 183; *pl. 196.*

DOURA-EUROPOS. An ancient city on the right bank of the Euphrates: originally a Hellenistic colony, then an important fortress of the Parthians. In AD 164 it was occupied by the Romans, and shortly after 256 destroyed by the Sassanids: 310; *map 450.*

DRUSUS THE ELDER (Nero Claudius Drusus Maior), 38-9 BC. Son of Livia: died fighting the Germanic tribes on the Elbe: 208.

DRUSUS THE YOUNGER (Julius Caesar Drusus Minor), *c.* 12-23. Son of Tiberius and Agrippina; died poisoned: 196; *pl. 404.*

DURONIA *(gens).* 33.

EGYPT. Last Hellenistic kingdom to be conquered by the Romans (31 BC), and thenceforth a province under the Emperor's direct control: 5, 18, 26, 93, 100, 138, 180, 262, 312, 336.

ELECTRA. 48; *pl. 48.*

ENTASIS. Slight convex swelling on Doric columns: 324.

EPHESUS. City on the coast of Asia Minor, 30 miles south of Izmir: an ancient Ionian colony, possessing a famous sanctuary of Artemis. By the will of Attalus III, the last King of Pergamum (133 BC), Ephesus passed into Roman hands, and was made the capital of the Roman province of Asia (from 129). Adorned with various monumental works of art under the Empire, the city later became an important Christian centre: 312, 315-316, 320; *pl. 351; map 450.*

EPICTETUS (*c.* 50-*c.* 130). Stoic philosopher, born in Hierapolis (Phrygia): founded a school at Nicopolis (Epirus): 226, 262.

EPIDAURUS. Greek city in the Argolid: 19.

EPIRUS. Region in the north-west of Greece: its king, Pyrrhus, allied himself with Tarentum against the Romans. Later (148 BC) Rome conquered the country, and in 31 BC made it an autonomous province: 25, 179.

ERECHTHEUM. Temple on the north side of the Acropolis in Athens, dedicated to Erechtheus: built between 420 and 406 BC: 274.

EROS. Greek god of love, the son of Aphrodite and Ares: portrayed with wings, bow, and arrows: 43.

ESTE. Italian town (Venetia), 20 miles south of Padua: 62, 67; *pl. 65, 76; map 450.*

ETEOCLES. Son of Oedipus and Jocasta, brother of Polyneices: *pl. 14.*

ETRURIA. That region of ancient Italy inhabited by the Etruscans: 3-6, 9, 11, 24, 28, 40, 80, 114, 202.

ETRUSCANS. A people probably of Anatolian extraction, but settled in Italy from prehistoric times, occupying the central region between two main rivers, the Tiber and the Arno. Afterwards they expanded, south into Campania, north to the Po Valley. By the seventh cent. BC they had evolved a highly developed culture, but a hundred years later they began to be absorbed by Rome: 3, 4, 6, 9, 11, 12, 19, 20, 23, 24, 72, 79, 80, 182, 265; *pl. 13, 14, 15, 16.*

EUPHRATES. Mesopotamian river flowing into the Persian Gulf: 18, 261, 310.

EURIPIDES. The youngest of the three great Greek tragedians (480-406 BC): 36, 302.

EURYSACES (Marcus Vergilius), first cent. BC. Important Roman master-baker from the end of the Republic, whose monumental tomb still survives in Rome, near the Porta Maggiore: 66, 93, 157; *pl. 73, 103, 164, 169.*

EUSEBIUS OF CAESAREA (*c.* 260-340). Bishop of Caesarea in 313, he wrote the first history of the Christian Church, the *Ecclesiastical History:* 338.

EUTROPOS. Sculptor of sarcophagi, who signed his name on a coffin now in the Urbino Museum: 316.

EVANDER. *See* AVIANUS.

EXEDRA. In Greek and Roman architecture, a room for conversation and meetings, equipped with seats arranged in a semi-circle: 114, 151, 238.

FABIUS (Marcus) and FANNIUS (Marcus). Names of characters in the oldest painting on a historical theme found in Rome, in a tomb on the Esquiline: 115; *pl. 117.*

FABIUS MAXIMUS CUNCTATOR (Quintus). Roman general and politician who, as Dictator, led the struggle against Hannibal when the latter descended on Italy with his army (217 BC): 36.

FABIUS MAXIMUS RULLIANUS (Quintus). Roman consul in 310; hero of the Second Samnite War: 115.

FABIUS PICTOR (Caius). Roman painter of noble family, who lived in the late fourth and early third centuries. He is mentioned in our literary sources: 115.

FABULLUS. Roman painter who decorated Nero's *Domus Aurea:* 132, 137.

FALERII NOVI (Santa Maria di Falleri). City of the Falisci, founded in 241 BC some four miles from Falerii Veteres, when the Romans forced the inhabitants to evacuate their ancient capital: 24; *pl. 27; map 449.*

FALERII VETERES. Capital of the Falisci, in Latium, near modern Civita Castellana: destroyed by the Romans in 241 BC: 12; *map 449.*

FALISCI. A people dwelling between Etruria and Latium (capital, Falerii), of Italian origin but influenced by Etruscan culture: 12.

FANNIUS (Marcus). *See* FABIUS.

FASCES. Insignia of the highest Roman magistrates (consuls, praetors), consisting of rods of birch or elm, tied together with straps, and with an axe inserted among them: 75.

FAUSTINA THE ELDER (Annia Galeria Faustina Maior), 105-141. Daughter of M. Annius Verus, and wife of the emperor Antoninus Pius: 286; *pl. 321, 422.*

FAUSTINA THE YOUNGER (Annia

Galeria Faustina Minor), 154-175. Daughter of Faustina the Elder and Antoninus Pius: married the emperor Marcus Aurelius: 312; *pl. 423.*

FAUSTULUS. According to legend, the shepherd who saved Romulus and Remus from the waters of the Tiber, and brought them up: 189.

FAYYUM. Province of Upper Egypt: 100; *pl. 109.*

FERENTINO (FERENTINUM). Ancient Italian town on the Via Latina: 238.

FIBULA. Metal pin (most commonly of bronze or gold); made in various shapes, but always with a catch, for securing garments: 20; *pl. 22.*

FICORONI (Francesco), 1664-1747. Italian scholar and collector who gave his name to a receptacle (the Ficoroni Cist), decorated with engravings and signed by Novius Plautios: 17; *pl. 17-20.*

FIDENAE. A town of Latium, in the Sabine country, between Rome and Veii (today the village of Castelgiubileo): 28; *map 449.*

FIUMICINO. A town in Italy in Latium: 239.

FLAMININUS (Titus Quinctius). Roman consul in 198 BC, he inflicted a crushing and decisive defeat on King Philip V of Macedon at Cynoscephalae, and proclaimed freedom and self-government for Greece at the Nemean Games, near Corinth, in 196: 37, 81, 152; *pl. 43.*

FLAVIANS. The emperors Vespasian, Titus and Domitian (69-96), who all belonged to the *gens Flavia*: 58, 74, 89, 146, 148, 158, 168, 209, 249, 273, 281; *pl. 184-187.*

FLORENCE (Firenze). Main city of Tuscany, in Italy, and great centre of the Renaissance: from the first cent. BC a Roman municipality: 107, 242.

FOLIGNO. A town in Italy (Umbria): 288; *pl. 324, 325.*

FORTUNE. Ancient Italian divinity of Chance and Luck, venerated especially at Praeneste (Palestrina): 43, 146, 148; *pl. 156, 157, 436.*

FRANÇOIS TOMB. An Etruscan tomb at Vulci, discovered by the painter Alessandro François; its murals are now in the Museum at Torlonia: 10; *pl. 13, 14.*

FRANK (Tenney), 1876-1939. American historian and Latinist: 38.

FRASCATI. Town of Latium, near Rome (ancient Tusculum): 305.

FREEDMAN. Slave liberated or manumitted (*libertus*) by his master: 58, 60, 105, 151.

FRONTO (Marcus Cornelius). Born at Cirta in Numidia: orator, and tutor to both Marcus Aurelius and Lucius Verus: 273, 309, 310.

GABII. Ancient town of Latium, between Rome and Praeneste; near the Lago Castiglione, and certain quarries which yielded a volcanic stone (*lapis gabinus*). Sulla founded a *colonia* there: 155; *map 449.*

GAETA (CAIETA). Town of Latium: 5; *map 449.*

GALATIANS. A people of Celtic (Gallic) origin, settled in the third cent. BC in Asia Minor, between Phrygia and Cappadocia, but under pressure from the kings of Pergamum. After 133 BC Galatia formed a client-kingdom of Rome's under an independent king; from 25 BC its territory was amalgamated with Paphlagonia to form a single Roman province: 302; *pl. 341, 343.*

GALBA (Servius Sulpicius). Roman emperor from June 68 until January 69; Nero's successor: 223; *pl. 409.*

GALEN. Famous Greek doctor from Pergamum, who established himself at Rome under Commodus (129-c.200): 311.

GALLI (GAULS). A Celtic people who, in the sixth cent. BC, occupied the area between the Rhine and the Pyrenees, and in the fourth pushed down to the Po Valley, making several attacks on Rome. From the beginning of the second century BC the Romans had them under control, and between 58 and 51 BC Gaul itself was subjugated by Julius Caesar: 23, 186, 203, 224, 282, 306.

GAVIUS RUFUS (Marcus). Owner of a house in Pompeii: 114; *pl. 116.*

GEOMETRIC STYLE. The characteristic style of Greek ceramic art from the eleventh to the eighth cents. BC: 250, 265.

GERMANICUS (Julius Caesar). Roman

general, adopted by Tiberius: 196; *pl. 401.*

GERMANY. 223.

GHIBERTI (Lorenzo), 1378-1455. Florentine sculptor, goldsmith and architect: 107.

GIGANTOMACHY. Mythical combat between the Giants (the sons of Earth and Heaven) and Zeus, aided by all the divinities of Olympus: a theme very often handled in both classical and Hellenistic art: 71.

GLADIATORS. Professional fighters, slaves, or condemned criminals who fought, with each other or against wild beasts, in the arena. This type of spectacle was introduced to Rome in 264 BC: 40, 60, 337; *pl. 64, 378.*

GLANUM. *See* SAINT-RÉMY-DE-PROVENCE.

GLYCON. Supposed reincarnation of Asclepius in the form of a human-headed serpent, whose cult flourished in the East during the reign of Antoninus Pius: 311; *pl. 352.*

GNOSTICISM. A religious phenomenon which appeared during the first and second centuries AD: Christianity with an admixture of philosophical and astrological elements: 311, 339.

GRABAR (André). French archaeologist and historian, born in 1896: 305.

GRACCHI, THE. Tiberius (162-133 BC) and Caius (153-121 BC), both sons of T. Sempronius Gracchus, consul in 177 and 163, and both tribunes; they attempted to carry out a programme of social and agrarian reforms, but were murdered by the patricians: 77, 114, 180.

GREECE. x, 5, 6, 8, 11, 19, 24, 35, 36, 38, 42, 44, 51, 72, 75, 87, 107, 108, 163, 177, 180, 202, 224, 261, 275, 338, 341, 342.

GRIMANI COLLECTION. A collection of antiquities assembled in Rome by the Venetian Grimani family during the first half of the sixteenth century: subsequently dispersed: 193.

GROTESQUES. Painted or stucco decorations to which Renaissance artists gave this title because of the paintings in the underground chambers, or 'grottoes', of Nero's *Domus Aurea* in Rome: 130.

HADRIAN (Publius Aelius Hadrianus),

76-138. Born in Italica (Spain), adopted by Trajan, and emperor (AD 117-138): 37, 94, 148, 157, 159, 175, 196, 223, 224, 226, 235, 250, 252, 255, 258-267, 270, 274, 275, 279, 281-284, 301, 306, 312, 316; *pl. 278, 292, 293, 299-309, 419.*

HADRIAN'S WALL. Fortification built by Hadrian between England and Scotland: 261.

HAMPTON COURT. Royal English residence, on the Thames: 114.

HARNOUPHIS. Egyptian priest connected with the 'miracle' of the rain, shown on Marcus Aurelius's Column: 325; *pl. 360, 361.*

HATERII. Roman family who built a tomb, decorated with sculptures, during Domitian's reign: 215; *pl. 180, 242-245.*

HECTOR. Hero of Homer's *Iliad*, son of Priam, King of Troy: killed by Achilles: 310.

HEIUS (C.). Roman citizen of Messina, who owned a collection of works of art referred to by Cicero during the prosecution of Verres: 43, 44.

HELENA (Flavia Julia, Saint), 247-324. Concubine of Constantius Chlorus, and mother of Constantine I, she became a Christian convert in 313: 185.

HELIOS. Greek god of light and the sun; there was a colossal statue of Nero as Helios: 130, 255.

HELLENISM. The period of Greek civilization between Alexander's conquests in Asia and Egypt, and the Battle of Actium (31 BC) which finally gave Rome complete supremacy throughout the Mediterranean (325-31 BC): ix-xii, 11, 27, 30, 38, 41, 43, 64, 72, 80, 83, 108, 114, 115, 117, 118, 130, 138, 177, 179, 192, 194, 202, 209, 238, 249.

HEPHAESTUS. Greek god of fire, son of Zeus and Hera, identified by the Romans with Vulcan: 139; *pl. 147.*

HERA. Greek goddess, daughter of Chronos and Rhea, wife of Zeus, and identified by the Romans with Juno: 281.

HERACLES. The most popular of all Greek heroes, the son of Zeus and Alcmene. In Italy and Rome, worshipped under the name of Hercules, and regarded as the protector of flocks and fields: 6, 36, 43, 146, 184, 262, 263, 292, 302, 337; *pl. 295, 331, 437.*

HERCULANEUM. Ancient Campanian town, buried by the eruption of Vesuvius in AD 79: 40, 41, 110, 114; *pl. 44, 115.*

HERMES. Greek god, son of Zeus and Maia, protector of traders, messenger of the gods, escort of deceased souls to the underworld (*Hermes Psychopompos*); assimilated to the Egyptian god Thoth, and, by the Romans, to Mercury: 5, 182, 325; *pl. 47, 195.*

HERMODORUS OF SALAMIS. Greek architect, who from 146 BC on was given several contracts for putting up public buildings in Rome: 146.

HERODES ATTICUS (L. Vibullius Hipparchus Tib. Claudius Atticus Herodes), 101-178. Vastly wealthy citizen of Athens, orator and sophist, who had public edifices constructed at his expense in several towns: 301, 339.

HEROÖN. A place or building (often containing a tomb) which was dedicated to a hero's cult or memory: 275, 312.

HIERAPOLIS. Ancient town in Phrygia: 226.

HIERON I OF SYRACUSE. Leading statesman of Syracuse (478-466 BC), who also won a great naval victory against the Etruscans in 474 BC: 9.

HILDESHEIM. Town in West Germany (Lower Saxony) where a valuable treasure of silver vessels was discovered: 208.

HIPPOLYTUS (Saint). Christian priest and theologian, chosen as antipope against Callistus, martyred about 236: 339.

HITTITES. A people of Asia Minor who, during the second millennium BC, extended their domination from Anatolia to Syria: 5.

HOBY. Small town in Denmark (Isle of Lolland) where a hoard of Roman silverware was found: 208.

HORACE (Quintus Horatius Flaccus), 65-8 BC. Latin poet, born at Venusia in Apulia, died in Rome; the friend of Virgil and Maecenas: 3, 41, 49, 177, 182.

HORATIUS COCLES. Legendary Roman hero who, single-handed, held the Pons Sublicius against King Porsenna's Etruscans: 4; *pl. 8.*

HUANG-HO (YELLOW RIVER). The largest river of northern China (over 3,000 miles long): 18.

ILIAD, THE. The great Homeric epic on the Trojan War: 114.

ILLYRIA. Mountainous region of the Balkan peninsula, on the northern Adriatic coast. The Romans were fighting piracy here as early as the third century BC. In 27 BC it became a Roman province with the name of *Illyricum*: 224.

IMAGO CLIPEATA. Medallion portraying some important person, whose head is set either on a shield, or else on some other similar support imitating it: 87, 89, 90, 93, 152, 219; *pl. 98, 100.*

IMPLUVIUM. In Roman houses, a sunk basin in the middle of the atrium, designed to catch rain-water: 89; *pl. 100.*

IMPRESSIONISM. Hellenistic and Roman style of painting which much resembles that of the nineteenth-century Impressionists: 109, 132, 139, 141.

INDIA. 18, 204.

INDUS. River of southern Asia along which developed the oldest civilization in prehistoric India: 18.

INSTITUTIO ALIMENTARIA. A device of Trajan's to help Italian smallholders: 235; *pl. 261.*

IO. Daughter of Inachus, King of Argos; transformed by Zeus, who desired her, into a gadfly: *pl. 134.*

ISERNIA. Italian town in the Abruzzi, formerly Aesernia (Samnium): 30; *pl. 32.*

ISIS. Egyptian goddess whose cult was introduced to Rome during the first cent. BC: 94, 123, 125, 336; *pl. 106, 128, 129.*

ISTHMIAN GAMES. Panhellenic festival celebrated at Isthmus of Corinth: 26.

ITALIANS (ITALIC). General name for those Indo-European peoples settled in Italy from the second millennium BC, including the Oscans, the Umbrians and the Latins: 18, 30, 79, 115.

IUS IMAGINUM. The right granted patrician families in Rome to preserve portraits (masks or busts) of their deceased relatives in some appropriate part of the house: 76.

JANUS. Latin god: *pl. 23.*

JAZYGES. A Sarmatian tribe settled on the Lower Danube: 261.

JEROME (Saint), 347-420. Father and Doctor of the Church: born in Dalmatia, lived in Rome, died in Bethlehem: 44.

JERUSALEM. Holy city of the Jewish faith, in Palestine; destroyed by Titus in AD 70: 38, 114; *pl. 238; map 450.*

JOHN (Saint) and PAUL (Saint). Two brothers, Roman noblemen, martyred at Rome in AD 362: 334; *pl. 316, 371, 373, 375.*

JOSEPH. Hebrew Patriarch, son of Jacob and Rachel: 194.

JOSEPHUS (Flavius). Jewish historian, and a protégé of Vespasian (hence the name Flavius); author of *The Jewish War*, a work composed in Greek, narrating events from the reign of Herod the Great until the destruction of Jerusalem by Titus: 114.

JULIA. Daughter of the emperor Augustus; married first Marcellus, then Agrippa, and finally Tiberius. Afterwards banished; died AD 14: 208.

JULIA (Flavia Julia). Daughter of Titus: married Flavius Sabinus: *pl. 414.*

JULII (the GENS IULIA). 49, 155, 249; *pl. 277.*

JULIO-CLAUDIANS. Roman emperors from Augustus to Nero: 42, 208, 238.

JULIUS CAPITOLINUS. Latin historian of 3rd-4th cents. AD: 311, 324.

JUNO. Ancient Latin divinity, worshipped both by Etruscans and at Rome; subsequently assimilated to Greek Hera. Wife of Jupiter; worshipped as the patron goddess of childbirth (*Juno Lucina*), and associated with Jupiter and Minerva in the 'Capitoline Triad': 5, 146.

JUPITER. Principal Latin deity, identified with Zeus: 5, 146, 240, 286, 324.

JUSTIN (Saint). Christian apologist, martyred between 163 and 167: 339.

KHNUM. Egyptian deity with a ram's head: 311.

KLEE (Paul), 1879-1940. Swiss painter: 107.

KLEOMENES. Sculptor who belonged to a group of classicizing artists, active in Rome about 40 BC: 47, 182; *pl. 47.*

KORE-PERSEPHONE. Greek divinity of the Underworld, the daughter of Zeus and Demeter: 32; *pl. 37.*

KRAUS (Theodor). Modern German archaeologist: 193.

LAESTRYGONIANS. Cannibal giants, mentioned by Homer in the *Odyssey*: *pl. 119.*

LAOCOON. Trajan priest of Apollo; about the time of Troy's capture he and his two sons were choked by a pair of enormous serpents that emerged from the sea: 249.

LARARIUM. In a Roman house, the niche which contained the images of the Lares (household gods): 90.

LARES. Roman divinities who protected families and cross-roads: 69.

LARINO (LARINUM). Italian town in the Abruzzi: *pl. 10; map 449.*

LATINS. A group of Italic tribes settled in Latium, and forming a League with its centre at Alba Longa. Finally subjugated by Rome in 340-338 BC: 3, 12.

LATINUS. Legendary king and eponymous founder of the Latin peoples: 8.

LATIUM. Region of central Italy between Tuscany and Umbria in the north, the Abruzzi in the east, Campania in the south and the Tyrrhenian Sea to the west: 4, 5, 8, 17, 24, 32, 93, 115, 152, 159, 202; *pl. 88, 101, 193.*

LATONA or LETO. According to Greek mythology, the paramour of Zeus, to whom she bore Artemis and Apollo: 38.

LAUDATIO FUNEBRIS. Panegyric pronounced over a deceased patrician by a member of his family, in the Forum: 76.

LAVINIA. Daughter of King Latinus, who – according to Roman legend – married Aeneas: 8.

LAVINIUM (Pratica di Mare). Ancient city of Latium, founded (as legend has it) by Aeneas, in honour of his wife Lavinia: 8, 118; *pl. 11, 12; map 449.*

LEHMANN-HARTLEBEN (Karl). German archaeologist, born in 1894: 249.

LEPIDUS (Marcus Aemilius). Roman consul in 46; together with Octavian and Mark Antony formed the political agreement known as the Second Triumvirate (died 13 BC): 79, 179.

LEUCAS. Ancient island in the Ionian Sea, now linked to mainland Greece: 179.

LIBERALITAS. Public distribution of largesse carried out by the emperor: 315; *pl. 355.*

LIBYA. In antiquity, that part of North Africa lying between Cyrenaica and the territories of Carthage: 281.

LICTORS. Roman officers bearing the fasces, who accompanied the magistrates (their numbers varied between six and twelve, and were later increased to twenty-four for a dictator or, after Domitian's day, for the emperor): 75.

LIGURIANS. A people of non-Indo-European origin, settled in southern Gaul and on the west coast of northern Italy: 51.

LIVIA (Livia Drusilla), *c.* 59 BC-AD 29. Augustus's wife and the mother of Tiberius: 125, 126, 196, 208; *pl. 130, 131, 133-136, 214.*

LIVY (Titus Livius), 59 BC-AD 17. Roman historian born in Padua: 19, 24, 35, 36, 38.

LOMBARDS or LONGOBARDS. A Germanic people who came down into Italy from the north in 568, under the leadership of Alboin: 310.

LONGIDIENUS (P.). Shipbuilder at Classis, the port for Ravenna: *pl. 96.*

LUCERA (Luceria Apula). Town of Italy (Puglia): 27; *pl. 30; map 449.*

LUCIAN OF SAMOSATA. Famous Greek writer and philosopher of the second cent. AD: 310, 311.

LUCILLA (Annia), *c.* 147-*c.* 183. Daughter of Marcus Aurelius and the Younger Faustina; married first Lucius Verus, and then Tiberius Claudius Pompeianus: 282, 312.

LUCULLUS (Lucius Lucinius). Consul in 74 BC. Conducted the war against Mithridates in Asia Minor, and became famous for his wealth: 49, 86.

LUDIUS (Marcus). Roman painter of the Augustan era, also known as Studius: 123.

LUNI. Ancient Etruscan city of Liguria: from 177 BC a Roman *colonia*. Near the modern town of Sarzana: 51.

LUPERCAL. Sacred grotto identified with that in which Romulus and Remus were sheltered and fed by the She-Wolf, at the foot of the Palatine Hill: 189.

LUSTRATIO. Purificatory ceremony: 52, 311.

LYCOMEDES. King of the Dolopians, on the island of Scyros, where Achilles was hidden dressed in women's clothes: 132.

LYCON. *See* PLAUTIUS.

LYONS (Lugdunum). 338; *map 450.*

LYSIPPUS. Famous Greek sculptor of Sicyon, in the second half of the fourth cent. BC: 93, 110, 179.

LYSTRA. Ancient city of Asia Minor, in Lycaonia: 182.

MACEDONIA. Region in the Balkans. As a kingdom it reached its apogee under Philip II and Alexander the Great; from 146 BC it was a Roman province: 11, 40, 74, 146, 202, 311.

MACELLUM. Market in which were sold vegetables, fish, meat, and various other foodstuffs: 163.

MACROBIUS (Ambrosius Macrobius Theodosius), fourth cent. AD. Latin scholar: 23.

MAECENAS (C. Cilnius), 69-68 BC. Augustus's adviser, and a distinguished patron of arts and letters: 126; *pl. 132.*

MAENADS. Women who followed Dionysus: *pl. 337.*

MAGNA GRAECIA. Collection of Greek colonies in southern Italy and Sicily: 5, 9, 12, 25, 28, 44, 152.

MAGNASCO (Alessandro), 1677-1749. Italian painter from Genoa: 123.

MAGNESIA-BY-SIPYLUS (Manisa). Town in Asia Minor (Lydia) near Mount Sipylus, where the Romans conquered Antiochus III, in 190 BC: 11, 37, 51; *map 450.*

MAINZ. Town in West Germany; its ancient name was Mogontiacum: 240; *map 450.*

MANIOS. Goldsmith who inscribed his name on a fibula found at Praeneste, which gives us the oldest known Latin inscription (sixth cent. BC): 20; *pl. 22.*

MANTEGNA (Andrea), 1431-1506. Famous Italian Renaissance painter at the court of the Gonzaga family: 114.

MARCELLUS (Marcus Claudius). Roman consul in 222, 215, 210 and 208 BC; conquered the Insubres in 222, and in 212 captured Syracuse: 36; *pl. 42.*

MARCELLUS (M. Claudius). Son of C. Claudius Marcellus and Octavia, the sister of Augustus: married Augustus's daughter Julia: died 23 BC: 152.

MARCIA. Concubine of the emperor Commodus: 339.

MARCOMANNI. Germanic tribe; after being defeated near the Rhine by Drusus, they founded a kingdom in Bohemia, and invaded Pannonia between AD 170 and 180: 261, 305, 311-312, 322.

MARCUS AURELIUS ANTONINUS (AD 121-180). Roman emperor (AD 161-180) in succession to Antoninus Pius; author of a work, the *Meditations,* in which his Stoic philosophy is expounded: 223, 224, 226, 273, 282, 284, 286, 306-316, 322-328, 337-339, 342; *pl. 319, 344-351, 353-367, 424.*

MARCUS PLAUTIUS (Lycon). *See* PLAUTIUS.

MARINO. Italian town in Latium, among the Alban Hills: 331; *pl. 372, 374.*

MARIUS (Caius), 156-86 BC. Roman politician, born near Arpinum, several times consul: reformed Rome's military organization: 77, 180.

MARS. Ancient Italic divinity, whose symbol was a wolf. Identified with Ares, the Greek god of war: 52, 184, 189; *pl. 198.*

MARTIAL (Marcus Valerius Martialis), *c.* 40-102. Latin poet, born in Spain, lived in Rome; wrote fifteen books of *Epigrams*: 90.

MASKS, FUNERARY. Wax death-masks obtained by taking a moulding from the features of a deceased person, which Roman patrician families kept in a cupboard or niche of the atrium in their houses: 75, 80, 90, 93.

MASTARNA or MCSTRNA. Etruscan name of King Tullius: 9; *pl. 13.*

MATIDIA (Vibia). Trajan's niece and the mother of Sabina, who married Hadrian: 95, 258, 282; *pl. 110, 431.*

MAURETANIA. Ancient kingdom of North Africa, corresponding to modern Morocco; made a Roman province under Claudius: *pl. 268.*

MAZZARINO (Santo). Italian historian, born 1916: 339.

MCSTRNA. *See* MASTARNA.

MELOS (Milo). Aegean island (south-west Cyclades): 184.

MENANDER (*c.* 342-*c.* 292 BC). Greek comic poet: 90, 125.

MENELAOS (Marcus M. Kossoutius). Classicizing sculptor, pupil of Stephanos, active in Rome during Tiberius's reign: 48, *pl. 48, 49.*

MERCURY. Italic god: protector of trade and commerce. Identified with Greek god Hermes: 130, 182; *pl. 249, 336.*

MESOPOTAMIA. Region of western Asia situated between the Tigris and the Euphrates: centre of the ancient Assyrian civilization. Hellenized by Alexander the Great; became a Roman province under Trajan (AD 116): 5, 18, 310.

MESSINA. Coastal city of north-east Sicily; Greek colony. Occupied by the Romans during the Second Punic War in 264 BC: 43, 114; *map 450.*

MID-ITALIC ART. Conventional title coined to describe the art of Campania, Latium and southern Etruria from the Hellenistic period (third cent. BC) until their Romanization: xii, 28-30, 52, 58, 59, 69, 70, 74, 80, 81, 83, 114, 115, 137, 141, 249, 275, 341; *frontispiece, pl. 81.*

MILO. *See* MELOS.

MINERVA. Italic divinity, protectress of workers, doctors and learning; identified with the Greek goddess Athena. She formed part of the divine Capitoline triad, together with Juno and Jupiter: 5.

MINOTAUR. Monster with human body and a bull's head, the child of Pasiphaë; human sacrifices were offered to him in the Labyrinth on the island of Crete: 110; *pl. 115, 116.*

MITHRAEUM. Underground sanctuary where the Mysteries of the Mithraic cult were celebrated: 331; *pl. 372.*

MITHRAS. Iranian god of light, whose cult was widespread among the troops of Rome's armies: from the second cent. AD they disseminated it through the West: 331, 336, 339; *pl. 374.*

MITHRIDATES IV. King of Pontus (Asia Minor), reigning *c.* 169-150 BC: 72; *pl. 386.*

MITHRIDATES VI, known as 'The Great', *c.* 132-63 BC. King of Pontus (Asia Minor), 111-63; conducted a stubborn defence against Rome's invasion, but in 64 was defeated by Lucullus and Pompey: 72; *pl. 387.*

MODENA (Mutina). Town in Cisalpine Gaul: Roman *colonia* from 185 BC: 51.

MOESIA. Region lying south of the Lower Danube: made a Roman province in Tiberius's reign (15 BC): 241, 308, 311.

MOROCCO. Region of north-west Africa: formerly the Kingdom of Mauretania, which was divided into two Roman provinces under the emperor Claudius: 281.

MUMMIUS (Lucius). Consul in 146 BC; defeated the Achaean League, captured and sacked Corinth: 36-38.

MUSES. The nine daughters of Zeus and Mnemosyne (Memory), who were patron deities of the arts and sciences: 38, 72.

MUSONIUS RUFUS (Caius). Roman Stoic philosopher of the first cent. AD, an Etruscan by origin: 224, 226.

MYNAS. Byzantine manuscript containing the treatise on siegecraft by Trajan's architect Apollodorus of Damascus: 239.

MYRON. Famous Greek sculptor of the fifth cent. BC: 43.

NAPLES (Napoli). Italian city of Campania, ancient Neapolis. Greek colony from the sixth century; occupied by Sulla in 82 BC: 4, 20, 86, 283; *maps 449, 450.*

NARBONNAISE (Gallia Narbonensis). Southern region of Gaul, roughly equivalent to Provence: colonized by the Greeks, and made a Roman province from 123-121 BC: 249.

NASIDIUS (Quintus). Friend of Pompey: 36.

NEAPOLIS. *See* NAPLES.

NEO-ATTICISM. Modern name for an artistic movement which evolved in Athens and was popular at Rome from the middle of the first cent. BC until the early part of the first cent. AD. The artists who flourished during this period imitated or copied works of the fifth and fourth centuries, but also drew inspiration from the archaic period: 58, 86, 179, 194, 198, 202, 203, 209, 210, 235, 249, 259.

NEO-CLASSICISM. An artistic trend which flourished in Europe during the late eighteenth and early nineteenth centuries. Its inspiration came from the classical forms of antiquity, and, by analogy, also drew on the cultural movement which evolved in Greece and Rome towards the end of the Hellenistic period, from 150 BC (*see* NEO-ATTICISM): 48, 108, 109, 203.

NEO-PYTHAGOREANISM. Philosophical school of the first to third cents. AD, which reinforced the ancient doctrines of Pythagoras with Oriental and Egyptian religions, and developed a tendency towards mysticism: 209.

NEPTUNE. Italic divinity of sea and water, identified as early as the fourth cent. BC with the Greek god Poseidon: 52, 336; *pl. 165.*

NERO (Nero Claudius Drusus Germanicus Caesar). Roman emperor (54-68), son of Agrippina the Younger, adopted by Claudius; renowned for his mad excesses, and in particular for the Great Fire of Rome (AD 64): 60, 94, 130, 132, 137, 139, 146, 148, 157, 159, 163, 167, 168, 173, 196, 208, 210, 255, 265, 283; *pl. 138-145, 173, 174, 408.*

NERVA (Marcus Cocceius). Roman emperor (96-98), chosen by and from the Senate: 209, 223, 238, 282; *pl. 191, 416.*

NICOPOLIS. City founded by Augustus in Epirus, near the Bay of Actium: 226.

NIGIDIUS FIGULUS (Publius). Neo-Pythagorean scholar and philosopher; died 45 BC: 60.

NIKE. Greek goddess of Victory: 286.

NILE. The great river of Egypt, which forms the Delta at its outflow into the Mediterranean: 18, 258.

NIOBE, NIOBIDES. Niobe, daughter of Tantalus, and her many children (the Niobides) were exterminated by Apollo and Artemis, whom they had offended: 38, 275; *pl. 312, 314.*

NOBILITAS. The privileged aristocratic status acquired among the Romans by the descendants of a senator or a consul: 77.

NOCERA INFERIORE. Italian town in Campania, near Pompeii (ancient Nuceria Alfaterna): 64; *pl. 70; map 449.*

NORICUM. Territory situated between the Danube and the Inn, inhabited by a Celtic tribe: partly in Austria, partly in Bavaria. From AD 15, during Tiberius's reign, it was a Roman province: 224, 308.

NOVIOS PLAUTIOS. Campanian craftsman, whose signature is on the Ficoroni Cist, executed by him in Rome (late fourth to early third cent. BC): 17, 29; *pl. 17-20.*

NUMICUS. Coastal river of Latium which flows into the Tyrrhenian Sea south of Rome: 119.

NUMIDIA. Ancient region of North Africa, inhabited by Berger nomads. From 200 BC it was the kingdom of Massinissa; annexed by Rome in 46 BC, it was organized as a province in AD 38: 281.

NY CARLSBERG COLLECTIONS. Art-collections in Copenhagen, both ancient and modern, made by the Danish patron of the arts Carl Jacobsen (1842-1914): 47, 212.

NYMPHAEUM. An edifice consecrated to the Nymphs: 273, 312; *pl. 138, 140.*

NYMPHS. Minor divinities in Greek and Roman mythology, symbolizing Nature in her diverse aspects: *pl. 217.*

OBII. A Germanic tribe who attacked the Romans in Pannonia: 310.

OCTAVIA. Sister of Augustus; married first Marcellus, then Mark Antony, who in 35 BC repudiated her. She died in 11 BC: 86, 110, 146; *pl. 213, 398.*

OCTAVIAN. Scion of a plebeian family from the Volscian region; born 63 BC, and adopted in 45 by his maternal uncle Julius Ceasar, at which point he took the name Octavian (Caius Julius Caesar Octavianus). In 27 the Senate conferred upon him the religious title of *Augustus*, and as Augustus he became the first Roman emperor, a position he held until his death in AD 14: 79, 80, 110, 123, 152, 153, 155, 157, 179, 180, 182, 183, 200; *pl. 194, 195, 197, 215, 216, 397.*

ODEUM (Odeion). A small covered theatre, or hall reserved for concerts and public lectures: 239.

ODYSSEY, THE. Homeric epic poem describing the adventures of Odysseus (Ulysses): 116; *pl. 119.*

OIKOUMENE. Symbol for the cultivated or inhabited areas of the Earth: 196.

OMPHALE. Queen of Lydia who made Heracles a bond-slave to her slightest whim: 184; *pl. 199.*

ORESTES. Greek hero, the son of Agamemnon, whom he avenged by killing his mother Clytemnestra, together with her lover, Aegisthus: 48, 275, 279; *pl. 48, 49, 311, 313.*

ORPHEUS. Legendary Thracian singer and musician, the son of Apollo and Calliope. In later times a mystical doctrine (Orphism) was attributed to him: 29; *pl. 31.*

OSTIA. Ancient commercial and military port at the mouth of the Tiber, and the first Roman *colonia* (between 350 and 335 BC). Subsequently it became a flourishing centre of commerce, until the fourth cent. AD. It has now been partially uncovered by archaeological excavations: 63, 66, 94, 137, 175, 239, 252, 259, 292, 301, 328, 334; *pl. 66, 69, 71, 98, 107, 146, 198, 278, 281, 288, 294, 299, 328, 335, 336, 338, 369, 370, 376, 377, 443, 444; map 449.*

OTHO (Marcus Salvius Otho), AD 32-69. Roman emperor (15 Jan.-16 April 69): 223; *pl. 410.*

PADUA (Padova). Italian city (Venezia), ancient Patavium, the birthplace of Livy, who in 49 BC received the *municipium,* or freedom of the city: 67, 242.

PAESTUM. Greek colony in Lucania, probably founded by Sybaris about 600 BC. Known at first as Poseidonia, it changed its name after being occupied by the Lucanians: 5, 115; *map 450.*

PAIDEIA. The ideal of education and culture in ancient Greece: 36, 310.

PALESTRINA. *See* PRAENESTE.

PALOMBARA SABINA. Commune in Italy (Latium): 94; *pl. 105.*

PAMMACHIUS. Built a sanctuary dedicated to the martyrs John and Paul in their house on the Caelian Hill: 334; *pl. 371, 373, 375.*

PAMPHILOS. Greek gem-engraver of the Imperial period, who worked in Rome: *pl. 212.*

PANNONIA. A region largely corresponding to modern Hungary; a Roman province from 9 BC: 224, 306, 309-310.

PAPHLAGONIA. Country in Asia Minor, south of the Black Sea: 311.

PARADEISOS. Originally a Persian word denoting 'enclosed garden' or 'park'; used in the same sense by the Hellenistic and Roman world: 125.

PARIUM. Coastal city of Mysia, on the Hellespont; a colony of Miletus: 311.

PARMA. Italian city (Emilia) on the Via Aemilia: made a Roman *colonia* in 183 BC: 51.

PAROS. Greek island (Cyclades), west of Naxos: 241.

PARTHIA. Region of Persia south-east of the Caspian Sea, inhabited by the Parthians: 223, 261, 262, 309, 310, 312, 324.

PASITELES. Classicizing sculptor from Magna Graecia; active in Rome in the first cent. BC: 48, 49.

PATERA. A shallow circular cup or dish, mostly employed at sacrifices or feasts: 188, 193.

PATRICIAN. Descendant of those ancient families who alone, at the very beginning, formed the city's population: 71, 72, 75, 77, 79-81, 86, 93, 180; *pl. 80, 84-87.*

PAUL (Saint), c. AD 10-67. A Jew from Tarsus in Cilicia; after his conversion to Christianity, he became its chief exponent in the Roman Empire: 182.

PAVONAZZETTO. A particular variety of Carrara marble, white veined with purple: 281.

PAX AUGUSTA. Divinization of peace, instituted by Augustus after his victory at Actium: 198.

PEGASUS. Winged and magical horse, born from the blood of Medusa: 194.

PELLA. Capital of the kingdom of Macedonia, and birthplace of Alexander the Great: 311; *map 450.*

PENATES (DI). Roman divinities who protected the house: 189; *pl. 202.*

PEPERINO, or PIPERINO. An Italian word designating a certain volcanic tufa employed as building material: 29, 148, 155.

PERGAMUM. Town of Mysia (Asia Minor), the capital of a Hellenistic kingdom; annexed by the Romans in 133 BC: 11, 43, 118, 193, 198, 202, 204, 235, 240, 250, 302, 311, 312, 315, 320; *pl. 257; map 450.*

PERISTYLE. Court or garden in a Roman house, with a portico round it: 175, 270.

PERSEUS. Last King of Macedonia (179-168 BC); defeated at Pydna by the consul L. Aemilius Paulus: 40; *pl. 385.*

PERSEPHONE. Greek divinity, daughter of Zeus and Demeter, Queen of Hades. Identified at Rome with Proserpine: 32; *pl. 37.*

PERSIANS. An Indo-European people from the Iranian plateau. They reached the zenith of their power under the Achaemenid dynasty, destroyed by Alexander the Great: X, 182.

PERUGIA. Italian city (Umbria), conquered by the Romans in 295 BC. Its ancient name was Perusia: 305; *map 449.*

PERUZZI (Baldassare), 1481-1536. Sienese painter and architect, a pupil of Bramante: 119, 301.

PETER (Saint). Leader of the Twelve Apostles, and the first Pope; martyred, probably at Rome, under Nero: 339.

PETRONIUS (Titus Petronius Arbiter). Roman writer, author of the *Satiricon,* probably to be identified with a Roman aristocrat who lived in Nero's reign: 60.

PHEIDIAS. The most celebrated sculptor of classical Greece, who lived between 490 and 430 BC: 44, 48, 107, 108, 177, 185, 274; *pl. 309.*

PHILIP V. King of Macedonia (221-179 BC), Hannibal's ally in the Second Punic War; decisively defeated in 197, at Cynoscephalae, by the Roman consul T. Quinctius Flamininus: 37, 51, 152.

PHILIPPI. Ancient Greek city of Thrace, near the Bay of Kavalla, where Octavian and Antony inflicted a crushing and final defeat on Brutus and Cassius (October 42 BC): 155.

PHILIPPUS. Gold coin minted by Philip II of Macedon, worth 20 drachmas: 38.

PHILISCUS. Greek sculptor of the Hellenistic Age (? second cent. BC), a native of Rhodes. According to the Elder Pliny, he was responsible for a series of statues of the Muses that were put up in Rome: 38.

PHOENICIA. Country of Asia, lying on the Syrian coast between Lebanon and the Mediterranean, and inhabited by the Phoenicians: 5.

PICENUM. Ancient region of Italy, between the Apennines and the Adriatic: 11, 29.

PIETAS AUGUSTI. Divinization of the Emperor's religious quality, or *pietas*: 314.

PIRANESI (Giambattista), 1720-1778. Italian architect and engraver: *pl. 301, 363*.

PIRATICUM BELLUM. War against the pirates (78-66 BC), fought and won by Pompey the Great: 79.

PISA. Italian city (Tuscany) on the Arno; made a Roman *colonia* in 180 BC: 51, 274; *map 450*.

PIZZOLI. Italian village, in the Abruzzi, near ancient Amiternum: 67; *pl. 75*.

PLATO (427-347 BC). Athenian philosopher; the disciple of Socrates and Aristotle's teacher. Composed a number of famous *Dialogues*: 72, 116, 287.

PLAUTUS (T. Maccius), 254-184 BC. Roman comic poet: born at Sarsina (Umbria), the author of numerous comedies: 177.

PLAUTII. A patrician family whose circular tomb stands a few miles from Tivoli, near the Ponte Lucano: 154; *pl. 172*.

PLAUTIUS (Marcus Lycon). Painter who decorated the temple of Juno Regina at Ardea, near Rome (second cent. BC): 116.

PLEBEIANS. Second-class members of the Roman population, who fought long and hard against the patricians before they obtained full political rights: 18, 23, 25, 58, 66, 67, 76.

PLINY THE ELDER (C. Plinius Secundus Maior), 23-79. Roman writer, killed during the eruption of Vesuvius; compiled the *Natural History*, a valuable encyclopedia of the ancient world:

36, 38, 40, 43, 44, 49, 52, 85, 90, 100, 105, 107-110, 114, 117, 121, 123, 130, 342.

PLINY THE YOUNGER (C. Plinius Caecilius Secundus), 61-113. Roman orator and writer, the nephew and adopted son of the Elder Pliny; lived under Trajan: 226.

PLOTINUS (204-270). The leading Neo-Platonist philosopher, active in Rome under Gallienus: 43.

PLOTINA (Pompeia). Wife of the emperor Trajan: 252; *pl. 280, 418*.

PLUTARCH. Greek writer under Trajan and Hadrian. Author of the *Parallel Lives* and the *Moralia*, together with various other works: 19, 24, 36.

PO. The principal river of Italy (some 400 miles long) which flows into the Adriatic after traversing the Po Valley, the largest plain in Italy, occupied in turn by the Etruscans, the Celts and the Romans: 23, 51, 86.

POLLUX. *See* DIOSCURI.

POLYBIUS (c. 201-120 BC). Greek historian, who wrote a general history of his times: 75, 76, 93.

POLYCLETUS. Greek sculptor of the fifth cent. BC; with Pheidias, the leading sculptor of his era: 44, 183; *pl. 196*.

POLYNEICES. Son of Oedipus and Jocasta, father of Eteocles: *pl. 14*.

POMERIUM. Territory encircling the Palatine, which formed the sacred city-boundary of Rome: 123.

POMPEY THE GREAT (Cn. Pompeius Magnus). General and politician of the first cent. BC: 36, 47, 49, 79, 152, 154, 180; *pl. 41, 392, 438*.

POMPEII. Italian town in Campania, destroyed by the eruption of Vesuvius in AD 79: 30, 41, 43, 45, 64, 90, 100, 110, 114, 118, 125, 129, 152, 204, 208; *pl. 45, 46, 50, 70, 100, 108, 116, 147, 225, 226, 249; map 449*.

POMPEIANUS (Tiberius Claudius). Marcus Aurelius's general and son-in-law: 311, 313.

POMPONIUS HYLAS. Owner of a hypogeum near the Porta Latina (first cent. AD): 67; *pl. 74*.

PONTIFF. Member of the leading Sacred College in Rome: 1, 25; *pl. 216*.

POPULAR and PLEBEIAN ART. Artistic trend, linked with the middle classes in the provincial municipalities: 114, 115, 141, 215, 239, 249, 263, 288, 306, 315, 323, 334, 341, 342.

PORTLAND VASE. *Pl. 192, 221, 222*.

PORTUS URBIS ROMANAE. Port built by Claudius at the mouth of the Tiber: 239.

POSEIDON. Son of Chronos and Rhea; god of all seas and waters: *pl. 51, 52*.

POSTUMIUS ALBINUS (A.). Brother of the consul Postumius Albinus Spurius: *pl. 388*.

POTHOS. A famous sculpture by Scopas, personifying desire: 44.

POZZUOLI. An Italian town in Campania, near Naples. In antiquity it was known as Puteoli, and one of the most important ports then existing: 265.

PRAENESTE (Palestrina). An Italian town in Latium, famous for its temple of Fortune: 17, 117, 148, 151; *pl. 89, 156, 157, 207, 436; map 449*.

PRAETOR. Roman magistrate charged with maintaining public order and justice: 75, 76, 77.

PRAETORIANS. The Roman Emperor's special guard, created by Augustus: 224, 288.

PRATICA DI MARE. *See* LAVINIUM.

PRAXITELES. Famous Athenian sculptor of the fourth cent. BC: 38, 43, 107.

PREVEZA. Greek port on the Gulf of Arta, in Epirus, off which the Battle of Actium was fought (31 BC): 179.

PRIAPUS. God of fertility, and latterly of viticulture and horticulture: *pl. 248*.

PRIMA PORTA. Roman suburb on the Via Flaminia: Augustus's wife Livia had a villa there: 125, 183, 200; *pl. 130, 131, 133, 197*.

PRINCEPS CIVITATIS. The 'first citizen', a title borne by the emperors from Augustus to Diocletian: 212.

PROCONSUL. Ex-consul who became governor of a Roman province: 49, 77.

PROCOPIUS OF CAESAREA. Byzantine historian of the sixth cent. AD, author of the *Histories*: 237.

PRO GLOSSARY-INDEX ROM

PROPLASMATA. Greek term employed by the Elder Pliny to indicate small-scale wax models: 49.

PRUSA-BY-OLYMPUS (Bursa). Ancient capital of Bithynia (Asia Minor): 224.

PTOLEMY II PHILADELPHUS. King of Hellenistic Egypt (285-246 BC): 26, 41.

PUNIC WAX. Material employed for encaustic painting: 90, 296.

PUY DE DÔME. 130.

PYDNA. Ancient city of Macedonia, where the consul L. Aemilius Paulus conquered King Perseus (168 BC): 40; *map 450.*

PYRGI (Santa Severa). Port of the Etruscan city of Caere: 23.

PYRRHUS (319-272 BC). King of Epirus, famous for his struggle against the Romans, who finally defeated him at Beneventum (275 BC): 25.

PYTHAGORAS OF RHEGIUM. Greek sculptor of the fifth century BC: 38.

QUADI. A Germanic tribe, driven back, along with the Marcomanni, by Marcus Aurelius: 261, 305, 311-312, 322, 325.

QUAESTOR. Roman magistrate, whose duties were financial or judicial: 77.

RABIRIUS. Roman architect, active under Domitian, for whom he designed the *Domus Flavia* on the Palatine: 168.

RAPHAËL (Raffaello Sanzio, known as), 1483-1520. One of the greatest Italian painters of the Renaissance: 119.

RAVENNA. Italian city (Emilia) on the Adriatic coast; a Roman naval station, and from AD 402 the capital of the Western Empire: 86; *pl. 96; map 450.*

REDEMPTOR. A contractor, especially a building-contractor: 215.

REMUS. Brother of Romulus, according to the legends dealing with Rome's origins: 6, 119, 189; *pl. 10.*

RENAISSANCE. A literary, philosophical and artistic movement, born of the rediscovery of the ancient world (fifteenth and sixteenth centuries): 107-109, 114, 119, 130, 137, 153, 161, 168, 209, 274, 291, 301, 326.

RHEA SILVIA. Mother of Romulus and Remus: 189.

RHEGIUM (Reggio di Calabria). Ancient Greek colony of Bruttium, on the Straits of Messina: 26; *map 450.*

RHODES. Main island of the Dodecanese group: *pl. 194.*

RIEGL (Alois), 1858-1905. Austrian art-historian: 109, 317.

RIZZO (Giulio Emanuele), 1869-1950. Italian archaeologist: 123.

RODENWALDT (Gerhardt), 1886-1945. German archaeologist: 68.

ROLL OF JOSHUA. Cod. Palat. Gr. 431 (tenth cent.) in the Vatican Library: 240.

ROME. City-state, and later capital of Empire: ix-xii, 1, 3, 4, 6, 8, 12, 17, 20, 118, 154, 190, 255; *pl. 3, 206, 284, 285, 450, 451; maps 449, 450.*
Aqueducts: 157; *pl. 169, 170.*
Ara Pacis: 69, 182, 186, 188, 189; *pl. 200-204.*
Ara Pietatis: 209; *pl. 228, 229.*
Arch of Augustus: *pl. 167.*
Arch of Constantine: 235, 262, 313, 314, 316, 323, 324; *pl. 255, 256, 258, 259, 291-293, 354-359.*
Arch of Titus: 69, 114, 213-215; *pl. 237-241.*
Aventine: 263
Basilica Aemilia: 152; *pl. 159, 440.*
Basilica Fulvia: 152.
Basilica Julia: *pl. 440.*
Basilica Maxentii: *pl. 440.*
Basilica (underground): 209, 210; *pl. 230, 231.*
Basilica Ulpia: 238; *pl. 440.*
Baths of Agrippa: 264.
Baths of Caracalla: 337; *pl. 378.*
Baths of Constantine: 107.
Baths of Titus: 130, 239.
Baths of Trajan: 239.
Caelian Hill: 130, 132, 334; *pl. 371.*
Campus Martius: 38, 146, 180, 186, 265, 286.
Cancelleria: 69, 212-213; *pl. 79, 236.*
Capitol: 1, 5, 12, 23, 62, 146, 154, 180, 314; *pl. 5, 247.*
Circus Flaminius: 52.
Coliseum: 130, 167, 168, 215, 255; *pl. 176, 178, 179, 181-183.*
Columbaria: 67, 103, 105; *pl. 74, 112.*
Column of Antoninus Pius: 242, 286-288, 306; *pl. 321-323.*
Column of Marcus Aurelius: 241, 322-328; *pl. 360-367.*
Column of Trajan: 114, 221, 229, 235, 237-250, 310, 322, 324; *pl. 253-254, 264-276.*
Domus Augustana: 159, 168, 173; *pl. 163, 184-187, 446.*
Domus Aurea: 130, 132, 137, 139, 157, 163,
167, 224, 239, 328; *pl. 139, 141-145, 173-175, 368, 445.*
Domus Transitoria: 132, 157; *pl. 138, 140.*
Emporium: 145.
Esquiline: 29, 115-119, 130; *pl. 114, 117, 119, 121, 122.*
Forum Augusti: 155, 238; *pl. 171, 440.*
Forum Boarium: 1, 336.
Forum Caesaris: 49, 154, 155, 238, 260; *pl. 161, 162, 440.*
Forum Olitorium: 1.
Forum Romanum: 1, 28, 146, 154, 168, 238, 255, 283, 313; *pl. 7, 155, 282, 283, 432, 440.*
Forum Traiani: 229, 235, 237-239; *pl. 430, 440.*
Forum Transitorium (Nervae): 238; *pl. 191, 440.*
Gardens of Sallust (Horti Sallustiani): 175; *pl. 188.*
Hippodrome: 168.
House near the Farnesina: 119, 121-123, 182, 210; *pl. 123-127, 195, 232.*
House of the Griffins: 117, 118; *pl. 120.*
House of Livia: 128, 129; *pl. 134-136.*
House of the Masks: *pl. 137.*
Insula Tiberina: 1, 19, 145; *pl. 6.*
Largo Argentina: 146.
Maecenas's recital-room: 126; *pl. 132.*
Markets of Trajan: 159, 238, 239, 312; *pl. 262, 263, 440, 447.*
Market-hall, large: *pl. 177.*
Mausoleum of Augustus: *pl. 439.*
Mausoleum of Hadrian (Castel Sant'Angelo): 265-266; *pl. 299.*
Palace of Domitian: *pl. 446.*
Palace of Tiberius: *pl. 168.*
Palatine: 1, 23, 117, 118, 123, 128, 129, 132, 159, 168, 175; *pl. 4, 120, 128, 129, 134-137, 163, 184-187.*
Pantheon: 148, 163, 264, 265; *pl. 296, 297, 448.*
Pincio: 175, 209.
Pons Sublicius: 3; *pl. 8.*
Ponte di Nona: *pl. 154.*
Ponte Mammolo: 210; *pl. 233.*
Porta Latina: 67; *pl. 74.*
Porta Maggiore: 66, 157; *pl. 73, 103, 164, 169.*
Porta Tiburna: 29.
Porta Triumphalis: 213.
Porta Viminalis: 275, 279; *pl. 311-314.*
Porticus Aemilia: 145.
Porticus Octaviae: 110, 146.
Quirinal: 107, 175, 238.
S. Lorenzo in Via Lata: 186.
S. Salvatore in Campo: 52.
Servian Wall: 23; *pl. 26.*
Stadium of Domitian: *pl. 434.*
Suburra: 155.
Tabularium: 146; *pl. 153.*
Tarpeian Rock: *pl. 5.*
Temple of Antoninus and Faustina: 291; *pl. 326, 327, 440.*
Temple of Apollo Sosianus: 69; *pl. 78.*
Temple of Caesar: *pl. 440.*
Temple of Concord: *pl. 428, 440.*

Temple of Hadrian: 282, 283; *pl. 317.*
Temple of Juno: 146.
Temple of Jupiter Stator: 146.
Temple of Mars Ultor: 155.
Temple of Neptune: *pl. 165.*
Temple of Romulus: *pl. 440.*
Temple of Salus: 115.
Temple of Saturn: *pl. 155.*
Temple of Venus Genetrix: 155, 260;
   pl. 290, 429.
Temple of Venus and Rome: 255, 258;
   pl. 286, 442.
Temple of Vespasian: *pl. 440.*
Temple of Vesta: *pl. 427, 435, 440.*
Temple of the Via S. Gregorio: 35.
Theatre of Marcellus: 152; *pl. 160.*
Theatre of Pompey: 152; *pl. 158, 438.*
Tomb of Caecilia Metella: 154.
Tomb of Eurysaces: 66; *pl. 73, 164, 169.*
Tomb of the Flautists: 29.
Tomb of the Haterii: 215; *pl. 180, 242-245.*
Tomb of the Plautii: 154.
Tomb of the Scipios: 26; *pl. 29.*
Tomb of the Statilii: 118, 119; *pl. 121, 122.*
Via Appia: 26, 40, 105, 154, 235, 296, 301,
   331; *pl. 334.*
Via Biberatica: 238.
Via Casilina: 215, 305.
Via Claudia: 311.
Via Flaminia: 125.
Via Labicana: 200; *pl. 216.*
Via Latina: 105, 224, 305, *pl. 251.*
Via Portuense: 66, 141; *pl. 72, 99, 149-151, 295.*
Via Praenestina: 35, 157; *pl. 73, 164, 169, 230, 231.*
Via Sacra: 213.
Via Salaria: 4, 18.
Via Statilia: 35, 93.
Vicus Aesculetius (Aesculetum Quarter):
   57.
Vigna Codini: *pl. 112.*
Vatican, Mausoleum of the Valerii: *pl. 332, 333.*

ROMULUS. Legendary founder of Rome:
   6, 119, 189; *pl. 10.*

ROSTRA. Orators' platform in the Roman
   Forum, decorated with the beaks
   (rostra) of ships captured during the
   Battle of Antium against the Latins
   (338 BC): 28, 75.

ROXOLANI. A Sarmatian tribe dwelling
   between the Black Sea and the River
   Borysthenes (Dnieper): 261, 305.

RUPILIA FAUSTINA. Daughter of Matidia: 282.

RUSTICUS (Q. Junius). Roman Stoic,
   tutor of Marcus Aurelius: 339.

RUTILIANUS. Proconsul in Asia under
   Marcus Aurelius: 311.

SABINA. *See* VIBIA SABINA.

SABINE TERRITORY. Region of Central
   Italy south of Umbria and north of the
   River Anio: 4.

SAINT-RÉMY-DE-PROVENCE. In antiquity, Glanum, in Gallia Narbon-
   nensis: 191, 249; *pl. 277; map 450.*

SALLUST (Caius Sallustius Crispus), 86-35
   BC. Roman politician and historian,
   born at Amiternum. Author of the
   Catilinarian Conspiracy and the *Jugurthine War:* 77, 175; *pl. 188.*

SAMNITES. An Italic people, speaking the
   Oscan tongue, who came down from
   the mountains into Campania at the
   end of the fifth cent. BC; held out
   against Rome through three stubbornly
   fought wars (343-341, 327-304, 298-290).
   Those who survived were destroyed by
   Sulla at the Colline Gate in 82 BC: 19, 79,
   115.

SAMNIUM: Ancient region of Italy, situated between Latium, Apulia, Campania
   and Picenum: 29.

SAMOSATA. Fortified town in Syria, on
   the Euphrates, capital of Commagene:
   311.

SAMOTHRACE. Greek island lying off the
   coast of Thrace: 89.

SANGALLO (Antonio Giamberti, known
   as Antonio da Sangallo the Elder),
   c. 1455-1534. Italian architect: 301; *pl.
   340.*

SANGALLO (Antonio di Bartolomeo
   Cordini, known as Antonio da Sangallo
   the Younger), 1483-1546. Italian architect: 310.

SANGALLO (Giuliano Giamberti, known
   as Giuliano da Sangallo), 1445-1516.
   Florentine sculptor and architect of the
   Renaissance: 301.

SAN GIOVANNI SCIPIONI. A village
   in the Abruzzi, 11 miles from Bovianum:
   74; *pl. 81.*

SAN GUGLIELMO AL GOLETO. Site in
   the province of Avellino: 59; *pl. 59.*

SANTA SEVERA. *See* PYRGI.

SAPPHO. Greek lyric poetess: *pl. 231.*

SARDINIA. Large island in the Tyrrhenian Sea; from 227 BC formed part
   of a Roman province, with Corsica: 26,
   114, 339.

SARMATIANS. A people established in the
   Ukraine who, from the fourth cent. BC
   onwards, began to occupy the Greek
   towns on the shores of the Black Sea,
   and penetrated as far as Armenia: 242,
   309, 312, 322, 342.

SARTI (Antonio), 1797-1880. Italian architect: *pl. 297.*

SATIRICON. Picaresque and satirical novel
   by Petronius, a Roman author who
   lived during Nero's reign: 60.

SATRICUM (Casale di Conca). Latin town
   in the territory of Antium: 12; *map 449.*

SATURN. One of the most ancient Italic
   divinities, the husband of Ops, and god
   of prosperity: assimilated to the Greek
   god Chronos: *pl. 155.*

SATYRS. Processional companions of
   Dionysus-Bacchus: 17; *pl. 18, 19, 20,
   217.*

SCHIAVI (E.). Modern Italian writer: 296.

SCHWEITZER (Bernhard), 1892-1966. Distinguished German archaeologist: 79.

SCIPIOS, THE. Members of the great Gens
   Cornelia (*See* CORNELIUS): 26, 152.

SCOPAS. Greek sculptor and architect of
   the fourth cent. BC: 38, 44, 52.

SCYROS. Greek island in the Aegean
   (northern Sporades): 132; *pl. 132-145.*

SEGUSIANS. A Ligurian tribe whose territory, the Cottian Alps, was turned into
   a province by Augustus (14 BC): 57.

SELE. Coastal river between Samnium and
   Lucania (near Paestum), at the mouth
   of which stood a great sanctuary of
   Hera (ancient Silaris): 5.

SELEUCIA-ON-THE-TIGRIS. A city of
   Babylonia, founded by Seleucus I Nica-
   tor in 312 BC: 11, 38, 310.

SELEUKOS. Greek name carved on the
   frescoes of a wall in the Roman house
   near the Farnesina, interpreted as the
   artist's signature: 121.

SELINUS-IN-CILICIA. A town in Asia
   Minor, later renamed Traianopolis:
   250; *map 450.*

SENATE. The highest Roman collegiate
   magistracy, whose members were elected by the Censors: 76, 77, 79, 85, 130,
   180, 182, 186, 209, 223, 224, 235, 281,
   314; *pl. 236.*

SENECA (Lucius Annaeus), (c. 4 BC-AD 65). Stoic philosopher, born at Cordova in Spain, and forced to commit suicide by Nero after the Conspiracy of Piso: 77.

SENTINUM. An ancient city of Umbria: 23.

SEPINO (Saepinum). Italian town (Abruzzi) on the right bank of the Tammaro: *pl. 77.*

SEPTIMUS (Caius). Roman legionary whose sepulchral stele is now in Budapest: 342; *pl. 381.*

SERAPIS. Divinity introduced to Egypt from Mesopotamia during the reign of Ptolemy I; his mysteries were also celebrated in Rome: 336.

SERVIUS TULLIUS. This sixth king of Rome was credited, traditionally, with having built the oldest city-wall, and having worked out a new constitution classifying citizens by centuries: 9.

SEVERE STYLE. Term used to describe Greek art between 480 and 450 BC: 121, 177.

SEVERUS. Nero's architect: 130, 163.

SEVIR. Member of a board of magistrates comprising six persons: 58, 60, 67; *pl. 58, 62-64.*

SHE-WOLF, CAPITOLINE. Ancient bronze statue of the Roman She-Wolf, which stood on the Capitol in Rome from the sixth century BC. In 65 BC it was struck by lightning: 6; *pl. 2, 9.*

SICILY. The largest island in the Mediterranean: colonized by Greeks and Phoenicians. In 227 BC it became a Roman province, except for the little kingdom of Hieron in the immediate vicinity of Syracuse: 5, 9, 11, 23, 25, 26, 43, 44, 77.

SICULI (Sicels). Ancient Italic population of Sicily: 6.

SILARIS. *See* SELE.

SILVANUS. Latin god of forests and herds, latterly assimilated to Pan: 262.

SIPYLE or SIPYLUS. A chain of mountains in Lydia (Asia Minor): 37, 51.

SIXTUS V. Pope from 1585 to 1590: 324.

SOCIAL WAR. War fought by the Italian Allies against Rome in order to obtain equality of civic rights (91-89 BC): 79; *pl. 33, 34.*

SOPHISTIC. A philosophical and cultural movement, rationalist in outlook, which was introduced into Greece during the fifth cent. BC: 72.

SOSIUS (Caius). Consul in 32 BC; Roman governor of Syria and Cilicia in 38: 38, 69.

SPAIN. The Iberian peninsula was occupied by Rome during the Second Punic War, and became a Roman province in 197 BC: 9, 40, 177, 186, 224.

SPARTACUS. Thracian gladiator who, in 73 BC, headed the Third Slave War against Rome: 40.

STABIAE. Town on the Gulf of Naples, destroyed by the eruption of Vesuvius in 79: now Castellammare di Stabia: 203; *pl. 218.*

STATILII. Ancient Roman family: 118, 119; *pl. 121, 122.*

STELE. Stone set up either to commemorate a deceased person, or else to mark some important event: 86, 94, 103, 105; *pl. 96, 102, 103, 381.*

STENDHAL (Henri Beyle, known as), 1783-1842. French writer: 52.

STEPHANOS. Classicizing sculptor, a pupil of Pasiteles, active at Rome during the second half of the first century BC: 48.

STOICISM. A school of moral philosophy founded in Greece by Zeno (301 BC), and disseminated at Rome during the first centuries of the Empire: 224, 242, 261, 309, 339.

STORAX (C. Lusius). Magistrate *(sevir)* of Teate (Chieti), whose funerary monument is preserved: 60; *pl. 62-64.*

SUETONIUS (Caius Suetonius Tranquillus), *c.* AD 70-140. Roman historian at the court of Hadrian: 163, 179.

SUEVI. Germanic tribe: 261.

SULLA (L. Cornelius). Roman politician and general. After his victory over Mithridates he got himself appointed Dictator (82-79 BC), in which capacity he strengthened the aristocratic party: 77, 79-81, 86, 118, 130, 146, 148, 151, 153, 180, 181, 203, 212, 265; *pl. 83, 389.*

SURA (Lucius Licinius), 1st-2nd cent. AD. An officer of Trajan's during the Dacian Wars: 229, 242; *pl. 253.*

SUSA. Italian town (Piedmont), ancient

capital of the Segusians: 57; *pl. 56; map 450.*

SYRACUSE (Siracusa). Sicilian city, a Greek colony from Corinth. Occupied and sacked by the Romans in 212 BC during the Second Punic War, and after the death of Hieron in 215: 26, 36, 37; *map 450.*

SYRIA. Kingdom on the shore of the Mediterranean, between Egypt and Asia Minor, conquered by Pompey in 64 BC, and made a Roman province a year later: 38, 177, 204, 237, 274, 311, 312, 341.

TABLES, THE TWELVE. The Romans' first written legislation, engraved on twelve plaques of bronze (traditional date, 450 BC): 20.

TACITUS (P. Cornelius), *c.* AD 55-120. Latin historian: 64, 77.

TARENTUM (Taranto). Italian city and port on the Ionian Sea (Puglia). Originally a Greek colony from Sparta, it was occupied by the Romans in 272 BC: 25, 26, 36, 74; *pl. 82; map 450.*

TARQUINIA (Tarquinii). Italian town (Latium), once a major Etruscan centre, with a vast necropolis containing painted tombs: 80, 115, 191; *pl. 92, 205; map 450.*

TARQUINS (Tarquinii). Etruscan kings of Rome: Tarquinius Priscus (the Elder Tarquin), and Tarquinius Superbus (Tarquin the Proud, the last king): 19.

TARRACINA or TERRACINA. *See* ANXUR.

TATIUS (Titus). Legendary King of the Sabines, supposed to have reigned with Romulus: 8; *pl. 382.*

TEATE MARRUCINORUM. Italian town (Abruzzi and Molise) some 4 miles from Pescara: main town of the Marrucini. Its modern name is Chieti: 60; *pl. 62-64.*

TELEPHUS. Son of Heracles and Auge: his story was represented on one of the sculptured friezes from the Great Altar at Pergamum (about 160 BC): 235; *pl. 257.*

TEOS. Small coastal city of Asia Minor, opposite Samos; its quarries provided the marble known as 'African': 155.

TERRA SIGILLATA. Roman crockery vases decorated with reliefs *(sigilla):* 40, 203.

TERRA (TELLUS). Personification of the Earth and its fecundity: 182, 190.

TETRADRACHM or STATER. Greek coin worth four times the basic unit of currency, the drachma: 38.

THEODOROS. Greek artist who signed his name to a sequence of reliefs epitomizing the *Iliad (tabula Iliaca Capitolina)*: 114.

THEODOSIUS THE GREAT (Flavius Theodosius), 347-395. Roman emperor (379-395): 42.

THERMOPOLIUM. Snack-bar where hot drinks were sold: *pl. 71.*

THERSITES. One of the Greeks who fought at Troy: 310.

THESEUS. Greek hero who killed the Minotaur, thus liberating the children whom Athens sent to Crete as annual tribute: 110, 281; *pl. 115, 116.*

THETIS. A Nereid, the mother of Achilles: 52.

THOTH. Egyptian divinity identified, in the Hellenistic period, with Hermes in his aspect of god of eloquence, wisdom, and guide to the dead: 182; *pl. 195.*

TIBERIUS (Tiberius Claudius Nero), 42 BC-AD 37. Roman emperor (AD 14-37); son of Livia, and adopted by Augustus: 123, 157, 192, 196, 208, 209; *pl. 168, 400.*

TIBUR. *See* TIVOLI.

TIBURTINUS LAPIS. Limestone quarried at Tibur (Tivoli): 146, 148, 154, 168.

TIEPOLO (Giambattista), 1695-1770. Venetian painter, chiefly famous for his frescoes: 215.

TIGRIS. One of the two largest rivers of Mesopotamia: 310.

TIMARCHIDES. A classicizing Athenian sculptor, active during the second half of the second century BC (another sculptor of the same name is attested for the first century BC): 38.

TIMOMACHUS OF BYZANTIUM. A painter who flourished in the middle of the first century BC: 155.

TITUS (Titus Flavius Vespasianus), 39-81. Roman emperor (AD 79-81), the son of Vespasian: 69, 94, 114, 167, 209, 213-215, 219, 338; *pl. 237-241, 413.*

TIVOLI (Tibur). Small Italian town in Latium, some 20 miles east of Rome, on the hills; a Roman summer retreat: 18, 83, 85, 146, 238, 264, 267-274; *pl. 93, 152, 172, 300-309, 437, 441; map 449.*

TOMIS (Constantza). City of Rumania, a large port on the Black Sea; Ovid's place of exile: 311; *pl. 352.*

TOREUTIC ART. The art of repoussé decoration, and of sculpting objects in precious metal or ivory: 38, 49, 188, 194.

TORLONIA (COLLECTION). An archaeological collection made by Alessandro Torlonia (1800-1886): 86.

TOWER OF THE WINDS. An octagonal edifice at the foot of the Acropolis in Athens, built to house a clock, and decorated with images of the Winds: 163.

TOYNBEE (Jocelyn). English archaeologist, born in 1897: 258.

TRAJAN (M. Ulpius Traianus), 53-117. Roman emperor (AD 98-117), born in Spain: 42, 69, 94, 155, 157, 167, 175, 221, 223, 224, 226, 229, 235-242, 249, 250, 252, 255, 260, 261, 263, 279, 281, 282, 301, 306, 310, 312, 320-324, 338; *pl. 250, 252-256, 258-276, 279, 281-283, 417.*

TRAVERTINE, *See* TIBURTINUS LAPIS.

TRIBUNES. Roman magistrates who, under the Republic, had the right – in the People's name – to veto the decisions even of the highest authorities of the State. This office reverted to the Princeps under the Empire: 77, 79.

TRIMALCHIO. Character in the *Satiricon*, a novel of the first cent. AD, who typifies the rich freedman: 60.

TRIUMVIRATE. A commission with three members, formed in 60 BC by Julius Caesar, Crassus and Pompey, and again in 43 BC by Octavian, Mark Antony and Lepidus: 79, 80, 93, 154, 179.

TROY (Ilium). Ancient city of Anatolia, scene of the war recounted by Homer in the *Iliad*: 8; *map 450.*

TUFA. A soft volcanic stone, easily worked: 18, 125, 146, 148, 154.

TUNISIA. North African republic. In antiquity its territory was colonized by the Phoenicians, who founded Carth-

age; later, from 146 BC, it became a province of the Roman Empire: 281.

TUSCULUM. Ancient town of Latium, 15 miles south-east of Rome, near modern Frascati: 43.

TYANA. A city of Cappadocia in Asia Minor, the birthplace of Apollonius: 311.

TYRE. A Phoenician city: 274; *map 450.*

TYRRHENIANS. Greek name for the Etruscans: 3.

TYRRHENIAN SEA. That part of the Mediterranean which lies between Corsica, Sardinia, Sicily, and the west coast of Italy: 3.

ULYSSES (Odysseus). Homeric hero, son of Laertes and Anticleia, husband of Penelope, King of Ithaca: 116; *pl. 119.*

UMAYYAD. Dynasty of Arab Califs established in Damascus, from 661 to 750: 238.

URBINO. City of central Italy (Marche): 316.

VALERII. Ancient Roman family, whose mausoleum is at present in the Grotte Vaticane: *pl. 332, 333.*

VEII. Ancient Etruscan city north-west of Rome: 3, 5, 6, 12, 23, 28; *pl. 25; map 449.*

VELLETRI. Italian town in Latium, on the slopes of Monte Artemisio: in ancient times Velitrae, the capital of the Volscians: 12; *map 449.*

VENICE. 80, 210.

VENUS. Roman goddess of love, identified with the Greek goddess Aphrodite: 49, 152, 184, 185; *pl. 198, 429.*

VERONA. Italian city (Veneto) on the Adige: made a Roman *colonia* in 89 BC. The birthplace of Catullus and Vitruvius: 312; *map 450.*

VERRES (C. Lucinius). Propraetor in Sicily from 73 to 71 BC, and prosecuted by Cicero, in a famous trial, on charges of extortion and misappropriation of public funds: 43, 44, 180.

VERUS (Lucius Aurelius). Roman emperor (AD 161-169); adopted by Antoninus Pius, associated in power with Marcus Aurelius: 223, 282, 284, 286, 308, 314; *pl. 318, 351, 425.*

VESPASIAN (Titus Flavius Vespasianus). Roman emperor (69-79), founder of the Flavian dynasty: 85, 110, 114, 167, 209, 212, 223, 224, 226, 241; *pl. 189, 234, 235, 412.*

VESTA. Roman goddess of the hearth, identified with the Greek deity Hestia: 8; *pl. 227, 435.*

VESTORIUS PRISCUS. Aedile whose tomb survives in Pompeii: *pl. 45.*

VESUVIUS. Active volcano some seven miles from Naples. Its eruption in AD 79 destroyed Pompeii, Herculaneum and Stabiae: 41, 110, 130.

VETTII, HOUSE OF THE. A house in Pompeii (Insula 15, no. 1): 89.

VIBIA SABINA. Daughter of Matidia and wife of the emperor Hadrian; died between AD 135 and 138: 261, 282, 284, 286, 287; *pl. 320, 420.*

VICOMAGISTRI. Under Augustus, junior magistrates responsible for the various quarters of Rome: 57, 69; *pl. 57.*

VICTORIA. Goddess of Victory, identified with the Greek goddess Nike: 119, 314.

VIENNA. *See* VINDOBONA.

VILLA. Country house or holiday residence for wealthy Romans: 41, 267-274, 296; *pl. 130, 131, 133, 152, 300-309, 334.*

VINDOBONA (the modern Vienna). Roman military settlement at the north-eastern extremity of the Empire, established in the first century AD. Marcus Aurelius died there: 312.

VIRGIL (P. Vergilius Maro), 70-19 BC. Born near Mantua, one of the greatest Latin poets, author of the *Aeneid,* the *Eclogues* and the *Georgics:* 44, 182, 192.

VITELLIUS (Aulus). Roman emperor for eight months in AD 69: 223; *pl. 411.*

VITELLIUS SUCCESSUS. For his funerary altar, *see pl. 113.*

VITRUVIUS (M. Vitruvius Pollio). A Roman architect who flourished in the first century BC. Author of a treatise on architecture: 116, 153.

VOLCACIUS MYROPNOUS. Unknown person, whose portrait, with an inscription, is now in the Ostia Museum: 292; *pl. 328.*

VOLSCIANS (VOLSCI). A people of southern Latium, subdued by Rome in 338 BC: 12, 19.

VULCI. Ancient city of Etruria: 11; *pl. 13, 14.*

WEBER (Wilhelm), 1882-1948. German historian: 338.

WEITZMANN (Kurt). Modern American art-historian: 240.

WICKHOFF (Franz), 1853-1909. Austrian art-historian: 109, 116, 141.

WINCKELMANN (Johann Joachim), 1717-1768. German savant, who lived many years in Rome; the founder of modern archaeology: 108.

ZENODORUS. Greek sculptor, probably a native of Asia Minor, who lived in the first cent. AD; created one colossal statue, of Mercury, in Gaul, and another of Nero in Rome: 130.

ZEUS. Chief divinity in the Greek pantheon, Father and King of the Gods; identified with the Roman god Jupiter: 281 (Olympian), 281 (Panhellenios).

Maps

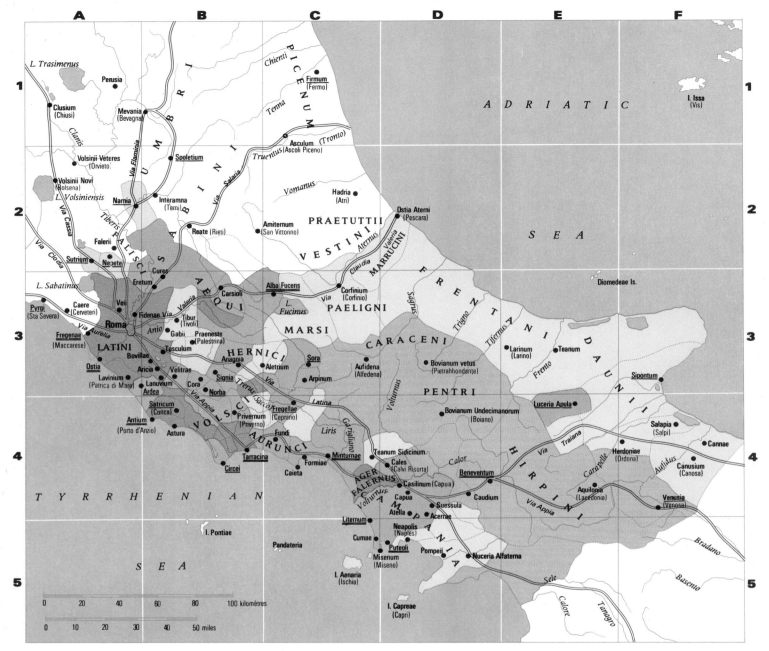

A B C D E F

1

L. Trasimenus

Perusia

Clusium
(Chiusi)

Mevania
(Bevagna)

Chienti

Firmum
(Fermo)

PICENUM

Tenna

A D R I A T I C

I. Issa
(Vis)

1

Volsinii Veteres
(Orvieto)

Spoletium

Via Flaminia

U
M
B
R
I
N
I

Asculum (Tronto)

Truentus (Ascoli Piceno)

Volsinii Novi
(Bolsena)

L. Volsiniensis

Narnia

Interamna
(Terni)

Via Salaria

Vomanus

Hadria
(Atri)

Ostia Aterni
(Pescara)

S E A

2

Via Cassia

Falerii

Tiberis
FALISCI

Reate (Rieti)

Amiternum
(San Vittorino)

PRAETUTTII

VESTINI

Aternus

Valeria

MARRUCINI

Claudia

Corfinium
(Corfinio)

PAELIGNI

Sagrus

FRENTANI

Diomedeae Is.

2

Via Clodia

Sutrium

Nepete

Cures

Eretum

Veii

AEQUI

Carsioli

Alba Fucens

L. Fucinus

Via Valeria

DAUNII

Trigno

Tifernus

Larinum
(Larino)

Teanum

Sipontum

L. Sabatinus

Caere
(Cerveteri)

Pyrgi
(Sta Severa)

Fidenae *Via*

Tibur
(Tivoli)

Valeria

MARSI

CARACENI

Aufidena
(Alfedena)

Bovianum vetus
(Pietrahbondante)

Frento

3

Via Aurelia

Fregenae
(Maccarese)

Roma

Anio

Gabii

LATINI

Tusculum

Praeneste
(Palestrina)

HERNICI

Anagnia

Aletrium

Sora

Arpinum

PENTRI

Bovianum Undecimanorum
(Boiano)

Luceria Apula

Salapia
(Salpi)

Cannae

3

Bovillae

Ostia

Anicia

Lavinium
(Patrica di Mare)

Velitrae

Cora

Signia

Norba

Trerus (Sacco)

Via

Latina

Fregellae
(Ceprano)

VOLSCI

Privernum
(Priverno)

Liris

Garigliano

Liris

Volturnus

HIRPINI

Via Traiana

Herdoniae
(Ordona)

Canusium
(Canosa)

Aufidus

4

Lanuvium

Ardea

Satricum
(Conca)

Antium
(Porto d'Anzio)

Astura

Tarracina

Circei

Fundi

Caieta

Formiae

AURUNCI

Minturnae

Teanum Sidicinum

Cales
(Calvi Risorta)

Casilinum (Capua)

Calor

Beneventum

Caudium

Aquilonia
(Lacedonia)

Venusia
(Venosa)

4

AGER
FALERNUS

Voltumus

Capua

Suessula

Acerrae

Via Appia

T Y R R H E N I A N

Liternum

CAMPANIA

Atella

Neapolis
(Naples)

Carapelle

Bradano

5

I. Pontiae

Pandateria

S E A

Cumae

Misenum
(Miseno)

Puteoli

Pompeii

Nuceria Alfaterna

Sele

Basento

5

I. Aenaria
(Ischia)

I. Capreae
(Capri)

Calore

Tanagro

0 20 40 60 80 100 kilomètres

0 10 20 30 40 50 miles

449 CENTRAL ITALY IN ABOUT 300 BC

ROMAN TERRITORY (FULL CITIZENSHIP)

ROMAN-OCCUPIED TERRITORY (CITIZENSHIP WITHOUT VOTING RIGHTS)

ALLIED TERRITORY

TERRITORY OF THE SAMNITE LEAGUE

——— ROADS

Double underlining indicates Roman colonies

Single underlining indicates Latin colonies

Acerrae	D 4	Interamna	B 2
Aenaria (Ischia)	C 5	Issa (Vis)	F 1
Alba Fucens	C 3	Lanuvium	B 3
Aletrium	B 3	Larinum (Larino)	E 3
Amiternum (San Vittorino)	B 2	Lavinium (Pratica di Mare)	A 3
Anagnia	B 3	Liternum	C 4
Antium (Porto d'Anzio)	B 4	Luceria Apula	E 4
Aquilonia (Lacedonia)	E 4	Mevania (Bevagna)	A 1
Aricia (Ariccia)	B 3	Minturnae	C 4
Arpinum	C 3	Misenum (Miseno)	D 5
Asculum (Ascoli Piceno)	C 1	Narnia	A 2
Astura	B 4	Neapolis (Naples)	D 5
Atella	D 4	Nepete	A 2
Aternus	C 2	Norba	B 3
Aufidena (Alfedena)	C 3	Nuceria Alfaterna	D 5
Beneventum	D 4	Ostia	A 3
Bovianum Undecimanorum (Boiano)	D 4	Ostia Aterni (Pescara)	D 2
		Pandateria	C 5
Bovianum Vetus (Pietrabbondante)	D 3	Perusia	A 1
Caere (Cerveteri)	A 3	Pompeii	D 5
Caieta	C 4	Pontiae	B 5
Cales (Calvi Risorta)	D 4	Praeneste (Palestrina)	B 3
Cannae	F 4	Privernum (Priverno)	B 4
Canusium (Canosa di Puglia)	F 4	Puteoli	C 5
Capreae (Capri)	D 5	Pyrgi (Sta Severa)	A 3
Carapelle	E 4	Reate (Rieti)	B 2
Carsioli	B 3	Roma	A 3
Casilinum (Capua)	D 4	Sabatinus, Lake	A 3
Caudium	D 4	Salapia (Salpi)	F 4
Circei	B 4	Satricum (Conca)	B 4
Cora	C 3	Signia	B 3
Corfinium (Corfinio)	C 3	Sipontum	F 3
Cumae	C 5	Spoletium	B 2
Cures	B 3	Suessula	D 4
Diomedeae	E 3	Sutrium	A 2
Eretum	B 3	Tarracina	B 4
Falerii	A 2	Teanum	E 3
Fidenae	A 3	Teanum Sidicinum	C 4
Firmum Picenum (Fermo)	C 1	Tibur (Tivoli)	B 3
Formiae	C 4	Trasimenus, Lake	A 1
Fregellae (Ceprano)	C 4	Tusculum	B 3
Fregenae (Maccarese)	A 3	Valeria	C 2
Fucinus, Lake	C 3	Veii (Veio)	A 3
Fundi	C 4	Velitrae	B 3
Gabii	B 3	Venusia (Venosa)	F 4
Hadria (Atri)	C 2	Volsiniensis, Lake	A 2
Herdoniae (Ordona)	F 4	Volsinii Novi (Bolsena)	A 2
		Volsinii Veteres (Orvieto)	A 2

THE ROMAN EMPIRE FROM THE SECOND PUNIC WAR
TO THE DEATH OF HADRIAN (201 BC TO AD 138)

Actium	D 3	Magnesia	D 3
Adrianople	D 2	Mainz	B 2
Aix-en-Provence	B 2	Marseilles	B 2
Alexandria	E 3	Messina	C 3
Antioch	E 3	Miletus	D 3
Apamea	E 3	Modena	C 2
Aphrodisias	D 3	Naples	C 2
Aquileia	C 2	Narbonne	B 2
Aquincum	C 2	Nicomeda	E 2
Arezzo	C 2	Nisibis	F 3
Athens	D 3	Numantia	A 2
Barletta	C 2	Odessus	D 2
Benevento	C 2	Paestum	C 2
Bologna	C 2	Palmyra	E 3
Brindisi	C 2	Paris	B 2
Byzantium	D 2	Pella	D 2
Cadiz	A 3	Pergamum	D 3
Caesarea	E 3	Petra	E 3
Cairo	E 3	Pisa	C 2
Capua	C 2	Pydna	D 2
Carnuntum	C 2	Ravenna	C 2
Carrhae	E 3	Reggio	C 3
Carthage	C 3	Rome	C 2
Cherchell	B 3	Sabrata	C 3
Cirta	B 3	Sagunto	A 2
Cologne	B 1	Salonae	C 2
Corinth	D 3	Saqqara	E 3
Crotone	C 3	Seleucia	E 3
Cuma	C 2	Seleucia in Pieria	E 3
Cyrene	D 3	Selinunte	C 3
Damascus	E 3	Silistra	D 2
Djemila	B 3	Spalato (Split)	C 2
Dura-Europos	F 3	Susa	B 2
Edessa	E 3	Syracuse	C 3
Ephesus	D 3	Tabarqa	B 3
Este	C 2	Tangier	A 3
Glanum	B 2	Taranto	C 2
Hadrumetum	C 3	Tarquinia	C 2
Halicarnassus	D 3	Tarragona	B 2
Hermopolis	E 4	Tebessa	B 3
Hildesheim	C 1	Thessalonica	D 2
Hippo	B 3	Timgad	B 3
Jerusalem	E 3	Toulouse	B 2
Karnak	E 4	Tours	B 2
Leptis Magna	C 3	Trèves	B 2
Lixus	A 3	Troy	D 3
London	A 1	Tyre	E 3
Luxor	E 4	Verona	C 2
Lyons	B 2	Volterra	C 2

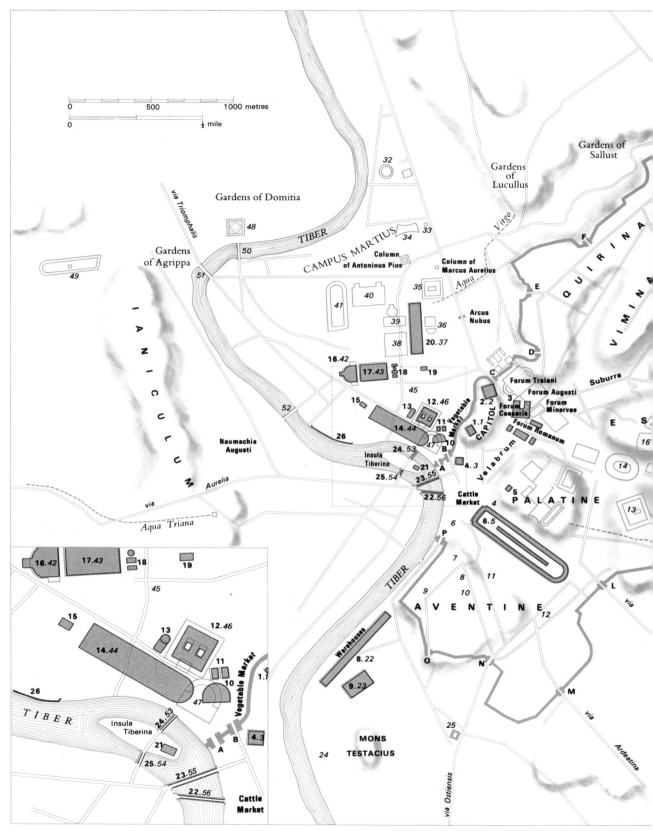

451   REPUBLICAN ROME (ABOUT 50 BC) AND IMPERIAL ROME IN THE AGE OF THE ANTONINES (ABOUT AD 138-92)

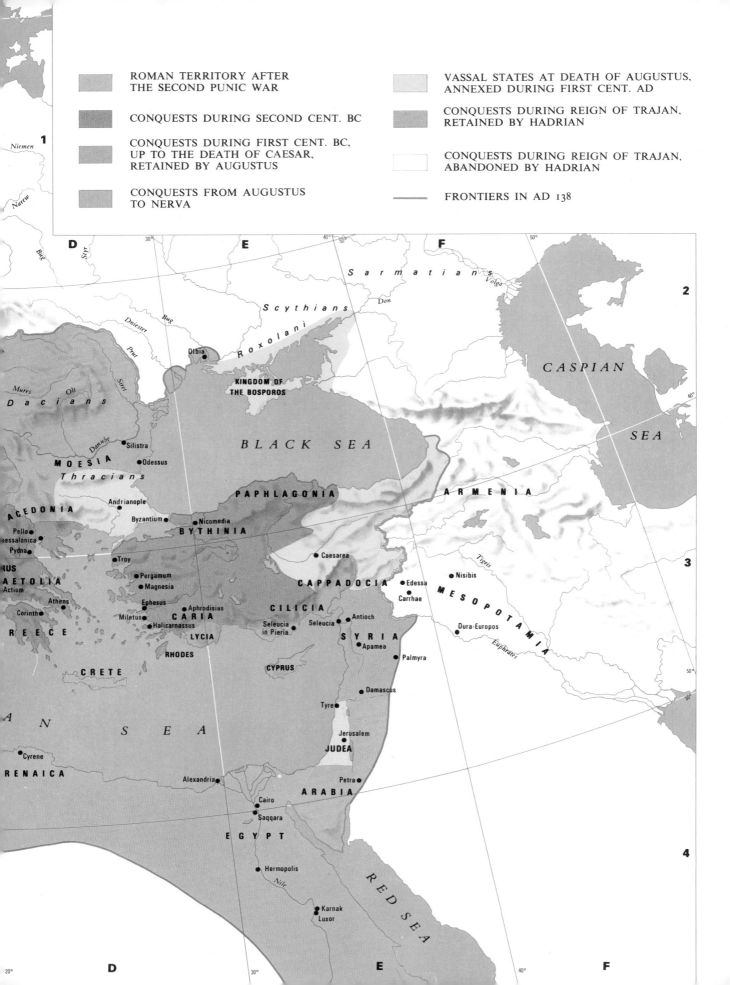

ROMAN TERRITORY AFTER
THE SECOND PUNIC WAR

CONQUESTS DURING SECOND CENT. BC

CONQUESTS DURING FIRST CENT. BC,
UP TO THE DEATH OF CAESAR,
RETAINED BY AUGUSTUS

CONQUESTS FROM AUGUSTUS
TO NERVA

VASSAL STATES AT DEATH OF AUGUSTUS,
ANNEXED DURING FIRST CENT. AD

CONQUESTS DURING REIGN OF TRAJAN,
RETAINED BY HADRIAN

CONQUESTS DURING REIGN OF TRAJAN,
ABANDONED BY HADRIAN

FRONTIERS IN AD 138

Niemen

Narew

1

D   30°   E   40°   50°   F   50°   2

Styr

Bug

Sarmatians

Volga

Don

Scythians

Dniester

Bug

Prut

Siret

Roxolani

Olbia

CASPIAN

KINGDOM OF
THE BOSPOROS

Mures

Olt

Dacians

Danube

Silistra

Odessus

MOESIA

Thracians

BLACK SEA

SEA

PAPHLAGONIA

ARMENIA

ACEDONIA

Andrianople

Byzantium

Nicomedia

Pella

essalonica

Pydna

BYTHINIA

Troy

Caesarea

3

Tigris

Nisibis

RUS

Pergamum

CAPPADOCIA

Edessa

AETOLIA

Magnesia

Carrhae

MESOPOTAMIA

Actium

Ephesus

Aphrodisias

CILICIA

Athens

Miletus

CARIA

Seleucia

Seleucia

Antioch

Dura-Europos

Corinth

Halicarnassus

in Pieria

REECE

LYCIA

SYRIA

Euphrates

RHODES

Apamea

50°

CYPRUS

Palmyra

CRETE

30°

AN

SEA

Damascus

Tyre

Jerusalem

Cyrene

JUDEA

RENAICA

Alexandria

Petra

ARABIA

Cairo

Saqqara

4

EGYPT

Hermopolis

Nile

RED SEA

Karnak

Luxor

20°   D   30°   E   40°   F

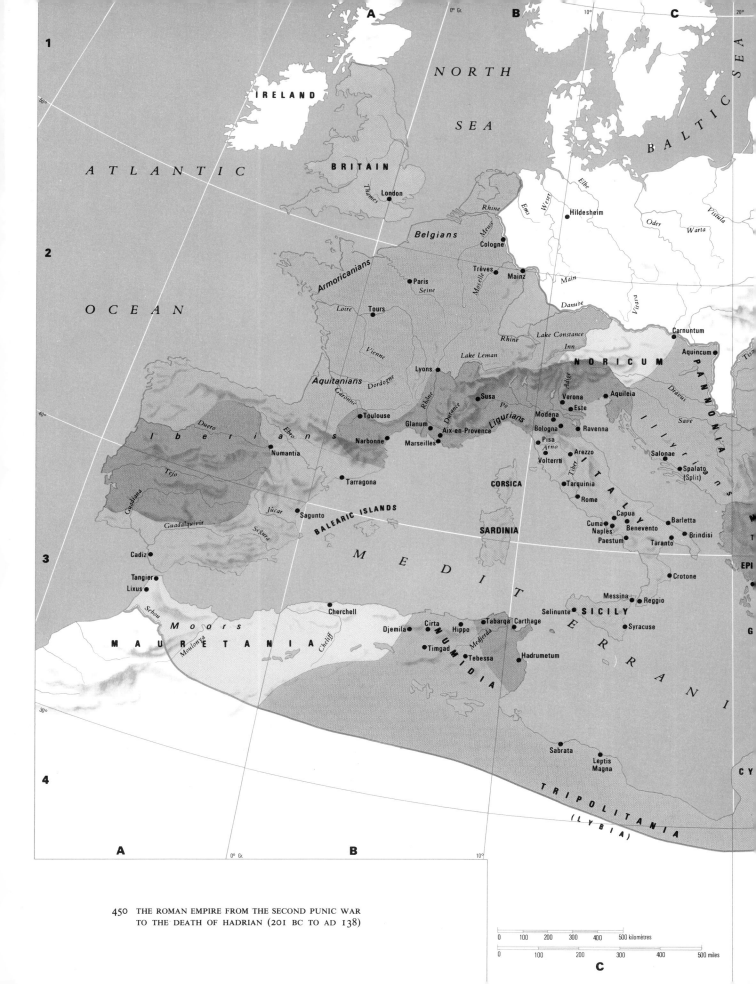

1

A

IRELAND

N O R T H

S E A

BRITAIN

A T L A N T I C

London

Thames

B A L T I C   S E A

Hildesheim

Ems
Weser
Elbe
Oder
Warta
Vistula

2

O C E A N

Belgians

Rhine
Meuse
Cologne

Trèves
Mainz
Main

Armoricanians

Paris
Seine

Moselle

Danube

Vltava

Loire

Tours

Vienne

Rhine
Lake Constance
Inn

Carnuntum

Aquincum

NORICUM

PANNONIA

Dravus

ILLYRIANS

Save

Lyons

Susa

Po

Aquileia

Verona
Este

Adige

Aquitanians

Garonne
Dordogne

Rhône
Durance

Ligurians

ITALY

Modena
Bologna
Pisa
Arno

Ravenna

Salonae

Iberians

Duero

Ebro

Toulouse

Glanum
Aix-en-Provence
Marseilles

Arezzo
Volterra

Tiber

Spalato
(Split)

40°

Narbonne

Tejo

Numantia

Tarquinia

Rome

Guadiana

Tarragona

CORSICA

Capua

Barletta

Júcar

Sagunto

BALEARIC ISLANDS

Cuma
Naples
Paestum

Benevento
Taranto

Brindisi

Guadalquivir

Segura

SARDINIA

3

Cadiz

M E D I T

Crotone

EPI

Tangier
Lixus

Sebou

Moors

Cherchell

Messina
Reggio

Selinunte
SICILY

Syracuse

M A U R E T A N I A

Moulouya
Cheliff

Djemila
Timgad

Cirta
Hippo
Medjerda
Tebessa

Tabarqa
Carthage

Hadrumetum

NUMIDIA

E R R A N I

Sabrata

Leptis
Magna

T R I P O L I T A N I A

(LYBIA)

CY

4

A

0° Gr.

B

10°

450   THE ROMAN EMPIRE FROM THE SECOND PUNIC WAR
      TO THE DEATH OF HADRIAN (201 BC TO AD 138)

| 0 | 100 | 200 | 300 | 400 | 500 kilomètres |

| 0 | 100 | 200 | 300 | 400 | 500 miles |

C

31

7. 21
Plain of
Sceleratus

G

29

30

H

Campus
Viminalis

via Nomentana

via Salaria

via Tiburtina

via Tiburtina

via Collatina

C I S P I U S

E N L I V S

I

19

20

Gardens
of Maecenas

18

17

15

J

27

C

A

K

Aqua Claudia

Valley of the Muses

Appia

Gardens of Lamia

Labicana

via

28

Aqua Julia, Tepula, Marcia

via Labicana

via Praenestina

Aqua Claudia

C A E L I U S

via Tusculana

26

via Latina

AREA OUTSIDE THE WALLS

LINE OF WALLS
COMMON TO BOTH PERIODS

AREA INSIDE THE WALLS

STRUCTURES BUILT DURING
THE REPUBLICAN PERIOD

STRUCTURES BUILT DURING
THE IMPERIAL PERIOD

STRUCTURES COMMON TO
BOTH PERIODS

AQUEDUCTS

REPUBLICAN ROME (ABOUT 50 BC)

GATES IN THE REPUBLICAN WALLS

A   FLUMENTANA
B   CARMENTALIS
C   FONTINALIS
D   SANQUALIS
E   SALUTARIS
F   QUIRINALIS
G   COLLINA
H   VIMINALIS
I   ESQUILINA
J   CAELEMONTANA
K   QUERQUETULANA (?)
L   CAPENA
M   NAEVIA
N   RAUDUSCULANA
O   LAVERNALIS
P   TRIGEMINA

STRUCTURES INSIDE THE REPUBLICAN WALLS

1   AEDES IOVIS OPTIMI MAXIMI...................TEMPLE OF JUPITER
2   AEDES IUNONIS MONETAE................TEMPLE OF JUNO MONETA
3   COMITIUM...COMITIUM
4   AEDES FORTUNAE ET MATRIS MATUTAE.........................
            TEMPLE OF FORTUNE AND THE MATER MATUTA
5   AEDES CIBELES.........................TEMPLE OF CYBELE
6   CIRCUS MAXIMUS............................CIRCUS MAXIMUS
7   AEDES FORTUNAE (?)....................TEMPLE OF FORTUNE (?)

STRUCTURES OUTSIDE THE REPUBLICAN WALLS

8   PORTICUS AEMILIA.........................AEMILIAN PORTICO
9   HORREA GALBIANA....................GRANARIES OF GALBA
10   THEATRUM AD AEDEM APOLLINIS........................
            THEATRE NEAR THE TEMPLE OF APOLLO
11   AEDES APOLLINIS ET AEDES BELLONAE.....................
            TEMPLES OF APOLLO AND BELLONA
12   PORTICUS METELLI......................PORTICO OF METELLUS
13   AEDES HERCULIS ET MUSARUM....TEMPLE OF HERCULES AND THE MUSES
14   CIRCUS FLAMINIUS.........................CIRCUS FLAMINIUS
15   AEDES NEPTUNI (?).....................TEMPLE OF NEPTUNE (?)
16   THEATRUM POMPEII.....................THEATRE OF POMPEY
17   PORTICUS POMPEIANA......................PORTICO OF POMPEY
18   AREA SACRA ('LARGO ARGENTINA')........................
            REPUBLICAN TEMPLES OF THE 'LARGO ARGENTINA'
19   AEDES LARUM.......................TEMPLE OF THE LARES
20   SAEPTA.........................ELECTORAL PRECINCT
21   AEDES AESCULAPI IN INSULA............................
            TEMPLE OF ASCLEPIUS ON THE INSULA TIBERINA

BRIDGES AND HARBOUR

22   SUBLICIUS (?)
23   AEMILIUS
24   FABRICIUS
25   CESTIUS
26   NAVALIA (ARSENAL)

IMPERIAL ROME (ABOUT AD 138–92)

STRUCTURES INSIDE THE REPUBLICAN WALLS

1   AEDES IOVIS OPTIMI MAXIMI...................TEMPLE OF JUPITER
2   ARX (AEDES IUNONIS MONETAE)..CITADEL (TEMPLE OF JUNO MONETA)
3   AEDES FORTUNAE ET MATRIS MATUTAE.........................
            TEMPLE OF FORTUNE AND THE MATER MATUTA
4   ARA MAXIMA HERCULIS................GREAT ALTAR OF HERCULES
5   CIRCUS MAXIMUS............................CIRCUS MAXIMUS
6   AEDES CERERIS.........................TEMPLE OF CERES
7   AEDES LUNAE........................TEMPLE OF THE MOON
8   AEDES MINERVAE........................TEMPLE OF MINERVA
9   AEDES IUNONIS REGINAE...............TEMPLE OF QUEEN JUNO
10   AEDES DIANAE........................TEMPLE OF DIANA
11   DOMUS ET THERMAE SURAE..........HOUSE AND BATHS OF SURA
12   AEDES BONAE DEAE.................TEMPLE OF THE GOOD GODDESS
13   TEMPLUM DIVI CLAUDII.............TEMPLE OF THE GOD CLAUDIUS
14   AMPHITHEATRUM............................AMPHITHEATRE
15   LUDUS MAGNUS.........................GLADIATORS' QUARTERS
16   THERMAE TITI.........................BATHS OF TITUS
17   THERMAE TRAIANI........................BATHS OF TRAJAN
18   NYMPHAEUM (AUDITORIUM MAECENATIS)......................
            NYMPHAEUM (MAECENAS'S RECITAL-ROOM)
19   ARCUS GALLIENI.......................ARCH OF GALLIENUS
20   AEDES IUNONIS LUCINAE...............TEMPLE OF JUNO LUCINA
21   AEDES FORTUNAE.........................TEMPLE OF FORTUNE

STRUCTURES OUTSIDE THE REPUBLICAN WALLS

22   PORTICUS AEMILIA.........................AEMILIAN PORTICO
23   HORREA GALBIANA....................GRANARIES OF GALBA
24   HORREA LOLLIANA....................GRANARIES OF LOLLIUS
25   SEPULCRUM C. CESTII....................PYRAMID OF CESTIUS
26   SEPULCRUM SCIPIONUM...................TOMB OF THE SCIPIOS
27   HORTI ANNIANI ET HORTI LATERANI.........................
            GARDENS OF ANNIANUS AND GARDENS OF THE LATERAN
28   NYMPHAEUM (TEMPLUM MINERVAE MEDICAE).................
            NYMPHAEUM (TEMPLE OF MINERVA THE HEALER)
29   CAMPUS COHORTIUM PRAETORIARUM.........................
            EXERCISE-GROUND OF THE PRAETORIAN GUARD
30   CASTRA PRAETORIA.............CAMP OF THE PRAETORIAN GUARD
31   AEDES VENERIS ERYCINAE.............TEMPLE OF VENUS ERYCINA
32   MAUSOLEUM AUGUSTI...............MAUSOLEUM OF AUGUSTUS
33   ARA PACIS..ALTAR OF PEACE
34   SOLARIUM AUGUSTI.....................SUNDIAL OF AUGUSTUS
35   AEDES DIVI HADRIANI.........TEMPLE OF THE GOD HADRIAN
36   ISEUM ET SERAPEUM.............TEMPLES OF ISIS AND SERAPIS
37   SAEPTA.........................ELECTORAL PRECINCT
38   THERMAE AGRIPPAE........................BATHS OF AGRIPPA
39   PANTHEON......................................PANTHEON
40   THERMAE NERONIANAE........................BATHS OF NERO
41   STADIUM DOMITIANI...................STADIUM OF DOMITIAN
42   THEATRUM POMPEII.....................THEATRE OF POMPEY
43   PORTICUS POMPEIANA.....................PORTICO OF POMPEY
44   CIRCUS FLAMINIUS.........................CIRCUS FLAMINIUS
45   THEATRUM BALBI........................THEATRE OF BALBUS
46   PORTICUS OCTAVIAE....................PORTICO OF OCTAVIA
47   THEATRUM MARCELLI...............THEATRE OF MARCELLUS
48   MAUSOLEUM HADRIANI.................MAUSOLEUM OF HADRIAN
49   CIRCUS CAI.........................CIRCUS OF CAIUS CALIGULA

BRIDGES

50   AELIUS
51   NERONIANUS
52   AGRIPPAE
53   FABRICIUS
54   CESTIUS
55   AEMILIUS
56   SUBLICIUS

THIS, THE FIFTEENTH VOLUME OF 'THE ARTS OF MANKIND' SERIES,
EDITED BY ANDRÉ MALRAUX AND ANDRÉ PARROT, HAS BEEN
PRODUCED UNDER THE SUPERVISION OF ALBERT BEURET, EDITOR-
IN-CHARGE OF THE SERIES, ASSISTED BY JACQUELINE BLANCHARD.
THE BOOK WAS DESIGNED BY ROGER PARRY, ASSISTED BY JEAN-LUC
HERMAN. THE TEXT WAS FILMSET BY FILMTYPE SERVICES LTD.,
SCARBOROUGH. THE TEXT AND THE BLACK-AND-WHITE PLATES WERE
PRINTED BY LES ÉTABLISSEMENTS BRAUN ET CIE, MULHOUSE-DORNACH;
PLATES IN COLOUR BY DRAEGER FRÈRES, MONTROUGE; PLANS AND
MAPS BY GEORGES LANG, PARIS. THE BINDING, DESIGNED BY MASSIN,
WAS EXECUTED BY BABOUOT, GENTILLY.